NAZI MILLIONAIRES

Books by Kenneth D. Alford

Spoils of War:
The American Military's Role in the Stealing of Europe's Treasures

Great Treasure Stories of World War II

Books by Theodore P. Savas

Silent Hunters:
German U-Boat Commanders of World War II (editor)

The Campaign for Atlanta & Sherman's March
to the Sea, vols. 1 & 2 (co-editor, with David A. Woodbury)

Nazi Millionaires

The Allied Search for
Hidden SS Gold

Kenneth D. Alford
& Theodore P. Savas

CASEMATE
Philadelphia & Newbury

Published in the United States of America and Great Britain in 2011 by
CASEMATE PUBLISHERS
908 Darby Road, Havertown, PA 19083
and
17 Cheap Street, Newbury, Berkshire, RG14 5DD

Copyright 2002 © Kenneth D. Alford and Theodore P. Savas

ISBN 978-1-935149-35-4
Digital Edition: ISBN 978-1-93514-968-2

Cataloging-in-publication data is available from the Library of Congress
and the British Library.

Printed and bound in the United States of America.

For a complete list of Casemate titles, please contact:

CASEMATE PUBLISHERS (US)
Telephone (610) 853-9131, Fax (610) 853-9146
E-mail: casemate@casematepublishing.com

CASEMATE PUBLISHERS (UK)
Telephone (01635) 231091, Fax (01635) 41619
E-mail: casemate-uk@casematepublishing.co.uk

To my guiding lights: my wife Edda, and my children,
Cheryl Thomas, Roger Alford, and Mark Alford

— Kenneth D. Alford

In memory of my pop, Michael Anthony Savas, who served his
country proudly over the skies of occupied Europe

— Theodore P. Savas

Map of Central Austria

Contents

Contents (continued)

Illustrations follow page 186

Preface

The prisoner was clad in reddish brown trousers, his white shirt open at the neck. With a minister leading the way, he walked steadily across the fifty yards separating his cell from the execution chamber, head erect and hands bound tightly behind him. He looked calm, remembered one witness, thin and older than his 56 years.

The gallows—the first ever used in the history of Israel—had been set up in a small room that had once served as living quarters for the prison guards. The condemned was ushered to a spot on the floor and instructed to stop. Israeli President Itzhak Ben-Zvi had refused to commute the sentence of death, and so the prisoner found himself standing on a black-painted trapdoor that had been cut in the floor in the fog enshrouded Ramleh prison, waiting for the inch-thick hemp that would snap his neck and choke the life from his body. As his executioners tied his ankles and knees, he exhaled loudly and looked about, surveying his earthly surroundings one final time.

"Can you loosen the straps a bit so I can stand erect?" he inquired.

The guard ignored him. "Do you have any last words?"

Even when confronted with death he refused to atone for his crimes, brushing aside the minister's request that he repent. Squinting, eyes almost closed, he looked to the side and down at the trapdoor upon which his brief future on this earth rested. And then the doomed man spoke:

> After a while, gentlemen, we shall all meet again. So is the fate of all men. I have lived believing in God, and I die believing in God. Long lives Germany. Long lives Argentina. Long lives Austria. These are the countries with which I have been most closely associated and I shall not forget them. I greet my wife, my family and friends. I had to obey the rules of war and my flag. I am ready.

A few seconds of silence lingered after his final words. A hood was offered. A shake of the head was his only reply.

The prisoner's four-month trial had been one long and painful public replay of Nazi brutality. His testimony—defensive, cold, calculating, and remorseless throughout—presaged his final rebuff of the Protestant minister's attempt at salvation. Visits to the death camps at Auschwitz, Treblinka, and a mass grave at Minsk, Russia, were coolly described with the words "Corpses, corpses, corpses. Shot, gassed, dead . . . they sprung out of the ground as the grave was opened. The stink . . . it was a fantasy of blood. It was an inferno, a hell, and I defy anyone to say that I wasn't going crazy from it." No words of apology. No admission of guilt. Not a whisper of contrition.

"Muchan!" barked the Commissioner. Ready.

A noose was slipped over the prisoner's head and secured snugly around his neck. Three men stood in a corner of the room hidden behind a tent of blankets. Each gripped a lever in his hand, rigged so that none of them could tell who actually controlled the trapdoor.

"Muchan!"

"Christ!" called out the minister. "Jesus Christ!" The words echoed for a few moments and then an eerie silence briefly filled the room.

The prisoner stiffened when a rustling sound was heard behind the partition. The trapdoor dropped open, and Adolf Eichmann was dispatched into eternity. In accordance with his Will and Testament, his corpse was cremated, its ashes scattered in the Mediterranean Sea—just outside Israeli waters.

It was a few minutes before midnight on May 31, 1962.[1]

*   *   *

On February 10, 1961, while Eichmann impatiently paced inside his cell awaiting trial, crystal chandeliers were swaying softly from the high ceiling in the banquet room of the old city hall in Bremen, Germany. Several large models of three-masted ships swayed gently between the magnificent light fixtures, a tribute to the vessels that had brought both wealth and power to the port city. The descendants of these merchants and sea captains, outfitted in their best clothes or crisp uniforms, together with a few other honored guests, were about to take their seats below the hanging models at long festively-arranged banquet tables. They were there to hear businessman Kurt A. Becher address them.

A member of the Seafaring House and one of the richest men in Bremen, Becher was the afternoon's main speaker at the annual Bremen Seafaring Association celebration, which for 416 years had been held each year on the second Friday in February. Like Adolf Eichmann, whom he knew well, Hamburg native Becher carried with him a not-so-secret burden. The canvas of his World War II past was smeared with a myriad of colorful connections to mass Jewish deportations, concentration camps, and mechanized murder. His tenure in Budapest offered Hungarian Jews and other "undesirables" life with one hand—if they filled it with gold—and deportation and death with the other. Unlike Eichmann, however, Becher was not considered one of the top tier of Nazis slated for immediate arrest and trial. Years had passed and Lady Luck, apparently, still hovered overhead.

The illustrious, tradition-laden event began at 3:00 p.m, when a glass bell rang six times, calling those in attendance to silence. The president of the board announced the traditional and rather mysterious phrase, "Working upstairs and downstairs, upstairs and downstairs working." A trio of raps on a carved oak door ensued, followed by orchestral strains of "Entrance of the Guests in the Wartburg." Those gathered in attendance stood up and slowly moved toward the banquet room, the tables arranged in the shape of Neptune's trident, the seating arrangements carefully planned well in advance. The meeting's first speaker addressed the attentive crowd. The next scheduled lecturer was businessman and multi-millionaire Kurt Becher. To the group's dismay, another was introduced in his stead. Murmurs of disapproval coursed through the angry and confused crowd.

One month earlier, on January 7, 1961, the *Weser Kurier* newspaper reported that Becher was about to be indicted for war crimes as a former member of the SS. The article noted that a legal action had been or would soon be filed against the businessman in a Frankfurt court. The indictment would allege that the former colonel had swindled a Jewish businessman out of $18,000 when he offered to save the man's brother from deportation to a concentration camp. Becher, claimed the paper, was paid the money but the doomed Jew rode the rails to death all the same. Rumors of even worse offenses persisted. Was Becher's absence related to this rumored indictment?

Rich and well connected, Becher was no stranger to the media and public spin. In an effort to stop rife speculation in the wrong circles of Bremen, a representative announced to the disgruntled crowd that a business emergency in South America had suddenly called him away. Becher, continued the spokesman, was genuinely disappointed that the crisis would not allow him to participate in the longstanding and honorable event. At least the last bit of verbal pirouette was true. Despite his bulging bank account and prominence in the community, Becher had waited years before finally being voted in as a member of the prestigious Seafaring House in 1959. Keenly aware of his criminal baggage, Becher hoped that admission to the private club would help him take another giant step on the road to social acceptance. His goal was to eventually serve as president of the Bremen Seafaring Association, and thereby gain access into the inner circles of Bremen aristocracy.

Until now, Kurt Andreas Ernst Becher (who, impressed by SS Reichsführer Heinrich Himmler's "King-Heinrich-craze" often used the middle name "Alexander" for Alexander the Great) had enjoyed a string of remarkable luck. A distinguished equestrian, Becher somehow always knew how to mount the right horse. During the war's early years, he had caught the eye of several important officers, including Himmler and SS Gruppenführer (Major General) Otto Hermann Fegelein. Because of their trust in him, Becher rose rapidly through the ranks from a lowly sergeant in the SS to Standartenführer (Colonel). His duties included everything from distinguished combat service on the Eastern Front to mundane desk work in Berlin; from stealing Jewish-owned properties in Warsaw and Hungary, to selling freedom passes for millions of dollars to thousands of Jews. A brief imprisonment after the war threatened to dim his personal star, but his fortune quickly took a turn for the better when he was released from custody two years later. Within a remarkably short time the poor grain merchant was a multi-millionaire—an amazing feat in the wake of Germany's near-total destruction and precarious economic situation. Was his personal fortune due simply to his knack for business and a bit of good luck? Or had he tucked away a fortune for later use during the war's waning months?

During the dark years of the Third Reich, Himmler and others shielded Becher and often acted on his behalf. In the postwar rise of the West German Bundesrepublik, Becher enjoyed the assistance of other influential friends, including Robert Pferdmenges, Chancellor Konrad Adenauer's friend and economic advisor. Certainly they were aware of his disreputable past. Rumors about Becher circulated freely. Some said he paid his personal Hamburg attorney a large annual retainer to keep the shadows of his past at a respectable distance. The dark stain remained, however, for not everything can be wiped clean with money and lawsuits.

*   *   *

Kurt Becher is just one of many men sketched in *Nazi Millionaires: The Allied Search for Hidden SS Gold*. Admittedly, it is a story whose end has yet to be written, its primary passages gleaned from careful study of thousands of pages of declassified memorandums, letters, reports, interrogations, and interviews. It details, as far as possible today, our investigation into the activities of Kurt Becher and other merciless former SS soldiers, like Franz Konrad, Wilhelm Höttl, Josef Spacil, and Franz Six. All of these men worked by day for their Führer, and by night for themselves. They executed their duties with a religious fervor with one hand, and lined their pockets with stolen loot with the other.

The overrunning of Europe and the western Soviet Union opened the door to the widespread sacking and raping of banks, churches, businesses, houses, and other personal property. The breathtaking scale of this ransacking would not have been possible without the mass deportation of European Jewry and the implementation of the "Final Solution." Every Jewish ghetto gave up warehouses full of artwork, gold, currency, rings, furniture, clothes, rugs, and other personal belongings. Every train crammed with men, women, and children destined for the concentration camps sprinkled about Europe represented thousands of people stripped of their worldly wealth, their dignity, and eventually, their lives. When Germany surrendered in early May 1945, only slivers of this golden mountain remained. What had happened to the rest?

From all accounts, a sizeable portion was in the hands of Adolf Eichmann and his fellow SS comrades in the RSHA (Reich Security Main Office) who, during the last weeks of the war, crammed trucks, trains, planes, and automobiles with gold, jewels, currency, and artwork, and made a mad dash for freedom. Few places were left to hide by April 1945. Americans were sweeping eastward from France and Italy into Germany and Austria. The dreaded Russians, with fire in their eyes for the war crimes committed on their soil (never mind their own government's horrendous crimes against its citizens) were driving westward, closing the Allied pincers in a grasp from which few would wriggle free. To the south, the mountains of Austria beckoned. There, the fevered minds of a few fanatics persisted, a last ditch defense could be waged. And there they flocked by the hundreds, staining the snowy white Austrian Alps with their presence—and their blood money.

A few of these men escaped capture. Most, however, were eventually arrested—but not before metal chests and cloth sacks had been buried, trucks pushed into fast flowing rivers, crates dumped into deep mountain lakes, and cellars and woodsheds filled with everything from currency to jars of gold. Determined and extensive searches by Allied investigators in the early months and years following the surrender recovered only a small fragment of this wealth. Was it really lost, or had much of it been safely stashed away for furtive future visits?

Unfortunately, the complete story of what many of these men did during the war will never be fully revealed. Twenty-five years of research has failed to satisfactorily penetrate the wall of silence erected as soon as the guns fell quiet in 1945. An entire network of police departments, law firms, politicians, and prominent and powerful citizens around the world voluntarily protected (and still continue to do so) many of these monsters of humanity, shielding them from their hideous yesterdays. Few people today realize that this protective network exists. Even organizations and individuals within the United States have unclean hands. During and after World War II, the American Counter Intelligence Corps (CIC), Criminal Investigation Division (CID), Central Intelligence Agency (CIA), Federal Bureau of Investigation (FBI), and even the Department of State, participated in the silence for reasons we may never know or fully understand. In 1965, Congress passed legislation authorizing the destruction of all 110,000 CID documents. These included hundreds of cases of paperwork relating to the investigation of *Americans* who had stolen, or had somehow been nefariously involved with, the plunder of Europe's treasures. Repeated Freedom of Information Act requests for particular documents the authors know exist have been refused under Exemption 6 and 7C of the Privacy Act, or Presidential Executive Order 12356, National Security. Persistent requests have also prompted return telephone calls threatening lawsuits. Still, our labors continue.

It was not our goal to write the definitive study of every lost World War II-era treasure, for such an accounting is impossible. Nor is this book intended as an exhaustive description of how Hitler structured his criminal Third Reich. Many other books have already plowed that ground well. Instead, we offer an account, reasonably thorough and hopefully interesting, of the vast amount of SS gold, jewelry, currency, and written documents that wound their way into Austria during the war's final weeks. Some of it was discovered in short order; most of it never, at least officially, was seen again.

In order to fully understand and appreciate this fascinating slice of history, we decided to introduce our subject with a general overview of Adolf Hitler's rise to power, and how that power was implemented in relation to the Final Solution. This portion of our study is based largely on secondary sources and admittedly breaks no new ground. Within this framework of understanding our principal characters mount the stairs, walk across the written stage, play their parts, and exit—some gracefully, some kicking and screaming. A few perish during the war; others eventually sit at the bar of justice and meet a state-sponsored death or spend time behind bars. Far too many live in freedom to a ripe old age in a grand fashion not one of them deserve. Few suffer the earthly fate each so richly merit; hopefully a higher justice awaits them. All of them have in common one thing: they used their positions of power over other human beings to steal and conceal wealth earned or owned by others, while their own shoulders brushed against, or their fingers operated, the Reich's organized machinery of death.

One might look upon this book as a builder looks upon a home. The foundation and general framework represent the government of the Third

Reich, the levers of the Holocaust, and the major players who shaped that unholy drama—like Adolf Eichmann, Heinrich Himmler, Reinhard Heydrich, and Ernst Kaltenbrunner. This aspect of our story is well known and has been visible to the world for some time. The front door of this rotten structure leads into a labyrinthine black interior decorated almost entirely with declassified manuscript sources few have seen and fewer still have read. Here, then, is our wallpaper and furniture in the form of detailed interviews, lengthy interrogations, intelligence and police reports, letters, and final accountings. These documents introduce us to a new cast of devilish characters, and augment our knowledge of other, better known, war criminals.

Who in the general reading public knows of SS officer Franz Konrad, his frenzied escapes, nocturnal burials of loot, and endless prevarications to avoid a Polish firing squad? Or of Walter Hirschfeld's remarkable interviews with General Fegelein's elderly parents in search of Hitler's diaries, followed by his out-of-control spiral while on the payroll of American Intelligence? How many have read of Josef Spacil's twisted attempts to obfuscate his wartime activities, and so keep his millions hidden away from prying Allied eyes? Or that part of "Operation Bernhard's" counterfeiting operation was so secret that even Berlin was not fully informed? Of all of the fresh revelations found within these pages, the bombshell regarding the exact nature of Walter Schellenberg's relationship with his friend, Count Folke Bernadotte of Sweden, will likely detonate with the most force.

It is our sincere hope that this study both enlightens and entertains. We hope it will encourage others to take up the lantern and search for new clues in dark corners. If we have shed additional light upon the corrupt activities surrounding atrocities of the past, and broken new ground in the process, then we will consider our mission a success.

Preface Notes

1. Lawrence Fellows, "Eichmann Dies on Gallows For Role in Killing Jews," *New York Times*, p. 1, June 1, 1962.

Acknowledgments

Authors are always indebted to others. And so it is with this study. Many people and institutions along the way helped with our research, copied thousands of pages of documents, answered endless numbers of questions, and responded to desperate pleas (often on short notice) for this letter or that picture. We could not have completed this book without this help. If we have overlooked someone, we apologize in advance. You know who you are, so pat yourself on the back and forgive our error.

Special thanks are due to Mike Bauman, Dallas, Texas; Julius Geönczeöl, Budapest, Hungary; Klaus Goldmann, Berlin, Germany; Willi Korte, Germany and Silver Springs, Maryland; and also to John Taylor, Richard Boylan, Rebecca Collier, David Giordano, and Vickie Washington.

The indispensable and hard working librarians and archivists at the U.S. Army Intelligence and Security Command, Fort Meade, Maryland, and National Archives and Record Services, Washington D.C., went out of their way to help us.

Thanks also are due David Farnsworth, our publisher and the head honcho at Casemate, for seeing value in this work in its early stages and having the faith and ability to shepherd it through to publication. We wish you nothing but the best with Casemate, a new and outstanding company with a bright future before it. We await our evening's worth of pints—dark, *cold*, and on your tab! Special thanks are also due to Holly Keane of Casemate, who read the manuscript and saved us from a number of embarrassing errors.

Finally, our loving wives, Edda Alford and Carol Savas. Both extended to us the time and solitude required to finish this project. Their love and encouragement, truly, keep us going.

Kenneth D. Alford
Richmond, Virginia

Theodore P. Savas
El Dorado Hills, California

Dramatis Personae

Apfelbeck, Albert (??-??). SS Captain and Bureau II depot leader. He helped Josef Spacil hide treasures in Taxenbach, Austria.

Augsburg, Emil (1904-??). SS Major, Einsatzgruppen officer, and senior assistant at the infamous Wannsee Institute, the SS think tank involved in planning the Final Solution.

Barbie, Klaus (1913-1991). SS officer and Gestapo man known as the "Butcher of Lyons."

Becher, Kurt (1909-1995). SS Colonel who mistreated Jews in Warsaw and Hungary. He made a deal with Jewish leader Rezsö Kastner to trade lives for gold.

Berger, Gottlob (1895-1975). SS General and Inspector General of Prisoners of War. Helped American agents recover a fortune in currency and gold.

Bernadotte, Count Folke (1895-1948). The beloved head of the Swedish Red Cross helped save thousands of Nazi concentration camp victims. But he also was Walter Schellenberg's friend. Their relationship was more complex and nefarious than heretofore believed.

Billitz, Wilhelm (1902-1944). A representative of the Hungarian Manfred Weiss Works at the time of the German occupation of Hungary.

Bober, Max (1896-??). Printing expert and concentration camp slave who forged English pound notes in Sachsenhausen as part of "Operation Bernhard."

Braun, Eva (1912-1945). Adolf Hitler's mistress and, on the last day of her life, his wife. Much of her private correspondence, jewelry, photos, and other valuable items were smuggled out of Berlin into Austria.

Conner, William J. (??-??). Master Sergeant, Military Intelligence Interpreter, Team 466-G Seventh Army. All efforts to discover more about this man have been unsuccessful. According to fellow CIC agent Robert Gutierrez, Connor had in his possession one of the most outstanding collections of Nazi memorabilia in the world.

Eichmann, Adolf (1906-1962). SS Lieutenant Colonel and Head of Bureau IV B4. Eichmann was the logistician who implemented the "Final Solution."

Eigruber, August (1907-1947). SS Governor of the Upper Danube in Austria who attempted to prepare the Austrian Alpine Redoubt for a final defense.

Fegelein, Gretl Braun (1915-??). The sister of Eva Braun and wife of SS General Herman Fegelein. She ended up with much of Eva's jewelry and some of her correspondence.

Fegelein, Herman (1906-1945). SS General and commander of the 8th SS Cavalry Division "Florian Geyer" in Russia. Fegelein committed war crimes in Poland and Russia, and later served as Heinrich Himmler's liaison officer with Hitler's bunker headquarters.

Göhler, Johannes (1918-??). SS Major on the staff of General Fegelein. He served in Russia and Warsaw.

Göhler, Ursula (??-1993). The young and attractive wife of Johannes Göhler. Ursula served as the secretary (and perhaps mistress) of an American CIC agent. She later claimed knowledge of a shipment of large quantities of Nazi-related materials (including Hitler's diaries) to the United States.

Greim, Robert Ritter von (1892-1945). Luftwaffe Field Marshal who flew out of Berlin with aviatrix Hanna Reitsch during the final days of the war.

Gutierrez, Robert (??-??). Special Agent, 970 CIC, who investigated the whereabouts of Adolf Hitler and many of nefarious personalities and hidden fortunes discussed in this book.

Haufler, Erwin (1907-??). SS Captain, commanding officer of Fischhorn Castle, and a close associate of Herman Fegelein.

Heydrich, Reinhard (1904-1942). SS General and the first head of the Reich Security Main Office (RSHA). Assassinated 1942 by Czech partisans.

Himmler, Heinrich (1900-1945). SS Reichsführer. His efforts made the Holocaust—and thus the widespread raping of Europe—possible.

Hirschfeld, Walter (1917-??). SS Second Lieutenant who worked closely with American Intelligence to arrest former SS men, and spy on former Nazis.

Hitler, Adolf (1889-1945). The Führer who employed many of the men found within these pages. His actions triggered the most deadly war in human history.

Höttl, Elfriede (??-??). The wife of Wilhelm Höttl. She ostensibly assisted American Intelligence officers in the search for concealed SS gold.

Höttl, Wilhelm (1915-1997). SS Captain and Deputy Chief of Bureau VI. One of Germany's most clever intelligence officers who knew much more about hidden SS loot than he ever revealed.

Kaltenbrunner, Ernst (1903-1946). SS General; second and last chief of the Reich Security Main office (RSHA). The tall, Chesterfield chain-smoking officer controlled the Third Reich's machinery of death.

Kalewska, Barbara (??-??). Polish Countess and Franz Konrad's mistress in Warsaw. She following him back to Austria when Poland was overrun by the Russians, and left for parts unknown a wealthy woman.

Kastner, (Rudolph) Rezsö (1906-1957). This fervid Hungarian Zionist made a deal with SS officer Kurt Becher to save his own life and those of his family, friends, and others suitable for emigration to Palestine to form a Jewish state.

Konrad, Agnes (??-??). Franz Konrad's wife.

Konrad, Franz (1906-1951). SS Captain and administrative officer who committed war crimes in Warsaw. Konrad hid several fortunes in gold, currency, and personal effects, including the uniform worn by Hitler during the July 20, 1944, assassination attempt.

Konrad, Fritz and Minna (??-??). Franz Konrad's brother and sister-in-law.

Krüger, Friedrich Walter Bernhard (1904-??). SS Major. He oversaw the counterfeiting scheme run at Sachsenhausen, popularly known to history as "Operation Bernhard."

Meier, Rudolf (??-??). Franz Konrad's nephew, who helped hide a fortune in gold, jewels, and currency.

Naujocks, Alfred (1901-??). An SS Officer and special operations man. Naujocks led the fake attack on the Polish radio station that triggered World War II, and helped initiate the "Operation Bernhard" forgery operation.

Ohlendorf, Otto (1908-1951). SS Colonel and head of Bureau III. Ohlendorf organized mass murders in the Ukraine in 1941-1942 with the notorious Einsatzgruppen.

Pichler, Willy (??-??). The husband of Franz Konrad's sister Minna. Willy's house was used to hide some of Konrad's loot.

Ponger, Kurt (??-??). U.S. Army Lieutenant, criminal investigator at Nuremberg, Soviet spy, and brother-in-law to Otto Verber.

Reitsch, Hanna (1912-1979). Nazi Germany's leading female pilot and admirer of Adolf Hitler. Reitsch piloted the plane that carried her and Robert Ritter von Greim out of Berlin after a sojourn in Hitler's bunker. She admitted taking out four letters with her.

Röhm, Ernst (1887-1934). The head of the powerful SA (Brownshirts) until Hitler ordered his ouster and murder in the summer of 1934.

Scheidler, Arthur (1911-??). Top administrative aide to SS RSHA chiefs Reinhard Heydrich and Ernst Kaltenbrunner.

Scheidler, Iris (??-??). Wife of Arthur Scheidler.

Schellenberg, Walter (1910-1952). SS Major General and head of Bureau VI (counter-intelligence operations). Schellenberg's well-known "official" relationship with Count Folke Bernadotte, the head of the Swedish Red Cross, was a bit more complex than history has thus far revealed.

Schiebel, Kurt (??-??). SS Lieutenant and adjutant to Josef Spacil.

Schlemmer, Gerhardt (??-??). German Army Captain and company commander of the 352nd Volksgernadier Division. He worked for the CIC in 1946 and 1947 as an undercover agent with Walter Hirschfeld.

Schwend, Friedrich (??-1980). SS Lieutenant General who organized a master network of agents for the distribution of forged English pound notes as part of "Operation Bernhard."

Six, Franz (1906-??). SS General in charge of Bureau VII, and a former Einsatzkommando who eventually crossed paths with Walter Hirschfeld.

Six, Marianne (1919-1946). Sister of General Franz Six who unwittingly played a hand in his apprehension.

Skorzeny, Otto (1908-1975). SS Lieutenant Colonel and special operations commando. During the closing days of the war, he amassed a fortune in gold and American and Swiss currency.

Smolianoff, Salomon (1897-??). Professional counterfeiter and forger who was located by the Nazis and sent to Sachsenhausen concentration camp to assist in the forging of English pound notes as part of "Operation Bernhard."

Spacil, Josef (1907-??). SS Oberführer (no U.S. equivalent) and head of Bureau II. Spacil was responsible for concealing vast sums of gold and currency at the end of the war.

Spitz, George (1893-??). A notorious Jewish swindler who helped Friedrich Schwend and his counterfeit operation.

Verber, Otto (??-??). U.S. Army Lieutenant, criminal investigator at Nuremberg, Soviet spy, and brother-in-law of Kurt Ponger.

Wisliceny, Dieter (1911-1948). SS Major, Adolf Eichmann's deputy, and one of Kurt Becher's superior officers in Hungary. Wisliceny was responsible for horrendous war crimes in Slovakia, Greece, and Hungary.

Introduction

The Rise of Adolf Hitler
and Nazi Germany

he rise of Nazism, personified by its leader, Adolf Hitler, triggered a conflagration that spread suffering, destruction, and death across the globe such as the world had never before witnessed. The vortex of war drew in, in one way or another, most of the world's countries. Few emerged in 1945 unscathed.

The prolonged and aggressive war waged by Germany overran most of Europe and large swaths of western Russia. In addition to improving Germany's strategic position, the obvious goal of these jackbooted offensives was the conquering of foreign soil for the acquisition of resources. Hovering below the radar screen and following in the Wehrmacht's wake were several thousand officers and men tasked with other, less obvious, objectives: plunder and murder. Most of those who participated in this massive organized sacking of Europe and western Russia were tethered to Germany's human enslavement and exter- mination industries. Like vultures circling dying prey, those responsible for pillaging cities and trafficking in human misery often sought a means to personally profit from the suffering of others. After the war, many were hunted down and imprisoned. Others, like Adolf Eichmann, were eventually executed for their crimes. Many more, however, secreted their fortunes from prying eyes and slipped quietly into the postwar world. Some recovered their gold and jewels; others did not.

How were so many able to plunder so widely for so long and reap untold millions in gold, jewels, and currency? The answer cannot be fully understood without appreciating the system within which they operated. The entire edifice rested upon the military–industrial complex erected by Adolf Hitler.

*   *   *

He was from humble origins, the son of an Austrian customs agent. Born on April 20, 1889 in Braunau am Inn, Hitler spent most of his youth in Linz. Much to the dismay and anger of his tyrannical father, Hitler proved to be an unfocused daydreamer and failure as a student. With dreams of becoming an artist, Hitler left secondary school in 1905 before graduation. Armed with but mediocre talent, however, he twice failed to acquire a seat in the Vienna Fine Arts Academy in 1907 and 1908. For the next several years the Austrian lived a Bohemian and apparently immoral existence scratching out an aimless living painting postcards and advertisements.[1] When World War I erupted Hitler joined the army and served as a courier throughout the long and bloody war on the Western Front. He was wounded seriously in 1916 and gassed in 1918. He was apparently decorated four times, once with the Iron Cross, First Class. Attrition alone should have forced him through the lower ranks, yet he never rose above the transitory level of corporal.[2]

Germany's defeat in 1918 was codified in the Versailles Treaty, a harsh peace that outraged and devastated many Germans and Austrians, Hitler among them. He emerged from the war a fervent militaristic nationalist. A year later, while still attached to his regiment, Hitler acted as an army political agent and joined the right-wing radicals of the German Worker's Party—the genesis of the Nazi Party. A few months later he was out of the army working full-time as a propaganda agent. Wracked by depression and political street wars, Germany teetered on the brink of anarchy. Hitler was keen enough to appreciate that turmoil offers opportunity to those ruthless enough to seize it. He worked tirelessly to transform the German Worker's Party into the National Socialist German Worker's Party (NSDAP), or Nazi party, and was elected its president in 1921. Surrounded by security thugs, the passionate and charismatic figure barked from street corners atop overturned boxes. The country's ills, he screamed, were the blame of communists, Jews, and the Versailles Treaty. Emboldened, he attempted to grab control of the Bavarian government in what is known as the Beer Hall Putsch. The effort ended in failure and imprisonment on charges of treason.

When the revitalized and unrepentant Hitler emerged from Landsberg Prison in 1921, he began transforming the NSDAP into a national organization. Six million votes later, the Reichstag found itself with 107 additional Nazi members in 1930. Within just a few years Hitler had risen to preside over the second largest party in Germany. The stunning victory convinced bankers, industrialists, and others with political interests and capital resources to back Hitler. A close but failed bid for president of Germany in 1932 against incumbent war hero Paul von Hindenburg earned Hitler additional power when his Nazi party picked up 37 percent of the vote and another 230 seats in the Reichstag. The end game was now in sight. Hitler held the reins of power of the largest party in the land, and von Hindenburg reluctantly appointed the son of a civil servant Chancellor of Germany.

With anti-Semitism firmly cemented in place as the keystone of his politics, Hitler moved quickly to solidify his power and revive the German military and industrial base. The Communist party was banned in 1933, and within a short time he managed to break apart and dismantle the remaining parties battling for control of Germany. In what was dubbed "The Night of the Long Knives," on June 30, 1934, Hitler purged many of his long time supporters who posed the final threat to the complete control he was seeking. Hindenburg's death that August opened up the presidency and Hitler climbed aboard, assuming the title "Führer" (supreme leader) of the Third Reich. Germany was now solely his own.[3]

Hitler executed his war plans with breathtaking speed. Within six years he tendered several violations of the Versailles Treaty. Troops marched into the demilitarized Rhineland without foreign penalties being levied. Naval terms with Great Britain were abrogated. The German army (Wehrmacht) and air force (Luftwaffe) were significantly expanded both in terms of numbers and weapons systems. Sovereign territory fell under his control when Austria was annexed in 1938. Desperate to avoid war, Britain and France forced Czechoslovakia to cede the Sudetenland to Hitler. While the rest of the civilized world wrung its collective hands in helpless dismay, the Führer signed a nonaggression treaty with his ostensible enemy, Josef Stalin's Soviet Union. This brilliant foreign policy coup allowed Hitler to operate elsewhere in Europe without having to worry about the Communist threat hovering beyond his eastern border.

War began in earnest on the first day of September 1939 with the invasion of Poland. To Hitler's dismay, Great Britain, followed by France, declared war on Germany, triggering a massive conflict well ahead of Hitler's timetable. Unfortunately for the brave Polish soldiers and citizenry, their British and French allies offered little more than threatening words in response to the invasion. The Poles were subdued within a few weeks. With his eastern boundary secure Hitler cast his covetous gaze to the north in the spring of 1940, jabbing an armored fist into Denmark and Norway. France, meanwhile, refused to engage Germany from the west with its large and potent army, remaining instead safely ensconced behind the Maginot Line. Ever more confident, a few weeks later Hitler's armies marched into the Netherlands, Belgium, and finally, France. The fall of the only continental power capable of standing up to Germany was breathtakingly swift. Within a few weeks Hitler's Wehrmacht was standing on the beaches of the Atlantic Ocean, his Luftwaffe soaring over the English Channel. England refused to come to terms. The Battle of Britain followed. The Luftwaffe, led ineptly by Hermann Göring, beat the courageous English down to one knee. To Hitler's dismay, capitulation was not in the cards.

Resigning himself to the fact that he was not strong enough to successfully invade the island nation, Hitler turned his attention to his ally, the Soviet Union. The decision to launch a massive attack in the east had been made years earlier. For Hitler, war with Stalin was unavoidable, and was driven by both a hatred of Bolshevism and a quest for resources, especially oil. But it was launched in the face of a spectacular failure of intelligence concerning the size, quality, and morale of the Russian forces. The assault, unleashed on June 22, 1941, was the largest offensive in history. The stunning, lightning-fast invasion swept the victorious

German armies to the very suburbs of Moscow and marched hundreds of thousands of Russians into prisoner of war camps. Courageous resistance and a bitter early winter snow ended the drive without a decisive German victory. With Hitler's massive army groups bogged down and freezing on the Russian steppes, the Japanese manufactured a blunder of similar proportion by attacking the United States at Pearl Harbor on December 7, 1941. Cobbled onto this double stroke of recklessness was yet a third major blunder—Hitler's most serious strategic faux pas: he declared war on America. The declaration tilted American industrial and financial might onto the side of the embattled British and Russians, who rightly hailed both the Japanese attack and the Führer's reckless response as a godsend.

Unbeknownst to the world, Germany's fortunes were nearing their apex. Gravity was about to glom onto Hitler's grand design. Field Marshal Erwin Rommel's Afrika Korps, with its associated Italian allies, experienced a few months of stunning success in 1942 in North Africa before suffering an equally striking series of reverses and ultimate defeat. The same pattern was repeated on the Eastern Front. Successful German air and land attacks tore titanic chunks of terrain from Mother Russia. Stiff Russian resistance and equally ferocious counter thrusts, however, eventually blunted and bloodied the Wehrmacht and Luftwaffe to a standstill. By late 1942, the Sixth German Army was trapped deep in Russia at Stalingrad on the Volga River. Hundreds of thousands of casualties and several weeks later Field Marshal Friedrich von Paulus surrendered. More than 100,000 Germans marched into captivity; German fortunes in the East waned forever. While von Paulus's men were fighting for their lives, German cities crumbled one by one under the relentless bombing campaign adopted by the Allies. Germany's sea war, too, experienced staggering early success followed by stiffening resistance and, eventually, abysmal failure. The fear housed deep in the hearts and minds of the Allies lessened when new anti-submarine weapons in 1942 began taking their toll on Admiral Karl Dönitz's U-boats. The breaking of the Enigma code and deployment of radar on aircraft and surface ships swung the pendulum decisively against Hitler's Wolfpacks, which lost the all-critical Battle of the Atlantic just three months after the Stalingrad fiasco. "Black May" of 1943 saw more than forty U-boats dispatched to the bottom of the sea and drove the remainder back to their pens in France, Norway, and Germany. By June 6, 1944, the date the Allies invaded France at Normandy, it was manifest that Germany could no longer win the war.

*   *   *

Operating in the wake of this colossal ship of combat and bloodshed were a handful of organizations and individuals tasked with objectives as odious as the men who implemented them. It is now time to introduce these men and their bureaucracies and explain who they were, where they came from, and how they operated.

At the forefront, standing tall on the graves of millions, was Heinrich Himmler and his SS henchmen.

Introduction Notes

1. Hitler's efforts painting postcards are today reaping large sums for those who own them. The least expensive unattractive green on green card sells for at least $6,000. Nicer ones with a postmark fetch $15,000. Any of his paintings sell today for more than $1,000,000. The largest collection of Hitler art is owned by collector Billy Price of Houston, Texas.

2. The issue of Hitler's rank, awards, and lifestyle are a minor mystery that is only now being understood by historians. Lothar Machtan, in his remarkable recent book *The Hidden Hitler* (New York, 2001), delves into these and many other issues surrounding Hitler's early years, friendships, rise to power, and sexuality. Machtan's work is based almost exclusively on police and army reports, diaries, letters, newspapers, and eyewitness accounts. His trenchant study seems to confirm that Hitler was awarded the Iron Cross under dubious circumstances, and was not promoted to higher rank because of his homosexuality. Ibid., 68-69, 71, 91.

3. Alan Axelrod and Charles Phillips, *The Macmillan Dictionary of Military Biography* (NY, 1998), pp. 165-166. The best biography of Hitler is Ian Kershaw's recent two volume set *Hitler: Hubris, 1889-1936* (New York, 1999), and *Hitler: Nemesis, 1936-1945* (New York, 2000). It is a meticulously researched and written study, but must be utilized in conjunction with Machtan's *The Hidden Hitler*.

Chapter 1

"In this hour I was responsible for the fate of the German people, and
thereby I become the supreme judge of the German people."

— *Adolf Hitler*

The Devil's Duo:
Heinrich Himmler and Ernst Röhm

A dolf Hitler was the most powerful man in Europe years before
the United States entered World War II. His chosen successor,
Reichsmarshall Hermann Göring, was also one of Germany's
most dominant leaders. However powerful the former air ace was as the
head of a mighty Luftwaffe at war—and notwithstanding his general
corruptness and megalomania—Göring was forced to operate within the
conventional framework of the armed forces, and all the restrictions that
system entailed. He had stood side-by-side with Hitler during the
Austrian's climb to power, and was first in line in responsibility for
victory in Poland and the Low Countries. But Göring's fortunes rested
upon a foundation of military successes. Humiliation over the skies of
Britain and the humbling experience above the steppes of Russia dimmed
his star.

Two other dominant personalities also played an important role in the
rise of Nazism and Adolf Hitler during the 1920s and 1930s. Their
quasi-military organizations were not hampered by traditional bureau-

cratic niceties or other such impedimenta. Laws and tradition existed only to be broken and extinguished. Only one of the leaders survived to witness the outbreak of war in 1939. His star rose during the heady days of 1939-1941—and kept on rising as setbacks in the east and west mounted. His position within the Third Reich was less conspicuous than that of Göring's, and the power he wielded was almost absolute.

*   *   *

The character of one of the Nazi regime's most brutal officers continues to fascinate historians. Despite his explicit and freely admitted responsibility for monstrous cruelty against his fellow man, the dichotomy that was Heinrich Himmler remains.

Born in Munich on October 7, 1900, Himmler was the son of a pious authoritarian Roman Catholic schoolmaster who had once been tutor to the Bavarian Crown Prince. His early career in life was singularly unimpressive. Education during his formative years was taken in Landshut. While a teenager, he trained as an officer cadet and served with the 11th Bavarian Regiment, but did not see active service before the end of World War I. Unlike Hitler, however, Himmler did not outwardly manifest vehement infuriation at the harsh outcome imposed by the Versailles Treaty. Returning home, he entered Munich's School of Technology in 1918 and emerged four years later with a degree in agriculture. The first few years of the 1920s passed quietly while Himmler labored as a fertilizer salesman and poultry farmer. Quiet, non-violent, and outwardly unemotional, the young man was described by one who knew him well as "an intelligent schoolmaster." But inside that calm schoolmaster's demeanor was something terribly wrong.

By 1923 Himmler had acquired a deep interest in German politics. Setting aside his quiet life of agriculture, he participated in Hitler's abortive Beer Hall Putsch and joined Ernst Röhm's criminal paramilitary organization, the *Reichskriegsflagge* (Reich War Flag). By 1925 he was a full member of the Nazi party as well as the black-shirted SS (*Schutzstaffeln*), Hitler's personal armed bodyguard. A succession of positions of power within the fledgling party were now open to him; promotions flew in his direction. In 1926 he became the party's assistant propaganda leader. After marrying in 1927 and briefly returning to poultry farming, Hitler tapped him to run the SS, at that time a small body comprised of about 200 men. The following year Himmler was elected as a Nazi Reichstag deputy. For the next three years he worked tirelessly on Hitler's behalf, guaranteeing his own continued rise to power.

After the Nazis seized the country's political machinery in 1933, Himmler was appointed police president in Munich and head of the Bavarian political police. This authority and control gave Himmler exactly what he had been seeking for years: the power base to broaden and deepen his SS and organize the *Sicherheitsdienst*, or SD, a separate ideological intelligence department within the SS under the command of Reinhard Heydrich. It also distanced him from Ernst Röhm's *Sturmabteilung*, or SA, Hitler's paramilitary police. Himmler took the opportunity to set up the first concentration camp at Dachau, where political opponents and undesirables were housed in what was euphemistically called "protective custody." Throughout these early years Himmler demonstrated an amazing organizational ability, especially with regard to the formation of political alliances within the Nazi hierarchy. The superficially cool officer was a survivor, an ambitious climber who craved power.[1]

According to one author, Himmler used his new powers in 1933 to begin constructing a "state within the state," a shadow government that answered to no one. Membership in his SS grew from 200 to more than 50,000 before the end of 1933. The ideology driving Himmler, and thus the SS, was an unhealthy preoccupation with religion, Nordic myths, and Aryan genealogy. As a result, the SS was constructed on the organized principles of the order of the Jesuits. The service statutes and spiritual exercises prescribed by Ignatius Loyola were emulated. Indeed, Himmler's title, "Reichsführer," was intended as the counterpart of the Jesuit's General of Order. The complete structure of the SS leadership was adopted from Himmler's studies of the hierarchic order of the Catholic Church. His domination expanded during this time when he secured the SS's independence from control of Ernst Röhm's SA, to which the SS was initially subordinated. Together with Reinhard Heydrich's SD, Himmler continued his ceaseless labors to consolidate his power. In September 1933 he was made commander of all the political police units outside Prussia and, though formally still under

Göring's control, became head of the Prussian Police and Gestapo on April 20, 1934. Up until now Himmler's rise within the party hierarchy had been little short of meteoric. Only one man stood in the way of his complete consolidation of power.

* * *

Like Himmler, Ernst Röhm was also born in Munich. Other than their mutual association with Adolf Hitler, however, similarities were few and far between. Röhm served honorably in World War I. By the time Germany surrendered in 1918 he was the recipient of three combat wounds and held the rank of captain. Like so many men after that disastrous war, Röhm's postwar goals were ill-defined at best. Yearning for structure he joined the Friekorps, a radical right-wing group of armed associations organized to defend the country's borders against the threat of communist invasion. After participating in the Friekorps's bloody slaughter of hundreds of communists and socialists in March 1919, Röhm steeped himself in nascent right-wing party politics. It was Röhm who secured the services of a young Adolf Hitler to spy on the German Worker's Party (GWP), which Röhm soon joined. Like so many others, Röhm found Hitler to be a charismatic comrade. At his urging, Röhm led a group of armed storm troopers in the failed Beer Hall Putsch in November 1923. Tried and found guilty of treasonable acts, Röhm escaped prison but was booted from the German army. Hitler was much smarter than Röhm. Instead of trying to defend himself on the few merits of his position, Hitler turned his trial into a political discourse that elevated his prestige even as he later languished in Landsberg prison.

In these early years of the Nazi movement Röhm's Brownshirts had been an indispensable element of Hitler's success, a magnet that had attracted thousands of disaffected recruits into the Party. From within Landsberg the future leader of Germany came to realize that Röhm's thirst for direct military confrontation with the German State was not the true course to power. He began to disassociate himself from a man he now viewed as an undesirable. Discarded by Hitler, Röhm withdrew from political life. The few jobs he held frustrated and bored him. Only an offer from Bolivia to serve as a military instructor preserved in Röhm some vestige of self worth. But history was not yet finished with the stocky native of Munich. The round chubby-faced ex-captain with a deep scar on one cheek, uneven mustache, and biting, porcine eyes, had one more act to play in the drama unfolding within Germany's borders.[2]

While Röhm toiled, Hitler plotted a new course for the SA. Shedding its paramilitary garb, Hitler honed the organization into a political weapon wholly subordinated to the NSDAP, or Nazi party. Hitler's significant electoral victory in 1930 prompted him to recall Röhm as the SA's chief of staff—though only after Hitler had assumed the position of Supreme Leader of the organization. Röhm rapidly expanded the SA into a popular army of street fighters, gangsters, and thugs. By 1934 the unemployed and disaffected swelled the ranks of the SA to several (loosely organized) millions. Röhm regarded this plebeian army of desperadoes as the core of the Nazi movement, the embodiment and guarantee of a permanent revolution. Under his leadership the SA fulfilled an indispensable role in Hitler's rise to power between 1930 and 1933. Spreading propaganda and terror, Röhm's brownshirts won the battle of the streets against the communists and other political opposition. As 1934 dawned, Röhm's private army was as powerful as the German Army itself. But while Röhm was conquering the streets for Hitler, the new Chancellor of Germany had again come full circle in his thinking: his SA chief was no longer necessary.

Indeed the SA chief was now a threat to Hitler. Röhm had become disillusioned with the Nazi revolution. The growing bureaucratic Nazi movement angered Röhm, who dreamed of a "soldier's state" and the primacy of the soldier over the politician. Provided a seat on the National Defence Council in 1933, Röhm vocalized his dissatisfaction over the use of his SA. In October he sent an ominous letter to Walther von Reichenau, the liaison officer between the German army and the Nazi Party. "I regard the Reichswehr [German army] now only as a training school for the German people. The conduct of war, and therefore of mobilization as well, in the future is the task of the SA." Röhm insisted on maintaining momentum in a socialist direction while talking openly about the conquest of Germany. His populist demagogy alienated the middle class and the industrialists, whose support Hitler was still seeking and desperately needed. Röhm failed to understand Hitler's concept of a gradual insurrection carried out under the cloak of legality. The real revolution, warned Röhm, was yet to come.

If Hitler did not readily admit and recognize it, his chief supporters did: Röhm had to go. The head of the SA overplayed his hand by antagonizing two dangerous rivals, Hermann Göring and Heinrich Himmler. Both feared the SA leader, who was potentially strong enough to crush them. Both pressured Hitler to reduce his power and exposure by utilizing the SS and the Gestapo to do so. Röhm's own conduct and that of his entourage, given to dissolute homosexual orgies and drinking bouts, loutish behavior, and wildly indiscreet remarks, made the task of his enemies that much easier. Still, Hitler hesitated. How could he eliminate his oldest comrade-in-arms, a man to whom he felt a debt of gratitude and a certain warmth—even though he had become a liability and even a danger to his regime?

In goose-stepped Heinrich Himmler and his SS. Together with several officers of the German army, Himmler plotted Röhm's spectacular demise. Heydrich, head of Himmler's SD arm, was ordered to compile a damning dossier. The SA leader, Heydrich "discovered," had accepted millions of marks from the French to launch a coup and oust Hitler. Hitler knew the record was untrue, but he saw the opportunity to finally be rid of Röhm—and seized it. Taken utterly by surprise, Röhm was arrested on June 30, 1934, in a private hotel at Bad Wiessee, a small Bavarian spa south of Munich where he was taking a holiday with other SA leaders. He was taken to Stadelheim prison, where he was executed two days later by firing squad after refusing to take his own life. It was an ironic end for the man who had once uttered, "All revolutions devour their own children."[3]

The bloody purge was kept secret until the middle of July, when Hitler mentioned the action during a speech and gave it a name that would resonate through history: "The Night of the Long Knives." Hitler publicly branded Röhm a traitor and accused him of having fomented a nationwide plot to overthrow the government. "In this hour I was responsible for the fate of the German people, and thereby I become the supreme judge of the German people," shouted Hitler in his explanation of why he did not use the German justice system to try Röhm. "I gave the order to shoot the ringleaders in this treason." Hitler professed outrage at the homosexual aspects of Röhm and his criminal entourage, although the leader's lifestyle had been well known and tolerated for many years. Scores and perhaps hundreds perished in the purge that both ended the influence of the SA and gained for Hitler the acceptance of the German officer corps and support of many industrialists. When President Paul von Hindenburg died five weeks later, the former World War I corporal became head of state.[4]

Himmler, too, was the beneficiary of a Nazi apparatus unfettered with the likes of an Ernst Röhm. The flow of SA blood paved the way for the emergence of the more military SS as an independent organization charged with safeguarding the embodiment of the National Socialist idea and translating the racism of the regime into a dynamic principle of action. The Reichsführer occupied a splendid villa in the fashionable Berlin suburb of Dahlem alongside other high Party officials, as well as a country home on the Tegernsee. However, neither location was suitable for the seat of his rising SS Order. His wandering eye fell upon Wewelsburg Castle, an impressive triple-towered renaissance-era citadel overlooking the Alme Valley ten miles southwest of Paderborn. The location and unusual triangular form of the castle, which had served as the secondary residence of the prince bishops of Paderborn in the early 1600s, was perfect for what Himmler had in mind. He viewed his black-shirted SS men as the reincarnation of not just the medieval order of the Teutonic knights, but also of King Arthur's Knights of the Round Table. Arthur had Camelot; Himmler would have Wewelsburg.

The SS rented the castle in 1934 from the district of Büren for a single Reichsmark each year. Himmler intended to transform the castle into a nucleus of support for the pseudo-scientific ideology of National Socialism and a sacred shrine for dead SS leaders. Improvement work on the Wewelsburg complex began immediately. The castle's focal point, a grand dining hall complete with a gigantic oak table that seated twelve, owed much to Arthurian legend. Coats of arms adorned the walls. Below the dining hall was a circular cellar called the "Ring of Honor." The room, intended as a crypt, was lighted by a few rectangular openings in the thick brick walls and sported a giant swastika embedded in the ceiling. Signet rings emblazoned with the horrendous "death's head" insignia were presented to the first 10,000 SS men and to senior commanders. Whenever an SS notable died, his ring was placed in a chest housed in the crypt. Select SS members were ordained into senior positions there.

Each of the rooms allotted to the knights in the castle commemorated Germanic heroes, decorated and furnished in period and provided with books and documents on their subject. Himmler's castle quarters were dedicated to Heinrich I, the tenth-century Saxon King who beat back Magyar horsemen pressing westward from the interior of Russia and formed the basis of the German confederation of princes which became, under his son Otto, the Holy Roman Empire.[5]

*   *   *

Reichsführer Himmler had successfully completed his bid to win control of the political and criminal police throughout the Third Reich when he became head of the Gestapo that had originally been established by Göring. Almost every level of power was now either under Himmler's command or within reach of his iron cold grasp. Now the only question was how that power would be wielded and the results that would flow from its use.

Chapter Notes

1. This general background of Heinrich Himmler is extracted from Peter Padfield, *Himmler: ReichsFührer-SS* (London, Cassell Publishers, 2001). See specific references within. Padfield's book is, by far, the best single source on Himmler's life and career under the Nazi banner.

2. Joachim C. Fest, *The Face of the Third Reich: Portraits of Nazi Leadership* (London, 1970), pp. 141-144.

3. Fest, *The Face of the Third Reich*, pp. 144-147.

4. Axelrod and Phillips, *Dictionary of Military Biography*, p. 166.

5. Padfield, *Himmler*, pp. 248-249.

Chapter 2

"We have achieved a complete victory and the SS is in
formation and awaiting further orders."

— Ernst Kaltenbrunner to Heinrich Himmer, March 12, 1938

Hitler's Rogues: Reinhard Heydrich and Ernst Kaltenbrunner

I n order to channel his authority and project his power into every
nook and cranny of the Third Reich, Heinrich Himmler created the
Reich Security Main Office, or *Reichssicherheitshauptamt*
(RSHA). The idea had been in the works for some time, but was finally
formalized with a decree on September 27, 1939, merging the SD
(*Sicherheitsdienst*) and the Secret State Police (Gestapo) into one
policing authority under the control of a single organization. With the
stroke of a pen Himmler consolidated his own power base and
simultaneously created an organization capable of carrying out murder,
deportations, and intelligence activities on a grand scale.

It proved a deft political stratagem.

* * *

The Reich Security Main Office was headed by Reinhard Tristan
Heydrich, one of the leading architects of the "Final Solution." Heydrich
was born in Halle, a provincial town in Prussia, on March 7, 1904. His

father was a Dresden music teacher and the founder of the First Halle Conservatory for Music, Theatre, and Teaching. Born too late to participate in WWI but craving a military career, Heydrich enlisted at Kiel in the much-reduced German navy in March of 1922. Service as a tar under Wilhelm Canaris generated a taste for intelligence work, but his naval career foundered in 1931. Heydrich was forced to resign for conduct unbecoming an officer after compromising the virtue of a shipyard director's daughter.[1]

Long-fascinated with racial ideologies and right wing politics, the out-of-work and disaffected Prussian seized the opportunity and joined the Nazi party and SS that same year. Tall, slim, blond-haired with a set of deep blue eyes, Heydrich with his military bearing, iron discipline, and icy hardness epitomized the Hitler-inspired Aryan Nazi mythology. Himmler had found the perfect right-hand man. He immediately took Heydrich under his protective wing and groomed him for special work. The result was a meteoric rise through the ranks. By Christmas Day he was a major. He established the intelligence department of the SS, the *Sicherheitsdienst*, or SD, in 1932. As Himmler's assistant, Heydrich spent much of 1933 and 1934 overseeing the unification of the political police. In 1934 he took control of the Prussian Gestapo in Berlin. Before summer's end, the 28-year-old was an SS Obergruppenführer (Lieutenant General), a reward for his murderously efficient services rendered during the liquidation of Ernst Röhm and his cronies. Two years later, in 1936, he was made chief of the newly formed Security Police (*Sicherheitspolizei*), or SIPO. The organization was part of the ministry of the interior, which meant Heydrich now had complete control over the Gestapo and the criminal police for the entire country. Himmler's able technician of power politics was indispensable to the rising masters of the Third Reich.

Heydrich's arrogant facade disguised a deep inferiority complex and pathological self-hatred that found an outlet in his morbid suspiciousness and boundless greed for power. Indeed, Heydrich suffered from a gnawing uncertainty as to his own racial origins. Some (including Heydrich) suspected he was part Jewish. Although his rivals were never able to establish a Jewish connection as a matter of fact, it added to Heydrich's innate sense of inferiority and aggravated his tendency to see treachery, intrigue, and potential hostility lurking around every corner.[2]

As head of the SIPO (Himmler's unified, centralized, and militarized security police), Heydrich acted with pitiless harshness in his dealings with those declared to be enemies of the state. His cynicism and contempt for human beings helped him spin a gigantic and intricate web of police surveillance throughout the Third Reich. Extensive dossiers were filed not only on enemies of the Nazi Party but on his rivals and colleagues. The police apparatus was utilized to pit his opponents against one another. Anyone who stood in the way of his duties or the goals of the State were arrested, tortured, and murdered—especially Marxists, Jews, Freemasons, Liberal Republicans, and religious figures.

Heydrich's expertise at political dirty tricks, scandalous intrigue and blackmail zeroed in on other convenient targets. Seeking a means of solidifying his control of the Germany army, Hitler unleashed his henchmen against two prominent commanders, Field Marshal Werner von Blomberg and Brigadeführer (General) Baron Werner von Fritsch. Trumped up charges and "proof" of homosexuality against the latter, coupled with a marriage scandal involving the former's wife, ousted both from power in 1938. Heydrich also masterminded the fake attack on the Gleiwitz radio station, which was used as a pretext for Hitler's invasion of Poland on September 1, 1939.[3]

The same month of the Polish invasion, which triggered WWII in Europe, Heydrich was tapped to command the Reich Security Main Office, or RSHA. The Prussian lieutenant general and Aryan poster boy now had absolute control of the entire secret police organization. This power was used for murderous purposes. In a directive dealing with the "Jewish question" issued on September 21, 1939, Heydrich distinguished between the "final aim, requiring longer periods of time" (and necessarily top secret) and the stages required for achieving it. Heydrich set about implementing the preliminary steps necessary to achieve the "Final Solution." After the conquest of Poland, he ordered Polish Jews concentrated into ghettoes and authorized the appointment of Jewish councils, a characteristically perfidious way of forcing Jewish communities to collaborate in their own destruction. Hundreds of thousands were stripped of all their worldly wealth. With the assistance of SS Obersturmbannführer (Lieutenant Colonel) Adolf Eichmann and other SS members, Heydrich began mass deportations of Jews and other undesirables from Austria and Germany into Poland.

On July 31, 1941, following the invasion of the Soviet Union, Hermann Göring, head of the Luftwaffe, commissioned Heydrich to find "a total solution to the Jewish question." Heydrich, in other words, was delegated to take responsibility for all the necessary organizational and administrative measures necessary to implement the destruction of European Jewry. Death camps were organized for this purpose (later called Operation Reinhard in his honor). Einsatzgruppen squads, or mobile killing units, were organized to follow in the wakes of the various victorious German armies. The sole purpose of these small squads was to round up and execute Jews, intellectuals, Soviet commissars and partisans, prisoners of war, and other undesirables. This enormous mass killing spree, carried out with the cooperation of many high-ranking Wehrmacht officers (who often did not approve but turned a blind eye to the murders nonetheless), took the lives of almost 1,000,000 people.[4]

The head of RSHA left his Berlin headquarters to assume the post of Deputy Reich Protector of Bohemia and Monrovia on September 23, 1941. Residence was taken up in Prague, Czechoslovakia, where he adopted what has been called "the policy of the whip and the sugar." Hitler wanted the Czechs mobilized into a slave labor base. Repression, arrests, torture, and executions were carried out at the same time he designed to win over workers and peasants by improving their social conditions. On January 20, 1942, Heydrich organized a top secret conference in the Berlin suburb of Grossen-Wannsee. The purpose of the meeting was to organize the various government agencies and streamline the process of implementing the "Final Solution." Although many high-ranking Party officials (like Heinrich Himmler, Hermann Göring, and Joachim von Ribbentrop) were conspicuously absent, in attendance were fourteen of the Third Reich's leading second-tier figures, including Adolf Eichmann and Heinrich Müller, the head of the Gestapo. In a speech rich in euphemisms but clearly understood by all in attendance, Heydrich methodically discussed the organized mass murder of Jews.[5]

The Czech government, operating in exile in England, was about to take matters in its own hands. A pair of specially trained men, Jan Kubis and Josef Gabcik, parachuted into Czechoslovakia on December 28, 1941. Partisans sympathetic to their cause guided the assassins to a country home in the village of Panenske Brezany. Heydrich had stolen the estate from its Jewish owner and placed his own family within its walls. Kubis and Gabcik figured out Heydrich's routine and somehow obtained a copy of his travel plans for May 27, 1942. Heydrich, they learned, was slated to meet Hitler in Berlin. In order to get there, however, he had to drive on a stretch of road that required him to slow down for a sharp turn. It was the perfect place for an assassination. At about 10:30 in the morning on May 27, "the Butcher of Prague" was in his car and slowing down for the turn when Gabcik jumped up and pulled the trigger on his pistol. It misfired. A shocked Heydrich drew his own pistol and fired at the Czech, while Kubis lobbed a grenade into the open car. The badly wounded general chased away his attackers with gun in hand before collapsing on the ground with damage to his lungs, spleen, and diaphragm. He lingered in agony for a week before dying on June 8, perhaps as a result of blood poisoning from the horse hair seat stuffing that had been embedded in his body. It was the only successful assassination of a major Nazi leader during the entire Second World War. The devil was eulogized at his funeral by Hitler, Himmler, and his old rival, Admiral Canaris.[6]

The reprisal for his death was swift and brutal, and ordered by the Führer himself. The assassins had supposedly been tied to a small village near Prague called Lidice. The Germans razed the entire town and executed most of its male inhabitants. Two hundred women and half as many children were shipped to concentration camps. Another Czech village, Lazaky, suffered a similar fate. Nearly 1,000 additional Czechs were condemned to death by a German court-martial in Prague. A "special action" in Berlin resulted in the death of another 152 Jews and more than 3,000 were deported from the Theresienstadt ghetto and eventually exterminated. In death, as in life, Heydrich's name was inextricably linked with terror and intimidation. But his passing did not derail or even slow down the German death machine. His replacement proved just as fanatical and soulless.[7]

*   *   *

Ernst Kaltenbrunner was born on October 4, 1903, in the valley of the Inn, near Braunau, the birthplace of Adolf Hitler. He was educated in Linz; Adolf Eichmann was one of his boyhood friends. Kaltenbrunner studied law at Graz University, following in the footsteps of his father and grandfather, both of whom were lawyers. He took his doctorate in law in 1926 and set up a practice in Linz. He was an unattractive giant of a man, tall with massive broad shoulders, huge arms, a thick square chin, and deep scars on his face from his student dueling days. Few would have guessed that twenty years later he would be dancing at the end of a rope as one of the world's most notorious war criminals.[8]

Active in one of the first groups of Austrian National Socialist students and, for a time, as a militant in the Independent movement for a Free Austria, Kaltenbrunner eventually joined the Nazi Party in 1930. By 1933 he was a member of the well-camouflaged Austrian SS, an organization forbidden in Austria at that time. He was arrested by the Dollfuss government in 1934 and again in May 1935. The bill for bad behavior was steep: six months in a prison cell on a conspiracy charge and the loss of his license to practice law because of his radical political activities. By 1937, however, things were looking up for the disfigured and disbarred Austrian colossus: Kaltenbrunner had risen to command the Austrian SS. The Anschluss, the annexation of Austria by Hitler's Germany, worked to Kaltenbrunner's advantage when he was given control over the SS and police for Vienna and the Upper and Lower Danube. By April 1941 he was also the lieutenant general of Police. Like Reinhard Heydrich, Kaltenbrunner created an impressive intelligence network. His efforts caught the attention of Himmler, who to the surprise of many, recommended in January 1943 that Kaltenbrunner head the Reich Security Main Office in Berlin.[9]

The result of this consolidation of power under the RSHA umbrella was organized and focused terror on a widespread scale. Kaltenbrunner had complete control of a substantial segment of the most powerful parts of the Nazi apparatus, including the Gestapo and the methods of extermination. And he enjoyed his work. Kaltenbrunner took a personal interest in the wide variety of methods employed to snuff out human lives, both individually and en masse. The use of gas chambers especially fascinated him. Under his relentless direction, his RSHA men hunted down and exterminated several million Jews. His resume also boasts responsibility for murdering Allied parachutists and prisoners of war.

In order to understand how the Reich Security Main Office operated, it is imperative to appreciate its complex internal structure. The RSHA consisted of seven bureaus numbered I through VII. For administrative purposes, each bureau was subdivided into groups and subsections. The whole was staffed by some 100,000 men. Admiral Wilhelm Canaris's Abwehr, which was responsible for all military intelligence and counter-intelligence, was absorbed into Bureau VI in February 1944.[10]

The Bureaus of intelligence and death overseen by Kaltenbrunner were organized and staffed as follows:

Bureau I: Personnel and Organization under the command of SS Standartenführer (Colonel) Erich Ehrlinger.

This section managed to gain a position of prominence rarely seen in a personnel section of any agency. Almost all the chiefs of the sections of the bureau maintained their positions due to political clout. Bureau I and its members were unpopular with the rest of the RSHA bureaus, but there was little love lost between any of the sections housed within RSHA, where intense rivalries and political intrigue thrived.

Colonel Erich Ehrlinger, born October 10, 1914, was plucked from his successful tenure as a commander with the Einsatzgruppen (or mobile killing squads) to head Bureau I. His eyes had overseen mass murder on an almost unprecedented scale while serving on the Russian front from 1941 through 1943. During the early months of the RSHA's existence, Bureau I acquired an incredible measure of power. The bureau's function was the appointment of personnel requested by the other bureaus. The transferees were initially assigned to a Waffen-SS division, and then sent to Bureau I headquarters for reassignment to other RSHA Bureaus.

Bureau I's primary claim to infamy was its creation of special units initially drawn from the SIPO (Security Police) and SD (Secret Police and Secret Service of the SS). The Einsatzgruppen, or as one author calls them, "itinerant killing institutions," were organized for specialized looting and murder instead of traditional warfare. Generally speaking, these insidious units operated in the wake of the advancing Wehrmacht armies. After entering a town or region, Jews and other undesirables were assembled and transported into the countryside, where they were shot to death, either individually or en masse. Although they managed to exterminate over 1,000,000 Russian Jews, gypsies, communist party leaders, and others deemed unworthy, no more than about 3,000 men at the outset served in the Einsatzgruppen; perhaps 6,000, all told, stood in its ranks before the war ended. Even in the midst of this ghastly business the RSHA managed to ring up a profit by combing through the stiff corpses for valuables and organizing the stolen property of those rounded up to die.[11]

Bureau II: Administration and Finance, under the command of SS Oberführer (no U.S. equivalent) Josef Spacil

This department administrated the funds allocated for all of Kaltenbrunner's Bureaus, including large amounts of gold and foreign currency. These funds were also used to purchase uniforms and weapons. Spacil's primary effort was directed at managing Operation Bernhard, a massive counterfeiting scheme designed (at least ostensibly) to flood Europe and Britain with fake notes generated in concentration camps.

Bureau III: Security Service, under the command of SS Obergruppenführer (Lieutenant General) Otto Ohlendorf

This branch of Kaltenbrunner's organization was directly responsible for the murders of hundreds of thousands of Jews and others deemed unworthy of life. Ohlendorf was born in Hoheneggelsen, Germany, on February 4, 1907, the son of a peasant. He studied law at the universities of Leipzig and Göttingen and graduated in July of 1933 with a specialty in National Socialism and Italian fascism. Ohlendorf was one of the first members of the newly constituted Nazi Party, which he joined at the young age of eighteen in 1925. He enlisted in the SS a year later and also fulfilled various SA duties in his home district. Highly educated in both law and economics, Ohlendorf joined the SD in 1936 as an advisor on economic matters and was promoted to major in 1938. The following year he was promoted as chief of Bureau III, a position he retained until the end of World War II.

Ohlendorf's security services provided rather unique intelligence by prying into the lives and thoughts of ordinary citizens in Nazi Germany and acting as a secret and candid chronicler of public opinion for the benefit of Party officials. Although Ohlendorf's research workers were secret police agents and they did their odious task well, Himmler disliked

Ohlendorf. The Reichsführer described him as "an unbearable Prussian, without humor," a rather ironic description coming as it did from a cold man also described by others as humorless. Ohlendorf was promoted to SS Obergruppenführer (Lieutenant General) in November of 1944. He eventually gained a small measure of favor as part of Himmler's twisted entourage, and suggested during the war's final weeks that the Reichsführer surrender to the Allies in order to vindicate the SS against the slander of its enemies. Himmler's right-hand man, Walter Schellenberg, proposed Ohlendorf (one of history's most heinous mass murderers) as the member of a new German cabinet for presentation to the Allies.

One of the projects of SS Colonel Albert Hohlfelder, who headed up Bureau III B (Public Health) and reported directly to Ohlendorf, was x-raying the German population, including minorities in the Balkan states. X-ray machines were placed into vans so that large numbers of people could undergo the procedure. The x-rays were ostensibly used to study diseases and defects in order to find cures for various illnesses. In reality, Hohlfelder used them to sterilize thousands of Jews so that they could be put to work for the Reich without procreation concerns.[12]

Bureau IV: Gestapo, under the command SS Obergruppenführer (Lieutenant General) Heinrich Müller

The son of Catholic parents and future head of the ruthless Gestapo was born on April 28, 1901. During World War I, Müller served as a flight leader on the Eastern front and was awarded the Iron Cross (First Class). After Germany's surrender, he made his career in the Bavarian police department, where he specialized in the surveillance of Communist Party leaders. Much of his tenure there was spent studying Russian police intelligence and investigative techniques. The reward for his expertise in this field arrived when Reinhard Heydrich selected him as his second-in-command of the Gestapo. From that day onward Heydrich's right-hand man virtually ran the Gestapo.

Oddly, Müller was not a member of the Nazi Party. This, coupled with the fact that during his stint with the Munich State Police he had worked against the Nazis, made him politically suspect to many influential Party members. Some of the doubts ceased when he was officially admitted to the Nazi Party in 1939. Short and stocky, with a dry wit and often expressionless countenance, the stubborn and opinionated Müller was highly regarded by both Himmler and Heydrich. Both admired his professional competence, blind obedience, and willingness to execute "delicate missions, spying on colleagues and dispatching political adversaries without scruples." Indeed, Müller was a model for the cold and dispassionate bureaucratic fanatic necessary to carry out the horrendous official state policies underpinning the Third Reich. The result of his efficient exertions was rapid promotion by Heydrich to Standartenführer (Colonel) in 1937, Brigadeführer (Brigadier General) in 1939, Gruppenführer (Major General) in 1940, and Obergruppen-führer (Lieutenant General) and chief of police on November 9, 1941.[13]

As the head of Bureau IV from 1939 to 1945, Müller became almost as deeply involved in the "Final Solution" as Heydrich, Himmler, and Kaltenbrunner. Some might argue he was more directly linked to the mass killings, if only because he was closer to the bloodshed in the chain of command. Working under Müller's direct supervision was Adolf Eichmann, who was in charge of Bureau IV B4. The SS officer was the Chief of the Jewish Office of the Gestapo. On him fell the task of implementing the Final Solution—the total extermination of European Jewry. Because so many later threads of this story intertwine with Bureau IV B4 and Eichmann, a biographical sketch is in order.

The man whose name would one day be synonymous with mass murder came into life near Cologne, Germany, on March 19, 1906. When his mother died, the family relocated to Linz, Austria, where Adolf passed his formative years. The Eichmanns enjoyed a good life in Austria, where a small mining company operated by Adolf's father generated a comfortable middle class income. The youth led a rather uneventful early life, attending schools without demonstrating any particular distinction. Paradoxically, his dark complexion earned him the nickname "little Jew" by his classmates. Unable or unwilling to complete his studies in engineering, Adolf accepted a variety of positions to earn a living. For a time he worked as a laborer in his father's establishment, and later as a traveling salesman for an American oil company.

Without significant ties to a career and without direction, by the early 1930s Eichmann was adrift in an uneasy world. On the advice of his friend Ernst Kaltenbrunner, Eichmann enrolled in the Austrian Nazi

Party and a short time later was on the rolls as a member of the SS. By 1934 he was serving as an SS corporal at Dachau, a concentration camp for political prisoners twelve miles north of Munich, Germany. The corrupting influence of both the Nazi doctrine and the individuals with whom he associated took a fateful turn for Eichmann that September, when he accepted a position with Reinhard Heydrich's already notorious SD, a powerful arm of the RSHA.[14]

Eichmann's RSHA career began rather inauspiciously, his days consumed as a desk clerk registering information about Freemasons. His assignment to a section investigating prominent Jews, however, seemed more to his liking and marked the beginning of what would evolve into a deadly passion for killing on a scale rarely imagined and never before implemented. As far as was possible, Eichmann immersed himself in Jewish culture. He appeared at Jewish meetings, studied the history of Zionism, and frequented Jewish sections of cities. Friendships and associations were cultivated with members of the community. There was a method to his madness: all the while he appeared interested in their faith and beliefs, Eichmann was busy scribbling copious notes that would one day be used for perfidious purposes. Within a short time, the German from Cologne (by way of Linz) was recognized by his superiors as a "Jewish specialist." Eichmann had found a direction and purpose in an otherwise aimless existence. The SD had found a dedicated man well suited to its purposes.

In August 1938, Eichmann was placed in charge of the Office for Jewish Emigration in Vienna, set up by the SS as the sole Nazi agency authorized to issue exit permits for Jews from Austria, then Czechoslovakia, and later Germany. In less than eighteen months, approximately 150,000 Jews were forced out of Austria to centers in the East. By March 1939 he was handling the deportation of Jews and other undesirables to Poland. After the war began that September, Eichmann was appointed special adviser on the evacuation of Jews and Poles. Before 1939 ended, a transfer to Bureau IV (Gestapo) of the Reich Security Main Office came about, where he took over Bureau IV B4 dealing with Jewish affairs and evacuation.

For the next five and a half years Eichmann's office was the headquarters for the implementation of the Final Solution. Initially this manifested itself in administrative efforts, deportations, and the establishment of ghettos. In accordance with Hitler's order to create a Jew-free Reich, Eichmann began organizing mass deportations from Germany and Bohemia. His system of convoys would eventually be replicated across Europe and carry millions of men, women and children to their deaths. Most would perish in the death camps that Eichmann began establishing in the summer of 1941. The death camp at Birkenau, one of three Nazi concentration camps that came to be collectively known to a horrified world as simply "Auschwitz," opened its assembly line murder factory in October 1941. Eichmann paid a visit and approved of the gassing technique adopted there. Heydrich's Wannsee Conference of January 1942, mentioned earlier in this study and attended by Eichmann, solidified his standing as the Reich's "Jewish specialist."

Unlike some of the prominent Nazi leaders, Eichmann had never been a fanatical anti-Semite or dedicated Nazi. Indeed, during his trial in Israel in the 1960s, he made a point of claiming that he "personally" had nothing against Jews, and apparently he was telling the truth. His methodical enthusiasm manifested itself in any number of bureaucratic ways. He constantly complained about obstacles in the fulfillment of the quotas set for his death camps, and lamented the lack of cooperativeness of the Italians and other German allies in expediting Jews for death. Nothing better illustrates Eichmann's zeal for his job than his refusal to comply with Himmler's moderated views during the war's final months. Eichmann felt utterly free to ignore the Reichsführer's order to stop gassing Jews because his immediate superiors, including Heinrich Müller and his old friend Ernst Kaltenbrunner, provided him cover to continue the killing.

Eichmann, as he saw it, was just doing his job.

Bureau V: Police Functions under the command of Oberführer (no U.S. equivalent) Friedrich Panzinger

All German police and police forces of occupied countries were under the command of the bureaus of the RSHA. This force, which numbered more than 2,000,000 men, was the eyes and ears of the SD, SIPO, and Gestapo. History has confirmed that some like the Gendarme of France were an enthusiastic group and provided the Germans with considerable assistance. On the other hand, the police of Denmark are known today for their obstinate behavior and obstructionist policies in dealing with the German occupiers.

Friedrich Panzinger, the future head of the powerful Bureau V, was born in Monaco on February 1, 1903. He returned to Germany and obtained a law degree, joined the Nazi party in 1937 and the SS two years later. Panzinger quickly became a Communist espionage specialist. In 1943 he took command of the Security Police and SD in the Baltic states as well as Einsatzgruppen A—one of the mobile killing squads. Panzinger looked as though one might imagine an SS murderer would—medium stature with a high forehead, immaculately groomed hair parted on the side, oval spectacles—and an icy cold mien. At the end of the war he went into hiding, but was arrested in Linz, Austria, in 1946, and imprisoned by the Soviet Union.

Bureau N: M.I. (Abwehr) Armed Forces, under the command of Admiral Wilhelm Canaris

Wilhelm Canaris, the German admiral of Greek descent who headed up military intelligence for the Armed Forces (OKW), was born in Aplerbeck, Germany, on January 1, 1887. The son of a Westphalian industrialist, Canaris entered the Imperial Navy in 1905. During World War I, he commanded U-boats in the Mediterranean and carried out espionage missions in Spain and Italy. In the early 1920s he was a naval staff officer in the Baltic fleet and rose to command the battleship *Schlesien*. Like so many during that period, Canaris appreciated Hitler's anti-Versailles program and apprehension of Russian communists, but disliked the mob violence and street thuggery aspects of Nazism. His resentment of Hitler's murderous behind-the-scenes politics increased after his appointment as Chief of the Abwehr on January 1, 1935.

Although Canaris was aligned with the anti-Hitler faction, his exact role within the Nazi regime is still debated today. Some argue that he was an incompetent dilettante whose judgment was consistently unsound and whose political and military information about the enemy proved minimal at best. A pessimistic recluse whose nerve failed before each major Nazi offensive thrust, only to evidence itself in effusive praise for Hitler once success resulted, Canaris was said to be constantly beset with doubts about his role. Others, like Abwehr attache and Canaris supporter, Hans Bernd Gisevius, argue that the admiral's perceived incompetence and seeming insecurity were simply techniques employed to fool Hitler and other high ranking leaders, which enabled him to maintain a powerful position and influence events.

Long suspected of treasonous activity, Canaris's dangerous game neared its end in February 1944 when the Abwehr was snatched away from him and placed under the control of the SD. A position in the economic warfare department followed, but the appointment was merely a sinecure that allowed Gestapo agents to keep an eye on his activities. The botched attempt to kill Hitler in July 1944 doomed Canaris when a conspirator confessed his involvement. In fact, he was not directly tied to the assassins, but his papers and diaries proved his perfidy against Hitler spanned many years. Canaris was arrested, tortured, and during the final days of the war hanged with several others on a makeshift gallows at Flossenburg concentration camp.

"Canaris hated not only Hitler and Himmler, but the entire Nazi system as a political phenomenon," wrote fellow Abwehr agent Hans Bernd Gisevius in a memoir published two years after the war. "He was everywhere and nowhere at once. Everywhere he traveled—at home, abroad, and to the front—he always left a whirl of confusion lingering behind him. . . . Extremely well read, oversensitive, Canaris was an outsider in every respect. In bearing and manner of work he was the most unmilitary of persons."[15]

Bureau VI: Military Intelligence under the command of SS Brigadeführer (General) Walter Schellenberg

Walter Schellenberg was the head of the Third Reich's espionage services and Heinrich Himmler's right-hand man during the war's final years. He was born in Saarbrücken on October 16, 1910, the seventh child of a piano manufacturer. After receiving his law degree at Bonn University (where he developed an ardent interest in Renaissance history and its political implications), Schellenberg joined the Nazi Party and the SS in 1933. Within a year he was part of the Gestapo apparatus. Young, handsome, ambitious, and fluent in both English and French, Schellenberg attracted the attention of both Heydrich and Himmler, who eventually made him their personal aide.

At the behest of his superiors, Schellenberg organized the Einsatzgruppen squads for use in the Austrian and Czech campaigns in 1938. Four years later, he negotiated on behalf of the RSHA with the Wehrmacht over the zones of authority in which the Einsatzgruppen could work to "execute their plans as regards the civil population." In other words, where the killing squads could operate freely against noncombatants without political or military interference.

By November 1939 he was the head of the Gestapo counter-intelligence division (Amt I'VE). The former lawyer had a passion and talent for military intelligence and counter-espionage. He led a detachment of armed Germans across the Dutch border to kidnap two British military intelligence agents. Barely thirty, he was decorated and promoted to the rank of colonel. His attempt to kidnap the Duke and Duchess of Windsor in Spain, however, was unsuccessful. In 1941 Schellenberg was selected to lead Bureau VI, the Foreign Intelligence Service. His efforts in this capacity unraveled the web-like network of Soviet intelligence operating within the Reich.

In February 1944, Schellenberg's division swallowed the foreign and counter-intelligence Bureau (Bureau N) of the Abwehr under Admiral Wilhelm Canaris, which was reduced to a branch of Schellenberg's Bureau VI office. His dedicated efforts earned an appointment as head of the SS and Wehrmacht military intelligence. He now stood second only to Himmler in the Gestapo hierarchy.

Bureau VII: Ideological Research, under the command of Brigadeführer (General) Alfred Franz Six

Franz Six was an academic. The Mannheim-born professor of sociology, politics, and philosophy graduated from the University of Heidelberg. Long enamored with the Nazi doctrine, he joined the party in 1930. Membership in the SA followed in 1932, and the SD in 1935. He also pursued a teaching career. As war was breaking out in 1939, he accepted a position as a foreign political science professor at the University of Berlin.

Six clasped hands with the devil in 1941. While Hitler's war machine was preparing to invade the Soviet Union, the scholarly professor from

Mannheim accepted a position as Chief of the Vorkommando Moscow. According to Six, the position was merely one of collecting documents when Stalin's capital fell. In fact, his role was to oversee mobile killing squads. Vorkommando Moscow, it was later proven, was part of Einsatzgruppen B. On November 9, 1941, Heinrich Himmler personally promoted Six for his "outstanding service in [the] Einsatz."[16]

Bureau VII was organized on July 1, 1935, by Himmler as an SS research institution for the purpose of furnishing a scientific foundation for the Nazi doctrine of German superiority. Himmler's fascination was Germanic prehistory. His political aim was to establish scientific proof of the theory of Aryan supremacy. Although Himmler was no scientist, he did demand facts and scholarly thoroughness. Therefore, the staff that made up Bureau VII was composed of scholars, scientists, and experts—many of them, like Franz Six, were professors of leading universities. Men capable of splitting atoms and designing rockets were engaged in rewriting the record of the past in order to influence the future course of history.

*   *   *

The information summarizing these various men and the bureaucracies within which they labored has been presented to help establish the background of both, and the overall framework within which these men and thousands of others operated during World War II. As most readers will have already recognized, most of the managers of these governmental entities were college graduates. In other times and in other places, these lawyers, professors, bank managers, civil engineers, and economists would have led ordinary and productive lives. History would never have found them. But the times within which they lived were not ordinary. Records from around the world and across the centuries reflect the sad fact that often, when men grip the reins of life and death over their fellow man, they devolve into beasts of evil. Just the *authority* to commit murder often leads to extermination on a massive scale. Few are truly ideologically motivated. Power and treasure are the aphrodisiacs that drive them.

The insatiable quest for profit ran on a parallel track with these bureaucracies of mass murder and intelligence gathering. As millions of people from across Europe were loaded onto trains and deported, lined up along ditches and executed, or stuffed into gas chambers and suffocated, men in positions high and low scrambled to line their pockets with gold. This was especially true for officers holding prominent positions of authority. SS officers in particular—because of their close association with the Final Solution and all that entailed—looted hundreds of millions in currency, bullion, jewels, artwork, and antiques. Others came into possession of valuable letters, documents, diaries, and other written memorabilia pertaining to important Nazi leaders.

The tide of war turned irrevocably against Germany in 1944 when the Allies landed in Normandy. Perhaps it turned even earlier. Regardless, by that time the final push to free Europe from the Nazi yoke was underway. As the Allies drove eastward, the Soviets were forcing the Germans, mile by bloody mile, out of the Soviet Union and back into Poland and ultimately, Germany. By the spring of 1945, Hitler's troops still held a sizeable chunk of territory, but the German war machine had been marched and bled to the point of exhaustion. It was no longer able to coordinate an effective resistance to the multitude of Allied advances. While Berlin and a score of other cities crumbled building by building under Allied bombing runs, trucks, jeeps, railroad cars, and planes loaded with treasures and other personal property stolen from death camp victims and conquered cities were on the move. Most of this moveable wealth was being shipped into the mountains of Austria. It was there that many of the SS's worst criminals hoped to wage a successful, or at least prolonged, resistance. Others concerned themselves with escape. Few prominent leaders trapped in Austria at war's end had any illusions of their final fate if captured.

The ensuing pages will introduce you to, and follow the fortunes of, some of the more fascinating characters associated with the Reich Security Main Office and the stolen treasures over which these men presided. Many were caught, their fortunes confiscated. Many more escaped with their treasures intact. A sizeable number managed to conceal their bullion and currency for subsequent unearthing. Millions remain unaccounted for and will perhaps never be found.

Chapter Notes

1. There are several good books dealing with Heydrich. Two of particular relevance are: Edouard Calic, *Reinhard Heydrich : The Chilling Story of the Man Who Masterminded the Nazi Death Camps* (New York, 1984), and Callum MacDonald, *The Killing of Reinhard Heydrich: The SS Butcher of Prague* (Da Capo, 1998).

2. For an interesting psychological examination of Heydrich, see Fest, *The Faces of the Third Reich*, pp. 98-110.

3. Dear, ed., *Oxford Companion to World War II*, pp. 526-527. Heydrich also probably took a hand in the Tukhachevsky Affair, which led to the purge of many top Red Army generals in the Soviet Union.

4. Daniel Jonah Goldhagen, *Hitler's Willing Executioners: Ordinary Germans and the Holocaust* (New York, 1996), pp. 148-153. According to the museum at Wannsee, Germany, Reinhard Heydrich requested the Final Solution assignment.

5. Adolf Eichmann testified at his trial in Israel that he sat in a corner with a stenographer and recorded "euphemisms," although Heydrich spoke "in absolutely blunt terms" regarding the killing of the Jews. Eichmann Testimony, Session 107, July 24, 1961; Padfield, *Himmler*, p. 357.

6. Fest, *The Faces of the Third Reich*, pp. 108-109.

7. William L. Schirer, *The Rise and Fall of the Third Reich* (New York, 1959), pp. 991-994.

8. Peter R. Black, *Ernst Kaltenbrunner: Ideological Soldier of the Third Reich* (Princeton, 1984), p. 14.

9. Dear, ed., *The Oxford Companion to World War II*, p. 642.

10. Dear, ed., *Oxford Companion to World War II*, pp. 969-970. The Germans referred to the individual bureaus as Amt. Thus, Bureau II, for example, would be listed as Amt. II.

11. Goldhagan, *Hitler's Willing Executioners*, p. 167.

12. Case No. 9, "The Einsatzgruppen Case." Ohlendorf's testimony can be found in RG 238, Entry 92, Box 1, vol. 2, National Archives.

13. Padfield, *Himmler*, pp. 127, 144-145.

14. Padfield, *Himmler*, pp. 198-200.

15. Dear, ed., *Oxford Companion to World War II*, pp. 189-190; Hans Bernd Gisevius, *To the Bitter End* (Boston, 1947), pp. 443-444.

16. Michael Musmanno, U.S.N.R, Military Tribunal II, Case 9: *Opinion and Judgment of the Tribunal*. Nuremberg: Palace of Justice. April 8, 1948, pp. 146-151.

Chapter 3

"If one of my SS men takes only as much as a pin from the Jewish
properties, I shall punish the man with the death sentence."

— Reichsführer Heinrich Himmler to Franz Konrad

Franz Konrad:
The King of the Ghetto

chloss Fischhorn, or Castle Fischhorn, is nestled deep within the
breathtaking Alps of Austria near the town of Zell am See. Its
walls tower over the shores of a deep crystal blue glacier lake of
the same name. When Japan bombed Pearl Harbor on December 7, 1941,
the 12th century fortress and surrounding farmland was owned by
Henrique E. Gildemeister, the Peruvian Minister to Austria. Peru,
however, severed its diplomatic relations with Germany following
Hitler's declaration of war against the United States. Fearing for their
safety, Gildemeister took his family back to their native land. The SS
eventually seized the castle and grounds and evicted its land manager.
They had refrained from taking title to the land and ousting him earlier in
fear that the Peruvian government would take similar steps against
German property within its own borders. During the latter months of
World War II, Fischhorn served as both a repository for stolen loot and
SS Headquarters for Equine Matters.[1]

Even before the Germans overran Europe, a plan had been crafted to
create a race of superior horses bred from the best blood on the European

continent. The intention was to form an elite cavalry corps—the finest ever fielded on any battlefield. These black riders from central Europe, so the fantasy went, would cut through rough terrain, move behind an enemy, and hold him until powerful mechanized units could be brought up for the kill. The improbable scheme was initiated as early as 1938 in Austria. The most famous stables in the world were looted, one by one, as country after country fell beneath the twisted cross of the Nazi banner. In France, two outstanding stables belonging to Baron Edouard Rothschild and the Aga Khan were seized. Every one of Poland's privately owned Arabians, generally recognized as the finest Arabian stock in the world, was confiscated. From Hungary, the Germans stole all the horses owned by the Hungarian government, including Pax, the winner of the Hungarian Oaks, and Taj Akbar, who came in second in the English Derby. To these were added the finest blooded horses the Germans had been able to purchase from England and America before the war. Most of these magnificent beasts were transported to Fischhorn castle during the final year of war. The result of this grand-scale horse thievery was a Salzburg province, Austrian stable complex that produced some of the purest and most magnificent foals in horse breeding history.

Neither adjective, pure nor magnificent, would ever be associated with the administrative officer who oversaw the equine operation during its final months of existence. SS Hauptsturmführer (Captain) Franz Konrad's road to Schloss Fischhorn was paved with crime, hardship, blood, death—and gold.

* * *

The early years of Franz Konrad's life were unremarkable. He was born in Vienna on March 1, 1906, into a middle class existence. After he finished school and obtained a business degree, he worked for a time as a bookkeeper for various export firms. He soon demonstrated his proclivity for criminal action when he was caught stealing money from his employer. Not only did he lose his job but he was also imprisoned for three months in 1932. Out of jail and out of work, Konrad drifted for a few weeks until his former defense lawyer helped him join the illegal Austrian SS in January 1933. Membership in the Nazi party followed before the end of the year. Party officials provided him with living expenses and helped land him a job with a highway construction firm. As the years passed Konrad advanced, rung by rung, up the party ladder. In December of 1939 he joined the elite Waffen SS and was assigned to Berlin.

Of the many characters covered in some detail in the study, Franz Konrad is perhaps the most physically unremarkable. Everything about him was ordinary. He was of average height, a bit frumpy looking with a tendency toward paunchiness; his hairline had receded above his chubby and round, but not altogether unpleasant, face. If he walked by on the street not a single head would turn to take a second glance. Unlike Otto Ohlendorf, Heinrich Himmler, or Franz Six, Konrad did not project an icy cold demeanor. Looks are indeed deceiving.[2]

In the German capital, Konrad's administrative duties brought him into close association with Hermann Fegelein, a callous SS officer about to be promoted to Obersturmbannführer (Lieutenant Colonel). Fegelein was tasked with organizing Waffen-SS cavalry units in Poland. Hitler's attack against that country on September 1, 1939, launched without any declaration of war following false claims that the Poles had assaulted Germany territory, had triggered the war's outbreak in Europe. To the surprise of Poland's leadership, Soviet troops swept in from the east seventeen days later. The Fascist and Communist armies smashed Polish opposition quickly. By the end of the month the country was partitioned by Hitler and Stalin in a treaty signed in Moscow. Now, the difficult task of administering the newly conquered territory began.

Germany assumed control of the western provinces, which were formally annexed in early October. Some 35,000 square miles and almost 10,000,000 new people were now officially part of Hitler's Third Reich. A far larger area, however, including the major cities of Warsaw, Cracow, and Lublin—100,000 square miles and 12,000,000 souls—was given a general government listing and classified as a "labor colony." As one writer describes it, "the Nazi occupation marked the beginning of almost six years of unspeakable horror for Poles." Intellectuals, political activists, Jews and other undesirables were rounded up and either shot or imprisoned. Polish culture was on the block and scheduled to be dismantled, piece by piece; those remaining alive in the end would be thoroughly Germanized. Concentration camps were established. Hell had come to Poland.[3]

In January 1940, four months after Poland fell to the Nazis, Konrad and Fegelein traveled by car from Berlin to Warsaw. Konrad's initial assignment was "Leiter für Werterfassung in the Warsaw Ghetto"— the official in charge of seizing possessions in the Warsaw Ghetto. His job was to provide furnished and decorated apartments for SS officers. In other words, he was ordered to steal homes and property. To accomplish this odious task, Konrad was assigned a Warsaw-born, Polish turncoat who worked for the Germans as a translator. According to Konrad, the Pole "knew where the rich Jews of Warsaw lived." On a typical outing Konrad and his associate would drive up to an apartment building and ask around if Jewish families were housed in the building. If the answer was "no," they simply looked at the directory mounted at bottom of the staircase. If a Jewish name appeared, they called in an SS military squad and confiscated the apartment and all its belongings. The family was thrown out in the streets, deported, or sent into the Ghetto. Konrad also used the telephone directory to search for Jewish-sounding names. He knew how the game was played, and he played it well. Konrad regularly pilfered items for his own use and enjoyed a lavish lifestyle of wealth and pleasure. His ability to produce exquisite wines, antiques, jewelry, and artwork at the snap of a finger was put to good advantage and cemented his relationship with Hermann Fegelein, SS Captain Albert Fassbender, and Reichsführer Heinrich Himmler.[4]

Albert Fassbender, nicknamed "sweetie" because his adoptive father owned a chocolate factory in Berlin, was a shiftless crook and drunk before the war. His association with Fegelein, whose morals and scruples were as low as his own, landed him the position of battalion commander of the 1st Reiter Regiment. The command, coupled with Fegelein's assistance, helped him achieve notoriety as one of the leading looters, womanizers, and criminals in all of Warsaw. And he had plenty of competition.[5]

Fassbender moved into an upscale department store owned by Maksimillian Apfelbaum, who had fled the country soon after the beginning of the war. One of his first acts was the seduction of former Apfelbaum model Slawa Mirowska. The beautiful model was half-Russian and the wife of a Polish officer. Like Fassbender, Mirowska delighted in a life of riches and luxury, especially if they were the result of the hard efforts of others. Realizing an opportunity to live well in the middle of a hard war, Mirowska signed on as both Fassbender's lover and accomplice. The pair transformed the Apfelbaum showrooms into a den for drinking parties and sex orgies. Many of the younger models, out of work and hungry, were enticed with food and expensive presents to ply their wares for German officers. Before long the once-respected Warsaw store was the best bordello in Warsaw. At some point during their liaison Fassbender discovered Mirowska was pregnant. He had her husband arrested by the Gestapo. A few days later he was shot in his prison cell. Fassbender's behavior, already horrendous, spiraled out of control.[6]

While German officers stole, drank, and engaged in debauchery, factory workers labored feverishly to keep up with the growing demand for luxury items—especially fur coats. Every friend of "Sweetie" Fassbender had a sweetheart or wife (or both) who wanted an expensive fur. Like other commodities, furs proved to be an effective way to buy friends and loyalty. Even Hans Frank, Hitler's appointed governor of Poland, pressed Fassbender to supply him with endless numbers of the expensive coats. Like Fassbender, the immoral duo of Konrad and Fegelein often ignored their duties in favor of endless playtime. Both also took girlfriends, although only the former officer was married. When Fegelein's mistress announced she was pregnant, he forced her against her will to abort the child.[7]

Ironically, it was the SS that clamped down on these activities. In early 1940 Dr. Konrad Morgen, an SS officer and judge, was put in charge of investigating cruelty and black market activities in conquered towns and concentration camps. Morgen's inquiry eventually wound itself to the doorsteps of Fegelein and Fassbender, as well as a number of other SS officers. Konrad, somehow, fell outside the shadow of suspicion. Fegelein's crime, or at least the only one deemed serious enough to investigate, was sending cash and other stolen Polish valuables to the SS cavalry school at Reim. A Gestapo search of Fegelein's home and grounds uncovered a plethora of purloined goods including a customized Mercedes, furs, antiques, furniture, and many other items of value. Demands were made for their return to their owners. Fortunately for Fegelein, Himmler intervened to discourage the investigation in an attempt to protect one of his favorite officers. The embarrassed Reichsführer was angry only because many of the officers involved were his beloved SS men. He scribbled "impossible conduct" in the margin of the final report, but refused to take any additional action against his young protégé. Himmler was not about to sacrifice Fegelein, one of the SS's rising stars, over stolen goods and sexual transgressions.[8]

As a result, the embarrassed Fegelein and Fassbender (with Fegelein's assistance), escaped serious punishment. Thus Konrad, as Fegelein's close associate and general thief, also managed to avoid Dr. Morgen's dragnet. For political reasons, however, Himmler had to at least pretend he was concerned about the level of corruption Morgen's investigation had discovered within his SS. Swift punishment, ordered the Reichsführer, must be meted out against unscrupulous SS officers. One of those unable to wriggle free was SS Obersturmführer (Lieutenant) von Sauberzweig, who, according to Dr. Morgen's report, was working hand-in-hand with Fegelein and Fassbender. The lieutenant was sentenced to death and executed by firing squad. When other SS officers were accused of similar crimes, they demanded to be treated by the precedent set by the Fegelein–Fassbender case, i.e., let off the hook. Himmler, however, showed little mercy.[9]

Even with Dr. Morgen's judicial inquisitions, life in Warsaw was wonderful—if you were a German. SS cavalry officers spent much of their time riding stolen thoroughbreds on Warsaw's famous racetrack, drinking wine, eating fine food—and rounding up Jews. Morgen's "investigation" did nothing to slow down SS criminal activities in Poland or elsewhere. A large section of Warsaw had been cordoned off to hold a growing population of Jews. By the summer of 1941 it was the largest such ghetto in Europe. There, 400,000 to 500,000 people awaited their fate, crowded, hungry, sick, and frightened. There was still money to be made in Warsaw—especially from the new Jews who arrived daily from other occupied countries. Each family, blissfully unaware of what was planned for them, carried with them their transportable valuables. Most of this currency, gold, and jewelry was confiscated within hours of their arrival in Warsaw.[10]

*   *   *

As both Konrad and Fegelein were about to discover, all goods things come to an end. On June 22, 1941, the gigantic German blitzkrieg known as Operation Barbarossa was launched against Soviet Russia. Fegelein was dispatched east with his 8th SS Cavalry Division *Florian Geyer* to participate in the massive invasion. To his dismay, Konrad was shipped out as well and assigned to Fegelein's outfit. The bureaucrat with a taste for cruelty was put in charge of a light truck transport responsible for supplying troops and horses with provisions. He remained in this position for about a year, experiencing combat largely behind the lines while Fegelein's troops mopped up bypassed enemy forces and carried on a ruthless extermination campaign against partisans and civilians alike.[11]

Hermann Fegelein was enough of a crook to realize that while he fought in the East, others were collecting millions in loot from the rapage of Poland. Together with his friend and assistant SS Standartenführer (Colonel) Kurt Becher, Fegelein arranged a closed-door meeting with Ferdinand von Sammern, the SS Police Führer of Warsaw. Fegelein informed von Sammern that he was "going to transfer Franz Konrad back to Warsaw." Konrad, he continued, was the best administrator of the SS Cavalry. His job would be to seize ghetto valuables. Kurt Becher, meanwhile, explained the details of the arrangement Fegelein was foisting upon von Sammern. A cut of the take, he said matter-of-factly, would be handed over to Fegelein for assigning Konrad to the project. Von Sammern, who was not in much of a position to disagree, quietly acquiesced to the new arrangement. And so Konrad departed the front lines of Russia in July 1942 and returned to Warsaw, which had by now become one of the primary logistical centers for the Eastern invasion. He threw himself back into his work with a new gusto. The valuables—rugs, paintings, antiques, and everything else normally found inside well-to-do homes—were plucked from their owners and loaded into cavalry trucks provided by Fegelein. Colonel Becher often accompanied Konrad on his rounds. After all, he too was slicing off a percentage for his own pockets.

Colonel Becher also ordered (probably with Fegelein's blessing) that Konrad assume the reins of Kohn & Heller, a Polish company that before the war produced a line of toiletry articles. Forced Jewish labor was utilized to enlarge the establishment and equip it to produce writing paper, cigarette paper, razors, shoe polish, batteries, uniforms, and the many items needed by German foot soldiers on the Russian Front.[12]

Konrad and Becher were busy honing the mechanics of their city-wide pillaging scheme when the extermination of Warsaw's Jews began in earnest. It was Konrad's duty (and pleasure) to seize everything of value he could lay his hands on. Anything left behind by those deported to Auschwitz or elsewhere was confiscated. Books, paintings, furniture, automobiles, machinery, and clothing filled to overflowing the fifteen warehouses under Konrad's control. Each storage facility was used to house separate items. For example, one warehouse contained pianos, furs and valuable carpets; another chemicals, paints, and medications. Eleven thousand Jewish laborers were required to oversee the mammoth pillaging operation. The Jews—and many Germans as well—heartily disliked Konrad, whose cruel streak, brusk manner in dealing with others, and tendency toward pompous display earned him the derisive title, "King of the Warsaw Ghetto."[13]

As the war dragged on and labor grew scarce, SS General Odilo Globocnik, Lublin police chief and the head of concentration camps in Poland, wanted to remove Jewish workers from Warsaw and use them to produce products for the German war machine. Globocnik petitioned Himmler to consider using Jews instead of sending them to the death camps. The Reichsführer paid a visit to Warsaw in early 1943 to observe firsthand the Jewish workers laboring there under Konrad's authority. He met with Konrad at Warehouse No. 2, where he viewed with some amazement the immense quantity of textiles, silver, porcelain, and small mountain of loose buttons accumulating under Konrad's watchful eye.

"Konrad," the bespectacled SS leader said, patting him on the shoulder, "if one of my SS men takes only as much as a pin from the Jewish properties, I shall punish the man with the death sentence."

Threats of death notwithstanding, many of the choicest valuables were set aside for Fegelein and others. Konrad himself acquired a large number of antiques, paintings, and other worthwhile items, including expensive stamp collections and several 700-year-old Torahs.[14]

The Jewish workers General Globocnik hoped to obtain as slave laborers to manufacture merchandise for Germany were removed from Warsaw on Himmler's orders—though not for the purpose Globocnik intended. The final evacuation and destruction of the Warsaw Ghetto began after the Reichsführer's visit and unfolded during the most sacred Christian holiday: Easter through the Pentecost. By this time some 300,000 Jews had already been taken to Treblinka or Auschwitz; 60,000 remained in Warsaw. Konrad stood by and watched as 3,000 Wehrmacht,

SS, and police, supported by tanks, armored vehicles, and machine guns, swept through the Ghetto to root out its inhabitants. Some of the Jews decided to go down fighting and launched a fierce building-by-building, block-by-block resistance. Caught flatfooted, the Germans suffered heavy casualties overcoming the fierce and unexpected opposition. Buildings were set on fire and the flames spread quickly. People of all ages climbed onto roof tops in a vain attempt to save themselves. As fire engulfed the structures the doomed, young and old alike, screamed from the heights overlooking devastated Warsaw or hung from window ledges in a futile attempt to escape. Some leapt to their deaths; most perished in the flames. One SS major was heard to whisper, "Those poor people." According to Konrad, the words of mercy landed the major in prison. Eight weeks later the Warsaw Ghetto was declared free of Jews. Bullets and fire had consumed 14,000 people. The Germans lost 400 killed and perhaps another 1,000 wounded in the uprising.[15]

Those Jews extracted alive from the Ghetto were herded into an assembly area, loaded onto trains, and shipped to the death camps. At one assembly point Konrad witnessed the execution of 2,000 Jews left behind because there were not enough to completely fill a train. They were lined up in small groups and shot in the back of the head with machine pistols. The corpses were dragged together and burned. Afterward, remembered Konrad, the piles of ashes were raked in the search for diamonds, gold coins, and any other valuables hidden or swallowed by the desperate victims that may have survived the hellish inferno.[16]

* * *

By 1945, Stalin's divisions were in complete control of the war in the East and driving relentlessly westward. Franz Konrad was still behind the lines in Warsaw, pillaging from innocents and living a comfortable life as a powerful SS officer. In early January, however, Fegelein decided it was time for Konrad and his staff—and his valuables—to evacuate. He ordered rail cars and trucks loaded with tons of valuables and shipped south and west to safer environs. Along with a handful of fortunate Jewish laborers, the SS officer and his associates beat a hasty retreat out of the war torn city and rode the rails south to the relative safety of north central Austria and Fischhorn castle, the SS gathering place outside Zell am See. He had been planning the move for some time. By the time he arrived, both Fischhorn and General Fegelein's private residence in Ravensburg were luxuriously furnished with possessions stolen from Warsaw's deported Jews.[17]

Chapter Notes

1. "Administration of Fischhorn Castle," signed Hans Schneider, August 25, 1948, RG 260, U.S. Forces Austria, NA.

2. "Personal Name File, Franz Conrad [sic]," RG 319/631/31-32/54-2/4-4, Box 31A, IRR Case Files, hereinafter referred to as "Personal Name File, Franz Konrad." See also, CIC, "Testimony of Franz Konrad, regarding his past doings in the Ghetto of Warsaw," pp. 1-5, January 4, 1946, NA, hereinafter referred to as "Interrogation of Franz Konrad."

3. Dear, ed., *The Oxford Companion to World War II*, p. 892.

4. "Personal Name File, Franz Konrad"; "Interrogation of Franz Konrad," January 4, 1946, pp. 6-10.

5. "Personal Name File, Franz Konrad"; "Interrogation of Franz Konrad," January 4, 1946, pp. 1-5.

6. "Personal Name File, Franz Konrad"; "Interrogation of Franz Konrad," January 4, 1946, pp. 6-10.

7. Von Kurt Emmenegger, *Sie und Er* (April 1963), KZ Ghetto Korruption, p. 22, Magyar Országos Levéltár, Hungarian National Archives, Budapest, Hungary.

8. Padfield, *Himmler*, p. 295; John Toland, *Adolf Hitler* (NY, 1976), pp. 773-774.

9. Toland, *Adolf Hitler*, pp. 773-774. According to Toland, Dr. Konrad Morgen brought 800 corruption cases to trial with 200 convictions. Morgen charged Karl Koch, the commander of Buchenwald, and his wife Ilse, with fraud and theft. Koch was convicted and executed; Ilse was acquitted. As astounding as this sounds, many SS personnel were imprisoned and executed because of Morgen's efforts. Later, many more SS officers faced Polish wrath even while the war was still being fought. For example, a group of six officials of the Polish death camp at Maidanek outside Lublin, including commandant Herman Vogel, were tried and put to death by a Polish Special Criminal Court in Lublin in 1944.

10. For an excellent study of the sad story of Warsaw and the subsequent uprising, see Israel Gutman, *The Warsaw Ghetto Uprising* (NY, 1994).

11. According to The Simon Wiesenthal Center, some 20,000 Jews and others, primarily partisans or surrendered soldiers, were killed during Fegelein's tenure in Poland and the Soviet Union.

12. Von Kurt Emmenegger, *Sie und Er* (April 1963), KZ Ghetto Korruption, p. 23, Magyar Országos Levéltár, Hungarian National Archives, Budapest, Hungary; "Personal Name File, Franz Konrad"; "Interrogation of Franz Konrad," pp. 13-17.

13. "Personal Name File, Franz Konrad"; "Interrogation of Franz Konrad," p. 31.

14. Hitler File, Volume I and II, two folders (no box number), Headquarters European Command, Intelligence Division, Receipt for Property, October 14, 1949, RG 319, G-2, NA; "Personal Name File, Franz Konrad"; "Interrogation of Franz Konrad," p. 33.

15. Dear, *Oxford Companion to World War II*, p. 1260; Gutman, *The Warsaw Ghetto Uprising*, selected references throughout; "Personal Name File, Franz Konrad"; "Interrogation of Franz Konrad," p. 33.

16. "Personal Name File, Franz Konrad"; "Interrogation of Franz Konrad," January 4, 1946, pp. 47-48.

17. "History and Identification of Polish Property," Salzburg, March 5, 1946, RG 260 USFA, NA; "Personal Name File, Franz Konrad"; "Interrogation of Franz Konrad," January 4, 1946, pp. 66-67.

Chapter 4

He agreed to help keep the Jews from resisting deportation and even
keep order in the collection camps if I could close my eyes and
let a few hundred or a few thousand young Jews emigrate
illegally to Palestine. It was a good bargain.

— Adolf Eichmann, speaking of Dr. Rudolf Kastner

Playing God in Budapest:
The Kastner-Becher Faustian Bargain

In the 1930s, Hungary was a country without a rudder, adrift in a
dangerous sea. The anti-fascist leanings of its *de facto* head of state,
Admiral Miklós Horthy, were balanced and eventually transcended
by a rising tide of right-wing fascist movements, the most powerful of
which was Ferenc Szálasi's Arrow Cross faction. By 1939 Hungary's
politics and strategic location linked its fate with Hitler's Germany. The
Führer's invasion of the Soviet Union in June of 1941 forced the hand of
Hungarian Premier László Bárdossy to declare war on Stalin. Within a
few months the Hungarians were also at war with England and the United
States. Horthy saw the decisions for what they were: a trap that could only
end badly for his beloved country.

Premier Bárdossy's successor, Miklós Kállay, strove mightily to
steer a middle ground by limiting Hungary's military involvement
without bringing down Hitler's wrath. For a time he succeeded in
walking the razor's edge. Because of the alliance with Germany,
Hungary's large Jewish population had thus far escaped the horrors of the

concentration camps. But a fateful line was crossed in early 1944: Kállay entered secret negotiations with the Allies to secure his country's withdrawal from the war. Hitler's fury erupted and his reaction was both predictable and devastating. That March, Wehrmacht troops swept into Hungary and seized control of the country. Admiral Horthy was forced to appoint a pro-Nazi government. In the wake of the occupation, the SS arrived to loot the country's industry and transportable wealth.

And then the killing of Hungary's Jews commenced.

* * *

When war erupted in September 1939, Kurt Becher was serving as a member of the Mounted SS reinforcing the police. Before the war, this son of a rich businessman and product of Hamburg society worked with a firm as an importer of grain and fodder. He transferred to the Waffen-SS and saw service as an infantryman during the Polish Campaign. There is some evidence that he was directly involved in the commission of atrocities there. By the spring of 1940, Becher was attached to the First SS Cavalry Regiment in Warsaw, and thereafter assigned to the Bad Tölz Cadet School for officer training. Back with his unit in time for the invasion of the Soviet Union in June 1941, Becher's outfit took part in the advance through northern Russia by way of Minsk, Bobruisk, and Smolensk. The offensive went well for the Germans during the summer and early autumn months. Stiffening Russian resistance and freezing cold weather changed that, and a bloody stalemate took root as 1941 approached its end. Fortunately for Becher, he fell sick and was shipped back to Germany and hospitalized in the Berlin-Lichterfelde Military Hospital. After his recovery he was dispatched to Warsaw to help streamline Franz Konrad's thievery efforts before returning to Berlin, where he was attached to the SS Leadership Head Office, Cavalry, and Transport Bureau. Becher's duties were to equip horse-drawn and mounted units with horses and other related equipment.[1]

Becher's new line of work was a vast improvement over the Russian front, and he happily remained in Berlin for several months. The bloody fighting in Russia, however, was chewing up Germans by the tens of thousands, and in December 1942 Becher was transferred back to the front lines and attached to General Hermann Fegelein's cavalry task force. By this time, Fegelein's command comprised a motley assemblage of Wehrmacht and Waffen-SS units, hastily patched together to stem the advance of grinding Russian counterattacks. Becher participated in the hard fighting that followed. When Fegelein was badly wounded and his command virtually destroyed, the remnant was disbanded and Becher was ordered back to Berlin. There, he returned once again to his administrative position.[2]

Becher, now a Oberturmbannführer (Lieutenant Colonel), was one of the many thousands of German soldiers sent in March 1944 to flood unfortunate Hungary with a heavy Third Reich military presence. He arrived in the lovely and largely untouched medieval city of Budapest as a staff member attached to the Cavalry and Transport Office. Ostensibly, he carried General Fegelein's orders to procure horses and equipment for the Wehrmacht and Waffen-SS. Fegelein had provided Becher with $125,000 in U.S. currency to speed along the acquisition process. Three large houses belonging to Manfred Weiss, the owner of the Manfred Weiss industrial organization, were allocated to Becher and his staff. To his delight, Becher found the houses crammed full of rich furnishings, art work, and other valuables. In order to develop a full inventory—and learn of other opportunities that might be waiting around the next corner—Becher summoned Dr. Wilhelm Billitz, a representative from the Weiss plant, to assist him.[3]

Dr. Wilhelm Billitz was born in Hungary in 1902 to Jewish parents. After receiving an education in law as well as political economics, he rose through the ranks and into a top management position with the Manfred Weiss organization. By the time the Germans arrived in Hungary in 1944, Billitz was the director of the Donau Airplane factory, a cooperative working under umbrella of the Herman Göring Works and a subsidiary of the Manfred Weiss industries. Dr. Billitz's wife was an Aryan who had represented Hungary as a skater during the 1936 Olympic Games in Germany. Billitz was the sole remaining manager from the entire Manfred Weiss complex that had not yet been arrested by the Gestapo.[4]

During the inventory, Billitz discovered that Becher was looking for horses and introduced him to Dr. Franz Chorin, a Budapest banker and connoisseur of fine equine stock. Chorin was also a major stockholder in the Manfred Weiss operation. Their discussions helped Becher acquire thousands of horses for distribution to Wehrmacht, Waffen-SS, and military police units. The Weiss family's large collection of art treasures also fell into his hands. Some of it was in Becher's possession at war's end. As time passed, however, the real reason for Becher's presence in Hungary bubbled to the surface. Seizing horses was purely a secondary concern—a thin veneer to hide his real purpose: Becher had been sent to Budapest, on the orders of Reichsführer Heinrich Himmler, to identify and confiscate major Jewish business concerns for the SS without the Hungarian government's knowledge. In return, he offered the displaced owners a chance to emigrate to Palestine or anywhere they chose—for a price. Failure to cooperate or pay for their lives earned them a one-way ticket to the death camps. His first victim was already in his sights: the mammoth Manfred Weiss industrial complex. His unwilling associate in the theft was none other than Dr. Billitz.[5]

*   *   *

SS Lieutenant Colonel Adolph Eichmann, the officer in charge of Bureau IV B4, arrived by train in Budapest on March 19, 1944. His overall task was simple to define; only the logistics behind it were complex: rid Hungary of its large population of Jews quickly and with as little trouble as possible. It seemed to Eichmann that there was insufficient time and inadequate resources to carry out his duties. The Russians were already drawing near Hungary's border. His own team of SS men numbered but 150, and only a modest number of Hungarian soldiers were available for assistance. This shortage of manpower to administer mass deportations was a critical problem for Eichmann—especially with the fiasco of Warsaw looking over his shoulder. There, a handful of armed Jews had defended themselves for weeks against German tanks and machine guns. In 1944, Budapest was home to 250,000 Jews. Another 650,000 were spread across the rest of Hungary. Many of Hungary's young Jewish males had military training from their service in the army. Active resistance was a very real possibility. The Germans had learned a bitter lesson in the cellars and on the rooftops of Warsaw; they had no intention of attending that school a second time.

Eichmann's final plan to achieve his objective was as brilliant as it was evil. Unlike the early years, by this stage of the war the Jews did not trust the Nazis or their representatives (in this case, the Hungarian authorities). There was only one way to implement a large-scale deportation quickly and efficiently: use Jewish leaders as tools in the demise of their own people. The Jews, after all, trusted their own. Eichmann decided to befriend Jewish community leaders and allow a small number of selected individuals, usually their friends or family members, to escape to Palestine or a neutral country of their choosing. In return, they agreed to remain silent and not share what they knew with the hundreds of thousands of men, women, and children who were dutifully boarding the trains and riding the iron rails bound for hell.[6]

*   *   *

While Eichmann quietly implemented his heinous strategy, Kurt Becher broke the news to Dr. Chorin about his first victim. The blood must have drained from the doctor's face when he was told that Germany would be taking over the Manfred Weiss Works. In return, Becher coolly continued, he would see to it that the members of the Weiss family would be able to safely leave the country. The industrial plants belonging to the Manfred Weiss Works employed 30,000 workers and produced virtually everything an army needed, from aircraft, trucks, and motorbikes, to artillery shells, grenades, and mortars. Hungary, of course, was not yet schooled in the ways of the Third Reich but Chorin—a banker and major stockholder in Weiss—quickly understood what was happening. The SS officer was suggesting a gigantic plunder of personal property.

After testing the waters with the experienced businessman, Becher squeezed Dr. Billitz into the negotiations. Billitz, the only top level manager available, was smart enough to know that resistance was futile. He tried as hard as possible to secure the best deal he could for his superiors and the Weiss stockholders. Between Becher, Billitz, Chorin, and Himmler, a final deal was hammered out transferring the Manfred Weiss Works to the Third Reich for a period of twenty-five years. Himmler formalized the blackmail in writing and drafted orders appointing Becher to the board of the organization. The Reichsführer was extremely pleased with the deal, which dovetailed with his long-term plan to acquire the means to make his precious SS completely self-sufficient by the time the war ended.[7]

As Becher later explained it, in return for their cooperation, the Weiss family—together with Billitz's mother, sister, and brother-in-law—were allowed to relocate to Portugal, a neutral country where Jews lived without fear of sudden death. Billitz and his own wife, however, were not so fortunate. The pair remained in Budapest as hostages. In exchange for the safety of his relatives, Billitz managed the company for Germany. (Becher knew nothing about the business or how it operated; he was merely a tool for its confiscation.) In addition to his own safety, another motive was in play. Billitz knew it was unlikely Germany would win the war and he wanted to keep the company—the basis of the Weiss family's wealth—unified in an attempt to preserve it for the postwar period. Since his wife was Aryan and of some renown, Billitz was under the impression that nothing would happen to him personally. Quiet negotiations continued. Himmler approved the exodus of an additional forty-eight people, including members of the Weiss family, Dr. Franz Chorin, and an extended circle of friends. Himmler also paid the Weiss family 3,000,000 Reichsmarks. On May 17, 1944, the Weiss family left their homes for freedom in Portugal.[8]

*   *   *

While Himmler smiled, Adolf Eichmann seethed. Becher's deal infuriated him. Eichmann had gone to great lengths to establish good relations with the Hungarian government, which expected to take over the ownership of confiscated Jewish property in return for not interfering with his deportations to the distant death camps. Viewed in that light, Eichmann's anger was justified because Becher's arrangement ran counter to established Nazi policy. Whether Becher knew it or not, Germany had a very specific procedure in place for dealing with Jews in foreign countries. In exchange for assistance in ridding their country of Jews, foreign governments were given the ownership rights to abandoned Jewish property. In return, Germany demanded only the costs for deportation and extermination. These costs varied from country to country. The Slovaks, for example, were supposed to pay 300 to 350 Reichsmarks per Jew, the Croats 30, the French 700, and the Belgians 250. As the war ground into 1944, however, the Third Reich needed more tangible items (such as industrial plants) instead of currency. Eichmann was aware that Hungary was to pay Germany in food, the amount based upon what each deported Jew would have consumed had he remained in that country. Thereafter, Hungarian officials would be free to seize Jewish assets. Becher's meddling had thrown a giant monkey wrench into this arrangement.

Eichmann and Becher did not see eye-to-eye on much of anything other than the righteousness of their terrible cause. The former was a bureaucrat, a cog in the mechanical wheel of the Third Reich machine. As far as Eichmann was concerned, his duty was nothing more or less than carrying out his assignment with as little deviation from his orders as possible. Becher, on the other hand, was a soldier armed with the mind of a shrewd businessman wrapped around a cold soul wholly devoid of conscience. He viewed his posting to Hungary as a godsend offering immense opportunity for acquiring wealth. Where the loot originated, or who suffered as a result of his aggrandizement, mattered not at all. Administrative bureaucrats like Adolf Eichmann made the task of making money all the more difficult for unprincipled miscreants like Becher.[9]

*   *   *

The successful Weiss transaction made Wilhelm Billitz a celebrity of sorts in Budapest's Jewish circles. He had, after all, secured the safety and freedom of dozens of Jews. Pleas for help from the Budapest Jewish Council poured in. Fearful of deeper involvement but willing to lend assistance as he might, Billitz was slowly but surely entangled in the expanding movement to rescue Hungary's Jews from extinction. Billitz's notoriety attracted the interest and efforts of Rezsö Kastner, who quickly learned of Billitz's connection with Becher and its subsequent tangible results.

A lawyer with a thick head of greased black hair, glasses, and a sharp hawkish gaze, Dr. Israel Rezsö (Rudolph) Kastner was the Chairman of the Hungarian Zionist Organization. In 1941, following the annexation of his hometown of Cluj, Transylvania, to Hungary, the 35-year-old relocated to Budapest. There, he helped found the Relief and Rescue Committee for the purpose of assisting the masses of Jewish refugees who had escaped the horrors of the Nazi regime in neighboring occupied countries. The German invasion of Hungary compelled Kastner to redouble his efforts on behalf of Hungarian Jewry. The Hungarian fascist party, Arrow Cross (whose inspectors carefully oversaw the process), refused to permit any exceptions to the mass round-ups and early deportations being carried out under Eichmann's direction. The Jews were only being relocated to Kenyermezo, Eichmann's minions explained. Kastner's misgivings increased. Perhaps turning to Becher and the German occupation authorities to save lives was a viable option? Billitz was the Jewish gatekeeper who held Kurt Becher's ear; Becher, in turn, held Himmler's ear. Kastner was about to cut a bargain that would haunt him for the rest of his life.[10]

Both Eichmann and Becher made Kastner's acquaintance, the former as early as May 22, 1944. By this time the trains were already rolling to Auschwitz. Eichmann told Kastner he had made an offer to the Allies to issue 600 Jewish exit visas in exchange for equipment and supplies. The idea captivated Kastner. The pair struck up a working relationship. "I concentrated on negotiating with the Jewish political leadership in Budapest," recalled Eichmann years later as he waited for death in his Israeli jail cell. "One man stood out among them." His name was Dr. Rezsö Kastner, "an authorized representative of the Zionist movement. He was a man, about my age, an ice-cold lawyer, and a fanatical Zionist. He agreed to help keep the Jews from resisting deportation and even keep order in the collection camps if I could close my eyes and let a few hundred or a few thousand young Jews emigrate illegally to Palestine. It was a good bargain. For keeping order in the camps," concluded Eichmann, "the price of 15,000 to 20,000 Jews . . . was not too high for me."[11]

Kastner was fully aware that death ultimately awaited every Hungarian Jew who could not escape Eichmann's foul net. Yet, he willingly remained quiet as families gathered in housing projects or other specified locations to await trains that would carry them to Auschwitz. Eichmann himself shed light on Kastner's motives. He was an "idealist" who willingly sacrificed hundreds of thousands of his fellow Jews to save "the best biological material." Simply put, Kastner's primary interest was to save select groups of Jews for emigration to Palestine. Kastner, explained Eichmann, "was not interested in old Jews or those who had assimilated into Hungarian society. The human material he was seeking had to be capable of reproduction and hard work." In other words

Kastner, the diehard Zionist, was only concerned with saving those who could help make the state of Israel a reality. "You can keep and kill the others," was Kastner's tacit agreement with Eichmann, "but let me have this group here." Eichmann's next statement was chilling. Kastner, he explained, provided the Nazis "a great service by helping keep the deportation camps peaceful." Kastner actively misrepresented to Hungary's Jews what was about to take place so there would not be a repeat of the Warsaw Ghetto uprising. Because of this cooperation, wrote Eichmann, "I would let his groups escape. After all, I was not concerned with small groups of a thousand or so Jews."[12]

Eichmann damning indictment of Kastner continues:

> Except perhaps for the first few sessions, Kastner never came to me fearful of the Gestapo strong man. We negotiated entirely as equals. People forget that. We were political opponents trying to arrive at a settlement, and we trusted each other perfectly. When he was with me, Kastner smoked cigarettes as though he were in a coffeehouse. While we talked he would smoke one aromatic cigarette after another, taking them from a silver case and lighting them with a little silver lighter. With his great polish and reserve he would have made an ideal Gestapo officer himself.

As he later told Kastner, "We, too, are idealists and we, too, had to sacrifice our own blood before we came to power."[13]

Negotiating "entirely as equals . . . trusted each other perfectly . . . would have made an ideal Gestapo officer . . . sacrifice our own blood." These words, written by the devil himself, are chilling to read even today. Kastner was playing God in Budapest—a role he had no right to assume. His failure to spread the word throughout Hungary *and the world* that the Nazi trains rolled in only one direction, to the gas chambers, resulted in the deaths of hundreds of thousands of people who might otherwise have survived.

*   *   *

After Eichmann had cemented the framework of the agreement into place, Kurt Becher implemented its details. He worked elbow-to-elbow with Kastner to save a handful of Jewish lives—for a price determined in advance for each soul saved. One transaction in particular stands out. In May, Eichmann had offered to free 1,000,000 Jews in exchange for 10,000 trucks and other items like soap and food. Joel Brand, another prominent Zionist, carried the offer to the Mideast but was arrested and incarcerated by the British. Kastner stepped into the diplomatic fissure to take up Brand's torch. Kastner told Eichmann the Allies had agreed "in principle" to his proposal, but wanted some show of good will before they would move forward. This could be obtained by letting a small number of Zionist leaders, say 750 (including many of Kastner's friends and relatives from his hometown of Cluj) emigrate to a neutral country. Eichmann agreed to the deal in exchange for a small number of trucks.

With Kastner's active complicity, the massive roundup of the rest of the Jews living in Budapest and elsewhere continued. These unfortunates were herded like animals into housing projects or crammed onto an island in the Danube River to await deportation to Poland. Others were also working hard, but with the intent of derailing Eichmann's plans. Some thirty partisans, trained in England, had recently parachuted into Europe to help organize Jewish resistance. Three of them were Hungarian Jews dropped into Yugoslavia in March 1944. One of the paratroopers was a young woman named Hannah Szenes, a poet and writer born in Budapest. She crossed into Hungary in June and was promptly arrested by Hungarian authorities, probably because of an informer. She was tortured for information and then executed by firing squad. The two other Hungarian partisans, Peretz Goldstein and Joel Nussbecher-Palgi, also slipped into Hungary and there made a fatal mistake: they contacted Kastner to seek his assistance. If these radical Jewish freedom fighters spread the word through the Jewish population, Eichmann would surely renege on his agreement to let Kastner's select trainload of Jews out of the country. In a savage double-cross, Kastner informed the Gestapo. Both men were seized and dispatched to Auschwitz. Goldstein perished there; Nussbecher-Palgi managed to escape and eventually make it to Palestine. Kastner's eventual attempt to explain why he failed to notify Swiss authorities of Hannah's capture or assist the partisans (discussed later in this book) outraged everyone who learned of it.[14]

Kastner's precious plan remained intact, but would the Allies actually turn over trucks and supplies to the Nazis? Eichmann had growing doubts. Frantic efforts in Switzerland and elsewhere failed to raise the funds necessary to buy the trucks and complete the first stage of the Eichmann-Kastner deal. Eichmann finally pulled the plug. On June 30, 1944, the train carrying Kastner's handpicked fortunates left Budapest for the concentration camp at Bergen-Belsen. The passengers, frightened beyond words, reached the camp on July 8 and remained there in what can only be described as a hellish limbo—hanging by a thread between life and death while others negotiated to determine whether they were worth saving.

In an attempt to grease the skids and get the ball rolling again, Kastner and Kurt Becher traveled to St. Margareten on the Swiss border on August 21. There, on a bridge linking Switzerland with Austria, the men met with several negotiators, including Saly Meyer, the Joint Distribution Committee's Swiss representative. When a letter of credit for ten trucks was finally produced, 318 of the Jews were shipped into Switzerland and freedom that August. The rest remained behind barbed wire within sight and smell of the crematorium chimneys, their fate still in doubt.[15]

The bribing for lives then began in earnest. Reaching agreement proved difficult. Eichmann himself got involved in the preliminary negotiations. "Characteristically, his price was the lowest, a mere two hundred dollars per Jew," explains one author who has written extensively on Eichmann's wartime activities in Hungary. Why did he ask such a low sum per head? This was not "because he wished to save more Jews but simply because he was not used to thinking big." Eventually, Kastner agreed that the Jews would pay Becher $1,000 per head, and the total number of people had risen to about 1,700. The ransom was collected from the Budapest Jewish underground in the form of gold and platinum bars, gold coins, diamond rings, necklaces, watches, and currency. The 1944 value of this treasure trove was $1,856,000—or almost $2,000 per person. For the chosen few, that was the price of life in Kastner's Budapest.[16]

Becher and Kastner, meanwhile, continued negotiating with Swiss authorities. Another meeting held in early September bore little fruit. A third encounter followed at the end of the month. Yet another, the fourth face-to-face meeting, was held during the first week of November in St. Gallen and Zurich. Roswell McClelland, a representative of the World Refugee Board and the United States government, joined the conference.

McClelland favored continuing the negotiations as a means of slowing down or stopping the Holocaust, but he was against putting a penny into the hands of Becher's SS. A final meeting on December 5, this one without Becher, broke the stalemate when the World Refugee Board decided to deposit funds into blocked accounts in a Swiss bank. That goodwill gesture, coupled with the large sum of money and gold Kastner had raised, convinced Eichmann to release the remaining Jews from the hell of Bergen-Belsen. A few days later almost 1,400 men, women, and children arrived in Switzerland.[17]

*   *   *

Although Kurt Becher had been dealing officially on behalf of the SS, he was unofficially negotiating on his own behalf to line his pockets. As events would later prove, a fortune in gold, jewels, and currency were miraculously discovered in a home he would come to occupy in Austria. Unfortunately for him, however, his money-making sojourn in Hungary was nearing an end. Soviet troops were rapidly closing in on the country from several sides. During a meeting with Himmler in Budapest in late November, Becher was ordered to remove everything of value under his authority from Hungary and transfer it to Germany. Entire factories with tens of thousands of workers were dismantled and shipped into the center of what was left of the Third Reich. Tons of raw materials and inventories from the Weiss Works and other plants were also loaded onto railroad cars and trucks and shipped out of Hungary.

Dr. Billitz remained in Budapest in an attempt to protect the operation and save the Weiss family fortune. Despite orders from Becher, Billitz did everything he could to slow down the breakup of the factory. With help from some of the plant's staff, he sabotaged the dismantling and evacuation process. While Becher was ripping the heart out of the Hungarian industrial base and scheming to transfer his loot to safety, Eichmann was providing his staff officers, including his adjutant SS Sturmbannführer (Major) Wilhelm Höttl, the green light to loot Jewish homes. Höttl took advantage of the opportunity to steal valuables from the palace belonging to Madame József Haatvany.[18]

A few days before the final Christmas of the war, Becher took wing and made for Vienna. Saving himself and safeguarding his accumulated wealth was more important than helping his old division, the 8th SS Cavalry Division *Florian Geyer*, now under the command of 35-year-old SS Gruppenführer (Major General) Joachim Rumohr, defend Budapest. The division was slaughtered in a useless effort to save the capital from the advancing Russians. Because the massive Weiss complex could not be efficiently utilized in Germany without the help of Billitz, Becher ordered him to ride with him to Vienna. There, explained Becher, Billitz would work for Germany and help create armaments that would be used against the Allies. Billitz refused. When Becher threatened him with force, Billitz disappeared with his wife. The couple hid with friends in fear for their lives until Becher, furious at Billitz's trick, left Budapest. Billitz returned home the next day, happy to be rid of the SS man. His joy was short-lived. Three SS officers were waiting. At pistol-point they ordered him to accompany them to Vienna. Left with little choice, Billitz packed a small suitcase and calmed his concerned wife. He was so sure he would eventually return that he decided not to tell his wife about any of his business dealings or financial affairs. He even took his own car and chauffeur, Geza Varga, with him. It was the last time Mrs. Billitz saw her husband.[19]

On Christmas Eve, Billitz and SS Obersturmführer (Lieutenant) Weber arrived in Vienna and checked into a small hotel. Weber ordered wine with dinner. Billitz drank a single glassful and complained aloud that he was not feeling well. The wine had not tasted right; perhaps it had gone bad. Within a short time he had spiked a fever and lost consciousness. A physician was called and Billitz was eventually transported to the Cottage Sanatorium.[20]

Rezsö Kastner was not about to remain behind in a Hungary about to be overrun by the Russians. He, too, fled for the relative safety of Vienna. There, he received news of Billitz's illness and paid him a visit on December 30. He found him in bed with a high fever. "I was taken from Budapest against my will by Becher's representatives," Billitz muttered in half-delirium. "Now," he lamented, "I am here all alone without my family. I only took the position beside Becher to save the Manfred-Weiss organization. In Budapest, I at least had the feeling that I was doing something for Hungary. Now, they expect me to help them fabricate weapons to be used against the Allied forces. What is Becher thinking?"

Nothing alleviated Billitz's condition. He lingered for several days before finally dying. The official cause of death was listed as "typhoid fever." He was buried in the Evangelical Central Cemetery in Vienna.[21]

*   *   *

On April 19, 1945, Kastner once again crossed over the Swiss border. This time he was not negotiating for ransomed Jews but seeking to establish residency in Geneva. Kurt Becher was also doing everything he could to save his hide. While the victorious Russians and Allies swept through what was left of the Third Reich, Becher retreated westward in the direction of Zell am See and Fischhorn Castle.

His caravan included a fortune in stolen loot.[22]

Chapter Notes

1. International Military Tribunal, Nuremberg, Frank Defense Exhibit 16.

2. Von Kurt Emmenegger, *Sie und Er* (December 1962), "Ein Schaffer Nicht," p. 17, Magyar Országos Levéltár, Hungarian National Archives, Budapest, Hungary.

3. Von Kurt Emmenegger, *Sie und Er* (December 1962), "Ein Schaffer Nicht," p. 17, Magyar Országos Levéltár, Hungarian National Archives, Budapest, Hungary. Like so many other SS officers, one of the first things Becher procured was a mistress by the name of Irene Polgar, a 37-year-old secretary employed by a rich, local industrial family.

4. Von Kurt Emmenegger, *Sie und Er* (December 1962), "Ein Schaffer Nicht," p. 18, Magyar Országos Levéltár, Hungarian National Archives, Budapest, Hungary.

5. Von Kurt Emmenegger, *Sie und Er* (December 1962), "Ein Schaffer Nicht," p. 17, Magyar Országos Levéltár, Hungarian National Archives, Budapest, Hungary. There was a secondary political motivation driving Becher's confiscation efforts. By taking over the Weiss complex, which was part of the Herman Göring Works, SS Reichsführer Himmler—through Becher—was asserting and demonstrating SS dominance over the Göring Works' officials.

6. Eichmann, "Memoirs," *Life Magazine*, Vol. 49, No. 23, December 5, 1960, p. 146.

7. Von Kurt Emmenegger, *Sie und Er* (December 1962), "Ein Schaffer Nicht," p. 18, Magyar Országos Levéltár, Hungarian National Archives, Budapest, Hungary.

8. Von Kurt Emmenegger, *Sie und Er* (February 1963), "Mord an Dr. Billitz?" p. 18, Magyar Országos Levéltár, Hungarian National Archives, Budapest, Hungary.

9. Hannah Arendt, *Eichmann in Jerusalem: A Report in the Banality of Evil* (London, England, 1994), pp. 141-142.

10. Von Kurt Emmenegger, *Sie und Er* (February 1963), "Mord an Dr. Billitz?" p. 19, Magyar Országos Levéltár, Hungarian National Archives, Budapest, Hungary.

11. Eichmann, "Memoirs," *Life Magazine*, p. 146.

12. Eichmann, "Memoirs," *Life Magazine*, p. 146. Much of Eichmann's contact with Kastner, and thus his subsequent assessment of him as related here, was the result of a lengthy negotiation designed to save a trainload of Jews of Kastner's choosing. This sad episode is explained in detail elsewhere in this chapter.

13. Eichmann, "Memoirs," *Life Magazine*, p. 146.

14. Alex Weissberg, *Desperate Mission: Joel Brand's Story* (New York, 1958), pp. 236-247; Ben Hecht, *Perfidy* (New York, 1961), p. 129. Joe Nussbecher-Palgi eventually became the head of El-Al, the Israeli national airlines.

15. Arendt, *Eichmann*, p. 143; "Bureau of State, Incoming Telegram, signed Acheson," June 21, 1946.

16. "Incoming Telegram, Signed Acheson," January 4, 1946, RG 59, State Department and Foreign Affairs, Bureau of State, National Archives.

17. Von Kurt Emmenegger, *Sie Und Er* (date and title missing, 1963), p. 89, Magyar Országos Levéltár, Hungarian National Archives, Budapest, Hungary.

18. Statement by Támas Bogyay, August 8, 1949, pp. 117-121, *Sacco Di Budapest*, compiled by László Mrvik (Egyetemi Nyomda Rt., Budapest, Hungary).

19. Von Kurt Emmenegger, *Sie und Er* (February 1963), "Mord an Dr. Billitz?" p. 18, Magyar Országos Levéltár, Hungarian National Archives, Budapest, Hungary.

20. Von Kurt Emmenegger, *Sie und Er* (February 1963), "Mord an Dr. Billitz?" p. 18, Magyar Országos Levéltár, Hungarian National Archives, Budapest, Hungary.

21. Von Kurt Emmenegger, *Sie und Er* (February 1963), "Mord an Dr. Billitz?" p. 18, Magyar Országos Levéltár, Hungarian National Archives, Budapest, Hungary.

22. Nuremberg Trials, Document 2605-PS.

Chapter 5

"If things go badly, and you are not able to get through, drive the truck over
a cliff. . . . But by all means deliver the suitcases and the trunk.
Fifty years from now the suitcases will make history."

— SS Hauptsturmführer Franz Konrad to SS Unterscharführer Johannes Haferkamp

Fischhorn Castle:
The Last SS Headquarters

Zell am See is a small resort village bordering a lake of the same
name three miles long, one mile wide, and 255 feet deep. Schloss
(Castle) Fischhorn crowns the south end of the lake just a
handful of miles southeast of Berchtesgaden. This picturesque setting
was the scene of frenzied activity during the final few weeks of World
War II. Seemingly everything and everyone converged upon the castle.
Automobiles and trucks came and went at all hours of the day and night.
Motorcycles roared in and out. Wehrmacht and SS officers and high
ranking party and state officials were seen everywhere in the small
Austrian village.

The goings-on around Fischhorn are particularly instructive for our
study. Every member of the SS knew their days of freedom were limited,
and the feeling of collapse triggered a frenzy of activity. Some went
steadily about their duties, working overtime to destroy evidence of
crimes or personal papers they did not want ending up in the hands of the
victors. Others, especially prominent SS officers who had played a role

either directly or indirectly in the Holocaust, thrashed about in a final mad dash for plunder to secret away for later use. As will eventually be seen, some of this last gasp effort was in vain. Much of it, however, was not.

*   *   *

It was in the almost impenetrable Alpine mountain region of Austria that Adolf Hitler's remaining faithful gathered at his request for a purported "last stand" against the relentless Allied advance. Fortifications were to be strategically arranged along ridges and hillsides bristling with machine gun nests, artillery pieces, and anti-aircraft guns. This entire defensive network would then be tied to Berlin and Berchtesgaden with an advanced communication system based on wireless transmission. Ammunition depots, repair workshops, and factories for the production of jet aircraft and missiles would be constructed in deep mine shafts and tunnels carved into granite mountains. Heavy fighting had already proven that mountainous terrain was readily defensible—during the winter of 1944, the Germans held nearly 300 miles of mountains and passes along the Italian frontier with a relatively small force. Unfortunately for the Germans, little of this Alpine dream had been realized by the time Hitler was trapped in Berlin. The Allies, who dubbed the region the "National Redoubt," saw such a stand as a real possibility and were moving with all speed into Austria to disrupt the enemy defensive effort.

In the middle of April 1945, Gruppenführer (Major General) Hermann Fegelein and his senior staff arrived at Fischhorn from Berlin for an important war conference. Amidst gloomy forecasts Fegelein adamantly proclaimed that the war was not lost because jet fighters were now operational. The war, he predicted, was about to take a dramatic new turn in Germany's favor. The Alpine Redoubt was defensible for two or three years, more than enough time to mass produce jets and wipe out Allied fighters and bombers. SS Hauptsturmführer (Captain) Erwin Haufler listened quietly. As he later recalled, "It was perfectly clear to me that this was impossible. But I am a soldier, and must accede to the orders of my superiors, no matter what my personal opinion may be." Much of the conference centered on the defense of the Alpine passes. Later, however, Fegelein took Haufler aside. "If things do get so bad that we must retreat into the mountains, hide everything you can, above all my personal belongings." Apparently Fegelein was not as sanguine of ultimate success as he would have others believe.[1]

Fischhorn was stocked and readied as a logistical center and fortress for Fegelein and his staff, who had temporarily returned to Berlin. Captain Haufler, in contact each day by phone with Fegelein, had four truckloads of the general's personal belongings evacuated from his home in Munich. He also arranged for a convoy of trucks to head south from Berlin stuffed with rugs, furs, and other valuables—much of it plundered from Warsaw earlier in the war. As the Allies advanced, phone connections were cut between Fischhorn and Berlin. Thereafter, Haufler drove each night 30 miles north to Hitler's southern headquarters near Berchtesgaden, the famed Berghof, in order to converse with Fegelein, who was working as Himmler's liaison officer between Führer Headquarters in the Reich Chancellery and the bunker.[2]

Many from Hitler's inner circle were staying at the Berghof. In addition to Dr. Theodor Morell, Hitler's personal physician, the group included the wives of several high-ranking Nazi officials. Among them was Eva Braun's plump (and pregnant) younger sister Gretl Fegelein, a generous and good natured woman with a deserved reputation as a nymphomaniac. Accompanying her was her good friend Herta Schneider, a petite dark-haired mother of two small children. Recently arrived were SS Sturmbannführer (Major) Johannes Göhler, Fegelein's 27-year-old adjutant, and SS Obergruppenführer (Lieutenant General) Julius Schaub, one of Hitler's closest adjutants. The pair had flown out of Berlin on a Junkers 290 aircraft on April 24. They were among the last to arrive at the Berghof.

Julius Schaub had served Hitler from his inauspicious beginnings. Born in 1898, Schaub took part in the 1923 Munich putsch and was sent to jail in Landsberg with the future leader of Germany. The pair struck up a friendship behind bars. From that point on, Schaub was responsible for Hitler's personal affairs, food, lodging, and the organization of many of his campaigns and speeches. Hitler valued nothing above absolute loyalty, and in Schaub he discovered his most faithful servant. The sycophant had been promoted regularly through the ranks of the SS well beyond his capacity for performance. Schaub had removed many of Hitler's personal papers from the Berlin bunker to the gardens above ground where, between the sporadic Russian artillery bombardments, he burned them. Thereafter, Hitler dispatched his trusted servant with the keys to his several large cabinets in the Berghof in southern Germany. Fly there and burn their contents, Hitler ordered. Schaub arrived at the Berghof drunk. According to witnesses he refused the help of two of Hitler's longtime secretaries, Johanna Wolf and Christa Schroeder, and instead, combed through the files with the assistance of his mistress. Supposedly he burned Hitler's belongings. Schaub may have refused help so he would have a free hand in concealing some of Hitler's private possessions and valuables. Neither woman thought much of the man, and now that it was obvious Hitler would never leave the bunker, they no longer had to be kind to him.[3]

It was during her final hours in Berlin that Christa Schroeder typed the last letter dictated by Eva Braun. The private message was intended for Gretl, her sister and Hermann Fegelein's wife. "How it hurts me to write such lines to you," Eva's letter began. Schroeder, who had worked for Hitler since 1933, was an intelligent and energetic assistant who had once taken dictation for several days and nights without an extended period of rest. She accompanied Hitler on almost all of his trips and was present during most of the important events of his life. As a result, Schroeder became Hitler's friend and confidant. He shared with her many of his most intimate thoughts. She recalled after the war that during their tea sessions each evening Hitler would repeat himself like a gramophone record, monotonously reliving his early days in Vienna and personal history. The monologues, she claimed, bored her to death.[4]

As the group of survivors gathered in the Berghof to await whatever was coming, Haufler made his way to the basement for his telephone call with General Fegelein. The call was made from a large switchboard. Under glass, on the switchboard desk, was a printed directory of important numbers. It was one of Haufler's last conversations with Fegelein. "Everything must be well prepared," the general informed his subordinate. "We must go through with the Werewolf plan [the code name for National Redoubt]. I can not go into more details on the telephone; you will soon receive detailed orders." According to Haufler, Fegelein's voice was curt and nervous, the conversation unusually hasty. The clear ring of authority always present in every syllable was noticeably absent. Haufler knew Fegelein as well as anyone. By the time he hung up the receiver he appreciated the import of the call: it was all over for Germany. Haufler was convinced the group in Berlin intended to withdraw into the Alpine Redoubt area and carry on a protracted defensive and sabotage campaign. The SS captain immediately began formulating a plan to hide food, ammunition, and other items for their use.[5]

Almost as soon as Haufler hung up the phone an air raid alarm sounded. Haufler, Gretl Fegelein, and Frau Mittelstrasser (a housekeeper at the Berghof) hustled into a shelter located behind the headquarters. At the foot of dozens of steps were long white-walled tunnels leading to a maze of elaborate rooms and storage areas. Haufler had never seen the place before. The two women walked the fascinated captain through the various rooms. The complex included living quarters with adjoining apartments for Hitler and Eva Braun. One wine cellar was stocked with thousands of bottles of superior vintages, pilfered from some of Europe's finest cellars. Storerooms held truckloads of books, many of them gifts to Hitler from party members and friends. On one shelf was a large enamel-covered picture book entitled *Itaila Imperia,* a history of the New Roman Empire. Inside were pictures of Hitler's visit to Italy.[6]

Eva Braun's bomb shelter bedroom was tastefully decorated with pastel-tinted walls, dainty flowered vases, and tinsel clothed dolls. In her study were built-in bookshelves containing a set of Shakespeare and, incongruously, a translated edition of the *Adventures of Tom Sawyer and Huckleberry Finn.* On her desk was light blue stationery with the letters "EB" embossed in the corner, together with some of her calling cards. Hitler's room was spartan by comparison. The only furniture was a combination day-bed couch and a desk. The room also contained some 5,000 phonograph records. Haufler picked up and examined several items bearing the initials "AH." Several large books were stacked on the desktop. The captain picked one up and flipped through it.

"What are these?" asked Haufler.

"Those are the diaries," replied Frau Mittelstrasser.

The rumor that Hitler kept personal diaries has been a popular one since before the war ended. According to Haufler, the books he picked up and flipped through were full of handwriting on very thin airmail-type paper, firmly bound or sewn into five large books. Haufler did not ask any other questions, and Frau Mittlestrasser did not say another word on the subject. When the air raid ended, Haufler left the Berghof and drove back to Fischhorn castle.[7]

*   *   *

On May 1, 1945, Gretl Fegelein asked Johannes Göhler, who had flown in to the Berghof with Schaub, to take charge of a large chest. "This contains about 200 letters between my sister Eva and Hitler," she told him. "They are hidden away in a cave near the Berghof."

"Yes, of course I will do whatever you ask," replied Göhler.

"I am traveling with Frau Schneider to Garmish-Partenkirchen and am unable to take care of these letters. I am expecting a child momentarily," added Gretl.

The SS major immediately placed a call to Captain Haufler at Fischhorn and instructed him to send a truck to the Berghof to pick up the chest. "In case of any danger," Göhler warned, "these items must be destroyed." Haufler agreed to do so. That same day Göhler made his way to Berchtesgaden, where he witnessed a disturbing event: "The personnel there were emptying the bunkers of the uniforms, photo albums, tablecloths, and other personal items belonging to Hitler and his close associates, and burning them." As Göhler explained it, "this was before any report had been made of Hitler's death. Ostensibly, the idea was to keep these items from the hands of the Americans."[8]

The truck sent by Haufler arrived the next night. Several other items in addition to the chest were loaded aboard. These included valuable paintings, a leather case with photo equipment belonging to Gretl Fegelein, and a small suitcase stuffed with Eva's clothing. A metal trunk and an open laundry basket were also packed aboard. The trunk contained several items, including a sketch book with drawings from both Eva and Hitler. Most of Hitler's sketches were pencil drawings of floor plans, churches, and other architectural renderings. The trunk also held a pair of badly ripped black trousers and a coat of field gray bearing a swastika. Hitler was wearing these garments on July 20, 1944, when a bomb exploded under his conference table and almost ended his life at his Wolfschanze headquarters in Rastenberg. The laundry basket contained 25 to 30 photo albums, some small framed pictures, and rolls of color movie film. Major Göhler and Ursula, his eye-catching young wife and mother of two children, accompanied the truckload of valuables to Fischhorn.[9]

Fischhorn castle was being utterly transformed from a lovely medieval fortress into a gigantic warehouse packed with everything imaginable. Daily convoys of trucks and trains arrived from Vienna and central and southern Germany. On May 3, a large steel chest about four feet square arrived under heavy guard. The locked, beige-colored strongbox belonged to Reichsführer Heinrich Himmler. The shipment also included many of the SS leader's uniforms from Berchtesgaden. Erika Lorenz, Himmler's tall, 40-year-old blond secretary accompanied the delivery. Himmler's former secretary, 30-year-old Hedwig Potthast, had trained Lorenz. In 1940, Potthast left her position as Himmler's secretary in order to give birth to his child. She remained Himmler's loyal and devoted mistress until the end of the war. Himmler refused to divorce his wife because of his Catholic background. He also believed that the shock of a divorce might result in her death. This from the squeamish exterminator of millions.[10]

On May 5, Haufler began burning the letters of Hitler and Eva Braun at Fischhorn. Each was read or at least skimmed before being tossed into the fiery central furnace. As the missives were going up in smoke, in walked SS Captain Franz Konrad—whom we met earlier during his ruthless Warsaw sojourn. It quickly became evident to Haufler that Konrad was searching for items of value to steal. The former king of the Warsaw Ghetto set his eyes on a small casket-like chest containing letters, stationery with the monogram of Eva Braun, and two other books. One was on Italian architecture, the other was a book full of collectable stamps. Konrad grabbed the chest and added the stamps to the gigantic collection he had stolen from Poland's Jews. After a few more searching glances he left. Haufler turned back to his task of burning correspondence. One letter, in particular, stood out from the others. The subject matter was the failed assassination effort in July 1944, and the handwriting was Hitler's. "My hand is still trembling from the attempt on my life," he wrote Eva Braun. It ended with the words, "I am full of hope for our coming victory." Haufler kept at least two pieces of correspondence, one a postcard from Hitler beginning with "Dear Tschapperl" (a Bavarian peasant pet name), and the other a letter from Eva beginning "Liebster" (beloved) describing a day in her life.[11]

While Haufler dutifully turned the Führer's love letters and those of his mistress into bits of ash, others in Fischhorn were also busy collecting materials slated for destruction. Erika Lorenz, Himmler's secretary, opened her boss's steel cabinet, removed the contents, and placed them on the floor. In addition to a large number of files were envelopes containing letters from Himmler's wife and parents. She packed all of this memoranda into a wash basin and, with the help of an unnamed SS sergeant, carried the papers to the castle's basement and threw them into the raging furnace. Whether Haufler was still at his job in the same furnace room is not known. During the sorting process the ubiquitous Franz Konrad made another appearance in the basement. Without a word he rifled through Himmler's materials, pulling out and setting aside several folders for himself. Of special interest to him were SS badges, the type Himmler awarded to SS maidens for their contributions to the breeding of a "superior Aryan race." Konrad took several handfuls. He later told Haufler, "Too bad you were not there; I read some really interesting correspondence between Hitler and Himmler."[12]

*   *   *

The Ghetto King had been a very busy man. Just a week earlier he and SS Unterscharführer (Sergeant) Johannes Haferkamp had driven a heavily-laden, wood-burning truck from Fischhorn castle to Konrad's brother-in-law's home in the little town of Schladming, Austria, a trip of about fifty miles. Konrad had selected Haferkamp because the sergeant was unmatched in his ability to handle the temperamental vehicle. By this late date gasoline was a scarce commodity in much of Europe, so many trucks had been converted to run on wood and charcoal. Oddly, Konrad used the wood-burning truck even though 80,000 liters of gasoline had been hoarded at Fischhorn. Willy Pichler was surprised when his brother-in-law woke him up just a few minutes before midnight. In keeping with his usual secrecy, Konrad introduced Haferkamp as "Karl Heinz."[13]

"I have my luggage, some foodstuffs, and some radio sets. I need you to take good care of my luggage." Konrad hesitated, then added. "The radios are my property. You should sell them."

Pichler merely looked on in amazement and agreed to do as Konrad suggested. There were twenty-four radio sets. In addition to the radios were several tin chests, three leather suitcases, and several boxes of food and liquor. The tin chests were the standard type used by German officers for their personal belongings. Haferkamp passed the cargo by hand from the back of the black truck to Konrad, who passed each piece through a window to Pichler, who in turn stacked the mysterious merchandise in the tiny cellar. The unloading took about thirty minutes.[14]

Afterward the men sat in the kitchen and conversed about the collapsing Third Reich and what it might mean for them. While a light meal was being served Konrad turned to Pichler's wife Miezi, who had heard the truck arrive, and said, "Just a moment, Miezi, I'll bring you something." The captain went back down into the cellar and returned a few minutes later with $1,000 in U.S. currency. Pichler asked Konrad if he had any additional money, and Konrad pulled out 5,000 Reichsmarks. Because it was late the men decided to stay the night. Konrad and the driver slept in the livingroom, one on a sofa and the other on some cushions on the floor.[15]

Pichler was up early the next morning, probably because he was a nervous wreck. His brother-in-law's nocturnal visit and deposit of what were obviously stolen items caused him no little concern. While Konrad slept Pichler walked briskly a few blocks to Fritz Konrad's house to tell him his brother Franz had arrived the night before. Fritz accompanied Willy back to his home, where the brothers greeted each other warmly. after a quick breakfast, they made their way into Pichler's small cellar. The food parcels Franz had stolen and deposited there were divided between Pichler and Fritz.

The brothers' mother, Frau Konrad, lived with the Pichlers but had been asleep when Franz had arrived the night before. After greeting her that morning at 9:00 a.m. he guided the elderly woman back to her room and gave her two suitcases, one containing film, and the other with four gold watches. The two suitcases were placed on top of her wardrobe chest, the small watch box hidden away inside.

"I am entrusting this to you," he told her. "Do not surrender it to anyone until I come to pick it up." Lowering his voice he whispered, "I have a large collection of Hitler's personal papers and have to find a safe place to hide them."

Additional conversation led his mother to believe that her son might have hidden the "personal papers" at Fischhorn castle, but that he would never let them fall into the wrong hands. It was shortly thereafter, about 10:00 a.m., when the family members gathered around the smoking and wheezing truck parked in front of the house. Frau Konrad noticed Franz clutching a suitcase. It was small and made of brown leather. When asked about it he told her not to worry about it. "I will take this with me," was all he said.

Franz placed the leather bag in the back of the vehicle and covered it with a tarp. There was nothing else in the truck. "I think that Franz did not want to leave it here with us because he would have involved us too deeply with it," Frau Konrad later told an Allied investigator. "I think he intended at first to leave it here, but then decided to take it back after all." With that Franz and his driver, "Karl Heinz" Haferkamp, returned to Fischhorn.[16]

Pichler wasted little time. He immediately turned to Fritz and pleaded with him to take some of the items to his home, claiming that his cellar was just too small to house all the cases. It was one thing to hide a few items; having an entire cellar crammed with stolen goods was something else altogether. Fritz readily agreed and the pair hauled out two or three tin chests and two small suitcases. The chests and suitcases were loaded onto a small hand-pulled wagon and hauled to Fritz's house. Some of the items were hidden away in the attic, where Fritz carefully lowered them down between the walls on a rope or wire. Neither man, Fritz or Willy, seemed to know exactly what it was they were concealing. At least, that is what they would later tell Allied investigators.[17]

On April 30, just two days after his hasty nighttime visit to his relatives in Schladming, Konrad was busy once again loading items into the back of a truck. This one was standing in the courtyard of Fischhorn castle. The vehicle's manifest included forty to fifty cases of Bols Liqueur, two large rugs, a few rifles, cases of foodstuffs, fifteen radio sets, two suitcases (one of which bore a tag with the name "Eva Braun"), and a large officer's trunk. These goods were also bound for Schladming, but this time Konrad did not accompany them. The Americans, after all, were closing in fast. "If things go badly, and you are not able to get through, drive the truck over a cliff," Konrad directed the trusty Sergeant Haferkamp. "But by all means deliver the suitcases and the trunk. Fifty years from now the suitcases will make history." As Haferkamp prepared to leave, Konrad changed his mind and walked around behind the truck and took off one of the chests. Haferkamp failed to notice the act; the only thing he saw was another SS officer removing one of the cases of Bols liqueur.

SS Sergeant Max Mayer accompanied Haferkamp on the second trip to Schladming. Unlike the first visit, this journey was not nearly as smooth and easy. Either because of bad timing or failure to plan ahead, the truck arrived at the Pichler house during daylight hours. Haferkamp and Mayer had just begun to unload the merchandise when some of the town residents stopped to watch them work. It did not take long for them to learn the truck was full of valuable goods. Someone got up the courage to jump up into the vehicle and grab a box. Another man vaulted up after the first, followed by still a third man. Before either Haferkamp or Mayer could stop them the truck was stripped of its precious cargo of liquor. The pair managed to unload the fifteen radios and two large rugs without any additional interruption. With that part of the mission behind them they throttled up the truck and headed the short distance to Fritz Konrad's house. With the help of the Konrads they unloaded what little was left on the truck and drove back to Fischhorn. Fritz Konrad knew the drill. After Haferkamp drove away he hid many of the goods between the walls of his home, just as he had two days earlier. This time Fritz and his wife Minna peeked into the heavy officer's chest. It contained his brother Franz's valuable stamp collection.[18]

On or about May 1, 1945, Franz Konrad left Fischhorn and drove to nearby Bruck to visit Martha von Broskowitz, his secretary and mistress. "He arrived with a package about 18 in. long, 6 in. thick, 4 in. wide, tied in colored paper and tied tightly with string," remembered Broskowitz.

"What is this?" she asked him.

"Just my personal letters," he answered. "I need you to hold them for me in case anything should happen to me."

The package was heavy and did not seem like the sort of box within which one would store personal letters. A reluctant Broskowitz agreed to hold it for him. She never saw him again. Weeks later, long after the war had ended, a member of the Fischhorn castle staff called on Frau Broskowitz and picked up the mysterious package Konrad had left behind. "I have been instructed to leave it with Nurse Ursula von Bieler at Aufausen, west of Zell am See," was all the unidentified man told her.[19]

*   *   *

While Konrad was busy running about secreting valuables and other items of unknown origin, enemy military forces were steadily squeezing what little life was left out of the Third Reich. Stalin's army was driving into Austria from the east and northeast, General George Patton's Third Army was approaching from the northwest, and General Alexander Patch's Seventh Army was closing in from the southwest. For men like Franz "King" Konrad, Göhler, Haufler, Kurt Becher, and others, the manner in which events were unfolding could not have been worse. Almost certain capture awaited them, and they all knew it. There was nothing they could do to alter the course of the war.

Their only hope was to save their own lives by fabricating new identities and lying about their wartime activities.

Chapter Notes

1. CIC "Interrogation of SS Captain Erwin Haufler," September 14, 1945.

2. 970th CIC "Report of Interrogation of SS Lieutenant Hans Schiffler," September 17, 1945; "Interrogation of SS Captain Erwin Haufler," September 29, 1945.

3. Arrest Report, Julius Schaub, May 11, 1945, 36th CIC Detachment, Kitzbühl; "Report of Conversation among Gretl Braun Fegelein, Frau Herta Schneider, and Walter Hirschfeld," September 25, 1945. Hirschfeld later served the Allies as an undercover agent, a fascinating story told elsewhere in this book.

4. 101st Airborne Division Headquarters, CIC, "Interrogation of Christa Schroeder," July 13, 1945.

5. "Haufler Interrogation," September 15, 1945.

6. "Haufler Interrogation," September 15, 1945.

7. "Haufler Interrogations," September 15 and 29, 1945; 1945.

8. CIC, "History of SS Major Johannes Göhler," Seventh Army Interrogation Center, August 6, 1945; Haufler Interrogation, September 15, 1945.

9. "Göhler History," August 6, 1945.

10. Seventh Army Interrogation Center, "Report: Hedwig Potthast, Reichsführer Himmler's Mistress," by Major Paul Kubala, May 22, 1945; 970th CIC, "Interrogation of Miss Erika Lorenz," October 17, 1945.

11. "Haufler Interrogation," September 15, 1945; "Konrad Interrogation," August 21, 1945.

12. "Interrogation of Erika Lorenz," October 17, 1945; "Konrad Interrogations," August 21, 1945, and October 29, 1945.

13. CIC, "Interrogation of Johannes Haferkamp," November 8, 1945.

14. CIC, "Interrogation of Willy Pichler," November 1, 1945; "Haferkamp Interrogation," November 8, 1945.

15. "Interrogation of Willy Pichler," November 1, 1945; CIC, "Interrogation of Frau Konrad," November 1, 1945.

16. "Interrogation of Frau Konrad, November 1, 1945.

17. "Interrogation of Fritz Konrad," October 31, 1945.

18. 970th CIC, "Interrogation of Mrs. Minna Konrad," October 31, 1945."

19. 970th CIC, "Interrogation of Mrs. Martha von Broskowitz," August 16, 1945.

Chapter 6

"Operation Bernhard was a name for a financial affair similar to Aktion I which they kept secret from Berlin. . . . As far as Berlin was concerned the name of the official currency operation was always Aktion I."

— SS Officer Josef Dauser to Allied Investigators

The Moneymakers

The end of the war was only days away when several large trucks roared to life and pulled out of Redl Zipf, a small town thirty miles northeast of Salzburg, Austria. Each truck was loaded with millions in counterfeit notes and other valuables, the result of one of the largest fraud schemes in world history. "In case of danger destroy contents" was clearly stamped on each box of ersatz currency.

Exactly how this operation ended up in the picturesque Alps, and who benefitted from it or suffered because of it, is a fascinating tale whose ending has not yet been written.

*   *   *

This stepped-up operation was a continuation of—though much more sophisticated and widespread—an ongoing effort named "Operation Andrew" or "Andreas," which also copied British currency.

The Reich Security Main Office (RSHA) had been involved in some form of counterfeiting since the late 1930s. Fake passports, rubber stamps, fingerprint cards, ration cards, postal stamps and the like had all issued forth; so had currency. Because of a general shortage of financial support, the German Secret Service decided to try and fund its activities abroad with forged notes. "This was no original idea," wrote a high ranking Secret Service officer who had viewed the effort from its epicenter. "The Secret Services of other countries, particularly that of the Soviet Union, had already used the same means to a considerable extent." The effort was tagged with the name "Operation Andrew" or "Andreas."[1]

This idea of stepping up the small and relatively unimportant RSHA forgery operation into something more substantial was the brainchild of SS Unterstürmfuhrer (Second Lieutenant) Alfred Helmut Naujocks, a native of Kiel, Germany. The a diehard fanatical Nazi and longtime member of the SS performed a prominent role on history's stage just before the outbreak of war. On the orders of Reinhard Heydrich, the chief of *Reichssicherheitshauptamt* (RSHA), Naujocks simulated a Polish attack against a German radio station near Gleiwitz on the Polish border. The date was August 31, 1939. Hitler used this incident as an excuse to invade Poland the next day, triggering World War II. Naujocks followed up this dramatic action with clandestine activities in Czechoslovakia, which included blowing up factories and possible assassinations—all on Heydrich's orders. A wild shootout over British agents during what became known as the Venlo Incident seems to have convinced Heydrich that Naujocks was too reckless and violent for his own good. When Hitler invaded the Low Countries in May 1940, Naujocks and his men donned foreign uniforms again, this time of Belgian and Dutch variety. The wild but brave officer seized key landmarks, including bridges and crossroads, and held them until the fast moving Panzers arrived. When the assignment was completed Heydrich, perhaps to be rid of Naujocks, quietly transferred him to the documents division of the SD.[2]

Forging passports as a desk-bound bureaucrat was not to Naujocks' liking. Flooding world markets with counterfeit currency, however, appealed to his sense of adventure and general wickedness. The concept of expanding and improving Operation Andrew was brought to Naujocks' attention later that year when a chemist friend produced several English five-pound sterling notes. Both agreed the English pound was one of the few stable currencies, respected and accepted the world over. If enough quality notes could be produced and put into circulation, the English economy was bound to suffer accordingly. Why work simply to fund secret service operations abroad when a more sophisticated and widespread counterfeiting effort could potentially cripple the enemy? The timing seemed right. The RAF had just dropped forged German auxiliary certificates of payment (50 Reichsfennig notes) utilized by the Wehrmacht over the occupied countries. The intent of the forgery, however, was not to damage the German economy but to badger the soldiers utilizing them. The notes were perfect in every respect except one: on the back of each was a typed sentence warning the holder of the evils inherent in following Adolf Hitler.[3]

Naujocks shared the idea with Heydrich. The idea of working to bring down Germany's enemy in that fashion fascinated Heydrich, who briefed the concept in a report to Hitler, but expanded it to include also forged American currency. Hitler, too, liked the idea but nixed the addition, writing: "No dollars; we are not at war with the U.S.A." Predictably, career German soldier-bureaucrats cringed at the notion of forging another country's money. It was, after all, unseemly and nonmilitary. German Economic Minster Walther Funk did not think much of the plan either, but for an altogether different reason. The English pound was the world's foremost currency. Attacking it in this fashion could trigger a creditor backlash on the world's economic stage and have the reverse effect of destabilizing the Reichsmark. Hitler, however, waved off warnings and signed off on the plan. Himmler, too, knew about and endorsed the effort. The entire matter was assigned by Heydrich to RSHA Bureau VI, and a new division named SHARP 4 was formed to oversee it. It was implemented, finally, in the summer of 1942 inside a pair of barracks in the Sachsenhausen concentration camp at Oranienberg, just north of Berlin. The man tapped to run the expanded forgery ring was SS Sturmbannführer (Major) Friedrich Walther Bernhard Krüger. The project became formally known in Berlin as Aktion I. It is more popularly (but incorrectly) known today as "Operation Bernhard."[4]

"Although the actual forging presented no very serious problem, the technical difficulty of producing the exact paper used in Britain proved to be very great," wrote Dr. Wilhelm Höttl, an Austrian working for Germany as an SS officer and intelligence operative. Höttl had it generally right, as the Nazis had already discovered. Quality counterfeit English currency was not easy to produce, but neither was it overly difficult. Experienced artisans were needed to craft exquisite plates, and printing experts had to be found to select paper, develop and handle inks, and oversee the complex printing process. Max Bober's profession ultimately saved his life when a search for these expert craftsmen was carried out across the Third Reich. Bober had been seized along with 2,000 other Jews in Berlin during one of the initial anti-Semitic roundups in 1938. Four years later only four of the 2,000 were still alive; 46-year-old Bober—a printer and machine compositor—was one of them. Without warning he was herded onto a railway car and transferred from the concentration camp at Buchenwald to Sachsenhausen. He was informed that because of his experience in the printing business he and sixty other Jews had been specially selected by the Gestapo to produce "official papers."

The work was performed in two barracks at Sachsenhausen, both isolated from the rest of the camp by three rows of electrified barbed wire. This secured area was heavily guarded outside the wire compound by members of the SS. Inside the buildings the men found waiting for them the very latest printing equipment, a photo lab, and everything they would need for what would become the greatest counterfeiting operation in history. The program was divided into five sections, each headed by a Jewish prisoner: printing, bookbinding, photography, photo-type, and engraving. The prisoners were given specific instructions about what was expected of them. Failure, they were told, would mean immediate death. The slightest attempt at sabotage would result in the immediate liquidation of each member of their counterfeiting section. Any communication with the guards or other prisoners was strictly forbidden and would result in summary execution.[5]

The division tasked with producing counterfeit English currency was the most important part of this new operation. The paper upon which the notes would be printed had to be perfect. Here Dr. Höttl's early quoted observation looms large, for reproducing the paper proved to be the single greatest stumbling block thrown before the counterfeiting effort. The same factory that manufactured paper for German currency tried to replicate English pound note paper but failed miserably in the attempt. Matching the color and texture seemed almost impossible. Months of experimentation followed without satisfactory results. Factory officials finally threw up their hands in defeat in early 1943 and urged that experienced craftsmen be found to produce the paper by hand.

Authorities turned to the Hahnemühl paper plant. In April 1943, the Hahnemühl factory set about producing a special paper made up of ninety percent cotton and ten percent linen for Bank of England notes in denominations of five to one hundred. After a series of failures, several former German craftsmen were located fighting on the Russian front and recalled for this special duty. Their assistance in the complex process produced an acceptable grade of paper after the SS discovered that the composition of Turkish currency was very similar to English pound notes. The factory delivered 120,000 sheets a month to the Sachsenhausen barracks, where the printing process was slated to occur. Each sheet was large enough for eight notes. Even with all this effort, the paper and final forged notes remained mediocre at best until an accomplished counterfeiter named Salomon Smolianoff arrived on the scene to unsnarl the mess.[6]

* * *

When he was not serving time in European jails, Salomon Smolianoff enjoyed a regal lifestyle laundering forgeries of English pound notes and American dollars at casinos in Monte Carlo. He was a Jew of Russian origin, born on March 26, 1897, in the southern part of the country. He had learned his engraving craft in 1926 when he met up with Erugen Zotow, a famous engraver whose work was displayed in the Hermitage Museum in St. Petersburg. Zotow, too, was a crook at heart and the pair launched a forgery ring. Smolianoff, operating under the alias "Soly," was arrested in June 1928 in Amsterdam trying to pass fake English notes. A brief prison sentence of a few months' duration was his reward. Another arrest followed in Berlin in 1936. This time he was sentenced to five years in prison, but was released shortly thereafter under strict monitoring conditions. Counterfeiting was like a virus in his blood, and "Soly" was caught two years later committing the same crime. A long stint in Dachau was prescribed for his disorder, but for a reason unexplained he was released only twenty days later. In 1940 he was again apprehended and incarcerated in a concentration camp outside Linz, Austria, called Mauthausen. Crafty and calculating, the gifted artist won favors from the SS guards by sketching their portraits in charcoal. His efforts pleased his captors, and in this way he avoided deadly slave labor duties or liquidation. Late in 1942, Major Krüger's staff stumbled across Smolianoff's amazing dossier. He was immediately transferred to Building 19 at Sachsenhausen, where the smiling Krüger was waiting to greet him. The SS officer carefully described his duties and told him he had to show them how to fix their mistakes and improve the overall process. "Otherwise," announced the major, "Himmler will withdraw his support of our operation, and everyone involved with it will be liquidated."[7]

Given that a few days earlier he had been languishing in disease-ridden Mauthausen, Smolianoff found his new employment more than satisfactory. The food and cigarette rations were adequate, the living arrangements as good or better than some of the jails he had visited, and armed guards policed the building in which he made counterfeit money. Smolianoff rolled up his sleeves and went to work. Krüger promptly arranged for "Soly" to work in a small private room when it became clear some of the prisoners disliked him intensely. He was an expert at engraving printing plates and understood the complex system of printing forgeries on glass plates with gelatin. Glass plates were used instead of metal because they were comparatively easy to make and were good for about 3,000 impressions. Within days he had streamlined and improved the process considerably.[8]

The procedure Smolianoff implemented was complex but workable. After the arrival of the paper sheets, Krüger gave Smolianoff and the printer an example of the exact signature, date, and serial numbers they were to use. Each set had to be synchronized exactly. How the Germans obtained this information is not known. Two prisoners were assigned to each counterfeiting machine. Each print run lasted between fifteen and twenty hours. It was a laborious process. The sketch of the Britannia seal in the upper left corner of the plates had to be meticulously cleaned after one hundred impressions. Finished sheets were carefully hung to dry for one week, at which time they were cut into single notes. Each was then painstakingly examined under a bright light on a glass plate. Many failed to pass the test and were set aside. Those that looked genuine were wrinkled, folded, unfolded, crumpled by hand, and rubbed on the floor in order to artificially age them. Some of the 100 pound notes were pierced with a needle in order to make it appear as though the notes had been pinned together by English bank clerks. Barracks 19 produced every circulated denomination, but the large five-pound note proved a favorite and accounted for forty percent of the total production. (In 1945 the five-pound note had a value of approximately twenty American dollars.) By the middle of 1943, Krüger's 140 employees were turning out almost 40,000 bills per month. By the end of the year, largely because of Smolianoff's efforts, this output increased to about 100,000.[9]

The notes made by the forgery operation were divided into four categories: perfect, near perfect, flawed (notes to be dumped by air over England, an idea later discarded), and outright rejections, which were set aside to be destroyed. Those deemed perfect were reserved for German spies to use in neutral countries like Switzerland and for circulation in Europe. The next best were packaged and provided to the SS and German collaborators for distribution in occupied countries. Notes that were flawed but still generally passable were also used in this manner, although in a more circumspect fashion. One attempt to see if the perfect notes passed muster involved a Nazi agent and a Paris bordello. Would the prostitutes, who had previously serviced British soldiers, readily accept the notes as payment? They did. This convinced the Germans that the notes could be passed in general circulation. Many were used to purchase gold, foreign currencies, and supplies critical to the war effort. But how good were these "perfect" notes? Eventually, reported Dr. Höttl, "such good forgeries were produced that they were accepted as genuine by banks throughout the world; only the Bank of England itself detected that they were forged." How the bank discovered the counterfeit note was itself remarkable. One of the notes turned up in the Bank of England in late 1944. By remarkable coincidence, the clerk holding the note noticed that it had the same serial number as another note in her other hand! Counterfeit experts working with the Bank of England could not readily determine which of the two was fraudulent. The counterfeit notes were so perfect that they could only be detected by matching them with the duplicate serial number of the original note—an obviously impossible task.[10]

The equivalent of some $4.5 billion, most of it in British pounds, was eventually shipped from Sachsenhausen to Berlin, and from there laundered all over Europe. Operatives used the forged notes to purchase legitimate objects, such as paintings, cars, furniture, bullion, and so forth. These items were then sold for Reichsmarks or converted into more stable world currencies like Swiss francs, English pounds, or American dollars. These currencies, in turn, were used by the Germans to pay their agents and purchase badly needed items abroad, such as penicillin or plastic explosives. Other counterfeit notes were distributed to German embassies in Norway, Denmark, Spain, Portugal, and Switzerland, where they were exchanged for local currencies. While some of these early transactions were successful, in order to have the intended effect of collapsing England's economy, a massive distribution of the forged notes had to be implemented. Initial efforts to pass counterfeit notes on a large scale, however, proved disastrous. German military administration officials in occupied countries actually discovered attempts to pass large quantities of counterfeit notes and arrested their own Aktion I agents! Because the program was top secret, the arresting agencies had no way of knowing the forgers worked for their own government.[11]

* * *

At some point the mission underlying Aktion I changed—a fact that has generally gone unrecognized by historians and students of the war. The possibilities of acquiring tremendous sums of personal wealth, which could be used in any number of ways, were simply too great to resist. The architects behind this reorganization were Heinrich Himmler and Obersturmführer (First Lieutenant) Gröbel, the Berlin head of Bureau VI. The new network they intended to create would operate in clandestine fashion within the existing structure of Aktion I. "Operation Bernhard," the name historians have used to describe the *original* counterfeiting operation, would launder the counterfeit funds on a grand scale, and Himmler, Gröbel, and others would skim the proceeds for personal use. Gröbel knew a man capable of running such a complex and dangerous operation. His name was Friedrich (aka "Fritz") Schwend. The controversial life Schwend led before his association with Aktion I (soon to be known in smaller circles as Operation Bernhard is fascinating.[12]

Friedrich Schwend's early years (and much of his career with the Nazis) is a virtual cipher. In the 1920s, he acted as an international arms dealer, shipping weapons to both China and the USSR. He married the niece of the Minister of Exterior, Baron von Neurath, and through this new family connection finagled a position as the personal administrator of the extremely wealthy Bunge family. In the late 1930s, Schwend was working out of New York City and managing the investments of Bunge & Born, the Argentina-based international wheat magnate. His business dealings also included substantial real estate holdings and banking affairs in Italy. Schwend was very good at what he did, for his pre-war income exceeded $50,000 a year. What he earned under the table from his activities selling Belgian weapons and German fighter planes to the Chinese is unknown.[13]

Schwend's activities during the war's early years are hard to fully decipher and require some educated conjecture. His naturally good luck slid a bit in 1941 when German officials asked Italian police to arrest him in Rome on charges of spying for the Americans. Whether he was actually snooping for the Yanks is doubtful, but the expungement of his files lends some credence to this allegation. He spent five months studying the interior walls of a German jail before he was finally able to purchase his way to freedom and return to Rome. Dr. Wilhelm Höttl may have had something to do with Schwend's release. His fingerprints seem to be all over Schwend's introduction to service with the RSHA. Schwend initially joined the Abwehr, or German military intelligence. Based out of Munich, his responsibilities included locating hidden foreign currencies. In July 1942, he was either forced out of the intelligence department or resigned. Schwend offered his services to the Munich head of Bureau VI, but was rebuffed. Later that year a new Munich bureau chief named Josef Dauser was installed. With the backing of Gröbel (who may have recognized Schwend's financial abilities and experience) or, more likely, the influence of Wilhelm Höttl, Dauser welcomed Schwend into the ranks of the Munich branch of RSHA Bureau VI in 1943.[14]

However Schwend came to be a part of Bureau VI, it was no accident. Gröbel (and likely Höttl) had decided to use Schwend as the paymaster of the money-laundering end of the counterfeiting scheme. That whole aspect of the forgery operation was so top secret that not even Munich Bureau chief Dauser was informed of its existence. As a cover for his clandestine operations, and in order to enable him to move freely about in Germany and its occupied territories, Schwend's identity was changed. He was now known as "Major Wendig." Papers were also drawn up showing him as both a member of the German tank corps and as a legal officer of the Gestapo. [15]

In September 1943, Schwend rolled up his sleeves and went to work in earnest. His first priority was to set up a large network of agents to launder the fake notes, and find someone in the RSHA who could reliably maintain bookkeeping responsibilities and keep the counterfeit notes within a small coterie of criminals. RSHA's Bureau II had long been involved in the counterfeiting business (passports, rubber stamps, and the like), but Schwend believed a new officer was needed to run the operation, someone with whom he could work. In the summer of 1944, Schwend decided SS Standartenführer (Colonel) Josef Spacil was the right person to head the bureau.[16]

Josef Spacil was born in Munich on January 3, 1907. His early years were as unremarkable as his physique. According to Allied records he had brown hair and brown-gray eyes, stood 5 feet 9 inches with a medium build, fair complexion, and a heavy Bavarian accent. The only known photograph of him—a grainy, poorly developed image—displays a mousy-looking oval faced man. Spacil had a wife, although details of his marriage are unknown. After he earned a business diploma in 1925 he labored in obscurity with his pen as a banker in Munich until 1930. The deteriorating economy finally shoved him into the ranks of the unemployed, where he marched for about one year.

Spacil's early political bent is a mystery, but the months he spent unable to earn a living likely hardened his views and pushed him to the right side of the political spectrum. On March 31, 1931, he joined the Allgemeine (Regular) SS. His first posting was as a guard at the Braunes Haus, the birthplace of the Nazi Party, in his native Munich. A few months later Spacil was offered a job as a stenographer for the Central Financial Administration of the SS. Three years later he transferred to Berlin, where he acted as a liaison officer between the SS in Berlin and the Reich Treasury. In 1936 Spacil returned to the Munich area to take a job as the finance officer at the Dachau concentration camp, which at that time was used to house political prisoners and petty criminals (and was not yet an extermination camp). The dutiful bureaucrat was transferred from the Allgemeine SS to the Waffen (Armed) SS in 1939. He held over the next two years a number of clerical positions within that organization. During the early months of Operation Barbarossa, the invasion of the

Soviet Union, Spacil served in southern Russia as a clerk and representative of the SS Main Bureau. By 1944 Spacil had proven himself to be a capable bureaucratic manager. He had also proven capable of participating in war crimes. Documents carrying his signature reveal his involvement in the organized German raping of Kiev, during which he coolly executed decrees demanding stocks of gold, silver, and raw materials. As a Standartenführer (Colonel) he was ordered to leave the front and take command of the RSHA's Bureau II in Berlin—the result of Friedrich Schwend's influence and string-pulling. The department administrated the funds allocated for all of Ernst Kaltenbrunner's bureaus. Spacil's staff members (who probably jumped for joy when they learned of their new posting) accompanied him from Russia to Berlin, where they and Spacil labored quietly on Schwend's behalf. "In the summer of 1944, Spacil was let into the conspiracy and operation name of Bernhard," recollected Spacil's private secretary Rudolf Guenther.[17]

Once Spacil joined the conspiracy, Schwend kicked the operation into high gear. Schwend's transactions were disguised to hide what was really going on. For example, if he wanted 1,000,000 forged English pounds, he would send Spacil a coded telegram requesting 1,000 kilograms. "Kilogram" was a code word, and each kilogram was a request for 1,000 British pounds. Spacil's private secretary, Rudolf Guenther, would pick up the counterfeit notes, debit Schwend's account for the proper sum, and deliver the currency to Schwend's special courier. When he received the notes, Schwend would distribute them into his network of agents—but not before raking thirty-three percent off the top for his own pocket.[18]

*   *   *

One of the great swindlers and double-dealers of the World War II era was an Austrian Jew named George Spitz. It is both ironic and fitting that he came to act as an agent for Schwend and his counterfeiting operation. Spitz was born about 1890 in Vienna. At a young age he traveled to the United States and went into the banking business with his brother in New York City. He did well in America. Before shipping off for Europe (under rather suspicious circumstances) he sold one-half of his interest to his brother for $500,000. Once back on the continent, Spitz's path crossed with a popular actress named Feran Andra. Before long the smooth-talking Spitz was both her manager and her lover. The pair lived primarily in Vienna and on the French Riviera, where Andra ripened her passion for gambling. Unfortunately, she was not very good at games of chance. Spitz's fortune was lost on the tables at the Monte Carlo Casino. Once the money was gone so was the actress. Completely broke but still his resourceful self, Spitz ended up in Switzerland as the founder of a bank called Maiser Holdings. Honesty, however, was not one of his long suits. Improper accounting procedures and other irregularities forced him to flee the country in 1936 just ahead of the Swiss police. Once safely over the border, he took up dual residences in Vienna and Berlin.[19]

Spitz was in Belgium when war broke across Europe in 1939. For reasons still unclear he decided to enter France, where he was arrested by the French Police in Strasbourg for outstanding criminal warrants. He was not released from jail until the Germans overran the country in 1940. Liberated but again penniless, Spitz traveled to southern Germany and moved in with a new mistress, Fraulein Bruckemann, the heiress to a wealthy and prominent Frankfurt family. It did not take long for the fast-talking Spitz to become gainfully employed—by the SS. This time the employment was not voluntary.

Gröbel and Schwend had asked bureau chief Dauser to find a man capable of selling English pounds for foreign currency. Gröbel may have hinted that the currency was forged, but the record is unclear on this point. In reality, Gröbel and Schwend intended to use this new man as a lead agent for Operation Bernhard. Dauser scoured the Munich branch of Bureau VI, but no one working there was deemed suitable for the position. Bertha von Ehrenstein, Dauser's secretary, either introduced George Spitz to her boss or informed on him. Either way, the paths of Dauser, Schwend, and Spitz converged. A meeting was held between the three during which Spitz was offered work as an undercover agent. Spitz wanted nothing to do with Dauser or Schwend and refused the offer. Afer all, he was a private sector criminal, not a bureaucratic crook. His rejection was unacceptable, and Dauser was not about to accept it. He coolly informed Spitz that he knew he was a Jew, that his papers were not in order, and that if he did not cooperate he and his family would be executed. Blackmailed into action, Spitz relented.[20]

It will be recalled that the money-laundering aspects of Operation Bernhard were not shared with Josef Dauser. Still, the man was not a complete fool and before long it dawned on him that Schwend and Spitz were working a scam. Schwend, the former Abwehr operative, brought the English notes into Dauser's Munich office by the suitcase full, where the currency was tied into bundles and stored away for future use. When it was needed, the money was stamped on the floor and "dirtied," activity sure to raise the eyebrows of thoughtful men. Within a short time Dauser could no longer keep his mouth shut.

"What exactly is going on here?" he inquired of Schwend during one of his frequent visits. "Are all of these notes counterfeit?"

"No," responded Schwend, "the money is genuine. It has been seized from prisoners."

Dauser refused to believe this explanation. "There is something wrong with what is going on," he shot back. "I think this is a private money-making operation, yes?"

Schwend, of course, could not reveal the true nature of his activities. "Himmler and Gröbel are involved," he responded carefully. "It is official business." In other words, it would be safer for Dauser if he backed off and kept quiet.

Dauser understood and backed away from pressing the matter. But he did not give up trying to discover what, exactly, was transpiring beneath his own nose. He discreetly continued his inquiry and discovered that another high ranking branch chief of Bureau VI was also involved in Aktion I, and that his agents were dealing with foreign currency exchanges within Schwend's network. Initially this seemed to satisfy him—it did appear, after all, to be a legitimate enterprise. Aktion I was a sanctioned RSHA operation. The more Dauser worked with Schwend and others, the clearer it became that all was not as it appeared to be. "Gröbel, Schwend, Dr. Höttl and his assistant, SS Captain Froelich, were retaining much of the money for their own pockets," Dauser told Allied investigators after the war. "Operation Bernhard was a name for a financial affair similar to Aktion I which they kept secret from Berlin. . . . As far as Berlin was concerned the name of the official currency operation was always Aktion I."[21]

We do not know how much information, if any, Schwend shared with George Spitz about Operation Bernhard. Perhaps Spitz believed all of his activities were legitimate operations carried out under the Aktion I program. What we do know is that Spitz turned in several stellar performances as a successful money laundering agent. After the war he made little attempt to hide his activities from Allied interrogators. He openly admitted working for "Wendig" (Schwend) but adamantly denied any knowledge that the money he was passing was fake. As he explained it, he only agreed to work for Schwend in order to avoid harm. At some point he discovered that Schwend's operation was extensive, and that fifty agents were under his employ. Spitz's story convinced his Allied captors that he was generally telling the truth.[22]

In late May of 1944 Schwend sent Spitz and Otto Kastner into Belgium and Holland. Kastner was the driver for Heinrich Hoffmann, Hitler's official photographer. The pair carried with them suitcases full of counterfeit notes to purchase local currency, gold, and valuable art treasures. From the renowned Goudstikker Collection, Spitz procured three expensive rugs for Schwend's castle in Meran, Italy, antiques, and numerous priceless paintings, including van Mierveld's *Portrait of a Lady* and Paulus Moreelse's *Woman and Child*. Exactly how Spitz stretched his tentacles into the prestigious Goudstikker Collection is a fascinating story.[23]

Wealthy collection owner, Jacques Goudstikker, did not enjoy a happy end. In late 1938, he married Austrian soprano Desirée. He had watched for some time the disturbing policies toward Jews bubbling within Germany and Austria. When Hitler invaded Poland in 1939, Goudstikker foresaw that the black tide would eventually sweep across all of Europe; it was time to leave Holland. Passage was booked for his wife and infant on the ship *Simón Bolívar*. For reasons unknown, when it came time to board he decided not to put his family on the ship. It was a good decision, because the *Simón Bolívar* was torpedoed and all aboard perished. On May 14, 1940, Goudstikker and his family boarded the *SS Bodengraven* in the port of Ijmunden, Holland. The ship was attacked by German airplanes as it crossed the English Channel, but none of the Goudstikkers were harmed. A short time later, Goudstikker was walking on deck when he missed his footing and fell through a hatch into the bowels of the ship. He did not survive. [24]

Although his wife and young child eventually reached America, the fortune they left behind never left Europe. Goudstikker had prudently formed a corporation to take over his houses and thousands of paintings and other priceless objects of art should he fall ill or die. Unfortunately, the person holding the power of attorney to operate the corporation died just before Goudstikker. During this confused period, when the ownership and control of the multi-million dollar estate was in flux, an art dealer named Alois Miedl slithered into the picture. The businessman had moved to Holland from Munich in 1932. One of Miedl's clients was Reichsmarschall Hermann Göring, the head of the German Luftwaffe. Göring was a voracious collector of art. Indeed, his hobby became an all-consuming compulsive endeavor, and Miedl fed Göring's addiction by sweeping Holland for pieces suitable for his collection. His interest in helping Göring was purely selfish: the Reichsmarschall had discovered that Miedl's wife was Jewish. Göring, never one to shy away from using his powerful position to advantage, offered to protect Miedl's wife. In return, the art dealer scoured Holland for priceless paintings, rugs, tapestries, and sculptures on Göring's behalf. Miedl utilized both his connections within the art world and Göring's clout to acquire a sizeable slice of the Goudstikker estate for the Reichsmarschall. The estate included one of Holland's historic castles, Kasteel Nijenrode, which contained hundreds of priceless paintings, many by the world's famous masters. Göring acquired the objects of art; Miedl took title to the real estate and he and his wife kept their heads. [25]

George Spitz, naturally enough, wanted to get his hands on some of the Goudstikker collection and launder some of his counterfeit money in the process. His opportunity arose when he discovered a man who knew Alois Miedl well enough to approach him with an offer. A doctor in chemistry with the surname of Kurz had known Miedl since childhood and introduced him to Spitz in Amsterdam. Acting as an intermediary, Dr. Kurz helped Spitz with the purchase of art and other financial transactions related to the collection. Spitz took full advantage of the introduction, acquiring the invaluable *Peasant's Dance* by Sir Peter Paul Rubens, as well as a Rembrandt. Transporting the valuable artwork without threat of robbery or discovery proved relatively simple. Spitz merely affixed SS stamps to a large traveling trunk. Tucked away in his pocket was a special pass personally signed by Himmler forbidding anyone from opening the trunk. The pass also gave Spitz the complete freedom to travel anywhere in Germany or the occupied countries without restriction. Spitz used this authorization to haul dozens of paintings from the Goudstikker and other collections to the Henkel Fabriken complex in Dusseldorf, as well as the Witzig storehouse in Munich. Because photographer Heinrich Hoffmann (for whom Kastner drove a car) was also employed by Reichsmarschall Göring, a large number of the paintings changed hands with Göring and other prominent collectors.[26]

Operation Bernhard, conducted entirely below Berlin's radar, was a stunning money laundering success. A large amount of the cleansed currency was eventually turned over to Dr. Höttl and his assistant, SS Captain Froelich. Just as it had dawned on Josef Dauser, Spitz (himself a swindler of the first order) eventually realized to his dismay that Höttl and Froelich were skimming a substantial amount of the money for themselves.[27]

In addition to being exchanged for other currencies, the counterfeit notes were used to purchase millions of dollars worth of weapons, ammunition, military equipment, liquor, gold, and jewelry. The military goods, including food, were mostly used within Germany proper. The gold and currencies were shipped to the Reichsbank; the chinaware, clothing, shoes, and furniture were shipped to three storage depots in Austria. Wherever the items ended up, once they were shipped an itemized bill was sent to Josef Spacil, who had his secretary, Rudolf Guenther, credit Schwend's account accordingly.[28]

In his capacity as the sole overseer for the distribution of the counterfeit currency, Schwend worked closely with Ernst Kaltenbrunner, the head of the RSHA and Gestapo, Kaltenbrunner's assistant, Lieutenant Colonel Arthur Scheidler, and Dr. Wilhelm Höttl. All the currency distributed to Italy, Croatia, and Hungary was delivered directly into Höttl's hands. These mammoth distributions enabled Schwend to satisfy the luxurious demands all three men placed upon him.[29]

*   *   *

The greatest forgery and counterfeiting enterprise of all time operated smoothly until the final days of the war. Despite its remarkable success it had no real impact on the war effort. The Bank of England suffered enormous losses as a result of the operation, but the British economy was never in danger of collapsing because of it. Operation Bernhard, however, did serve to feather the nests of those officers smart enough to realize the war would eventually end one day, and that Germany was not going to be on the winning side of the ledger. Schwend and company continued utilizing the Sachsenhausen barracks until early April 1945, by which time the advancing Russian army posed a serious threat to Berlin and the surrounding region. Himmler wanted to discontinue the operation altogether. However, Major Bernhard Krüger, who oversaw the project at Sachsenhausen, insisted that the production of the forged currency continue. As far as he was concerned, his efforts were helping the war effort while guaranteeing that high ranking Nazis would be well funded when they made their escape to safety after the war. Himmler relented and agreed to let the operation persevere.

Unbeknownst to Himmler, Krüger had other reasons for keeping the forgery team intact. He had been told that his Jewish staff would be executed when his operation closed shop. Krüger informed his prisoners of the order and advised them to keep working. They did not have to be told twice. The counterfeiting plant would continue, but in another more tenable venue. Twenty large army trucks were loaded with printing presses and equipment and placed onto a train. In that manner the entire operation moved by rail from Berlin by way of Mauthausen to a large underground chamber at Redl Zipf, a small village nine miles from Vokklabruk, Austria, and just thirty miles from Zell am See and Fischhorn castle. Krüger and his team arrived there on April 18, 1945.[30]

Austria, however, offered only a brief respite from the Allied armies. Seven days later Krüger was notified that American and Russian forces were closing in from three sides. The last thing he intended to do was be captured by the Russians. He and his mistress from Berlin, Hilde Möller, an attractive 24-year-old blond, packed their bags and sped away from Redl Zipf in an Alfa Romeo convertible. The 40-year-old Krüger, 5' 7" tall and with a nervous twitch in his left eye, was well prepared for flight. He carried with him all the forged documents he would need, together with a large supply of English pound notes. In his glove compartment were two passports, one Swiss and the other Paraguayan.[31]

The work continued even after Krüger's departure. According to Oscar Stein, Operation Bernhard's head bookkeeper and himself a Jewish prisoner, the men were put to work burning incriminating papers and destroying rejected English pound notes with an estimated counterfeit value of 60,000,000 pounds. The perfect English notes were packed into large heavy wooden boxes about 2' x 2' x 7'. It took four prisoners to carry and load each box onto a waiting truck. After each truck was fully loaded it rolled in the direction of Zell am See and Fischhorn castle. On the nights of April 30–May 1, 2, and 3, remembered Stein, the trucks hauled away hundreds of boxes containing 61,000,000 pounds of perfect counterfeit English notes. Each wooden container was stamped "In case of danger destroy contents."[32]

Some of this cargo ended up at the bottom of Lake Toplitz, dumped in a secret nocturnal rowboat operation witnessed by a single civilian woman who lived to tell the story. Early one morning on or about May 1, 1945, 21-year-old Austrian farm girl Ida Weisenbacher was roused from her bed with a sharp knock and a shout. "It was five o'clock in the morning, we were still in bed when we heard the knock on the door," remembered Weisenbacher. "Get up immediately hitch up the horse wagon, we need you!" shouted an SS officer. Actually, the Germans needed a wagon more than they needed Ida. Their large four-ton Lancia truck and trailer were loaded full with wooden crates. They had intended to drive it to the edge of the lake and dump the contents into the cold deep water, but the narrow road leading in that direction ended far short of the shore—and near Ida's home. "A commander was there," Ida recalled. "He told us to bring these boxes as fast as possible to Lake Toplitz." Ida saw each box, which was stenciled with bold-painted letters and a corresponding number. The woman hitched up a wagon and organized a trio of wheeled trips to the water's edge. "When I brought the last load, I saw how they went on to the lake and dropped the boxes into the water. . . The SS kept shoving me away but I saw the boxes were sunk into the lake," she said.

The contents of the boxes remained a mystery to her for fifty-five years. In 2000, a search of the deep lake with advanced underwater technology turned up the remains of several wooden boxes as well as thousands of pounds in counterfeit currency. Ida, now 78, still lives in the same small house near the edge of Lake Toplitz where one early morning a truckload of SS soldiers woke her from a deep sleep to play a small role in the dying hours of Operation Bernhard.[33]

Once the trucks were gone, Oscar Stein and his Jewish comrades were directed to hide a few boxes of currency in a home near Redl Zipf. Still under guard and facing a rapidly-approaching date with death, the prisoners were escorted several miles northeast to Ebensee concentration camp. They were told they would be gassed upon arrival. At Ebensee, the Jews were turned over to Wehrmacht soldiers and their SS guards promptly fled the scene. They, too, had every intention of avoiding Russian captivity. Krüger's Jews, it seems, lived a charmed existence. The Americans arrived at Ebensee the next day, May 6, 1945, and liberated them just hours before a one-way trip into the gas chamber. Without the timely arrival of the GIs, none would have lived to tell their remarkable story. A CIC agent asked one of them in a postwar interview what he thought of Bernhard Krüger. The answer surprised him. "He was very decent to us," he answered.[34]

*   *   *

What happened to the remaining trucks loaded with counterfeit currency? They were originally headed west and southwest out of Redl Zipf, thirty miles northeast of Salzburg, in the hope of reaching the Zell am See region. Because of the advancing Allies, however, the convoy could not take the direct route through Salzburg. To avoid the enemy, the trucks turned south through a gorge on a narrow road next to the Traun River, and then west on another constricted byway paralleling the Enns River. They never made it to Zell am See. Three trucks, two full of notes and the third crammed with valuable antiques and related loot pilfered from Russia, were purposely driven into a deep narrow gorge, where they plunged into the cold water of the River Inns not far from the village of Pruggern. The cases burst open and the swift water distributed the forged pound notes and loot as far as ten miles down river.

The truck that had made it to Ida Weisenbacher's home near Lake Toplitz left with its trailer partially loaded for the camp at Ebensee, where some of the notes were burned. Other trucks were driven to Gmündner, their contents dumped into Lake Traun. One of the trucks from Redl Zipf joined a winding line of trucks and cars filled with valuables from Berlin.

This particular convoy was under the command of Josef Spacil, the head of RSHA Bureau II who had recently relocated to the state of Salzburg, Austria, to carry out another, more desperate, directive.[35]

Although some of the counterfeit money was accounted for, the fate of tens of millions of pounds of "perfect" notes remains a mystery. Some of the money was hidden away in attics and barns, basements and fields; crates full of the fake currency were dumped into deep Austrian lakes. Millions were eventually recovered, but most of it was not. Given what we know today, it is likely that a large portion of the remainder was deposited into Swiss and Spanish banks (or otherwise hidden away) and used after the war by those SS officers and others lucky enough to escape arrest and conviction for their wartime crimes against humanity.

Chapter Notes

1. Wilhelm Höttl, *The Secret Front: The Story of Nazi Political Espionage* (New York, 1954), pp. 85-86.

2. "Contents," p. 2, signed by Major J. McNally, Chief, Counterfeit Detection Section, undated; Heinz Hohne, *The Order of the Death's Head: The Story of Hitler's SS* (New York, 1970), pp. 295-297.

3. "Contents," p. 2, Major J. McNally, undated.

4. Höttl, *The Secret Front*, pp. 85-86; Wilhelm Höttl Testimony, Nuremberg, October 28, 1945. According to Höttl, Walther Funk "succeeded in preventing any wholesale distribution of the forged notes in countries under German domination, and operations were therefore confined to enemy territories." *The Secret Front*, p. 86.

5. Höttl, *The Secret Front*, p. 85; CIC, "Report of Former Jewish Prisoner Max Bober," unsigned and undated. The number of Jews working on the project quickly rose from 60 to 140.

6. Germany lost Turkey as an ally in August 1944. This interrupted the free flow of goods between the two countries, including the precious linen imported from Turkey that had become indispensable to the manufacture of paper for the counterfeiting process. Although the Germans improvised, the forged notes produced in 1945 were not nearly as good as those produced in 1943 and 1944.

7. Murray T. Bloom, *Money of Their Own: The Great Counterfeiters* (New York, 1957), p. 245.

8. "Contents," p. 5, Major J. McNally, undated.

9. "Complimentary Report of Counterfeiting of British Banknotes," Attachment, S. G. Michel, July 25, 1945, Captain, French Army; "Contents," p. 9, Major J. McNally, undated. Krüger came up with a remarkable idea in order to keep up the morale of those laboring under a death sentence: he awarded medals to his most deserving workers. Six employees, including three Jews, were bestowed the Iron Cross, Second Class, and twelve other prisoners, almost all of whom were Jewish, accepted a lesser decoration. Krüger's superior had initially shot down the idea. Krüger, however, pulled some strings with Ernst Kaltenbrunner's aide-de-camp and made it appear as though all those receiving the award were German. Kaltenbrunner signed the papers without examining them closely. Although some of the SS guards grew incensed when they spotted Jews wearing German awards, Kaltenbrunner was amused (a rare state for him) by the whole affair when he discovered what Krüger had done.

10. Headquarters Counter Intelligence Corps, Fifteenth Army Group, 430th CIC Detachment, "Memorandum for Officer in Charge," Special Agent Richard W. Lindsey, July 13, 1945; Detachment A-2, 2677 Regiment OSS, "Subject, Documents, Counterfeit," Civilian OSS Erick A. Harris, June 22, 1945; Höttl, *The Secret Front*, pp. 85-86. At the end of the war the British withdrew all the five pound notes from circulation and replaced them with a fresh series. The only certain way to distinguish the forged notes from the originals is the watermark. In the original, the line into the bottom "N" of "England" is slightly offset. This "error" was inadvertently corrected in the German version, where the line runs into the middle of the bottom "N" of word "England." It has been estimated that by war's end some 40% of the British notes in circulation were forgeries.

11. CIC, "Report on Interrogation of Walter Schellenberg," June 27, 1945, and July 12, 1945; Bloom, *Money of Their Own: The Great Counterfeiters*, p. 251.

12. PIR, No. 96, USFET MIS, Lieutenant George Wenzel, January 17, 1946.

13. Friedrich Schwend's files have been carefully and intentionally purged. The United States acquired all the SS personnel files in our Berlin sector immediately after the war ended. Today, Schwend's file—and his RuSHA file—are not among them. The RuSHA (Race and Settlement Main Office) file was also known as the "purity" file, a genealogy certificate stretching back five generations for SS members and their wives. Accepted "purity" was 1/5 Jew, or

less. A microfilm copy of these SS files, RuSHA files, and the captured Nazi Party membership list (captured by the U.S. Seventh Army from Munich) are all available at the National Archives, complete with a master index. Both Schwend's Nazi Party index card and his Nazi Party file are missing. Someone went to considerable trouble to expunge his background. Perhaps he bribed a high ranking American officer to pull the card and files, or perhaps someone in the Intelligence service or U.S. Army was ordered to remove the information. The result is that the little information available on Schwend is derived from third party files and secondary sources.

14. CIC, "Interrogation Memorandum of Josef Dauser," May 30, 1945.

15. "Interrogation Memorandum of Josef Dauser," May 30, 1945. Gröbel was killed by partisans near Trieste, Italy, in September 1943.

16. PIR, No. 96, United States Forces European Theater, Military Intelligence Service, Lieutenant George Wenzel, January 17, 1946.

17. Headquarters U.S. Forces European Theater, Interrogation Center, Prisoner O/Fuerher Spacil, Josef, Chief of Amt. II, RSHA," August 4, 1945; PIR, No. 96, USFET MIS, Lieutenant George Wenzel, January 17, 1946; CIC, "Interview with Rudolf Guenther," conducted by George Wenzel, February 8, 1946.

18. CIC, "Interview with Rudolf Guenther," conducted by George Wenzel, February 8, 1946.

19. Undated statement signed by Mr. Erna Hoffmann (the wife of Adolf Hitler's photographer Heinrich Hoffmann).

20. Memorandum, "Sale of Foreign Currency by the RSHA," May 17, 1945. According to Spitz, ibid., Friedrich Schwend was at the meeting and also threatened him with harm if he refused to act as his agent. See also, "RSHA Financial Operation," Memorandum compiled by Lieutenant Winston Scott, USN, to Sir Edward Reid, MI5, June 13, 1945.

21. "RSHA Financial Operation," June 13, 1945. Josef Dauser's reference to Obersturmführer Gröbel is curious because that officer was killed in Trieste, Italy, in the Fall of 1943. Dauser's secretary kept the accounts in the Munich branch and was, according to Dauser, "well informed on the whole plan." Exactly what "well informed" meant is open to some debate. He may have told her everything once he came to fully realize several men were pulling a gigantic scam and that the operation was being carefully hidden from Berlin's prying eyes.

22. "RSHA Financial Operation," June 13, 1945.

23. CIC, "Sale of Foreign Currency by the RSHA," May 17, 1945; "RSHA Financial Operation," June 13, 1945; Edgar Breitenbach, "Goudstikker Paintings and Rugs bought by George Spitz," November 11, 1949, U.S. Army. All art transactions conducted with Germans after 1939 were considered invalid and the pieces, if located, were returned to their country of origin.

24. Lynn N. Nicholas, *The Rape of Europa* (New York, 1994), pp. 83-85.

25. Wealth has its privileges. Joseph Kennedy, the U.S. Ambassador to England, obtained visas to America for the widow, Desirée Goudstikker, and her child. Office of Strategic Services, Art Looting Investigating Unit, "The Göring Collection," by Lieutenant Theodore Rousseau, September 15, 1945.

26. "RSHA Financial Operation," June 13, 1945; "The Göring Collection," by Lieutenant Theodore Rousseau, September 15, 1945.

27. "RSHA Financial Operation," June 13, 1945; "Report on Interrogation of Walter Schellenberg," June 27, 1945, and July 12, 1945.

28. "RSHA Financial Operation," June 13, 1945; "Interrogation of Rudolf Guenther," February 6, 1946. Notorious Einsatzgruppen commander Otto Ohlendorf claimed after the war that Josef Spacil spent considerable effort placing forged British banknotes into circulation for the purchase of black market items in southern Europe. CSDIC (UK) GG Report, SRGG 1322 C , July 7, 1945, IRR File Ohlendorf, National Archives. The gigantic Nazi criminal bureaucracy made it relatively easy for unscrupulous men to stockpile fortunes beyond their wildest dreams; Operation Bernhard proved that conclusively. During his postwar trial Ohlendorf explained how several Nazi party district leaders, particularly in Poland, plundered the system. Erich Koch, the Gauleiter of East Prussia, created a foundation in his own name of which he was the sole member, manager, and director. He protected his little fiefdom by lavishing senior officials and officers, like Hermann Göring and Heinrich Himmler, with expensive gifts. Koch absconded to Flensburg aboard a ship "loaded with riches," Ohlendorf testified in May 1945. Koch eluded capture until 1949, when he was tried by the Polish government and sentenced to death. His sentence was later commuted and he died in prison in 1986 at the age of 90. Another similar operator was Arthur Greiser, the Gauleiter of Posen, who was connected "with shady dealings in gold articles which originated from the Lodz ghetto." According to Ohlendorf, Greiser bought luxurious houses and a big country estate. Ibid.

29. CIC, "Interrogation of Walter Schellenberg," June 27-July 12, 1945.

30. Unpublished report, "Interrogation of Harry Stolowicz," by W. Rukin, Chief Inspector, Criminal Investigation Department, New Scotland Yard,

September 7, 1945. Although Great Britain did not suffer unduly, several prominent but unsuspecting victims did suffer as a result of the counterfeit operation. Miedl & Co. Bank of Amsterdam dealt in foreign exchange on the Iberian Peninsula. One of its prestigious customers was Hermann Göring. Another victim was Dalmann shipbuilders of Sweden, which purchased nautical material from Great Britain with the counterfeit pound notes and in turn sold seafaring supplies to the German Navy. PIR, No. 96, USFET MIS, Lieutenant George Wenzel, January 17, 1946.

31. "Interrogation of Harry Stolowicz," by W. Rukin, September 7, 1945.

32. CIC, "Report of Jewish Prisoner, Max Bober," May 6, 1945.

33. www.cbsnews.com/now/story/0,1597,251320-412,00.shtml.

34. "Interrogation of Harry Stolowicz," by W. Rukin, September 7, 1945. There seems to be good reason why the Jews in Sachsenhausen liked Bernhard Krüger. According to the O.I.P.C. (Interpol), some 300 people eventually worked in the concentration camp on the counterfeiting operation. Blocks 18 and 19 were only built to accommodate half that number. Krüger stuffed Jews into the barracks, worked them hard—but by doing so saved their lives. Few summary executions seem to have taken place on his watch, even though warranted under German law. One Jewish prisoner known only has "Gutig" pilfered several sheets of English notes, although what he intended to do with them inside a concentration camp is anyone's guess. Instead of a bullet to the head Gutig was ordered to return the notes and never repeat the crime. Another prisoner, "Sukenik," was not so fortunate. He contracted tuberculosis. In an effort to prevent the disease from spreading through the counterfeiting operation, the prisoner was immediately executed (probably on Krüger's orders) and his body incinerated.

35. 430th CIC Detachment, "Counterfeit Money Statement by Eric Victor Doubrava," July 13, 1945, Appendix E.

Chapter 7

"[I] was besieged by requests for supplies, money, and
quarters, most of them impossible to fulfill."

— SS Oberführer Joseph Spacil, April 1945

A Bureaucrat and His Gold:
Josef Spacil's Final Days of World War II

pril 1945. The world was collapsing on the Thousand-Year
Reich. With each passing day, it resembled a sinking ship
settling a bit further in the water, the rats scurrying from within
the dying vessel in a vain attempt to save themselves in the rigging. As
the Reich disintegrated, so too did the layers of criminally-imposed
"legal" accouterment, which had for so long offered protective cover for
the Nazi leaders who had run the machinery of death, enslavement, and
plunder. But now, in the spring of 1945, these same men were consumed
with the hunger for self-preservation.

SS Oberführer Josef Spacil's connections with the plunder and
killing of European Jewry were suddenly too close for comfort. Like so
many of his SS comrades, he had also taken the opportunity to feather his
nest in anticipation of a cozy postwar existence. Unlike so many of his
comrades, however, his cache consisted of more than just counterfeit
notes or stolen liquor. Spacil, it will be recalled, was the head of RSHA
Bureau II. He had helped launder millions in fake English pounds. Within
his charge were millions in gold, jewels, and currency, both foreign and

domestic. He was also burdened with documents and personal items belonging to Adolf Hitler and Eva Braun, and had close associations with several others bearing similar items of interest to the Allies.

For Spacil, escaping the fusing enemy pincers closing in on Germany and Austria was of no little urgency.

*   *   *

For the first time in many years Ernst Kaltenbrunner was all but powerless. The head of the Reich Security Home Office (RSHA) and chief of the Secret Service keenly appreciated the collapse of the Nazi regime meant certain arrest and a likely death sentence for war crimes. That is, if he were caught by the Allies. At this late date, the only viable means of escape was to change his identity and blend into the population of southern Germany or Austria. Alas, final obligations to the dying State remained, including the dilemma concerning the immense wealth his bureaucrats had managed to steal and hide under a fraudulent account named Max Heiliger. What was Kaltenbrunner to do with these millions? A final decision was made to transport the wealth south into the relative safety of the supposed "Alpine Redoubt." In April 1945, he ordered Josef Spacil to organize and oversee the transfer of the account. Perhaps as a reward for the impossible task with which he was suddenly burdened, Spacil was promoted to Oberführer on April 20, 1945, a rank between that of colonel and brigadier general, which has no equivalent in the United States Army.[1]

The Max Heiliger account, the fortune tucked under Spacil's wing of responsibility, was comprised of funds laundered through yet another account named "Melmer." This ring of theft was as elaborate as it was macabre. The wealth, long housed in the German Reichsbank, originated in gold looted from the occupied nations of Europe. Most of it was snatched from Jews and others persecuted by the Nazi regime. In order to disguise the origins of this fortune from the wrong eyes, the RSHA created what became known as the Melmer Account, named after SS Hauptsturmführer (Captain) Bruno Melmer. In stereotypical German fashion, Melmer maintained a precise recording of what was stolen from Nazi Holocaust and other victims between 1942 and 1944. According to Melmer, the gold (which came from watches, jewelry, coins, bullion, and dental fillings pried out of the mouths of the dead and living alike) was collected, inventoried, packaged, and shipped to the Berlin Reichsbank monetary gold reserve. The financial institution logged it in and sent it on to the Degussa smelting company, which processed the metal into bars for easy storage and shipment. Once smelted into bars the SS gold no longer contained the scent of blood, for it was now indistinguishable from other bullion stolen from central banks in occupied Europe. Gold was not the only asset funneled into the Melmer account. Truckloads of silver, diamonds, artwork, antiques, and many other items of tangible value were sold or consigned to pawn shops, and the currencies deposited in the account. As a means of covering the original source of these ill-gotten gains, this wealth was credited, or laundered, into the Max Heiliger account, a phony ledger entry owned wholly by the Reich Ministry of Finance. Some of this gold has today been traced to Swiss bank accounts.[2]

By April 1945, much of the wealth contained in the Heiliger account had already been removed from Berlin. Allied bombing raids had compelled it. The bulk of RSHA's non-working assets had been transferred in October 1944 from the Berlin Reichsbank southwest to Bad Sulza, in the state of Thurginia. Packed carefully into small steel safes and stored in a special air raid shelter in Bad Sulza, designed for RSHA employees, the account consisted of gold bars and coins, rings, jewels, Reichsmarks, and other currencies. By late April some of the Bad Sulza loot had already been dispersed. What remained, however, was enough to make even Spacil's jaded jaw hit the floor. In addition to the gold and coins (200,000 napoleons and Swiss francs stored in ten large jute sacks and small chests), were at least 5,000,000 Reichsmarks in 100 Mark notes, and other foreign currencies—a fortune worth an estimated $25,000,000.[3]

A much smaller sum remained in Berlin, but Spacil was not about to leave it behind. He dispatched one of his Bureau II subordinates, SS Untersturmführer (Second Lieutenant) Ertl, to withdraw the remaining RSHA funds housed there in the Reichsbank. Ertl returned on April 21 with gold, pound sterling, American dollars, Swiss francs, Danish crowns and more, all worth more than 1,000,000 Reichsmarks. "The Reichsbank was giving up all its foreign assets," he reported to Spacil, and Ertl had received "more than what was in the RSHA account." Three sacks of gold francs and a large amount of mixed funds, worth about 350,000 marks, were given to Otto Ohlendorf, the notorious head of RSHA's Bureau III (Security Service). The balance, together with a large portion of the Heiliger hoard, was shipped to Austria under the watchful eye of Spacil's trusted adjutant Kurt Schiebel, who crammed it into sacks and chests and loaded up every square inch of space in three large passenger cars. Spacil also saw to it that some of Eva Braun's personal belongings were tucked away in the shipment for safekeeping. Accompanied by Gretl Biesecker, Spacil's mistress of two years, the trio of autos headed south for Salzburg. Another truck loaded to the gills with the balance of the Heiliger gold and currency was driven from Bad Sulza to Salzburg by a securities expert from Bureau II named Pfeiler.[4]

Spacil did not personally accompany these RSHA valuables. Instead, he and twenty other high-ranking RSHA officials and their families flew from Berlin to Munich on April 22. By that time flying over Germany was a dangerous proposition because of the close proximity of American military forces. That fact was almost fatally confirmed when American fighter planes were discovered in the skies around Munich, strafing everything remotely deemed a military target. Spacil and his party flew low—often at tree-top level—and landed instead in Salzburg, Austria, at 11:00 a.m. Once Spacil set foot in Salzburg the pace of his war picked up considerably. For him and the rest of the high command, one day merged into the next. Each was a disaster and on each passing day their circumstances appreciably worsened.[5]

An inspector with the SD and head of RSHA in Salzburg, Oberstrumbannführer Dr. Franz Josef Hüber, greeted Spacil and his associates and "arranged to care for [their] needs." The first thing Spacil did was leave his mistress in Salzburg and journey to Bad Ischl to visit his wife. There, Spacil was able to reach Kaltenbrunner by telephone and a brief but vigorous conversation ensued. What was discussed is unknown but it was serious enough to prompt Spacil to jump into his car and drive on to Altaussee to see the RSHA chief personally. Unfortunately, Spacil later reported, "he could see me only briefly." During that short time Kaltenbrunner heaped additional responsibilities upon Spacil and his adjutant Schiebel, including "distributing food, supplies, money and valuables, clothing, and if possible weapons to the remaining RSHA agents in the Salzburg area." Boiled down to its coarsest purpose,

Kaltenbrunner was attempting to bribe with food, gold, and currency as many officers and soldiers as possible to remain in the so-called Alpine Redoubt area to protect what little was left of the collapsing southern front of the Nazi Reich. Kaltenbrunner hoped Spacil's effort would buy him time to complete preparations for his own escape which, as it later turned out, was wretchedly planned. According to Spacil, Kaltenbrunner's final vague instructions were that "we should all conduct ourselves in accord with the tactical situation."[6]

On April 23, the bureau chief drove north to Munich, where he met up with Schiebel and his mistress Biesecker. Unable to remain there, the trio braved the roads again and drove back to Salzburg, where on April 24 Spacil attended a series of meetings with a variety of high ranking RSHA officials including two of Kaltenbrunner's primary subordinates, Gestapo chief Heinrich Müller and Oberführer Friedrich Panzinger, the head of Bureau III (the criminal police). Although no one noted it for posterity's sake, the morale at the meetings could only have been low. The prime topic of discussion was how to safely and thoroughly evacuate the region in the face of the advancing Allies. The most secure area seemed to be the few square miles surrounding Zell am See. Spacil ordered Pfeiler, his securities expert, to establish a pair of stations there, three miles apart. Spacil's financial Alpine Redoubt strategy involved housing the bulk of the Heiliger loot in one station, while the other served as a paying post to purchase equipment and other necessaries, pay soldiers and others, and thus sustain the war effort. Communications between the posts would be carried out by motorcycle. It was a clever arrangement. Even if the pay station fell into the hands of the rapidly advancing enemy, Spacil and his agents would have advance warning and thus time to salvage the bulk of the valuables stored at the main cache. Pfeiler arranged for the loot to be hauled from Salzburg to Breitweis with trucks. Spacil, meanwhile, turned his attention to other pressing concerns. Long hours were spent driving to one point after another in order to meet with a variety of officers and key civilian leaders.[7]

Exhausted and overwhelmed by his myriad of duties, Spacil arrived back in Salzburg on April 25. By this time many RSHA personnel knew that the head of Bureau II was in the area and flush with RSHA wealth. "[I] was besieged by requests for supplies, money, and quarters, most of them impossible to fulfill," Spacil later recalled. The following day, he ordered SS Hauptsturmführer (Captain) Schuler, a high-level administrator associated with Bureau VI, to turn over 5,000 carats of cut and uncut diamonds and foreign securities to SS Obersturmbannführer (Lieutenant Colonel) Otto Skorzeny. Skorzeny's headquarters were at Radstadt, Austria, on the Enns River some twenty miles south of Salzburg and fifteen miles east of Zell am See. Skorzeny had recently been appointed head of Bureau VI, Mil D, and placed in charge of Military Intelligence for the last ditch effort to continue Nazi resistance in the Alps. As Spacil was well aware, Skorzeny was valiantly trying to keep his men in the ranks and in some semblance of military order to slow down the advancing Russians. If anyone could accomplish the impossible it was Skorzeny. The indefatigable and brave SS man was one of Hitler's personal favorites, a hero whose name and exploits were well-known in both German and Allied circles. His forte was special operations. Skorzeny was the mastermind behind the daring rescue of Italy's dictator, Benito Mussolini. On September 13, 1943, he had heroically kidnapped the leader from his holding place at Gran Sasso in the Abruzzi Mountains in central Italy. Other special operations in Hungary and the Ardennes later in the war, coupled with his unwavering loyalty to Hitler, redounded to the benefit of his military career. By 1945 he had become one of the most popular men in Germany. None of this made a bit of difference to Captain Schuler. The bureaucrat departed Spacil's temporary headquarters bound for Radstadt. He never arrived. The heavyset distinctive looking blonde officer (he had not a single eyebrow hair) was last reported in Innsbruck a few days later. Neither he nor the fortune in diamonds were ever seen again.[8]

Schuler's treacherous actions struck a blow against Skorzeny's efforts to keep his SS men in the field. He needed supplies to feed his men and money to keep them fighting; he had few of the former and had exhausted the latter. Skorzeny could not afford to wait long for the missing Captain Schuler. Twenty-four hours after he expected the captain's arrival, Skorzeny dispatched his staffer, Hauptsturmführer (Captain) Radl, to Salzburg with orders to tap into Spacil's Heiliger account. Spacil steadfastly refused to believe that Schuler had absconded with the jewels. Armed with his orders, Radl adamantly demanded 2,000,000 Reichsmarks in foreign exchange. "Impossible!" shouted

Spacil, dismissing the request out of hand. Spacil was schooled deeply in Nazi bureau politics, however, and the last thing he wanted was to be tagged by history as the man responsible for Skorzeny's collapse. He appreciated the commando's tenuous situation. Yielding, Spacil offered Radl 50,000 gold francs stuffed into a pair of jute sacks. Radl promptly accepted. The officer was climbing into his car when the still optimistic Spacil told him "to expect Schuler with additional funds."[9]

Reconstructing exactly *what* transpired next within Spacil's sphere of influence, and the sequence of these events, is an extremely difficult task. Contradictory testimony, the general confusion of the final few days of the war, and the passage of more than half a century has muddled things considerably. Indeed, we will never know exactly how much money was distributed during the closing days of the war, who received it, and its ultimate fate. Much of the confusion surrounding when a particular cache of loot was buried, who concealed it, and where it was hidden is the result of a disinformation campaign undertaken by many of the key players in this drama. Postwar interviews and interrogations are replete with wrong names, dates, and places. Few were willing to openly admit their full involvement in transporting and hiding gold and other valuables stolen from their rightful owners—many of whom had been murdered in cold blood. Most of the primary participants were members of the SS who worked for the RSHA—constituents of a notorious order employed by a criminal organization operating within a criminal state. Few men proudly admitted as much after the surrender. Most appreciated that they would be arrested when the war ended, which was why so many cloaked themselves in new identities in an effort to escape detention. Thankfully, enough credible evidence courses through the documentation to allow us to construct a general framework of understanding of what took place.[10]

*   *   *

There are few places in the world more lovely in late April than Salzburg, Austria. But in 1945, Spacil could have come up with many other adjectives to describe the medieval city. His final three days of the month there were a nightmare punctuated with extreme chaos, a lack of rest, and a multitude of requests for everything—currency, gold, diamonds, food, ammunition, weapons. He knew he had to parcel out his wealth carefully, and he did the best he could given the deteriorating circumstances. Much of what was asked for—or, as in Captain Radl's case, demanded—was simply beyond his power to provide. Spacil's life was about to get even more complicated.

On the last day of the month Spacil drove to Bad Ischl, where he paid his wife a brief visit. Another telephone conference with Kaltenbrunner awaited his return. The discussion, he later remembered, was "very unsatisfactory." Once again we do not know exactly what the two men discussed, but it is not difficult to speculate as to the general gist of the conversation. The war was lost, both men knew it, both were under increasing stress, and both were linked, directly or indirectly, to a whole host of war crimes—Kaltenbrunner especially. The call convinced Spacil to again jump into his car and drive to Altaussee to meet with the head of the RSHA in person. Kaltenbrunner, however, was mired in a conference and unable to see him until 12:30 a.m. on May 1. The drive was for nothing. "I have no further information or instructions!" replied the testy giant when Spacil inquired as to his duties. When he tried to fill in his superior with data as to what he had thus far accomplished, Kaltenbrunner snapped back, "Spacil! I have no time for details!" Spacil never saw the RSHA chief again.[11]

Good bureaucrat that he was, Spacil continued carrying out duties that his boss now cared little about. The pace was frenetic. By 9:00 a.m. on May 1 he was back in Salzburg. There, to his dismay, he learned what had happened with Pfeiler, the securities expert he had entrusted many days earlier with a truck full of valuables and orders to establish a pair of stations in the Zell am See area. For reasons that remain unclear, Pfeiler reached the area but did nothing thereafter. Perhaps the proximity of Americans forces unnerved him; perhaps he simply did not work well when discretion and initiative were demanded. Spacil ordered Pfeiler to turn over the truck filled with gold and currency to another officer and member of Bureau II, Untersturmführer (Second Lieutenant) Menzel, who was told to safeguard the loot until further orders.[12]

After dismissing Pfeiler and safeguarding what was left of the Heiliger Account, Spacil drove to Wald in Pinzgau, where he conferred with Hauptsturmführer (Captain) Fichtner, the head of a Bureau II depot, regarding the transfer of goods from various places in Austria and the hiding of valuables. Their talk was interrupted by a crackling radio message at 10:00 p.m. announcing the news that their beloved Führer, Adolf Hitler, was dead. Any doubts Spacil may have been harboring about the war's outcome were forever shattered that evening. As midnight approached the fatigued officer climbed back into his car for the drive back to Salzburg. There, on May 2, he reported to one of Kaltenbrunner's primary subordinates, Oberführer Panzinger, the head of the criminal police. If he was hoping for some guidance in his duties he was once again disappointed. Panzinger waved Spacil away. Report to Kaltenbrunner "for further instructions" was his only and utterly unhelpful response.[13]

Bouncing back and forth like a yo-yo, without much direction or accomplishment, Spacil conscientiously drove back to Altaussee. One can only imagine his mounting frustration when he scribbled in his diary the five words, "unable to see the Chief." Kaltenbrunner's adjutant, remembered Spacil, told him that "the Chief would [not] be available at Bad Alt-Aussee until further notice," and that "he had no further instructions." Another nighttime drive back to Salzburg via Bad Ischl awaited Spacil. He stopped in the latter village to see his wife and throw down a cup of tea before resuming his drive to Salzburg, which he reached about 9:00 a.m. After a brief rest he reported again to Panzinger. Spacil summed up his meeting with the Gestapo officer in a single word: "Indecision." There was a good reason the Oberführer was deep in the grips of vacillation. His world was crumbling around him and he was trapped in Austria, the Americans on one side and the dreaded Russians on the other. Like Kaltenbrunner, Panzinger knew he was a wanted man. The Russians were not about to forget his merciless actions in the Baltic region earlier in the war. More likely than not they were already measuring his thick neck for a noose. If he fell into American hands they surely would turn him over to their Russian allies. Unwilling to waste more time with Panzinger, Spacil hastened back to Taxenbach "to expedite the burying of the treasure." He was relieved somewhat when he learned that the work there "was already in progress." Meanwhile, he noted, "It had been decided to remove the RSHA headquarters for the Southern area to Zell am See, since the enemy was approaching Salzburg."[14]

The "work in progress" to which Spacil referred was the effort to arrange for the burial of the gold, currency, and other valuables he had originally intended to use to establish the pair of stations around Zell am See. The situation was collapsing too quickly now to bother with the stations. Spacil was enough of a bureaucrat to know that his job responsibilities had changed. He now had to make sure what was left of the Heiliger account was hidden from the Allies, and yet readily available should something transpire to radically alter the course of the closing hours of the war. He stopped his car outside Taxenbach at Pulzel's sawmill and climbed out, surveying the wooded and hilly landscape. The remote site had recently been selected for a new depot by Sturmbannführer (Major) Schuster, a Bureau II administrative officer and one of Spacil's key subordinates. According to Schuster, Spacil asked him "where two or three reliable men could be found for the purpose of hiding a treasure." Schuster provided him with two names. "Wimmer," a Volkssturm official from Zell am See, and SA member "Reisinger," a forester and Ortsgruppenleiter of Taxenbach. Later, probably that same day, Schuster introduced Spacil to his deputy, SS Hauptsturmführer (Captain) Albert Apfelbeck, a Bureau II depot leader. Earlier in the war Apfelbeck had suffered a serious skull injury in a motor accident and been assigned a non-combat role in the RSHA bureaucracy. Spacil needed him "to report the location of [each] cache." He was also to establish a chain of agents for each group of valuables to make it more difficult for the Allies to locate all of them should any one person be arrested and spill the beans during an interrogation. Spacil returned to Taxenbach satisfied each man understood his assignment.[15]

Time was running out for Spacil and others of his ilk. Despite Kaltenbrunner's earlier order and Spacil's best efforts, men of every rank were dispersing to the winds; command and control had all but ceased to exist. While Schuster was making arrangements to receive the bulk of the Heiliger Account at Pulzel's sawmill, Spacil drove on to Zell am See late on May 3. The entire area was awash in chaos. "The Staff had been dissolved and was strewn to the wind," he lamented. When he asked officers about the new plan to relocate RSHA headquarters in Zell am See, no one seemed to know about it. Indeed, "no one said anything about the plans of the day before." Spacil tried to get in touch with other commanders operating in the area, including Brigadeführer Karl Schultz, the former head of Bureau I in 1943. Even that proved impossible because no one seemed to know where his headquarters was located. Even more alarming was the sight of hundreds of soldiers, some armed, some not, marching along the snowy roads in melancholy silence. No one seemed to be in charge anywhere. Refugees, burdened with what few belongings were left to them, added to the disorder clogging the roadways. The situation was spiraling out of control. Unable to accomplish anything in Zell am See, Spacil returned through Taxenbach and arrived late that night in St Johann, where he found Dr. Hüber and Salzburg Gauleiter Gustav Scheel deep in a conference that did not end until just before 1:00 a.m. on the morning of May 4. Hüber, remembered Spacil, "explained the general situation," which was little short of catastrophic. American forces, moving in from the west and north, had or were about to capture Salzburg and much of the surrounding area. Innsbruck to the southeast was lost. Berchtesgaden, the Führer's mountain retreat in the deep southern tip of Germany, was being looted by ecstatic GIs. Vienna and much of Austria's northeastern quadrant was in Russian hands. The news was even worse than Spacil and his comrades knew. Within a few hours Hitler's designated successor, Admiral Karl Dönitz, would surrender the Netherlands, Denmark, and northwestern Germany to the British.[16]

With Salzburg in the hands of the Americans, Spacil drove back to Taxenbach at 3:00 a.m. He made the place his "CP [Command Post] from then on." A quick side trip to Zell am See produced "no information." The next day, May 5, Captain Fichtner, the head of a Bureau II depot, arrived in Taxenbach for a conference with Spacil. We made a "decision," explained Spacil, probably relieved that something approaching a plan was finally in the works. "In case of the approach of the enemy, either over the Gerlos Pass [at the eastern end of the Tirol leading into the Salzburg province] or over the Pass Thum [leading down in the valley of Brucht] we would turn over the contents of the depot to the Bürgermeister. In that case officers and men were to be regarded as discharged, since I could give no further instructions and the Chief [Kaltenbrunner] was no [longer] available." The universe available within which the Germans could operate freely was shrinking by the hour. [17]

May 5 was both an interesting and vexing day for Spacil. He drove to meet SS Hauptsturmführer (Captain) Franz Konrad at a small inn in the Alpine village of Mittersill near Taxenbach. The SS captain, it will be recalled, was a member of General Fegelein's staff and had been posted in Warsaw, where he earned his keep stealing homes and valuables from Jews slated for deportation to the death camps. Konrad's most recent posting was at Fischhorn castle. Parked about 100 yards from the inn on the left side of the road was a five-ton diesel truck. Spacil opened the back of the vehicle and pulled out 5,000 Swiss francs, about $1,000 in U.S. currency, and 500,000 Reichsmarks. But Konrad also wanted gold—and he had good reason to believe Spacil had access to a healthy supply of the precious metal. A few days earlier an officer dressed in "civilian clothing" had arrived at Fischhorn castle in search of Spacil. Konrad told him that Spacil was not there, but that he occasionally made an appearance. Frustrated, the officer handed Konrad an unsealed letter marked "Top Secret" and walked away. According to Konrad, the letter confirmed that Spacil had in his possession 28,000,000 Reichsmarks and 100,000 gold franc coins. Konrad's attempt to extract gold ended in failure. The coins, Spacil told him, had already been dispersed.[18]

It was at that point in the meeting that their conversation took a strange twist. Exactly what transpired is subject to some debate, since later accounts provided by both officers to Allied interrogators differ on several fronts. According to Spacil, Konrad confided to him that he had "the uniform" the Führer was wearing when he was killed in Berlin, as well as other important items.[19]

The news naturally intrigued Spacil, who had already heard that Hitler was no more. "He is dead? You are sure?" he inquired.

"Yes. He was killed by an attack on the Chancellory bunker by Russian dive-bombers. He was fatally wounded by fragments which entered his whole right side, particularly the right thigh. The uniform was tattered by shell fragments, and bloodstained." Spacil was incredulous. Although rumors were flying thick and fast about Hitler's fate, he had yet to hear anything so concrete from such a seemingly reliable officer.

"I also have the Führer's diary," continued Konrad, "the correspondence between Hitler and Eva Braun, and several boxes of secret papers."

"What are you going to do with all these things?" Spacil supposedly asked Konrad.

"I have orders to hide the diary and the suit, and to destroy the letters and other papers, which I have already done. I had a zinc box made for the uniform, and one for the diaries, which were written on very thin paper." Konrad also told Spacil that he had many of the gifts given by Hitler to Eva Braun, which he also "destroyed." Konrad did not elaborate on the exact nature of these gifts.

According to Spacil, he did his best to convince Konrad to disclose the location of the zinc boxes. "No, I cannot tell you," Konrad replied. "I have orders not to tell anyone. Only the two of us know this," he cautioned. "It is not to travel any further."[20]

Konrad later admitted that a conversation with Spacil had indeed taken place, and that Spacil had provided him with money. However, he strongly disputed Spacil's version of the substance of the discussion. "I know nothing about any diaries," he told American investigators after his capture later that spring, although he admitted burning a suit of clothes that had supposedly belonged to Hitler, as well as some correspondence between the German leader and Eva Braun.[21]

Flush with currency, Franz Konrad returned to his temporary headquarters at Fischhorn castle. What he thought about on the drive back will never be known. Perhaps he pondered on his earlier crimes in Poland and elsewhere. Certainly he considered it likely the Allies would be interested in getting their hands on him. His time, too, was almost at an end. Once at the fortress, Konrad used 5,000 of the Reichsmarks Spacil had provided to satisfy back pay due Fischhorn personnel and several SS officers, including Hermann Fegelein's brother, Waldemar. The younger Fegelein, age 33, was recovering from a wound suffered during the fighting for Budapest. He had led a regiment of the 8th SS Cavalry Division during the siege, where the Russians managed to encircle the 35,000 German defenders. Waldemar was one of approximately 700 who managed to break free and escape. Konrad also gave SS Hauptsturmführer (Captain) Erwin Haufler, another of General Fegelein's staffers, 5,000 Swiss francs, several gold coins, a few diamond rings and gold watches, and 100,000 Reichsmarks. Haufler later averred that he found Konrad's attempt to dump the wealth into his lap worrisome. "I do not want these things for myself," he claims to have told

Konrad, "and I don't wish to enrich myself this way." According to Haufler, he knew that eventually he would be held to account for the loot, and that he frankly told Konrad as much. Given his wartime activities and proclivities, Haufler's explanation rings wholly untrue. It is difficult to picture any SS officer with his connections and vitae turning down gold and jewels ever—regardless of their origin.

As they were splitting the booty, Konrad rambled on about using the money to establish a farm in Peru. Haufler listened in impatient silence while he packed his share into a laundry bag. Later that day he delivered the treasure to his wife in nearby Hoegmoos for safekeeping.[22]

*   *   *

The fifth of May also marked the first day the Heiliger Account, or at least a portion of it, was entombed. Its concealment took several days, the assistance of many individuals, and the cloak of darkness to accomplish. While Spacil was meeting with Konrad, his subordinate Major Schuster oversaw the operation. Lieutenant Menzel had driven his large truck of valuables to Pulzel's sawmill. The vehicle was enclosed with a metal body, like a moving van, and had a five-ton hauling capacity. A smaller truck, covered with canvas with a three-ton capacity, accompanied him. Who drove that truck is not known. "Apparently only the larger vehicle contained treasure," Schuster later recalled, "for the smaller [truck] was simply parked and left untouched." Schuster also remembered looking inside the back of Menzer's vehicle and finding "it was filled to capacity." The rear of the load, or at least that portion visible to Schuster, was jammed with "canvas sacks" containing currency.[23]

Once the grounds of the sawmill were covered in darkness Schuster and his crew got to work. Wimmer, Reisinger, and Menzel worked together to unload the contents of the truck, which was packed tight into three passenger cars—a Fiat, BMW, and Mercedes. Only one car was used at a time. The cargo consisted of jute bags about two feet tall, small and medium sized heavy iron or tin chests, a bed mattress stuffed with English notes, and other valuables. Once the first auto was full, Wimmer and Reisinger drove off into the darkness and buried the loot. The men repeated the routine the following evening, May 6, and again after dark on May 7.[24]

The dawn of May 6, 1945, brought with it for Spacil some sense of relief in the knowledge that at least a portion of the Heiliger Account was now hidden away. What he did not know was that May 6 was also the last full day of the war without a signed surrender document harking to the final capitulation. Just hours earlier Admiral Dönitz had tried to negotiate a surrender with General Dwight D. Eisenhower in Rheims, Germany. One of his goals was to capitulate to the Americans rather than to the Russians. Eisenhower rebuffed Dönitz's efforts. Anything other than a simultaneous unconditional surrender on all fronts was unacceptable. General Alfred Jodl, Hitler's military advisor, would find the negotiating on May 6 just as difficult. When Eisenhower rejected similar pleas, Jodl bowed to the inevitable and agreed to sign an unconditional surrender the following afternoon.

Spacil was in Taxenbach when SS Brigadeführer (Brigadier General) Erich Naumann dropped by unexpectedly to pay him a visit. Naumann was more than just a brigadier general: he was a mass murderer. Naumann had operated Einsatzgruppen B in Russia from 1941 to 1943, one of the notorious killing squads that had proudly slaughtered tens of thousands of men, women and children. In late 1944, Naumann was named head of the SD for Nuremberg. Like Kaltenbrunner and so many others, Naumann knew his days were numbered unless he could make good an escape. He called at Taxenbach because "he was looking for the Chief (Kaltenbrunner)," recorded Spacil. When Spacil told him he did not know Kaltenbrunner's whereabouts, but he was headquartered in Altaussee, "Naumann decided to try to reach him personally [there], and promised to report back."[25]

After Naumann left Taxenbach, Spacil drove to Pulzel's sawmill to check on the status of the disposal of the Heiliger fortune. He arrived as darkness was falling and just in time to meet up with Schuster and his skeleton crew as they were preparing to dispose of the second carload. Schuster later claimed he overheard a discussion between Spacil, Wimmer and Reisinger "about the possibility of sinking something in a pond." He did not know if the subject of their discussion was part of the treasure or an entire car full of loot. What the three eventually decided upon, if anything, Schuster could not (or would not) say.[26]

Spacil did not have to wait long to see the former Einsatzgruppen leader. Naumann returned early the following morning, May 7. He was "in bad humor," remembered Spacil, and there was good reason why: Kaltenbrunner would not see him. The only person he had been able to speak with was Kaltenbrunner's adjutant, who said that he had "no information over future operations." As far as Kaltenbrunner was concerned, Naumann belatedly realized, it was every man for himself. In an attempt to drum up some news of what was happening, Spacil and Naumann jumped into a car and drove together to Radstadt. They discovered little reliable information. "There were only rumors that a capitulation was to take effect on 8 May 45 at 0001," Spacil wrote, "and that the border line for the capitulation zone was to lie west of Radstadt. The only concrete news of value was that Otto Skorzeny and his "special train" were a handful of miles away in the direction of Schladming. In order to "get further facts" the pair drove the eight miles to see if they could get a conference with the officer.[27]

The meeting with Skorzeny took place in a railroad car pulled onto a small siding. It was about three in the afternoon on May 7. Skorzeny, explained Spacil, "knew nothing further because his adjutant [Radl] was not yet back from Army Hq. with the latest reports." Once again we know little of what was specifically discussed. The issue of an approaching capitulation likely dominated the agenda. It is doubtful any loot changed hands given the circumstances surrounding the conference. The meeting lasted but one hour. Spacil described its anti-climactic ending with a short journal entry: "at 1600 Skorzeny took his leave and left for parts unknown." The SS combat officer departed for the village of Annaberg. Before he left, Skorzeny had removed his SS officer's uniform and changed into a German army sergeant's garb.[28]

Spacil and Naumann left as well. About 6:00 p.m. that evening they "found army columns were fleeing westward from the vicinity of Liezen." When asked what going on, one of the soldiers told them that the enemy had entered Liezen a few hours earlier. There would be little mercy shown to any German soldier unlucky enough to fall into Russian hands, and all of them knew it. Now, putting as much distance between that place and the Russians was a high priority for every soldier. "In order to check the report," Spacil explained, "[I drove] back to Schladming without Naumann." Nothing but disorder greeted him. "I determined nothing. All I saw was retreating columns. No one knew what was true and what was not, and everyone was trying to cross the supposed surrender line, which was said to lie west of Radstadt." Just before midnight Spacil and Naumann met again for the last time. Spacil explained that the situation was fluid and no one knew what was happening. The pair split up, never to meet again.[29]

While Spacil and Naumann had been watching despondent columns of soldiers trudging westward to escape the flood of advancing Russians, Major Schuster in Taxenbach was overseeing the final burial of his portion of the treasure. After Spacil had left the previous evening the second carload had been hidden away without incident. Now, as darkness fell again over Austria on May 7, the final carload of gold and currency was prepared for burial. When Captain Apfelbeck arrived at the sawmill earlier in the day, he found the Mercedes (the last of the three treasure cars) parked in the mill yard. Unsure of what was to transpire, and perhaps irritated that he had to participate in the concealment, he asked Schuster, "Now, what am I to do with all this stuff?" According to Schuster, the mill owner's 18-year-old son (whose name is unknown) climbed into the Mercedes "and drove it up a steep slope behind the buildings to the sawmill located on the slope." Apfelbeck believed the car was driven behind the outbuildings "to protect it from the curious glances of those in the vicinity." The Mercedes remained there for about four hours until Pulzel's son climbed back inside and drove it down the hill "and on the road toward Taxenbach."[30]

At 10:00 p.m. that night Reisinger "picked me up with another car, and we went up the hill near Rauris," Apfelbeck told his Allied interrogators. "Upon arriving, I saw Wimmer and another man, a forester, who probably was a friend of Reisinger." In all likelihood the "forester" was Pulzel's son. Armed with picks and shovels, "Reisinger and the forester went into the woods . . . to dig a hole; I remained at the car with Wimmer. After some time the other three began carrying the valuables away, while I stayed at the car." The men were overseeing the burial of a king's ransom. "As I remember, there were three or four heavy jute sacks, one heavy iron chest . . . two small light sacks containing currency, and a very large bed-tick of blue checkered ticking filled with white English pound notes." The mattress was stuffed with money. When Apfelbeck's cohorts lifted it from the car, the mattress burst open, showering the ground with its contents. "The notes were gathered up and carried to the hole," Apfelbeck told his Allied captors. "Thereafter I went to the cache, so I could describe the location to Spacil. When we arrived back at the sawmill, Spacil was there and I reported to him."[31]

Spacil did not arrive at the sawmill until about 3:00 a.m. on the morning of May 8. The news he had for his men was not good, or as he succinctly put it, "I told Schuster and Apfelbeck about the surrender." Schuster paints a more detailed reconstruction of the meeting. Spacil told us "that the Americans were in the vicinity, that the German armies had surrendered, and that he . . . intended to disguise himself as a non-com in the Wehrmacht." Spacil apparently advised Schuster and Apfelbeck to do the same, but both men refused. Spacil then mumbled something about a vehicle that "went into the water." He did not elaborate about the cryptic statement and, if we are to believe Schuster, he did not ask any further questions.[32]

While Schuster, Wimmer, Reisinger, and Apfelbeck had been concealing the treasure-laden Mercedes on May 7, Lieutenant Menzel and his two-truck convoy was heading east for Graz, Austria, in the southeast corner of the country. The region, Spacil believed, was the last area still in German hands. Menzel's orders were to take his truck and trailer to Graz; his assignment was to turn the load over to the RSHA staff there, or else to destroy it." Schuster's account provides additional information. The trucks left "in an easterly direction," and from what he gathered from discussing the matter with Apfelbeck and others, "one or more other trucks were to join the convoy." These additional vehicles, apparently waiting "in the town of Lent," were "loaded with ammunition and weapons." Kurt Schiebel added that Menzel's destination was "Corps Hausser," one of the few viable German military organizations still believed operating in that area. Menzel, he claimed, "among other items . . . was carrying several million RM [Reichsmarks] to pay off the personnel." The truck was carrying more than a few million in German currency. Menzel's trailer, wrote Spacil, was loaded with counterfeit notes produced at the Sachsenhausen concentration camp, "the property of Bureau VI." Packed in one hundred chests or crates, the forged British pounds were comprised "of notes of from one to fifty pounds denomination." They had been turned over to Spacil "because those responsible for them were at a loss as to what to do with them."[33]

After he met with Schuster and Apfelbeck early on the morning of May 8, Spacil drove on to the SS horse farm at Fischhorn castle. There, he met up again with Franz Konrad and shared once again the news of the German surrender. "Konrad already had the information, and showed me the written order," remembered Spacil. "At that point the war ended for me." The bureaucrat without a bureau to operate drove back to Zell am See a few hours later. "An American sentry and a German sentry with a white arm band were already standing in the street," he recalled with some amazement. When he inquired about what was happening, the German told him the GI "had been put there to protect him from French" soldiers who were also in the vicinity. Marching past was a long column of soldiery. On the flanks marched American guards. Blending into the mass of thousands was his only hope of escaping his prominent SS past. If Spacil could trick the Americans into giving him a discharge as an enlisted German soldier, he would probably avoid arrest.

Spacil parked his car in a meadow with other vehicles abandoned by the German army and quietly eased his way into the procession. He attached himself to the 352nd Volksgrenadier Division. The captives were heading for the Fürstenfeldbrück POW camp. After a few hushed questions he located the unit's commander, Captain Gerhardt Schlemmer. Could he join his company? Spacil asked. "My name is Sergeant Aue." In fact, Aue was Spacil's stepfather's name. When Schlemmer hesitated, the SS officer did his best to impress upon him the urgency of the matter by explaining that he was the treasurer of the SS Security Main Office, in charge of all payments to the Gestapo, the *Sicherheitsdienst* (SA) and other agencies. Whether this news influenced Schlemmer or not is unknown, but he agreed to let Spacil remain with his outfit.[34]

* * *

And so it came to pass that "Sergeant Aue," the man who had operated RSHA's Bureau II for so long, whose extravagant wartime existence had been dependent on the death and deportation of hundreds of thousands of civilians, walked without power or privilege with thousands of other German soldiers into what he hoped would be an anonymous captivity. Only time would tell whether his sojourn in American hands would be temporary or long-lived.

Chapter Notes

1. G-2 (Intelligence) Records Section, undated memorandum, "Concerning Spacil," page stamped 210294-95.

2. For a full account of this remarkable story, see selected indexed entries in Adam Labor, *Hitler's Secret Bankers: The Myth of Swiss Neutrality During the Holocaust* (New York, 1997). Just before this book went to press, author Kenneth Alford discovered a two-page consignment from the Melmer account to the Municipal Pawn Brokerage, 111 Central Office, Berlin N 4, Elsaesser St 74, dated September 15 1942. It has about 6,000 pieces of gold, diamonds, platinum, and silver jewelry listed, and is broken down into ten categories, each weighed by kilogram gross. The instructions read: "We submit to you the following valuables with the request for the best possible utilization." International Military Tribunal, "Nazi Conspiracy and Aggressors," Document 3948-PS, Volume supplement A (U.S. Printing Office, 1946-1949), page 677.

3. Special Investigations Squad, 970th CIC, "Ownership and Disposal of Effects Recovered as a Result of Interrogation of Oberführer Wilhelm (sic) Spacil, Head of Amt. II, RSHA," by Robert Gutierrez, February 4, 1946.

4. "Concerning Spacil," page stamped 210294; CIC, "Interrogation of Kurt Schiebel," July 5, 1945; CIC, "Interrogation of Kurt Schiebel in Camp 71, Ludwigsburg, Germany," undated.

5. Undated and untitled CIC Memorandum; "Interrogation of Kurt Schiebel," July 5, 1945; "Ludwigsburg Interrogation of Kurt Schiebel." One of the more interesting items stashed aboard Spacil's plane was microfilm of the original papers used in proceedings filed against those accused of plotting to kill Adolf Hitler in the July 20, 1944, assassination attempt. The film was removed from Berlin for safekeeping on Ernst Kaltenbrunner's orders.

6. "Interrogation of Kurt Schiebel," July 5, 1945; 307th CIC Document, "Diary of Spacil Concerning Period Under Investigation." It is unclear whether Kurt Schiebel's description of the responsibilities given to Spacil and himself were assigned at this meeting, as described in the text, or before Spacil left Berlin for Salzburg. Our research suggests the specific tasks were ordered after he landed in Salzburg. This initial meeting with Kaltenbrunner in Altaussee—even though Spacil does not elaborate on it in his diary entry—seems the most likely scenario. Regardless of when this order was assigned, we know for a fact that Kaltenbrunner ordered it, Spacil knew of it, and that he acted accordingly.

7. "Undated Memorandum Concerning Spacil," page stamped 210296.

8. Exhibit B, "Spacil Diary," p. 40. For a fascinating insight into Skorzeny's career and how he viewed his service for Hitler's Nazi Germany, see Otto Skorzeny, *My Commando Operations: The Memoirs of Hitler's Most Daring Commando* (Schiffer, 1995). According to one Allied record, Schuler had kept considerable funds belonging to Bureau VI at his office in Innsbruck. These funds, concluded the report, "were probably given to Otto Skorzeny and consisted of approximately 2 million Reichsmarks and a considerable quantity of dollars." They were never accounted for. See "Undated Memorandum Concerning Spacil," page stamped 210294.

9. Exhibit B, "Spacil Diary," p. 40. According to Kurt Schiebel, Skorzeny's staff officer was given 10,000 Swedish crowns, $5,000 U.S. dollars, 5,000 Swiss francs, and 5,000,000 Reichsmarks—in addition to the 50,000 gold francs. "Interrogation of Kurt Schiebel," July 5, 1945. Regardless of what Captain Radl received during his short visit to Spacil's headquarters, it is unclear whether these funds were utilized to pay troops and purchase supplies, or whether they were concealed for later use.

10. A good example of just how freely fortunes were paid out is offered by Josef Spacil himself, who admitted that many of the heads of various RSHA offices turned over their "liquid assets" to him at Salzburg. He, in turn, "distributed them to persons urgently requesting funds." One member of Heinrich Himmler's staff received 500,000 Reichsmarks. Several different amounts were paid to the commander of the Salzburg garrison "and the last of the gold and foreign exchange went to Kurt Scheidler." None of these funds were officially logged, and it is impossible to discern exactly when these transactions occurred. The ultimate fate of the money is unknown. "Undated Memorandum Concerning Spacil," page stamped 210294. Spacil's adjutant, Kurt Schiebel, told Allied interviewers that almost immediately after they were in Salzburg three agents received large sums of money. One was handed 10,000 gold francs, $1,000 in U.S. dollars, 2,000 Swiss paper francs, and 1,000 Swedish crowns. His assignment, remembers, Schiebel, "was to retreat to the hills above the town of Lent and to continue resistance." Whether these funds came out of the Heiliger account or some other slush fund provided by Kaltenbrunner or other RSHA officials is unclear. Even the recipient is unknown. "CIC Interrogation of Kurt Schiebel," July 5, 1945.

11. Exhibit B, "Spacil Diary," p. 40.

12. "Undated Memorandum Concerning Spacil," page stamped 210296.

13. Exhibit B, "Spacil Diary," 39.

14. "Spacil Diary," p. 39.

15. "Intermediate Interrogation Report," August 8, 1945, pp. 26-27. Menzel, Wimmer, and Reisinger made forays into the countryside surrounding Taxenbach on three successive nights to conceal the valuables in their possession. Exactly when they did so is open to some speculation. Some documents suggest the nights of May 2-4, 1945. There is some evidence indicating that Apfelbeck, et. al., buried only one load of treasure on May 7, 1945. Both scenarios are possible, but not consistent with available evidence. Although Spacil wrote in his diary on May 2, 1945, that he drove back to Taxenbach "to expedite the burying of the treasure," and that the "work was already in progress," he was almost certainly referring to the preliminary work necessary to collect the gold and valuables and organize their concealment. See "Spacil Diary," p. 39. This supports the Allied report of events found in the "Undated Memorandum Concerning Spacil," page stamped 210296. Albert Apfelbeck's account of the burial of loot on May 7, 1945, found in the undated "Interrogation of Albert Apfelbeck," refers only to the third installment in the process. The documentation found in the "Intermediate Interrogation Report," August 8, 1945, pp. 27-28, lends support for this conclusion. The nocturnal activities of May 7, 1945, are treated in detail elsewhere in this chapter.

16. "Spacil Diary," p. 40; Dear, *Oxford Companion of World War II*, p. 486.

17. "Spacil Diary," p. 40.

18. "Spacil Diary," p. 39; "Interrogations of Franz Konrad," April 21 and 25, 1945; "Interrogation of Kurt Schiebel," undated; Emanual E. Minskoff, U.S. Treasury Investigation, 1945.

19. Konrad was mistaken. The suit of clothes he had was the one Hitler had been wearing during the July 20, 1944, assassination attempt at the Wolfschanze.

20. "Memorandum of the Interrogation of Spacil," CIC Headquarters Seventh Army, July 5, 1945.

21. "Interrogation of Franz Konrad," April 21, 1945.

22. "Interrogation of Erwin Haufler," September 14, 1945.

23. "Intermediate CIC Interrogation Report," August 8, 1945, p. 27. According to American agents, Schuster knew a lot more about the burial of the RSHA treasure than he told interrogators. Although he feigned apathy as to what was transpiring around him, claiming "he did not wish to become too involved in the matter," none of the investigators believed him. "Schuster was at the place where all arrangements were made for the disposition of these caches; he should have more information than he has revealed." Ibid., p. 28.

24. "Intermediate Interrogation Report," August 8, 1945, p. 27. Spacil used cars to transport his loot to secret locations for two reasons. First, moving large trucks about on open roads was a dangerous proposition that often attracted the deadly attention of Allied fighter planes. Schiebel mentioned in his interrogation that strafing interfered with their activities and prevented a number of trucks from arriving at their preassigned destinations. "Interrogation of Kurt Schiebel," July 5, 1945. If these treasure-laden trucks were damaged or destroyed on open roads, their contents would be looted by anyone passing by. Second, even if the trucks managed to avoid enemy fire, they were too large for the small and rough trails leading into the meadows and woods where Spacil intended to bury the gold and currency. Even so, the cars suffered heavily as a result of the poor roads, which badly damaged all three vehicles.

25. "Spacil Diary," p. 39.

26. "Intermediate Interrogation Report," August 8, 1945, p. 27. Apparently Captain Albert Apfelbeck was not present on the evenings of May 5 and 6, when the first two carloads of treasure were buried. Why he was absent is unclear.

27. "Spacil Diary," pp. 39-40.

28. "Ludwigsburg Interrogation of Kurt Schiebel"; "Spacil Diary," p. 40.

29. "Spacil Diary," p. 40.

30. "Intermediate Interrogation Report," August 8, 1945, p. 27; "Interrogation of Albert Apfelbeck." Although there is not a hint of it in any of the documents, it is more likely than not that Pulzel's 18-year-old son was working for Spacil. Otherwise, he would not have been allowed anywhere near a car full of RSHA loot.

31. "Interrogation of Albert Apfelbeck." The next day Kurt Schiebel (Spacil's adjutant) and Albert Apfelbeck gave the owner of the sawmill 100,000 Reichsmarks. Mr. Pulzel was instructed to surrender 4,000 Reichsmarks "to any man who appeared with a written request from either Schiebel or Apfelbeck containing the code word 'sonne' (sun)." Pulzel, Apfelbeck recalled, retained 16,000 Reichsmarks "for his pains in the matter." When Pulzel was questioned a few weeks later by Allied investigators, he admitted having only 46,000 Reichsmarks left, "but he made up the shortage from his bank account and handed over the 100,000 Reichsmarks to the CIC at Zell am See. According to Pulzel, "Apfelbeck had originally left with him a large manila envelope containing jewelry and perhaps foreign securities, but that on the night of 9 or 10 May 1945 Apfelbeck came back and got the envelope." It seems certain that Captain Apfelbeck knew a lot more than he ever revealed to his captors. "Undated Memorandum Concerning Spacil," pages stamped 210294-95.

32. "Spacil Diary," p. 40; "Intermediate Interrogation Report," August 8, 1945, p. 28.

33. "Spacil Diary," p. 39; "Interrogation of Kurt Schiebel"; "Intermediate Interrogation Report," August 8, 1945, pp. 27-28, 30. Spacil later claimed Menzel was hauling "38 million Reichsmarks . . also Italian lira, Lithuanian currency, Russian Rubles, Ukrainian currency, and francs" (ibid.), and "300 million marks of English foreign exchanges." "Spacil Memorandum," July 27, 1945. Spacil is the only one who claimed that Menzel's truck had a trailer. None of the other key participants mention it. He may have been referring to the second small truck. More likely, however, he was trying to deceive and confuse his Allied interviewers.

34. 307th Counter Intelligence Corps, "Report of Robert A. Gutierrez on Josef Spacil," July 23, 1945.

Chapter 8

"I was once the administrative head for southern Russia,
and I know a little something about the Hungarian
state treasure, and about the burning of Jews."

— SS Oberführer Josef Spacil

Betrayal: The Discovery of Josef Spacil

I n the early morning hours of May 1, 1945, twenty-five Americans riding in fifteen jeeps crossed into Austria through the Brenner Pass. The men were part of the 430th Counter Intelligence Corps, or CIC. Austria has long enjoyed a deserved reputation as a mecca for spies and conspirators; certainly few countries offered a more enchanting backdrop for espionage operations. The agents, a new breed of spies and investigators, opened CIC offices in Salzburg, Linz, Vienna, and Braunau am Inn, the birthplace of Adolf Hitler. Their uniforms bore US insignias only. No rank or other means of verifying identity were visible. Along with a list of sixteen directives relating to counter intelligence operations, the agents were ordered to seek out and arrest not only high-ranking Nazis, but anyone who had been affiliated in any way with Heinrich Himmler's murderous SS.

These agents, who were soon joined by other CIC teams, fanned out across Austria's entire breathtaking expanse. Together they would arrest one of the war's leading Nazis, investigate the largest counterfeiting ring in world history, search for tens of millions in lost gold, jewels, and currency, and hunt tirelessly for Adolf Hitler's correspondence and diaries. Their indefatigable efforts would also help break up many of the remaining pockets of pro-Nazis and eradicate resistance efforts.

*   *   *

Even before the surrender of Germany, American intelligence officials had been preparing for the counterintelligence duties the occupation of Germany and Austria would demand. The general mission of the CIC was to contribute to military operations "through the detection of treason, sedition, subversive activity, and disaffection, and the detection, prevention, or neutralization of espionage and sabotage within or directed against the Army Establishment and the areas of its jurisdiction." Teams of officers from Interrogation of Prisoners of War, Military Intelligence Interpretation, and other G2 Intelligence units had been assigned to help the CIC. The importance of CIC operations had begun to overshadow other intelligence efforts even as combat continued to rage during the war's final months.

In late 1944, the British established a two-week intelligence training class in Italy at Castellamare for agents who would one day be assigned to work counterintelligence operations in Austria. American CIC officers attended these classes in an old castle overlooking the historic bay of Naples. The agenda was thorough. The history of the Nazi Party and its para-military organizations were studied in detail. What was the SS? The SD? What did RSHA stand for? How was it organized? What were its functions? Who ran the bureaus? What was the task assigned to each bureau and sub-bureau? Which departments and personnel were tied, directly or otherwise, to the deportation and extermination of Jews? (The Allies knew the Germans were killing Jews, but whether they fully realized the extent of the crime is still subject to debate.) Where were the priceless treasures and hundreds of millions of dollars worth of personal property looted from European Jewry and others deported from their homes? Once the agents had been carefully briefed on these and related matters their attention was directed to Austria and the study of its geography, history, and culture.

In order to ensure that United States counterintelligence missions were properly organized and staffed, the 430th CIC was formed from CIC units of the 85th, 88th, 91st and 92nd Infantry Divisions, as well as other units operating in Italy. The 970th CIC was created in Germany. On May 10, 1945, partial CIC units from fifty-five army divisions were transferred to the 970th. Although headquartered in Frankfurt, this large unit undertook various assignments in Austria. Much of what they would uncover would remain secret for more than fifty years. A substantial number of files remain locked away, or their contents redacted if requested by members of the public. Much of this material has been "lost" or destroyed.[1]

On May 8, the day after the Germans signed the capitulation agreement ending hostilities in Europe, the U.S. Seventh Army occupied Zell am See and took over the SS nest at Fischhorn castle. It was there, deep in the beautiful alps, that a unique pair of German aviators surrendered to the Americans. Their harrowing and macabre experiences in the Berlin bunker during the war's final days served to fan the flames of Allied inquisitiveness. What, exactly, did these fliers take out with them? And if they could get out, did Adolf Hitler and others escape as well?

*   *   *

The last hours of World War II were a surreal experience for Hanna Reitsch and Obergruppenführer (Lieutenant General) Robert Ritter von Greim. The Nazi notables ended a bizarre air voyage at Fischhorn castle that had originated in war-torn Berlin. They arrived at Zell am See on May 8, 1945—just hours ahead of the Allies.

The war had just a few days left in it when Adolf Hitler promoted von Greim to the rarified rank of Field Marshal to replace the disgraced Hermann Göring. He was the last man promoted by the Führer to that esteemed rank, and one of only a half-dozen Luftwaffe Field Marshals. Von Greim was a zealot Nazi and unyielding follower of the Führer, but one must wonder what crossed his mind when his obviously ailing leader told him deep within the embattled Berlin bunker to take over command of the now non-existent Luftwaffe. The promotion was well deserved. His remarkable vitae included artillery and air experience in the Great

War, a stint as a stunt pilot, the organization of Chiang Kai-shek's Nationalist air force in China, command of the Luftwaffe's first fighter wing, several important top administrative positions in the Western Theater (which earned him a Knight's Cross) and, finally, stellar command performances during four long and bloody years on the Russian Front. The only blemish on his otherwise outstanding military vitae was his undying devotion to a madman.[2]

Accompanying the newly minted Field Marshal was his much younger mistress, Hanna Reitsch, Germany's most illustrious test pilot. Born in 1912, the adventurous Reitsch studied medicine in the hopes of becoming a flying missionary doctor. After the limiting Versailles Treaty clipped her wings, she took to flying gliders. In 1932 she became one of the first pilots to soar across the Alps in one of the silent planes. Five years later the neophyte German air wing hired her as a civilian test pilot. Reitsch ended up testing almost every aircraft engineered during the Third Reich including the Focke-Achgelis, a crude version of the helicopter, and a manned prototype of the V1 rocket. Her tests of the Messerschmitt 163, an experimental rocket-powered interceptor, shot her 30,000 feet into the air at 500 mph—the fastest any human had ever traveled up to that time. Although her fifth mission aboard the rocket almost killed her, her trials garnered the prestigious Iron Cross, First Class, from Hitler himself.[3]

The genesis of the von Greim–Reitsch journey from Berlin to Fischhorn took life in the wake of Reichsmarshall Hermann Göring's now infamous April 23, 1945, telegram from Berchtesgaden to Hitler's Berlin bunker. With Hitler trapped and proclaiming he would fight to the end, Göring asked for permission to assume the Reich's reins of leadership. His application, though not unreasonable under the circumstances, outraged Hitler. Martin Bormann, the Führer's private secretary and one of Göring's most dangerous enemies, convinced Hitler that the telegram was an open act of treason. Hitler stripped the Reichsmarshall of all authority and ordered the Gestapo to arrest him. With a steadily diminishing pool of personnel from which to choose replacements, Hitler cast about for someone to supersede the decadent flyboy from World War I. An order flew out of the bunker on April 24: General Ritter von Greim was to report to the Reich Chancellery as soon as possible.

The order for von Greim to appear demonstrated just how removed from reality Hitler was by late April 1945. Like the horns of a great Zulu army moving forward to engage the enemy on the undulating terrain of southern Africa, the Russians had swept forward and around the once-magnificent German capital, all but surrounding it. Enemy infantry was pressing forward, artillery shells splattered at will into the few buildings left standing, and tanks were grinding forward, block by block against stiff and bloody opposition. A journey into central Berlin to the underground bunker a few blocks south of the Spree River was not only dangerous, but by now almost impossible. Hitler had demanded it; the dutiful soldier would comply.

The pilots flew from Munich to the airbase at Rechlin about 60 miles northwest of Berlin. Reitsch had intended to complete the trip to the besieged capital in a helicopter, but the only remaining machine was too damaged to fly. The trip was instead made in a Focke-Wulf accompanied by a large fighter escort. They landed at Gatow airfield—the only Berlin airstrip still in German hands. Gatow was in the eastern section of the city about fourteen miles from the Reich Chancellery and Hitler's bunker. Russians stood between them and downtown Berlin. Demonstrating their loyalty to the man who had singlehandedly navigated Germany to ruin, the general and the aviatrix hopped aboard a Fiesler-Storch and flew at tree top level in the hope of finding a landing spot close to the bunker. Heavy anti-aircraft fire tore out the bottom of the plane and severely injured von Greim's right foot. Illustrating yet again why she had earned the Iron Cross, Reitsch brought the plane down safely on a rubble-strewn street in front of the Brandenburg gate. From there the pair hitched a ride in a staff car. Once in the bunker von Greim, who was in great pain, was taken to an operating room so Hitler's physician could tend to his wounded foot. To his complete surprise he learned of Göring's alleged betrayal and his new appointment as the Luftwaffe chief, all in the same breath. It was the evening of April 26, 1945.[4]

Everyone associated with the moment knew the appointment was in name only. There was no effective air force left to command. In order to demonstrate their honor to the Fatherland and Hitler, von Greim and Reitsch decided to remain in the bunker and die with him and his remaining disciples. A pleased Hitler agreed—demonstrating again that his summons of von Greim was nothing but an empty and symbolic gesture. Both aviators were provided with a vial of poison and instructions from Hitler to destroy their bodies so that nothing recognizable remained. They agreed that when the time came, they would ingest the cyanide and simultaneously pull the pin from a grenade and hold it tightly between their bodies.

Almost three long days would be spent slinking around the bunker. Reitsch's contact with most of its inhabitants was inconsequential. She split her time between nursing and conversing with von Greim and entertaining the six children of Dr. and Mrs. Goebbels in the upper bunker. The children, ages three through twelve, were the only bright spot in the otherwise dark and tomblike bunker. Reitsch taught them songs to sing for both "Uncle Führer" and the injured Field Marshal. The aviatrix amused the children by telling stories about flying airplanes, all the wonderful places she had visited, and how to yodel. Her underground sojourn in Berlin allowed Reitsch, herself a Nazi zealot, to witness firsthand the pathetic disintegration of Hitler and his cronies.[5]

On April 28, Hitler shuffled into von Greim's sick room and ordered him to leave the bunker and return to the airbase at Rechlin. Exactly what his orders were is open to some speculation. Some claim the Führer directed von Greim to organize air cover for a massive ground counterattack about to be launched by General Walther Wenck's nonexistent Twelfth Army. Others assert he was to join Admiral Karl Dönitz in Plön, whom Hitler had just named his successor. Unlike Hitler, however, the wounded Field Marshal understood the true state of affairs and knew the German state was no longer able to mount a meaningful assault or establish a working government before the final collapse. Still loyal to the Führer, von Greim agreed to leave the bunker. Hitler also ordered the new Luftwaffe chief to have Heinrich Himmler arrested as a traitor for contacting the Americans and British in an effort to end the war. It was sometime after midnight on April 29 when von Greim and Reitsch left the bunker for good, supplied with their master's best wishes and letters from Eva Braun, Martin Bormann, and Goebbels and his wife—all of whom remained behind to meet their fate.[6]

The SS troops guarding the bunker produced a small armored vehicle to carry the lovers through the ruined city to an Arado 96, a small training aircraft hidden near the Brandenburg Gate. Only 1,200 feet of pavement was available as a runway. The Field Marshal and the test pilot strapped themselves in and took off into a hail of Russian anti-aircraft fire, which popped and whizzed around the plane as soon as it cleared the buildings. Enemy searchlights locked onto the small aircraft. Their luck held when a cloud bank at 4,500 feet hid them from view. A few minutes later both occupants looked down into a sea of flame feeding off the remains of what was once one of Europe's most beautiful cities. Reitsch circled around at 20,000 feet and headed north. Fifty minutes later she landed the Arado safely at Rechlin. The pair flew on into southern Germany, where resistance against the Russians would rage until May 9. For a few difficult days Hitler's last Field Marshal directed part of the futile effort there before he and Reitsch flew on in a Dornier 217 to Zell am See.[7]

Robert Von Greim and Hanna Reitsch surrendered without incident when the Americans drove into Zell am See. Still in a great deal of pain, von Greim was taken to a hospital in Salzburg. On May 24 the proud veteran of the First World War, Luftwaffe air ace, and holder of the Knight's Cross reached into his pocket and removed Hitler's final gift—a small ampule of cyanide. He inserted the capsule into his mouth and snapped it between his teeth. His lover, however, had a stronger desire to live. Eschewing suicide, Reitsch instead turned her dose of toxin over to Captain Robert E. Work, a U.S. Air Division interrogator. Reitsch was not about to kill herself but her parents had no such reservation. A few days later an American intelligence officer paid a visit to their home. Both committed suicide rather than face enemy questions. When asked why she had not done the same, Reitsch explained her only reason to stay alive was for "the sake of the truth." The truth must be told about Göring, she explained, "the shallow showman," and Hitler, "the criminal incompetent." She also wanted to explain to the German people the dangers inherent in dictatorial government.[8]

Reitsch was carrying more surprises than just a poison capsule courtesy of her Führer. In her possession CIC agents discovered two letters, one penned by Josef Goebbels and the other by his wife, Magda. In truth, exactly what they took with them from the bunker is unknown. Reitsch admitted carrying four letters out of the embattled city. Two from the Goebbels' and one each from Eva Braun and Martin Bormann. After reading them, she explained, she and von Greim agreed to destroy the Braun and Bormann letters. The latter, Reitsch said, was simply an official communication questioning why Berlin had not received radio communications from southern Germany. Braun's letter was destroyed because Reitsch felt "that the text was so glaringly theatrical and in such poor adolescent taste that only odious reactions would result should the letter ever fall into German hands . . . and the German reader might eulogize Braun as a Nazi Martyr." The Goebbels letters, neither of which were noteworthy, were intended for Magda's son from a previous marriage. In May 1945, "Harald" was one of the lucky young German males, still alive and sitting in an Allied prisoner of war camp in Algiers. With his dying pen strokes Goebbels could not resist dipping his pen in vitriol and spewing forth more Nazi diatribe about country and Führer. "Farewell my dear Harald," he wrote with his usual thespian flair. "Whether we shall ever see each other again lies in the hand of God." This from a man who had helped foster the entire Holocaust climate, lived a life of opulence while millions were herded into gas chambers or shot and thrown into ditches, and then, in the end, murdered his own children. Magda's letter explained that life was not worth living without the world envisioned by the Führer and National Socialism. "God grant that I will have the strength to accomplish the last and most difficult task of all," she wrote while preparing to slaughter her offspring. "I put my arms around you with the deepest, most heartfelt mother's love. This letter is to go out. Hanna Reitsch will take it along. She is to fly back out again."[9]

*   *   *

Josef Spacil was not a happy man.

His beloved Germany had been defeated and his efforts to distribute RSHA funds in the Alpine Redoubt had been a dismal failure. Much of the loot, worth millions of dollars, had been hastily hidden to keep it out of Allied hands. And now, in a final blow to his inflated pride, SS Oberführer Spacil found himself inside a crowded prisoner of war camp at Ebersburg masquerading as a lowly Wehrmacht sergeant named "Aue" in order to avoid detection, arrest—or worse. There were two good reasons Spacil was pretending to be an obscure foot soldier instead of an important RSHA and SS officer. First, everyone who had served in the SS was subject to automatic arrest. Second, and even more important, were his intimate associations and connections to those involved in criminal activity up to and including the implementation of the "Final Solution." These associations tarred him with the same murderous brush that coated Ernst Kaltenbrunner, Heinrich Müller, Adolf Eichmann, Franz Konrad, and others. Though no evidence has ever surfaced that he pulled a trigger or ordered the death of a single person, Spacil's RSHA Bureau II had administered the assets everyone knew had been stolen from those shipped off to slave labor and death camps. Spacil had issued a flurry of decrees aimed at extricating wealth from overrun cities and territories in the East. He knew well the origins of the treasure over which he presided. And now Spacil was a marked man. Escaping from the Allied net in which he now found himself entwined was his highest priority. As bad as his circumstances were, they were about to get much worse.[10]

Oberführer Spacil had become separated from SS Hauptsturmführer (Captain) Gerhardt Schlemmer, the commander of the 352nd Volksgrenadier Division who had allowed Spacil to slip unnoticed into his outfit. After a brief period in the prison pen at Ebersburg, all SS personnel had been transferred to Fuerstanfeldbruck and an area known as the Oklahoma PW Cage. Cloaked in the garb of a Wehrmacht soldier, Spacil was left behind. When Schlemmer left Obersturmführer (Lieutenant) Walter Hirschfeld, his former student at the training school for SS officers in Bad Tölz, Germany, went with him. There, Schlemmer told Hirschfeld about his earlier conversation with Spacil, who had claimed to be an important RSHA officer and the secretor of vast sums of money belonging to the German treasury. Spacil, he explained to Hirschfeld, had offered him a large sum of money if he would contact an American officer and buy a discharge from the U.S. Army. Both men agreed they should turn him in.[11]

On June 5, 1945, Schlemmer approached John E. Alter, an American military intelligence agent. An important officer, he explained, had asked him "before the German capitulation to take him into his company as a corporal in order to conceal his identify." His interest aroused, Alter hurried Schlemmer away to a secure area so that they could speak freely. There, Schlemmer revealed the important SS Oberführer's true identity. "He offered to reward me out of a hidden treasure."

"What is it he wants you to do?" asked Alter.

"He wants me to approach an American officer and buy a discharge for him, me, and Hirschfeld," came Schlemmer's reply.

"Why would you turn in a fellow SS officer?" The intelligence officer was smart enough to be skeptical.

Schlemmer claimed a general loathing for the top brass who had led them all to disaster. "Neither of us," he emphatically explained, referring to himself and Hirschfeld, "want to see an important Nazi party member go free while less important Germans sit in captivity."[12]

In an effort to bolster his own credibility, Schlemmer explained to his suspicious interrogator that he had been thrown out of the SS early in the war and jailed, but reinstated later when the need for manpower had become overwhelming. By revealing Spacil's identity and plan, Schlemmer and Hirschfeld hoped to improve their own situation and perhaps earn an early release themselves. Convinced Schlemmer was telling the truth, Alter and other intelligence agents, including Lieutenant Claus K. Nacke, devised a plan to trap and arrest the officer. Spacil would be picked up at Ebersburg and taken to the Oklahoma PW Cage. There, Schlemmer would convince Spacil he was buying a discharge for his freedom. The invaluable paper Spacil was trying to purchase was a single page Certificate of Discharge. The form exhibited a black thumb print, a statement in English that "the holder of the certificate is not verminous or suffering from any infectious or contagious disease," and the signature of an American officer. The word "Official" was stamped across the paper. The simple and straightforward certificate was Spacil's ticket home. With it he could walk out of the POW camp and into private life. But the price was steep: "1,000,000 Reichsmarks in American currency and gold." Schlemmer was also instructed to "obtain all pertinent information possible" about his role during the war and the location of his concealed treasures.[13]

On or about June 8, Spacil was transferred from Ebersburg to Fuerstanfeldbruck and reunited with Schlemmer. The CIC agents saw to it that the pair were housed in the same tent. It did not take long for the informant to gain the complete confidence of the former Bureau II chief by acting as a diehard SS man. "Schlemmer was now playing the part of a fanatical Nazi," reads one CIC memorandum, "and since he was Spacil's commanding officer [as part of the 352nd Volksgrenadier Division], and was also acting as an intermediary with the Americans, Spacil's future was more or less at Schlemmer's mercy." Blissfully unaware of the trap being set, Spacil shared a substantial amount of personal information about himself, his role in the war, and much more. All of it was captured in detailed notes when Schlemmer passed along the information to Americans investigators each evening.[14]

"I have to gain my freedom as quickly as possible," Spacil emphatically told Schlemmer, "otherwise my whole network of agents will fall apart." If the former Oberführer was to be believed, his wartime role was as important as it was extensive. When prompted for more information, Spacil confided that he had organized a web of agents all over the Third Reich who had procured vast amounts of valuables for him. The agents included several French, Swiss, and Italians—and even one American. The latter agent, explained Spacil, had a good grasp of international finance and was friendly to Germans, but had always steadfastly refused to have anything to do with matters that might adversely affect the American war effort. Despite Schlemmer's best efforts, Spacil refused to reveal the American's identity. Other information flew thick and fast from his lips. When Schlemmer explained that he was in bad financial straits, Spacil told him, "you need not fear for the future," and that he would fix him up "with a fund of several million marks to be used at your discretion." But you must get expert assistance when attempting to exchange the securities, cautioned Spacil, "to avoid being discovered." As part of the continued effort to fool the Americans, Spacil gave his confidant the code name "Drogerie." His own code name was "Lech." "Once you are free," he continued, give this code name to Frau Anna Ho—in Munich, to get in touch with [my] circle."[15]

Copious bits of information were revealed to Schlemmer, who continued to feign deep interest in his new friend's wartime role; Spacil loved the attention and dug his hole deeper. "I was once the administrative head for southern Russia," Spacil disclosed, "and I know a little something about the Hungarian state treasure, and about the burning of Jews." "The Reich accounting office would probably like to catch up with me," he continued. "At the end of April the last remaining funds and foreign securities belonging to the Reichsbank in Berlin were removed at the point of a gun on my order." This loot, he added, was "buried in the Tyrol, Austria, and is worth 23 million gold marks."[16]

"So a lot of valuables were stashed away near the end?" prodded Schlemmer.

"Yes. I am very worried about a truck containing 300 million marks of English foreign exchange notes in chests."

"Where is this truck now?" asked Schlemmer.

"I left it in charge of a capable Untersturmführer, but I fear this officer might act incautiously. I did receive a reassuring report about this man when he was in Taxenbach."

"Who is he?" asked Schlemmer.

Spacil hesitated. "I cannot say."

Changing gears, Schlemmer inquired about his associates. "You must have worked with a lot of people to hide all this treasure," he said.

"Yes, but I fear that my secretary [Gretl Biesecker, in the custody of the CIC Seventh Army] might be arrested," he whispered. "That would be very dangerous for me."

"Why is that?" asked Schlemmer.

"Because she is acquainted with most of my secrets." Many of Spacil's "secrets" were already floating around in the public domain.[17]

One day, Spacil displayed a much higher level of nervousness and irritation than usual. He excitedly waved a newspaper clipping in front of Schlemmer concerning the discovery of foreign currency in a barn near St. Johann, Austria. The article also described how one of the largest gold finds in history was unearthed nearby. Spacil's anxiety was understandable: the uncovered treasure was in the immediate vicinity of a large cache of loot he had hidden away. The more he read, the more agitated he became.

*   *   *

The story, and eventual discovery, of the treasure that so concerned Spacil began on April 17, 1945, when SS General Gottlob-Christian Berger reported to Reichsführer Himmler's headquarters in the old Ziethen castle in Wustrow. The 48-year-old Berger, who had risen steadily through the ranks to become one of Himmler's top generals and a recipient of the Knight's Cross, was recognized primarily as a racial selection "expert." He had served for a time on the Russian front and as chief of staff for the military SS and head of the SS main leadership office. When the war was winding down, Berger was named Inspector General of the Prisoners of War Administration. Himmler disclosed to Berger that eleven bags of currency were sitting in the Vereins Bank in Munich. Sealed by the Reichsbank, each sack contained a slip of paper indicating it was the property of the Reichsführer, held in the name of the Ministry of the Interior. A code word and secret number were provided to Berger so that he could obtain the money; the Reichsführer ordered him to hide it.

With Germany collapsing on all fronts and Hermann Göring long out of favor with the Führer, Himmler issued commands largely at his own pleasure. On April 22, Himmler made Berger his representative on the Southern Group's staff. Berger dutifully left his position in northern Germany and headed toward Munich. The trip was detoured by a telephone call from Hitler's bunker. Berger was to report to the Führer before leaving for his new post. Like von Greim, who would arrive a few days after him, Berger walked into a macabre scene orchestrated by a director gone mad. During their interview, the pair discussed what to do with the tens of thousands of British and American prisoners of war. "Shoot them all, shoot them all!" Hitler repeated over and over. We don't know exactly how Berger responded to the order. We do know, however, that at great personal risk he ignored Hitler's directive to execute Allied captives. In fact, many senior Allied POWs were transferred by train to Switzerland. It was 1:00 a.m., April 23, when an exhausted Berger climbed into Himmler's personal four-engine plane and left for southern Germany. A barrage of Russian artillery shells danced dangerously close to the aircraft as it lifted off into the black night. The general's luck, however, was about to run out.[18]

One week later U.S. army forces captured Berger. On May 22 (while Josef Spacil was sitting inside a detention center) an army military intelligence officer named Major Paul Kubala interrogated Berger. During this routine questioning, Berger nonchalantly mentioned the fact that he had worked directly under Heinrich Himmler, who had given him a large sum of money to hide. When pressed on the issue Berger claimed the currency did not belong to either Himmler or himself but to the Reichsbank. He even offered to show the Americans where he buried it. The following morning Berger and intelligence officer Lieutenant William S. Scheuer met Captain Harry Anderson at St. Johann. Berger led the pair to a chief forester's home, which was connected to a barn. He entered the structure, fell to his knees, and began removing floorboards. The soil was loose, and after digging down several feet he extracted eight large cloth sacks and one large metal box. The officers raised their eyebrows in astonishment: Berger's loot—foreign currency from more than two dozen countries—was worth about one million dollars. Not a single bill was of United States origin. The currency was sent under guard to the Foreign Exchange Depository in Frankfurt, Germany, stamped shipment number 27D.[19]

Berger had additional interesting information to share with his captors. During a second round of questioning by Lieutenant Scheuer, the SS officer revealed that twenty-five boxes of gold had been hidden in the vicinity of Mittenwald, Germany. Berger's story was assigned to Lieutenant Eloy F. Perez. Armed with specific information gleaned from Berger, Perez traveled to Mittenwald and contacted the CIC Detachment at Garmisch-Partenkirchen. On June 7, 1945, American agents located nine men to interrogate on the subject. The first eight professed complete ignorance of both Berger and any hidden Nazi gold. Hauptsturmführer (Captain) Heintz Rüger, however, came clean. "I think I can help locate the gold. I and my men unloaded the gold on the night of April 25 and 26 and if you take me with you, I think I may be able to locate the spot where it is buried."[20]

The following morning, June 8, Lieutenant Perez and his team drove to the foot of Altloch Berg and hiked up a trail for approximately twenty minutes. When the group reached a fork in the path, Rüger requested a minesweeper for use on the left branch of the track. It was almost too easy. Ten yards from the fork and five yards off the trail, the minesweeper detected the presence of metal spread out over an area six feet square. The recently dug money pit was well camouflaged with a tree stump surrounded by a thick bed of moss. A couple soldiers began digging and about fifteen minutes later one shovel nicked a bar of bright and shiny yellow gold several feet down. Excited by the discovery, Perez left a guard and transported the single bar to 10th Armored Headquarters. From there, he called Seventh Army Headquarters to report his find. Additional U.S. military personnel arrived at the scene to continue the excavation. Each shovel of dirt exposed more of the precious metal. By the time the men were through digging and lifting, 728 bars of pure gold worth millions of dollars were in the custody of the 10th Armored Division. The bullion was turned over to the Foreign Exchange Depository on June 10, 1945.[21]

*   *   *

With a display of disgust Spacil dropped the newspaper article about General Berger's treasure trove and looked up nervously at Schlemmer. "Everything I have worked so hard, my entire network, is going to be discovered," he lamented.

As he was waiting for his forged papers to be completed, Spacil revealed information even more amazing and in many ways more interesting to the Allies than stolen gold and currency: he boasted of his intimate knowledge of the fate of Adolf Hitler and Eva Braun and their personal papers.

"I know Hitler is, without question, dead."

"You are sure of this?" asked Schlemmer.

"Yes. The official version is that he fell in combat outside the Reich Chancellery with a machine pistol in hand, and that Gruppenführer [Hermann] Fegelein fell by his side." Later, Spacil changed his story. "In reality," he whispered, "the Führer's bunker was hit by a bomb which penetrated into the interior. It killed him and many of his staff. His entire right leg was said to be shattered," continued Spacil, "and his upper left breast was hit by bomb splinters."

"When did this happen?" asked an incredulous Schlemmer, who did not know whether the story Spacil was weaving was true or false.

"Just 48 hours before the Russians overran the bunker."

"What happened to the Führer's body?

"I hear it was possible to embalm and remove it from the Chancellery," Spacil replied, "but I don't know the men who embalmed his body. Only four men know the details of the burial. Two remained in Berlin and were probably killed; the other two got out safely."

"Where was he buried and who were these men?" asked Schlemmer.

Spacil knowingly shook his head. "I can't tell you that information. You really can't demand that of me." But then he continued, hinting that he was one of the four men. "We did it in the simplest manner. It is impossible that the Führer's body [could] fall into the enemy's hands."

"I am not sure the Führer is really dead," replied Schlemmer.

"Oh, you can believe me," Spacil promptly cut in. "I have seen the Führer's tattered trousers, his blood-drenched coat, his diaries, and his letters to and from Eva Braun."

"Where are these things now?" Schlemmer inquired.

"They are in the possession of a confidential agent in Zell am See," reported Spacil. "They are hidden away to preserve them for posterity. He intended to burn the letters and diaries but I urged him not to do so. I don't think he destroyed them." He paused, then added, "I hope they never find these things. That would cause a great sensation."

"You have seen the Führer's personal diaries? asked Schlemmer.

"Yes. He kept them since 1923. They are written in his own handwriting on very thin airmail paper."

Schlemmer was turning in an Oscar-worthy performance as the sympathetic and dedicated Nazi SS officer. When he commented that he must have known Hitler well, Spacil rambled on for several minutes about the Führer's poor health during the war's final months, and that he had continued believing in complete victory until just a few weeks before his death.

Believing he had tapped out that line of questioning, Schlemmer turned to Eva Braun. "What of Eva Braun? Did she perish in Berlin as well?"

"No," replied Spacil with authority and confidence, turning in an equally impressive performance. "She left Berlin at the last minute in a Fiesler Storch aircraft, taking off from the East-West Axis to join her sister Gretl in Zell am See. You know of course she is married to Gruppenführer Fegelein. Eva loved the Führer deeply, and in my opinion she will [eventually] take her own life."

"According to the Allied reports, they were married in the bunker."

"That is nonsense! Completely untrue!" Spacil answered with a wave of his hand and look of disgust. "A long time ago I spoke to the Führer on this very subject—the possibility of marriage. It was thoroughly discussed. Hitler told me he would not think of placing any woman in such a dangerous position as his wife would occupy. 'When I am with Eva, you can be sure that I am as good as married,' he told me."

Unable to stop spinning tales in an effort to enhance his image in the eyes of the one man who now held his fate in his hands, Spacil continued rambling on. "The Führer ordered me to assist Eva Braun regarding several private matters," he said in all seriousness. "I visited her several times in Munich taking to her, among other things, a large amount of transparent blue silk cloth from France. She intended to make it into a long gown with a train. The Führer especially liked such things."[22]

Unbeknownst to Spacil, of course, Schlemmer was regularly feeding this information to the Allies. As Lieutenants Scheuer and Perez were working with General Berger to locate his concealed millions, American agents Alter, Nacke and others were receiving Schlemmer's reports while simultaneously reconstructing Spacil's life and activities as they built their case against him.

In an effort to pay for his freedom, Spacil furnished a signed letter and the password "sun" to Lieutenant Nacke, both of which were necessary to enable him to contact those who knew where his treasures were hidden. On June 9, Alter, Nacke, and former SS officer (and Schlemmer's subordinate) Walter Hirschfeld traveled to Taxenbach to contact Spacil's liaisons. As instructed, the trio attempted to make contact with two men at Pulzel's sawmill about eight miles south of Zell am See. Their names were "Captain Apfelbeck" and "Wimmer." Neither man could be located. However, a forester named "Reisinger" who lived in Taxenbach and who was sympathetic to the Nazi cause was found. Nacke showed Spacil's letter to the skeptical forester, spoke the password, and convinced him he had Spacil's authority to remove the hidden valuables. Reisinger led the men to the home of a man named Urschunger, who lived in nearby Rauris southeast of Zell am See.

Josef Spacil had wildly exaggerated his limited contact with Hitler, but his tales of buried fortunes proved absolutely true. Gold bullion was found under the floor of a barn; millions in currency was discovered stashed away behind a brick enclosure in Urschunger's attic. Other separate caches of loot were recovered on a steep incline along the Rauris-Taxenbach highway, buried under some trees about 100 yards off the road. The foreign currency had not been well protected, and the recent rains had soaked the money sacks. According to the agents, the sacks appeared to have been "hastily or carelessly buried." On June 18, Lieutenant Nacke and ex-SS officer Hirschfeld loaded part of Spacil's fortune—nineteen bags of gold coins and bars, three bags of silver, two boxes of coins, and $117,752 in currency—into a jeep and trailer. Like all the other recovered caches, these valuables were sent to the Foreign Exchange Depository for safekeeping. During the return trip, a jeep driven by intelligence officer John Alter was involved in a serious accident that landed him in the hospital in Munich. There, the doctors discovered Alter was a rich man. Inside his field jacket were 220 gold francs, 280 gold lira, 850 English pounds, nine rings, four watches, and a jeweled cross encrusted with diamonds. Exactly how the U.S. authorities handled this delicate matter is not known. A wall of silence was erected around the case. When he recovered, Alter was quietly transferred to another unit.[23]

Captain Apfelbeck, the assistant who had helped Spacil hide much of the stolen loot, was located and apprehended near Taxenbach. The information he shared with investigators convinced the agents on June 12, 1945, that the time had arrived to officially arrest Spacil. According to one report, the ex-SS bureau chief (who still did not know he was being duped by Schlemmer) was "dejected, on the verge of nervous collapse, and apprehensive of being discovered by the Americans." Worried that he might commit suicide if he learned what was going on, the CIC men continued addressing him as "Sergeant Aue." Since he was a non-commissioned officer, they intoned, arrangements were being made for his discharge. Spacil was ecstatic. All released prisoners, they explained, had to submit to a physical examination before being released. A CIC agent posing as a doctor examined Spacil while other agents searched his personal belongings hanging in another room. Their suspicions were confirmed when three cyanide capsules were found sewn into the lining of his clothes. Spacil nearly fainted when the CIC told him he was under arrest for both serving in the SS and running Bureau II of the RSHA. Both Spacil and Apfelbeck, his partner in crime during his last few days in power, were vigorously interrogated by U.S. Intelligence officers. Apfelbeck quickly revealed most, if not all, of what he knew.[24]

The same cannot be said for Josef Spacil, who continued to stonewall his captors. He professed to know little or nothing about hidden caches of stolen gold and currency, nor did he know the names and whereabouts of the top brass of criminals with whom he had freely associated for so many years. His tongue loosened a bit over the course of several interrogations. The fascinating (and occasionally fantastic) tidbits of information offered investigators, however, were riddled with inconsistencies, half-truths, and outright falsehoods. Assembling them into a coherent mosaic of his final days of the war proved difficult, but not wholly impossible. Interviews with Apfelbeck and others bridged many gaps and filled in a handful of gray areas. Investigators continued rooting about, but they inevitably began running up against dead ends. There were too many other officers to interrogate, too many other leads and rumors to run down. In 1947 they closed the books on Spacil and walked away from the table. Many secrets remained behind. Most of them were locked away inside the former Oberführer. A reasonable estimate of the loot hidden by Spacil is $25,000,000. Nacke's single jeep and trailer load was valued at approximately $600,000—only a sliver of the whole, all of it buried in the scenic region surrounding Zell am See.

Officially, nothing more linked to Josef Spacil was ever recovered by U.S. forces.

*   *   *

Notwithstanding Spacil's steadfast reticence and verbal roadblocks, he did offer liberal (if occasionally untruthful) testimony regarding two men in particular: SS Captains Franz Konrad and Erwin Haufler. Both, he explained, were carrying valuables, including a mass of personal papers smuggled out of the bunker belonging to Adolf Hitler, Eva Braun, and others. Was this possible? The daring end-of-war flight engineered by Hanna Reitsch and Robert Ritter von Greim convinced many agents that it was conceivable that vast amounts of documents may have been smuggled into Austria.

Spacil steadfastly maintained that was the fact, and the Führer's personal diaries were among them.

Chapter Notes

1. The History of the Counter Intelligence Corps, The U.S. Intelligence Center (Baltimore, 1950), unpublished manuscript, Pages XXV–1 thru XXV–6.

2. Unfortunately, there is not a substantial body of readily available information on Robert Ritter von Greim. A good, though brief, account is found in Samuel W. Mitcham, Jr., *Hitler's Field Marshals and Their Battles* (London, 1988), pp. 355, 359-61.

3. James P. O'Donnell, *The Bunker: The History of the Reich Chancellery Group* (New York, 1978), pp. 152-153.

4. Mitcham, *Hitler's Field Marshals*, p. 360.

5. O'Donnell, *The Bunker*, p. 153. The Goebbels children were later murdered, one by one, in the bunker by their parents, who were themselves slain by a staff member on Dr. Goebbels's orders.

6. O'Donnell, *The Bunker*, pp. 153-154; Mitcham, *Hitler's Field Marshals*, pp. 360-361.

7. Mitcham, *Hitler's Field Marshals*, p. 361. The sources on the final few days of von Greim's wartime career conflict. This seems to be the most plausible account of his activities.

8. "The Condemnation of Göring by Hanna Reitsch," Captain E. Work, November 16, 1945, Air Division, Headquarters U.S. Forces in Austria. The Germans manufactured more than 5,000 cases of these thin glass cyanide ampules hidden inside rifle cartridges modified with a screw top.

9. CIC, "Interrogation: Introduction Summary of Hanna Reitsch," November 1, 1945. Reitsch's explanation as to why she destroyed Bormann's letter is not persuasive. At that late date it is unlikely she would have gone to the trouble of destroying a letter of such little consequence.

10. Some of the CIC documents concerning Spacil refer to him as "Wilhelm Spacil." His given name is actually "Josef." In addition, some of the documents say he was disguised as a corporal, when in fact he was dressed as a sergeant.

11. 307th Counter Intelligence Corps Detachment, "Interrogation Memorandum, Josef Spacil," July 27, 1945, hereinafter cited as "Spacil Memorandum"; Document 3839-PS, "Statement of SS-Oberführer Josef Spacil," The Nizcorp Project, http://www.nizkor.org.

12. CIC, "Headquarters Seventh Army Memorandum," June 16, 1945. Although this document does not offer the actual conversation between Schlemmer and Alter, it is detailed enough to reconstruct the exchange.

13. CIC, "Headquarters Seventh Army Memorandum," June 16, 1945; "Spacil Memorandum," July 27, 1945.

14. CIC, "Wilhelm Spacil Information Regarding the Discovery of Shipment 31," page stamped 210298; CIC, "Headquarters Seventh Army Memorandum," June 16, 1945; "Spacil Memorandum," July 27, 1945.

15. "Spacil Memorandum," July 27, 1945. The Allies were aware of a group of agents led by an American who worked under the code name "Wendig." The association, which specialized in securities (mostly counterfeit), worked out of northern Italy. SS General Friedrich Schwend, alias "Wendig," the distributor of

the counterfeit English pound notes, operated briefly at this time near his home in northern Italy. He was introduced in detail in an earlier chapter.

16. "Spacil Memorandum," July 27, 1945. Spacil is likely lying about draining funds from the Reichsbank "at the point of a gun on my order."

17. "Spacil Memorandum," July 27, 1945; "Memorandum for the Officer in Charge of the Interrogation of Josef Spacil," July 5, 1945. Though he did not reveal the name of the "capable Untersturmführer," Spacil was referring to Menzel, who left Taxenbach for Graz, Austria on May 7, 1945. Like so many captured SS officers, Spacil was prone to exaggeration and outright lying. He claimed to have firsthand information about the concealment of the Third Reich's historic insignia, which consisted of Charlemagne's golden apple, crown, ball, and scepter (also known as the imperial crown jewels). Spacil claimed the priceless artifacts had been seized by the Gestapo and dumped "in a lake near Zell am See" inside zinc caskets. In reality, they had been hidden inside the Paniers Platz bunker in downtown Nuremberg in four copper containers. For more information on this fascinating story, see Kenneth D. Alford, *Great Treasure Stories of World War II* (Savas Publishing, 1999), pp. 129-133.

18. Seventh Army Interrogation Center, "CIC Interrogation of Gottlob Berger," June 5 1945; "Interrogation of Otto Ohlendorf," by Henry Schneider, December 14, 1945, p. 30; Hugh R. Trevor-Roper, *The Last Days of Hitler* (New York, 1947).

19. "Interrogation of Gottlob Berger," June 5 1945.

20. "Interrogation of Gottlob Berger," June 5, 1945; Elroy P. Perez, "Chronological Report on Mittenwald Mission," June 9, 1945.

21. 10th Armored Division, "William R. Geilu Memorandum," June 6, 1945; Telephone Memo File, June 11, 1945, "Call from Frankfurt" (U.S. Foreign Exchange Depository) confirming the expected convoy of gold and foreign currency, and that it arrived yesterday evening as expected. "All the material was safely delivered and checked into the currency section of the Reichsbank." Also entered on the U.S. Foreign Exchange Depository books on June 10, 1945.

22. 307th CIC, Headquarters Seventh Army, "Memorandum for Officer in Charge," July 27, 1945; "Spacil Interrogation," July 27, 1945. Although Spacil did not reveal the name of the agent supposedly holding onto Hitler's and Braun's personal papers, he was almost certainly referring to SS Hauptsturmführer (Captain) Franz Konrad.

23. "Wilhelm [sic] Spacil Information Regarding the Discovery of Shipment 31," page stamped 210298; 307th Counter Intelligence Corps, "Report by Richard C. Cahoon," June 16, 1945.

24. "Report by Richard C. Cahoon," June 16, 1945.

Chapter 9

"Throughout the four interrogations Konrad has deliberately falsified the majority of his statements. He has only admitted that which he has been forced to admit because of being confronted with the facts. At present this unit is in possession of some of the items which he still insists he burned."

— CIC Special Agent Robert A. Gutierrez

Ghetto Konrad's Hidden Wealth

After Hanna Reitsch and Robert Ritter von Greim surrendered to the Americans, SS Hauptsturmführer (Captain) Franz Konrad was the only former German SS soldier allowed free reign on the grounds of Fischhorn castle. Dressed in civilian clothing he enjoyed hot meals, cigarettes, and liquor, and was on friendly terms with many of the victorious GIs. This comfortable existence stretched into days; two weeks passed without complication. Feigning cooperation, Konrad offered the Americans any assistance he could provide. Gracious to a fault, the chameleon-like captain was a smooth operator indeed, changing with the times in an attempt to distance himself from himself. Initially Agent Robert A. Gutierrez of the Counter Intelligence Corps promised Konrad continued freedom and a job with the CIC. Konrad began to breathe a little easier. The door of freedom beckoned.

But information from other sources was slowly oozing into the house of cards Konrad had constructed at Zell am See. For the former king of the Warsaw Ghetto, freedom would prove fleeting.

*   *   *

What Konrad did not know was that Agent Gutierrez was feigning as well. He and his intelligence team already knew a lot about him and his crimes in Warsaw, Poland. They also knew he was withholding valuable information from them. Offers of comfort, friendship and employment were intelligence tactics intended to put him at ease and loosen his tongue. There was very specific information Konrad had that the Allies craved: the location of perhaps millions in gold, silver, jewelry, and currency. And there were other items that intrigued the Allies even more—Adolf Hitler's and Eva Braun's personal letters and the Führer's supposed diaries. When the Americans learned that Polish authorities were also seeking the SS captain for war crimes, their strategy to move slowly with Konrad had to be abandoned. An order for his arrest was issued.

Without any advance warning, a group of American soldiers arrived at Fischhorn on May 21, 1945. Several people were rounded up for questioning and detention. Konrad had no idea his cover was blown until he asked a simple question.

"May I retrieve my toilet articles?" he inquired of a young American officer.

"What is your name?"

"Franz Konrad."

"No, you don't get anything," the officer replied sharply. "You will be imprisoned for 10 or 15 years, for sure." Konrad later reported seeing "hatred in his eyes."

At that moment the SS officer knew he was in big trouble. "If even this very young man makes such pre-judgments," he thought to himself, "what will become of me?" Given his past, Konrad had a pretty good idea. A prison sentence was the best outcome he could hope for once the Poles got their hands on him. If he did not escape his captors he would one day face a firing squad or find himself standing on the trap door of a gallows erected in his honor.[1]

Exactly how Konrad managed to slip out of the jail at Zell am See is unclear. What we do know is that four days after his arrest on the night of May 25, Konrad made it outdoors, climbed a steep hill in a pouring rain, and slogged his way to the home of a former SS nurse named Ursula von Bieler. The woman lived in Aufhausen, a small town west of Zell am See.

The knock roused her from bed. To her shock, she looked out and saw a saturated Konrad standing in her doorway in the middle of the night. Bieler pulled him inside, listened to his plight, and agreed to help him. She notified a former German soldier the next morning who supplied the SS captain with a gray hat, gray trousers, gray jacket, and a pair of climbing shoes with cleats. Dry and refreshed, Konrad decided to gamble with his luck and hike the few miles to a tavern in Bruck owned by Franz Schutzinger. Konrad had rented a small room there during the American occupation, and his swift arrest had prevented him from retrieving his rucksack. CIC agents later learned that Schutzinger knew Konrad well and was sympathetic to his plight. After eating supper the pair quietly made their way to the small hotel, which was occupied by U.S. soldiers of the 101st Airborne Division. They entered through a back door and walked quietly upstairs to the room. Once safely inside, Schutzinger opened a bottle of wine and the men drank deeply. Schutzinger spoke first.

"I have heard from several SS men that Polish officials are in the area." He looked intently at Konrad. "They are looking for you."

"Yes, I know. Thank you for the information." Konrad opened the rucksack and removed 50,000 Reichsmarks. He gave them to Schutzinger. "Thank you again for helping me," he said before getting up and leaving the same way he had entered.[2]

Konrad's probable goal was to slip into Switzerland. He walked from Zell am See along the banks of the Salzach River and crossed several fields in order to arrive back near Aufhausen just before dawn on May 27. Ursula von Bieler had directed him to a safe house on the Dollinger farm, not far from her own home. Konrad remained hidden for two days. When he left the farm he had with him his rucksack, together with two other packages, one about eighteen inches long and narrow, and the other about fifteen inches long and square. Someone probably delivered the boxes to Konrad. How he arranged it is not known. No one besides Konrad knew their contents. From the Dollinger farm, the escapee made his way to the former German army barracks at Aufhausen. Officers who had been living at Fischhorn during the war were being housed there. A whispered conversation or two turned up another friendly contact in the form of SS Captain Erwin Haufler, who had been in command of the SS horse farm at Fischhorn Castle. Konrad had given Haufler a cache of Swiss francs, gold coins, and thousands of Reichsmarks before the war ended. An evasive (and probably lying) Haufler told Konrad that he no longer had the money. Disappointed, Konrad asked him to obtain forged German army papers. Haufler agreed to help him and left. A few hours later another officer appeared with "a blank form with a seal and a signature." Using a typewriter, Konrad typed in the name "Franz Meier," slipped the paper into his pocket, and left Aufhausen. Haufler, too, was a hunted man. Before the end of the summer he would be arrested and sent to a camp at Bad Aibling, Germany.

After Konrad left Haufler, he struck out for Kirchberg. There, on or about May 30 he reached the home of his nephew, Rudolf Meier. The Meiers were as stunned to see Konrad as Ursula von Bieler had been. Once safely inside, the exhausted SS man wolfed down a hot meal prepared by Meier's wife, changed clothes, and then told his hosts for the first time about his plight.

"I have escaped from the U.S. authorities at Zell am See," he explained, "and am being hunted. I have good forged papers, and do not think I will be found. My name is now Franz Meier." Konrad dug into his pocket and produced the forged document, which he handed over for inspection to his dubious nephew. Frau Meier said nothing. An uneasy silence lingered between them.

The one-sided conversation continued with Konrad working overtime trying to impress his relatives with stories of his wealth. "I have a large Austrian stamp collection—forty folios, worth hundreds of thousands of Reichsmarks," he said. "These can easily be sold." He would buy their cooperation if they would not willingly provide it.

Meier watched nervously as his uncle removed clothing, shoes, canned food, coffee, and tea from his rucksack. His interest heightened significantly when a final pair of items were extracted from the sack. The first was wrapped inside a large German military map. Instead of string, the package was bound with telephone wire. The second bundle was wrapped in black packing paper. Konrad threw this parcel into a coal bucket and handed the map-covered package to Meier.

"Take good care of this for me," he cryptically ordered. He did not tell Rudolf how to take care of it or what was inside. "I need a place to stay for a while until I can make a few arrangements. Can I stay here with you and your family?"

Rudolf wisely declined. "No, you cannot remain here. I cannot risk my family's safety by sheltering a wanted SS officer—even if you are my uncle." Or at least that is what he later informed Allied investigators he had told his uncle.

"Alright, I understand." Rebuffed, Konrad gathered his few belongings and left, walking towards the hospital in Kirchberg. Whether he simply forgot the package in the coal bucket or intended to leave it behind, Konrad departed without either of the two mysterious parcels.

Meier opened the package wrapped with the map and almost dropped it on the floor. Inside were four smaller packages of 100,000 Reichsmarks, each with a 1945 value of about $10,000. Meier was examining the fortune residing in his lap when his wife, forgetting about the smaller package in the bucket, lifted the container and shook some coal into the stove. When Meier spotted the black package steaming in the flames he plucked it out and unwrapped it. To his amazement it contained Swiss francs, Swedish kronen, American currency, gold coins, and two rings. Unsure of what to do, he carried the valuables out to the woodshed behind his home and hid them in a stack of firewood.[3]

His uncle, by now exhausted and a nervous wreck, made it to the hospital in Kirchberg and checked himself in as a patient. A day or so later Americans arrived, discharged all the patients, and closed the building. No one questioned the ex-SS officer, who simply walked to a nearby hospital at St. Johann and landed a job as an attendant. An attic above an abandoned military barracks that had recently housed German tank personnel served as his living quarters. Konrad blended into the local population. Weeks passed without incident. Gaining confidence, "Franz Meier" made a few day trips to Kitzbühl, a small village lying within the French zone of control. Exactly what he did there is unknown. He also returned several times to Kirchberg to visit the relatives who had shunned him. The large sums of money he left with them on each occasion went a long way toward patching over the awkwardness Rudolf Meier experienced during his uncle's first nocturnal surprise visit.[4]

On August 11, 1945, agent Robert A. Gutierrez and Master Sergeant William J. Conner of CIC Team 970/45 were assigned to apprehend former SS officers Franz Konrad and Erwin Haufler. Both agents had been involved with the interrogation of Josef Spacil, who had revealed that Konrad and Haufler had been in charge of a number of personal items belonging to Adolf Hitler, Eva Braun, and the family of SS General Hermann Fegelein. These items, Spacil had told them, included correspondence between Hitler and Braun, the trousers and tunic worn by Hitler during the July 20, 1944, assassination attempt, jewelry, gold, and of supreme importance to the Allies, Hitler's diaries. Lieutenant Walter Hirschfeld, Captain Gerhardt Schlemmer's former student at the SS officers' training school in Bad Tölz, Germany, agreed to work with Gutierrez and Conner. Hirschfeld was assigned the mission of hunting down Konrad, and his initial interviews in the region provided him with several viable leads.

On August 13 Hirschfeld posed as an undercover SS fugitive and paid a visit to Ursula von Bieler. The former SS nurse who had assisted Konrad on the night of his escape from the Zell am See jail trusted him completely. She told Hirschfeld the entire story of how she helped Konrad avoid detection. She also told him his alias was "Franz Meier." It was now a simple matter for the CIC agents to follow Konrad's tracks. A trip to the Dollinger farm house produced an additional lead that took the agents to Schladming on or about August 14, where they met and interviewed Konrad's brother Fritz, his wife Minna, and her brother, Willy Pichler. Other than obtaining the address of Franz's wife Agnes, who lived in Liezen, wrote the agents, the interviews with the relatives proved "fruitless." According to Gutierrez, "the wife [Agnes] gave only the address of a relative named Meier, at Kirchberg, near Kitzbühl, Austria." Rudolf Meier, she told the agent, was Franz Konrad's nephew. If Gutierrez was concerned his investigation was going nowhere, his anxiety was about to lessen considerably.[5]

The CIC agents paid a visit to the Meier homestead on the afternoon of August 21. Both Rudolf Meier and his wife were interviewed. The couple initially denied any knowledge of Konrad, but after repeated questioning broke down and admitted he had paid them a visit three months earlier.

"He came by with a rucksack at the end of May, I think," said an obviously nervous Rudolf Meier.

"What was in the rucksack?" asked Gutierrez.

"I don't know, all he took out were a pair of shoes, some clothing, and a shelter half," he lied.

"What did you learn in your conversation with him?"

Meier proceeded to fill in several blanks, telling the investigators about Konrad's itinerary, a valuable stamp collection he said he owned, and the places he had visited. The man was seemingly forthcoming, but his information was vague enough to be of little use.

"Did he ask you to do anything for him?" inquired the agent.

"Yes," the nephew answered nonchalantly. "He asked me to stop in Schladming and inquire of his mother, his brother, his sister, and his brother-in-law, and see what had happened to the two truckloads of goods he had sent there."

This news electrified the agents. "Did he say what he took there?"

"Radios, foodstuffs, and liquor. He also said he once sent other items, but he did not explain further. He mentioned in this connection leather-lined trunks." The agents had struck the equivalent of informational gold.

"When was the last time you saw him?" inquired Gutierrez.

Meier looked nervously at his wife and then back at his interrogator. "This morning. He took a train from Kirchberg to Innsbruck a few hours ago." The Americans had missed nabbing the SS man by a handful of hours!

"When is he coming back?" asked Gutierrez.

"Tonight. He is coming back tonight," replied Meier.

The agents thanked the family for their cooperation and left. Rudolf Meier walked to the woodshed and removed the money his uncle has been bringing to them on each of his visits. The fortune was carefully divided into several large tin sugar cans and buried in the garden behind the house, safely away from prying Allied eyes.[6]

The Americans, meanwhile, made plans to recapture Konrad. Long anticipated, the event proved anticlimactic. Gutierrez waited until dark at the station. The Innsbruck train arrived at 9:00 p.m. and Konrad stepped onto the dimly lit platform. He was wearing German army trousers and a civilian shirt and jacket. The arrest was accomplished without fanfare. In his possession were numerous forged papers in the name of Franz Meier. Konrad was immediately transported to the Marcus Orr Internment Camp in Salzburg, Austria. An intense but largely unproductive interrogation followed late that night. Konrad cooperated on minor issues of fact only, such as his name and date of birth. He worked hard at steadfastly refusing to divulge useful information. What little he did provide was contradictory, evasive, incomplete, and misleading. One bit of information slipped out: he confirmed his nephew's statement that he had taken a few minor items "to my relatives in Schladming."[7]

After the frustrating interrogation Konrad was housed in solitary confinement and placed on a diet of bread and water. Three more intense interrogation sessions followed. The isolation and starvation fare did little to loosen his tongue. Konrad continued offering conflicting and evasive stories concerning his involvement with missing valuables that had been stored at Fischhorn castle and elsewhere. Armed with information supplied by Josef Spacil, the agents managed to pry out of Konrad that he had acquired a large sum of money from Josef Spacil, the former chief of RSHA Bureau II. Working with fragments of truth wrapped inside giant lies and misinformation, the veteran investigators pieced together the Konrad puzzle. The interrogations, coupled with other intelligence gleaned from Walter Hirschfeld's efforts, convinced Gutierrez that Konrad had disposed of a fortune in gold, currency, jewelry, important letters, diaries, and other valuables after his escape from Zell am See. The clues as to where some of this loot was hidden pointed solidly in the direction of Schladming. It was time to pay Konrad's relatives another visit.[8]

On August 24, Gutierrez and another CIC agent surprised the Schladming branch of the Konrad family. This time their trip paid off handsomely. Although no memorandums of either this visit or interrogations of the parties have been found, a listing of items recovered has been located. Inside Fritz Konrad's home Gutierrez and company found the following items:

> — The suit of clothes worn by Adolf Hitler during the assassination attempt on his life on July 20, 1944;

> — One chest of photo albums belonging to Adolf Hitler, Eva Braun, Gretl Braun Fegelein, and their friends depicting their private lives, including notes from Eva Braun's letters to Hitler, and artistic photos of both Hitler and Braun;

> — A chest of silverware with the emblem of the Polish crown. The silver was stolen in Poland during the occupation;

— Silverware monogrammed with the initials "E.B." [Eva Braun];

— Part of a valuable stamp collection consisting of fifty-one albums "obtained illegally by Konrad while with the SS at the Warsaw Ghetto (Jewish quarter). Konrad estimates that the collection in peace time is worth 80,000 RM [Reichsmarks]."

All of these items were turned over to the CIC Seventh Army on August 29, 1945.[9]

Gutierrez and other CIC agents spent the next several weeks investigating Franz Konrad's and Erwin Haufler's interrogation statements, talking with witnesses, and searching for additional clues. Trying to discern the extent of the stolen loot and what they had done with it was a laborious task. "Throughout the four interrogations," wrote one agent, "Konrad has deliberately falsified the majority of his statements. He has only admitted that which he has been forced to admit because of being confronted with the facts. At present this unit is in possession of some of the items which he still insists he burned." On the basis of this intelligence, CIC agent William Conner decided to drive to Ammerland am Starnbergersee on September 20 to interview Haufler's wife. She confessed almost immediately to possessing ill-gotten booty. Within a few minutes a fortune was removed from its hiding place and deposited in front of Conner. It included 91,000 Reichsmarks, a sum of English pounds and Swedish kronen, 5,000 Swiss francs, three gold rings encrusted with large diamonds, and four expensive gold watches. According to Conner, "The money and jewelry [were] part of the RSHA funds given by [Josef] Spacil to [Franz] Konrad" during the fading hours of the war. Frau Haufler acknowledged that Konrad had given the merchandise to her husband, who in turn had given it to his wife "for safe keeping." The entire cache was turned over to the CIC Seventh Army.[10]

A few weeks after Conner's discovery at the Haufler home Gutierrez and Conner dropped by Fritz Konrad's house in Schladming for another visit. The unannounced October 11 call caught the relatives unaware and struck pay dirt a second time. The Konrads sung the same tune initially, claiming they had nothing else of interest hidden away. After the agents summarized what else they had learned, however, the Austrians realized the Americans knew almost everything. They had little choice but to cooperate. Several containers from the Konrad cellar and a small chest from Konrad's mother's wardrobe were brought forward. Other valuables were also discovered and removed from the house. The agents thoroughly scoured the place. Virtually everything moveable was carried outside and carefully examined. The cellar containers held twenty-eight reels of color film depicting the life of Hitler and Eva Braun. The small chest contained four gold men's watches, a woman's gold watch set with 50 diamonds, and two pairs of expensive gold cuff links. Other parcels were found stuffed with 1,000 U.S. dollars and English pounds. Even more stamps were found. The items we recovered, reported Gutierrez, "had been left by Franz Konrad with his mother in Schladming." Konrad's relatives had been laboring under the impression the Americans would not return because they had already thoroughly searched the house back in August. After they convinced themselves it was a safe haven, Gutierrez explained, "the items were brought to the home" from another location. These things, too, were turned over to the CIC Seventh Army. When pressed on the whereabouts of Hitler's diaries, however, Fritz and Minna Konrad strenuously denied having any knowledge of their existence.[11]

The agents were not through searching for Konrad's stolen fortune. On October 22 Gutierrez and Conner returned to Kirchberg to question Rudolf Meier and his wife. "We know Konrad visited you and believe he left a large sum of valuables here with you," Gutierrez accused them. "What did he leave with you? Did he ask you to hide anything for him?"

"No, Konrad brought nothing here!" Rudolf Meier adamantly replied.

"We know you are lying. If you don't tell us everything, you will be in as much trouble as he is in." Gutierrez paused. "We found out all about what he left with his brother in Schladming. Now they are in trouble for lying to us. What did he leave with you and where is it?"

Konrad's nephew was well aware that Austrians and Germans had been detained or arrested for offenses far less important than sheltering an SS agent wanted for war crimes and hiding stolen loot. He decided to come clean and started talking.

"Very well, I will tell you," he responded. "Konrad brought here 400,000 Reichsmarks, some foreign money, and some jewelry." He asked if we might bury it here."

"When was this?"

"That was when he first appeared here with his rucksack. He did not bury this himself; I did that for him later. I put the money and the jewelry in tin cans—sugar cans—and buried them in my garden."

"Tell me about the currency. What was it and how was it packed?" inquired Gutierrez.

"The 400,000 Reichsmarks were in 100 notes, packaged in bundles," Meier answered, now almost relieved that the secret was out in the open. "The foreign currency consisted of Swiss francs, dollars, and Swedish crowns." He hesitated a moment, and then continued. "I'm not sure of the individual amounts. He did not give me the foreign money to bury. It was in a little packet which he had tossed into the coal bucket. Later, I took them out and buried them, too. As far as I remember, there are two rings and some gold dollars buried, too. But I don't know just how many dollars." Meier was not only cooperative, but full of information. But was he telling the officers the full truth?

When asked to do so Meier led the agents to the spot where the valuables were hidden. They were quickly and easily retrieved, stored away in four large sugar cans exactly as he had described. The fortune consisted of gold U.S. coins, thousands in Swiss francs, hundreds of thousands in Reichsmarks, Swedish kronen, a fragmentary diary kept by Eva Braun, and more. In one of the cans were two large gold and diamond rings. One was encrusted with twenty-nine diamonds and a sapphire cross; the other held three large diamonds. The German currency was all in 100 denomination notes, just as Rudolf had told them.[12]

"Did he offer you anything for your assistance?" asked Gutierrez.

Meier nodded. "Yes, he said I might keep 100,000 of the 400,000 Reichsmarks."

"What else can you tell us?

"Frau Konrad was here about one week ago," Meier revealed.

"Franz's wife Agnes?" asked Gutierrez.

"Yes."

"What did you talk about?"

"What else?" he responded. "My uncle and what has been going on. She told me she had visited her in-laws at Schladming. She was very upset that he had sent money and food to his mother and brother instead of to his wife and children."

This interested Gutierrez, who continued his questioning. "Did she say anything about any valuables or personal papers or letters Konrad might have been carrying or had hidden elsewhere?"

"Yes. Some time before that—I don't know exactly when—when she was in Schladming, she told me her sister-in-law [Minna Konrad] told her that the Americans had already been there several times and had picked up some of Konrad's possessions, including his stamp collection." Meier stopped talking. He had more to tell Gutierrez.

"What else did she tell you?" he asked.

"Her sister-in-law, Minna, told her that the glass jars with the writings and the gold were still buried, and the Americans had not yet found them," answered Meier. "She told Frau Konrad she would rather be shot than give those items up." He paused. "She also told me that she had 12,000 Reichsmarks at her disposal, which represented what she earned selling the radio sets Konrad had sent to her on two trucks in Schladming."

Fritz and Minna Konrad, apparently, were still concealing stolen items. "Did she mention anything else about the 'writings'?" asked Gutierrez.

"She talked about them and some photos and private effects of Eva Braun," Meier replied. "I don't know whether these items were the ones the Americans had already picked up, or whether they are still there."

"Did you bury or hide anything else?" he inquired further.

"I did not . . . other than the four cans." Meier paused and thought a moment. "One time Konrad came here on one of his visits and picked up a sum of money. I don't know just how much. I dug one can out, and then re-buried the remainder of the money in the same can."[13]

"Did he tell you why he needed the money? Did he hide anything else around here?" asked the agent.

"He said he wanted to buy a rug," answered the nephew. "I don't know whether he buried or hid anything himself near here. I did not see him bury anything."

"Did he ever mention to you how he obtained all of this money or what he needed it for?" queried Gutierrez.

Meier shook his head and continued. "He told me in the last days before the capitulation he had large sums of money under his control. I think he spoke of several million. He also stated that he had paid all the

Fischhorn personnel six months' salary in advance. He gave 100,000 Reichsmarks to one man—he did not say whom—and he said that man had burned the money."

"Did he take anything else to other places to hide them?"

The nephew shrugged in response. "He did not say whether he had taken anything to other places, or buried or hidden anything else. He only said that he would have liked to have sent to me the items which he had sent to Schladming [to his brother's house], but that he had not dared, because he did not know me well enough."

"Is there anything else you have forgotten to tell us?" asked the American.

"Yes, " he answered. "Shortly after you were here the first time, two women, foreigners, Slavic types, were here asking for Konrad. I had an impression they had an appointment with him."

This was an interesting new development. "What did you tell them?" asked Gutierrez.

"I told them Konrad had been arrested. They were shocked. I told the French military authorities about this at once," he added. Meier did not say why he felt the need to do so, and Gutierrez apparently did not ask him.

"Yesterday two other women were here," he continued. "The younger one was one of those who had come before. They asked what we knew about Konrad. I did not talk to the women but my wife did. This woman said that Konrad had to be helped, and that she would try to get to talk to him."

"Why did she want to speak with him?" asked the agent.

"She said that he was the only man in Warsaw who had tried to help the Jews and the Poles, the only one who had dared enter the Ghetto without a weapon. She also said he was greatly liked." Meier hesitated. "The older woman asked whether he had buried anything here at my place."

Gutierrez might have been more on his guard at this moment. The last bit of information—about Konrad helping Jews and Poles in Warsaw—contradicted everything he had learned about the ex-SS officer. Who was lying, Meier or the mysterious woman? "How did your wife answer her?"

"She told her no. She also told her about an article we had seen in the Salzburg paper that a Polish countess had received pictures valued at 700,000 Reichsmarks from an SS man from Fischhorn, out of [Reichsmarshall Hermann] Göring's collection. The woman then asked [my wife] whether the Polish countess had been named Barbara." Meier hesitated before adding, "My wife told me later that she thinks this woman was the Polish countess." With that exchange the second meeting with Rudolf Meier came to an end.[14]

It did not take agents Robert Gutierrez and William Conner long to locate two Polish women in the small village of Kitzbühl. They were found later the next afternoon. Frau Meier's intuition was correct. The "older woman" was the tall, raven haired, 29-year-old Polish countess named Barbara Kalewska. The younger girl was her sister, Kristina Kalewska. The countess had been Konrad's mistress during his tenure in Warsaw. The CIC agents listened carefully and took notes while Kalewska recounted her story. She had met Konrad in the Bristol Café in Warsaw, and in order to save herself and her family, which included her three small children, she manipulated him during the war years to guarantee their safety. As the CIC agents surmised, the "manipulation" meant she had become his mistress. Konrad, she continued, had intervened to save her brother, a Polish freedom fighter, from a German firing squad. He also helped move her two sisters and brother-in-law, Gricor Danturian, from Warsaw to Vienna, to Berlin, and finally to Kitzbühl.

When asked about his activities in Warsaw, Kalewska pleaded ignorance. "All I know about Konrad's activities is that he was working in the Ghetto, and that he was requisitioning furniture and other effects from the Jews. . . . I have never been afraid," she added, "but I was always sure that some day I would be questioned about Konrad." It was an odd statement, and one she would not have made if she believed he was just an administrative officer performing an innocuous job.

"I love him," she wistfully added, "and I will never forget that I owe my brother's life to him. I knew that I could not marry him, and that his place is with his wife and children, so I married Abbas Ali Kahn Rassul-Zade a few months ago." The marriage proved disastrous. "He was always drunk and very nervous," she claimed.

"Why did you marry him in the first place?"

"I never knew much about my husband," the Countess answered, looking rather dejected. "He said he was 37, but looked much older. I married him because I am no longer young and wanted someone to look after me. We had an unhappy life together."

Gutierrez wasn't sure she was telling him the whole truth. "Konrad was holding valuables for you, wasn't he?"

Kalewska looked puzzled and after a few moments answered. "While still in Warsaw I gave Konrad some things for safekeeping: a suitcase with underclothing, three pictures, and some jewelry—two bracelets and some rings. The pictures were by an Armenian painter. They are not particularly valuable."

"Did you give him any gold or currency?"

"I did not give him any gold coins to hold for me. I got the jewelry back from Konrad already in Vienna."[15]

Satisfied, the agents decided to let the Polish war refugee off the hook and continue their investigation in Schladming. As for the countess, she had nowhere to go and no way of making a living. They felt sorry for her. As it turns out she had no need to make a living. When the small house in which she was living later caught fire, Kalewska—the poor, broke Polish refugee—removed several chests of gold from the charred ruins and returned to Vienna. She was never heard from again.[16]

If Gutierrez and Conner had learned anything in their quest for Nazi loot it was that the primary players were rarely, if ever, fully forthcoming. Both men suspected Rudolf Meier had not revealed everything he knew or produced everything he had hidden away. The following day the agents returned unexpectedly for another round of questions. The Meiers sang from the same sheet of music, denying having anything else related to Konrad's visits. A series of sharp questions followed and Rudolf repeated much of what he had already told them. A few minor but interesting and potentially helpful details were thrown into the Konrad stew.

"On his first night here," remembered Meier, "he told me he had stopped to see some people who have a tavern in the vicinity of Zell am See. The Schutzingers I think is the name."

"How did he know them?"

"Their daughter had been employed at his office in Fischhorn," said Meier. "He had the package with the money with these people, and they had tended it well for him—I remember him telling me that. They were sympathetic to him, and he trusted them."

"How long was he there? Did he leave anything else with them he could not take with him?"

"I don't know. He mentioned nothing about it. I don't remember anything else except that he said they helped him contact the German military commander in Zell am See and had gotten a discharge paper in the name of Franz Meier."

"It is true, isn't it, that Konrad brought you money often?"

"Yes. Not only the 400,000 Reichsmarks. I saw he had 20,000 or 25,000 more marks with him. He always said to me, 'Here, take this too, I don't need it.' I put it with the rest of the money. He often returned to pick up sums of money."

"Did you ever ask where he got his money or any of the jewelry?"

"No."

Meier related once again, this time with more detail, Frau Agnes Konrad's visit a few days earlier. "She mentioned the gold Konrad had taken to Schladming. Her sister-in-law told her she would lie about it and never give it up. She said the same thing about some of Eva Braun's jewelry, which was still hidden in Schladming. Her relatives said they would not surrender this, either. Frau Konrad also spoke of preserving two jars of gold. Whether she had it herself or had been told about it, I don't know."

"These relatives in Schladming are still holding a lot of items and valuables delivered by Konrad, aren't they?" asked Gutierrez.

"I don't know. I remember now that Frau Konrad said, 'I also heard in Schladming that Franz sent diaries and writings there. The Americans found all that, however.' But she said further she did not know what exactly had gone to Schladming, and that her relatives there did not want to tell her everything."

Gutierrez queried him further about Hitler's diaries. Meier admitted some confusion about the details. "I know Konrad never mentioned diaries to me. He did often speak about 'writings' which 'might be very valuable some day.' In this regard he mentioned chests and suitcases, some of which were 'wonderfully packed.' He also told me a great many papers had been sent to Fischhorn. These he sorted and sent the most important to Schladming."

"Have you told me everything you know about Konrad?" inquired Gutierrez.

"Yes. I have told you everything," answered Meier. "I have hidden nothing further from him, and know of nothing else that Konrad himself hid. I don't believe that he buried or hid anything here at my place."

This time Gutierrez believed him. But he did not believe Fritz and Minna Konrad—or her brother, Willy Pichler. They had more to share with the CIC, of that Gutierrez was certain. On Halloween day, Gutierrez and Conner drove yet again to Schladming for another visit with them. He summarized the information gleaned since his last visit and demanded they turn over the rest of the stolen gold and written items. Fritz and his wife staunchly denied knowing the whereabouts of anything other than what the American agents had already found weeks earlier.

"Look, I know you are lying. Rudolf Meier told me you are still holding on to other items of value given to you by Franz Konrad," accused Gutierrez, who described Konrad's activities in detail, specifically mentioning personal letters and other "writings."

Fritz was clearly disgusted by the return visit. "If you are here looking for writings, I don't have any," he sighed. "You have seen everything which I had. I have no gold here, either."

"Then how did the film and other items we recovered get here after our first and second visits?" asked Gutierrez sarcastically. "You told us both times you had nothing more to turn over to us."

"After you were here the first time," Fritz explained, "we inquired of my brother-in-law what he still had and they gave us the films and the little suitcase."

The agents grilled the Konrads hard about the trucks his brother had sent and the items off-loaded. The writings and gold particularly interested them. Minna Konrad was angry and argumentative throughout the entire interview. "Do you think that we have the suitcase with the writings? But we really don't have it, nor did we ever get it!"

"Who said anything about a suitcase?" asked the agent.

"You told us yourselves you were looking for a suitcase with writings! You saw everything we have. We have nothing still hidden!" she shouted back at him.

When asked whether they were still concealing gold and jewelry, Frau Konrad denied the charge vehemently. "We have no more jewelry or gold! We never did have any gold, only the jewelry [watches] we already turned over to you."

"How did that get here after our first visit?" asked Gutierrez.

"When you were here you said that the films and jewelry were still missing. That evening I went to my mother-in-law and told her that. She gave me the jewelry in the box which I turned over to you."

"Who did you tell about the gold in jars you still have buried away?" asked Gutierrez.

"I am supposed to have glass jars filled with gold?" Minna Konrad asked incredulously, her voice rising almost to a yell. "This is not true! I never got anything of the sort. I said to no one that we had anything further hidden or buried! If I still had anything I would turn it over to you immediately, so we would finally have some peace!" she declared emphatically.

Fritz related the same basic story. Both husband and wife steadfastly denied having anything else of interest to the investigators. The agents nosed around the place but found nothing else out of the ordinary. With that, the final CIC interview with Franz Konrad's brother and his family ended.[17]

The next day the agents interviewed Franz Konrad's mother and Willy Pichler. The elder Frau Konrad substantiated the general story line told by her family and denied having anything left of value. It was a lengthy interview from which the agents squeezed little of substance.

"Franz was always in contact with Hitler and Fegelein, and he himself said that he had the letters, but he did not bring them here," she told Gutierrez. "He said he was taking them elsewhere. He said that Hitler's letters must disappear from Fischhorn. He said they would never be discovered."

"Did you ask him where he was taking them?" asked Conner.

"No. At that time that did not interest me."

"Why did he tell you these things?"

"Well, after all," she said with some surprise, "I am his mother! He can tell me things like that. I can swear to it that there are no letters here! No one else was present when Franz told this to me."

Willy Pichler had even less to share with the CIC agents. Except for some minor details his rendition of events of how the merchandise originally ended up in Schladming matched well with everyone else's version. He pled general ignorance throughout the interview. "Believe me," he told them, "had I had any idea what was included in the items which Franz sent here, I would never have accepted them."[18]

*   *   *

While the agents searched, Franz Konrad sat in his cell, utterly unaware that the Americans had recovered any of his loot from Schladming. Each time he was interrogated he was caught lying. The recovered film, for example, was just one instance of his routine prevarication.

"What happened to all the film of Hitler and Eva Braun you had in your possession," inquired Gutierrez. "We know you had the film."

"I burned all the film," he replied adamantly, confidently. "I know for sure. I know for certain that I burned the film personally. I remember that clearly because I was able with the film to get a good fire going in the furnace." The film, of course, had been seized from his brother's home in Schladming. He was lying again.

The agents began to suspect Konrad was a pathological liar. One nugget of truth was squeezed out during these interrogations. When asked about Hitler's damaged clothes Konrad responded, "I told Spacil about Hitler's suit because I wanted to have someone to share the secret. I was interested in keeping the relic for the German people. It is possible that decades later I might have been able to sell them in America for a large sum of money."

The longer Konrad remained in Allied custody, the more precarious his personal situation grew. Weeks and then months passed. News filtered into his cell that the Polish government was demanding he be extradited to Poland for war crimes committed in Warsaw. Damning evidence of his past continued to mount. In March of 1946 four Polish Jews came forward and offered evidence against him to the CIC. "All four were former inhabitants of the Jewish ghetto of Warsaw, Poland," reported one CIC officer. The Jews there called him "Ghetto Konrad," as a way of distinguishing him, as the chief of the "werteerfassung" (collector of possessions) from another SS officer in Warsaw named Conrad Franz. According to these witnesses Konrad "had ordered the execution of seven men in 1942." The victims had been members of a work crew "found by Konrad to have stolen some jewelry during their work in the house at Nowolipi Street 4, Warsaw." The rumor on the street amongst Germans in Warsaw, they testified, was that "Konrad possessed more gold than the Reichsführer SS [Himmler] himself." One of the four witnesses, Abraham Szulmann, testified that he "was present at the beating and slaying by Konrad of a Jewish boy on Nalewki Street in Warsaw in September 1942." He also "saw Konrad beat an old Jewish woman to death in front of the house on Leszno 72 in Warsaw, also in September of 1942." The agent who took the information "turned [it] over to the War Crimes Investigation Team 6836 for appropriate action."[19]

* * *

Gutierrez and his fellow CIC agents knew their time with Konrad was nearing an end. Pressure was being exerted by the War Crimes Commission, and Polish officials were becoming increasingly vocal about extraditing him to Poland. Still, they were convinced Konrad knew much more than he had divulged. If they turned him over to the Poles it was unlikely he would ever return. A last ditch effort to extract additional information from the Austrian native was organized. The strategy was kicked off in the summer of 1946 when Konrad was transferred on June 5 from the Marcus Orr camp to the prison at Regensburg, Germany. On July 2 Konrad's old nemesis Robert Gutierrez paid him a visit. The agent has a specific plan in mind. "It was not [to be] an ordinary interrogation," he later reported, "because that had been done so frequently by me and other people that there must be whole batches of his statements. I tried instead to appeal to his conscience."

"Konrad," he began softly, "we both know what will happen to you if the Poles get their hands on you. I can see that you are not extradited if you tell us the whereabouts of the remaining things we are after."

"I would accept this offer any time I could," Konrad replied. "I already know that I am to be delivered to Warsaw. I see my chance very well, what you offer me, however, I cannot take it although I would like to, because I do not own anymore or have owned anything except as you have found." He paused and then continued: "What would keep me just now [from] telling you if I really did own anything more?"

"Isn't it true you told Josef Spacil you had Hitler's diaries, suit, and correspondence?"

"Yes, I admit I told him that. I wanted to have another person to know about it. When the conversation took place, these things were already burned." Konrad was not going to play Gutierrez's game. His face remained "expressionless" as he wove the same tale he had spun a score of times before.

More questions and word games followed. "I never told Spacil I had Hitler's diaries," he added in an attempt to clarify his position. "Only that I had *diaries*. I don't know at all that Hitler kept diaries."

Although unsatisfactory, Gutierrez continued what he described as "word-play in the hope that he would catch himself or that he would makes mistakes, but he held to the description which we know well already, and which he tells with as much assurance as a poem learned by heart." By the time he finished, Gutierrez reported that, in his opinion, "Konrad can be (1) an entirely fanatical Nazi whom not even imprisonment and an impending death sentence can bring to speak, or (2) he really does not have anything else."

Feigning anger, Gutierrez ordered Konrad into solitary confinement. For eleven days he sat "incommunicado," living only on bread and water in a 3' x 3' x 7' cold basement cement box marked "No. 9." Operating on the theory that misery loves company, Gutierrez placed a German named Karl Albers into the box next to Konrad. Albers, who went by the undercover name "Peter Holtman," worked for Gutierrez. The scheme worked perfectly. Within a short time the pair struck up a confidential relationship even though they could not see one another. Albers encouraged conversation and Konrad was anxious to talk to someone other than American intelligence agents. The former SS officer told Albers "much about his past life." He confided to the German about his activities in Poland, and particularly his connection with the liquidation of the Warsaw Ghetto. Whether Konrad shared details about valuables or other items he may have hidden away is unclear.[20]

Albers sympathized with Konrad, telling his new friend that "all was not lost." Then Albers did something rather odd: he admitted he worked for the CIC. "You might be given a chance to work for the Americans, and I will help you get some assignment [with them]," he told him. Konrad was surprised by the revelation, but he did not think much of the idea. While he and Albers commiserated about the former's plight, Polish authorities demanded Konrad's speedy extradition to Poland. He was to be tried there as a war criminal, together with three women who had allegedly committed atrocities at Auschwitz. When he learned of the pending transfer Konrad told Albers that escape was his only chance to avoid a death sentence, and he would attempt it "at the first opportunity." Albers conceded that, given his Warsaw record, a trip to Poland would be a one-way journey and that escape was probably his only viable, if unlikely, option. According to official reports, "when our agent [Albers] realized that Konrad was determined to escape, he attempted to direct Konrad's movements in such a way that he could be recaptured if his escape attempt succeeded." Albers agreed to help him and gave Konrad "an address where he would be able to go into hiding." The address belonged to one of Albers' friends, a family named Wilhelm, who lived near Amberg. Albers told Konrad that he was slated for release soon, and that he would join him there should Konrad make good his escape.[21]

On September 4, 1946, Konrad and the three women were herded out of the prison and loaded into one of three boxcars filled with another seventy-five other alleged war criminals extracted from other prison camps. Almost immediately one of the occupants told Konrad that "he had removed one loose plank from the floor of the car, and that he planned to make an escape." By the time the train began its long and tortuously slow journey to Poland a hole had been ripped into the floor large enough for a man to pass through. Freedom beckoned anew. Konrad and two others slipped through the opening and onto the steps of the boxcar. The men jumped off the train as it slowed for a crossing north of Regensburg. The three separated immediately. Without money or papers Konrad knew he was unlikely to remain free for long. He had little choice but to contact Albers' friends. By walking and hitchhiking he made it to the Wilhelm safe house in Amberg.[22]

On September 21, 1946, Konrad made his last mistake as a free man: he wrote a letter to Albers and had Wilhelm's daughter deliver it. Albers immediately reported the contact to CIC officials, who learned that Konrad was living in the Wilhelm house near Amberg under his old alias of "Franz Meier." CIC agents placed the safe house under surveillance. Their hope was not only that they would apprehend Konrad, but that he would lead them to additional buried valuables or personal contacts. Konrad, however, did not budge. For two days nothing happened. On September 23 Albers paid a visit to the Wilhelm home and "asked whether 'Franz Meier' was still there." When they admitted he was, Albers assured his friends that his presence with them "was perfectly all right." Another two days passed. The CIC dispatched an American agent to the Wilhelm house who asked "whether they had guests living with them." Konrad overheard the conversation. As he later explained it, "When I heard that I knew that I was referred to and that I was in for it now. I considered the possibility of taking off for Austria, but decided . . . to stay." A few hours later he was arrested without incident and returned to the city jail at Regensburg.[23]

Konrad was vigorously interrogated over the next two days by Agent Ben Gorby. "Why did you go to the Wilhelm house and just sit there?"

The SS man was not as composed as usual. "I could have tried to get into the Russian zone of Austria where the Americans would not have gotten hold of me. However, since I trusted Holtman [Albers] completely, I set all on one card and proceeded to Amberg."

"Did you tell our agent all about your activities in Warsaw?" asked Gorby.

"What activities?" asked Konrad.

"You admitted to him your role in the liquidation of Jews in the Warsaw Ghetto, didn't you?" Gorby asked casually.

"No! I told him I might be shipped to Warsaw upon the request of the Polish authorities as a witness in the trial of a former SS officer in charge of the Ghetto," he retorted, "not as a war criminal!" Gorby remained silent. "My conscience regarding Warsaw is clear," Konrad added without much conviction. "That is why I had not tried to get away into Russian territory in the first place. If, however, you think you have to take me to Warsaw, I will not try to escape a second time." He was feeling the rough caress of hemp tightening around his neck. Konrad offered to work for the Americans. "I offer you my services again and assure you that you will find in me a determined fighter who wishes to break all the bridges with his past."

"Really? What bridge from the past are you trying to escape?" At that Konrad remained silent.[24]

The Ghetto King's last bit of luck ran out in Amberg. The Americans bundled him tightly, signed the extradition papers, and shipped him off to Poland.

*   *   *

Based on the outstanding undercover work of Walter Hirschfeld and the determined investigation conducted by Robert A. Gutierrez and Master Sergeant William J. Conner, the Seventh Army's Criminal Intelligence Corps recovered a fortune in currency, gold, silver, and jewels, personal items that had once belonged to Eva Braun, diamonds stolen from their rightful owners by Hermann Fegelein, photographs and motion pictures depicting the life of Braun and Hitler, a large pilfered stamp collection, and the clothes worn by Hitler during the attack on his life on July 20, 1944. Officially, all these valuables were turned over to the CIC. Eva Braun's belongings were removed to the Foreign Exchange Depository, Frankfurt, Germany, on November 8, 1945, designated as shipment number 76.[25]

The whereabouts today of many of these items seized by U.S. intelligence agents is unknown. Part of Shipment 76, for example, Eva Braun's small suitcase containing $1,000, was never accounted for in the final disposition of U.S. currency. As late as 1949, Mr. Ernst A. Jaffray, agent of the Bureau of Justice, was trying to locate the personal belongings of Hitler and Braun that had been confiscated and logged in by CIC officials. They were never located. Many of the photographs ended up in the National Archives. Recent inquiries by the authors as to the whereabouts of the more valuable items have been consistently shuttled aside. According to the government, these items are either in the thousands of crates stored in the Pentagon or have been stolen by U.S. Army personnel. In other words, they have no idea.

* * *

Franz Konrad's wartime activities in Warsaw and elsewhere, together with his close connections with the men who administered the deportations of Jews, gave him ready access to as much wealth as he could carry away. Only a small percentage of this was ever located by American officials.

Chapter Notes

1. "Interrogation of Franz Konrad," August 21, 1945. Konrad specifically mentioned his thoughts when the American officer predicted his fate for him.

2. CIC Report, "Apprehension of Hauptsturmführer Franz Konrad," undated. Schutzinger was questioned by American investigators and held for two days. He confirmed only that Konrad had lived in his hotel, left his rucksack there, and returned to retrieve it. He denied receiving anything from Konrad. After Konrad was apprehended and questioned investigators returned to talk with Schutzinger. The 50,000 Reichsmarks Konrad had left behind were discovered and confiscated. "Interrogation of Franz Schutzinger," November 3, 1945.

3. "Interrogations of Rudolf Meier," October 23 and 25, 1945.

4. "Interrogations of Rudolf Meier," August 22 and October 25, 1945.

5. [CIC Memorandum, "Apprehension of Franz Konrad," undated.]

6. "Apprehension of Franz Konrad," undated.

7. "Interrogation of Franz Konrad," August 21, 1945.

8. "Statements Made by Ursula von Bieler to Walter Hirschfeld," August 18, 1945.

9. CIC Memorandum, "Ownership and Disposal of Effects Recovered as a Result of Interrogation of Oberführer [Josef] Spacil, head of Amt. II, RSHA," February 4, 1946.

10. "Ownership and Disposal of Effects Recovered as a Result of Interrogation of Oberführer [Josef] Spacil, head of Amt. II, RSHA," February 4, 1946.

11. "Ownership and Disposal of Effects Recovered as a Result of Interrogation of Oberführer [Josef] Spacil, head of Amt. II, RSHA," February 4, 1946. The color film footage shown routinely on The History Channel of Hitler and Eva Braun enjoying a few private moments together is from the film Konrad stashed away with his relatives.

12. "Interrogation of Rudolf Meier," October 25, 1945; CIC Memorandum, "Recovery of Funds Pursuant to Investigation of Hauptsturmführer Franz Konrad," October 24, 1945. The questions posed by Agent Robert Gutierrez in this book are reconstructed from the responses recorded by those interrogated.

13. "Recovery of Funds Pursuant to Investigation of Hauptsturmführer Franz Konrad," October 24, 1945. Gutierrez recovered 365,898 Reichsmarks, leaving a difference of 34,102 marks. Konrad retrieved some of the currency during at least one of his frequent visits, which likely accounts for the discrepancy.

14. "Interrogation of Rudolf Meier," October 23, 1945.

15. CIC, "Interrogation of Barbara Kalewska," October 23, 1945. This interview is long and much of it does not apply directly to the subject at hand. Consequently, some of the quoted material is pieced together to provide readers with a clearer picture of Kalewska's relationship with Franz Konrad and her conversation with Agent Gutierrez.

16. CIC Report, "Frau Johannes Göhler, Bruck Bei, Zell Am See," August 14, 1945, unsigned; "Interrogation, Ursula Göhler," August 14, 1945.

17. "Interrogation of Fritz Konrad," October 31, 1945; "Interrogation of Minna Konrad," October 31, 1945.

18. "Interrogation of Frau Konrad," November 1, 1945; "Interrogation of Willy Pichler," November 1, 1945.]

19. The four Polish Jews working at Fischhorn and interrogated by the CIC included Abraham Szulman, Josef Kolnierzyk, Gerdalje Piernik, and Abraham Granas. See CIC "Memorandum for the Officer in Charge: Subject Konrad Franz," prepared by Meir Ben-Horin, Special Agent, March 26, 1946.

20. "CIC Memorandum Concerning Franz Konrad," by Special Agent Ben J. M. Gorby, September 27, 1946; "CIC Memorandum Concerning Franz Konrad," by Special Agent Ben J. M. Gorby, November 5, 1946.

21. "Memorandum Concerning Franz Konrad," September 27, 1946; "Memorandum Concerning Franz Konrad," November 5, 1946.

22. "Memorandum Concerning Franz Konrad," September 27, 1946; "Memorandum Concerning Franz Konrad," November 5, 1946.

23. "Memorandum Concerning Franz Konrad," September 27, 1946; "Memorandum Concerning Franz Konrad," November 5, 1946; "Counter Intelligence Arrest Report for Franz Konrad," September 26, 1946. There is some question as to whether Albers was a reliable undercover agent or truly sympathetic to Konrad's predicament. The reports are ambiguous on this point. Special Agent Ben J. M. Gorby may not have fully trusted him. Language such as "Our agent claims . . ." and "our agent admitted . . ." does not manifest firm reliance on his testimony. According to one report, agents refused Albers' later help in re-arresting Konrad. The probability that Konrad could escape was next to impossible. Just because he was "committed" to trying does not justify Albers' excuse—"in order to gain his trust"—for blowing his undercover status. Was Albers lured by riches Konrad had hidden away and offered to him in exchange for his help? Perhaps he was sympathetic to the German cause and the SS officer's personal plight. When he received the September 21st letter, Albers—wise in the ways of counter intelligence—may have suspected he was

being set up. If the Americans were on to him and had read the letter, he would be arrested unless he acted. Guided by this fear, therefore, Albers reported that Konrad was hiding in Amberg. However, it is also plausible Albers acted exactly as ordered. Konrad's escape was almost too easy. Did the CIC arrange it so they could track him to his hidden valuables and others in his network? Did the CIC arrange for him to be placed in an unguarded boxcar with a loose floor board and a ready-made stranger (agent) to guide him to it? We may never know. It should also be noted that Albers went out of his way to convince the CIC that the Wilhelm family "had no knowledge of Konrad's background," and that the ex-SS man had merely "introduced himself to them as [his] personal friend." Ibid., November 5, 1946. It is impossible to determine whether the Wilhelms were complicit in the affair.

24. "Memorandum Concerning Franz Konrad," September 27, 1946; "Memorandum Concerning Franz Konrad," November 5, 1946;]

25. CIC, "Report," by Robert A. Gutierrez, October, 14, 1945; "Report of Conversation with Mr. and Mrs. Fegelein," compiled by Walter Hirschfeld, September 22, 1945; Eva's Jewelry Ordered Sent to Washington," *Stars and Stripes*, December 5, 1945.

Chapter 10

"Eva sent me her jewelry at the end of the war with a
will naming me as principal beneficiary."

— Gretl Braun Fegelein

Walter Hirschfeld and the Search for Eva Braun's Jewels

Tracking down the myriad of leads, rumors, and clues strewn in the wake of World War II about the fates of individuals and individual fortunes was a Herculean task. The best way to accomplish this job was to infiltrate postwar German society with undercover agents—a difficult proposition indeed. Somehow informants with credibility had to be located, men who would be welcomed and trusted by a skeptical German populace and thus shepherded into otherwise closed circles.

The discovery of Oberführer Josef Spacil cowering behind a common soldier disguise in a prisoner-of-war camp opened the door for the CIC to employ one such individual. This former SS officer was willing to utilize his in-depth knowledge of the structure of the SS and personal blood tattoo to unlock the door and spy for his former enemies. His assignments would prove fascinating, frustrating, and productive. And in the end they would destroy him.

*   *   *

Walter Werner Hirschfeld is one of the more intriguing minor players and scoundrels in the drama of World War II. The native of Grossröhrsdorf, Germany, was born on July 21, 1917. His association with the Hitler Youth in 1933 subjected the lad to a steady stream of propaganda describing the advantages of joining the neophyte SS. Living as he was in a time of financial instability, the impressionable youth enrolled in Heinrich Himmler's paramilitary organization in January 1936.

His first assignment was to the Waffen-SS *Totenkopf* (or "Death's Head") Division and a posting as camp guard at Sachsenhausen concentration camp during the late 1930s, normal duty at that time for that SS Division. In 1939, his battalion was sent to Danzig, Poland, to stage demonstrations in favor of the return of that beleaguered city to Germany. Service with the division during the September 1939 invasion of Poland followed, as did active campaigning into the Low Countries in the spring of 1940.

Private Hirschfeld remained in France until June 1941, stationed on the coast of the Bay of Biscay. When a bomb fragment wounded him, Hirschfeld was transferred to Berlin and assigned to a desk job as an inventory control clerk. In this post he administered the confiscation of household goods stolen from Jews. He looked on as expensive furniture and priceless works of art were stripped away from beautiful villas and delivered to the lavish apartments of Reichsführer Heinrich Himmler and other high-ranking SS members. Hirschfeld also spent time procuring champagne, wine, whiskey, refrigerators, and pictures. Most of these items were dispatched to various command headquarters on the Russian front. While German infantry fought and died in extreme heat and cold on the steppes of Russia, the brass wined and dined in luxury. The obvious double standard disgusted the private.[1]

Unable to remain quiet any longer, Hirschfeld unloaded on his battalion commander. A violent argument ensued concerning the luxurious field headquarters of Himmler and his cronies. Fortunate he was that more severe punishment was not meted out in his direction. Hirschfeld was sentenced to the guardhouse in September 1942. Three weeks later he was released and transferred to an 88-mm antiaircraft unit on the Russian front just before the cold winter set in. There was a shortage of qualified antiaircraft officers, however, so he was detoured to an SS officer's training school at Bad Tölz, Germany. There, Hirschfeld met Captain Gerhardt Schlemmer, one of the instructors who would impact his life in a way Hirschfeld could not have imagined. When his instruction ended, Hirschfeld was reassigned to the 16th SS, or *Reichsführer* Division. Bloody fighting ensued in the defense of Italy, and later in the campaign to protect inland bridges and artillery positions from Allied dive-bombers.

In August of 1944, after suffering under a heavy shelling for three days, Hirschfeld asked for permission to withdraw his antiaircraft unit to a less exposed position. His commanding officer, drunk and sequestered in the safety of a cave with several Italian prostitutes, refused his request. A prolonged argument ensued before Hirschfeld finally received orders to reposition his unit near the front in the area of Pisa, Italy. A shell exploded in front of his Volkswagen jeep, which overturned and spilled him onto the pavement, fracturing his skull. The wound proved to be more than merely physically debilitating. Transfers in and out of a number of hospitals and sanatoriums followed before he finally ended up in an SS insane asylum in Giessen, Germany. When he was finally released in March 1945, Germany desperately needed every man who could walk and shoulder a weapon. Hirschfeld, however, had lost his stomach for fighting. Returning to the front lines to be killed in a losing effort was the last thing he intended to do. Instead, he worked overtime acquiring a venereal disease that would require hospitalization. He returned to his military unit briefly and was dispatched to Munich for treatment. When he was released, the war was nearly at an end. By May 8, he was marching into captivity along an Alpine road with thousands of his comrades.[2]

As we learned earlier, within a few weeks Hirschfeld and his former superior officer, Gerhardt Schlemmer, were cooperating with their Allied captors in the investigation of Oberführer Josef Spacil. The ever resourceful Hirschfeld ingratiated his way into the ranks of the CIC and finagled a job working for the 970th Counter Intelligence Corps, U.S. Seventh Army. Informing on Spacil's activities related to the RSHA was only his first assignment as an undercover operative. Convinced he was a valuable and reliable intelligence asset, CIC agents arranged for Hirschfeld to work undercover tracking down former SS members. Locating Franz Konrad was his first formal assignment outside the confines of an American detention facility. Hirschfeld had a natural talent for clandestine work and the know-how to pull it off. He was armed with a unique knowledge of both the Nazi regime and structure of the SS. In addition, the SS blood type tattooed under his left arm provided him ready entry into otherwise closed circles of German and Austrian society.

In September 1945 he was given another difficult task: establish contact and gain the confidence of Hans Fegelein and his wife. The Fegeleins were the parents of SS Gruppenführer (Major General) Hans Georg Otto Hermann Fegelein. The shadow of the younger Fegelein has intermittently crossed these pages. Now it is time to meet him.[3]

* * *

The ruthless officer who preferred to be called by his middle name, Hermann, was born in a small Bavarian village on October 30, 1904. The pursuit of a technical education held little interest for him. Horses—even more than booze and women, both of which would later lead to his downfall—were the passion of his life. He looked down on the world from the towering perspective of a saddle at a very early age. By the time he reached his teen years he was both a skillful rider and an outstanding jockey. He spent much of the 1920s crisscrossing Europe to participate in riding and racing competitions. When earning a living finally demanded his attention he spent a pair of loathsome years serving as a police officer in the Bavarian Territorial Police. Although Fegelein's early political outlook is largely conjecture, he saw his own path clearly after an influential friend from Monaco introduced him to the Nazi Party around 1930. On May 15, 1933, he joined the SS. His dedication to duty and chiseled Aryan features impressed Heinrich Himmler, who made Fegelein the director of the SS riding academy in Munich from 1936 until 1939. Himmler proudly looked on at the 1936 Olympics, in which Fegelein participated as a member of the German Equestrian Team.

When the war erupted in Poland Fegelein was dispatched to Warsaw to organize the first Waffen-SS cavalry units. His debauched behavior there almost cost him his rank and his life; only the timely intervention of Himmler saved his head. Service in Russia followed, where he led a cavalry brigade. Acting on the orders of the Reichsführer, SS Obergruppenführer (Lieutenant General) Erich von dem Bach-Zelewski, the Higher SS and Police Chief for the center section of the Eastern front, and the chief of the Anti-Partisan Units, directed Fegelein to commit mass murder. He and his men, explained Bach-Zelewski, were to clean up the lingering partisan problem behind the front lines and round up Jews. The men were to be shot, the women and children driven into the swampy region bordering the Pripet River and drowned. Fegelein executed his duties with breathtaking speed and efficiency. The marshy land (known as the Pripet Marshes) was not deep enough to drown the victims herded there, so bullets were used indiscriminately to massacre partisans and civilians by the thousands. Promotions followed.

The year 1943 was a pivotal point in his life. A severe wound earned him a one-way ticket back to Germany. Privilege and higher rank raced in his direction the following year when Fegelein married the plump but cheerful Gretl Braun, Eva's sister. His fanatical dedication to duty, close ties to Himmler, and marriage to the sister of Hitler's faux mistress catapulted him into the Führer's inner circle. During the final months Gruppenführer Fegelein worked as the liaison officer between Himmler (who referred to him often as "My Dear Fegelein") and Führer headquarters. The overseer of the Pripet Marshes cleansing exercise vanished in Berlin during the war's final hours. As Hirschfeld learned from CIC agents, they had reliable (if sketchy) information as to Fegelein's fate. The whereabouts of Adolf Hitler, however, remained an open question. If Fegelein was alive, he would have the answers. Almost certainly Hitler was dead, for U.S. authorities had interrogated eyewitnesses regarding his suicide. Only the Russians, however, who had overrun Berlin and the Reich Chancellery seemed to know for sure, and they remained tight-lipped about the entire affair. The surviving elder Fegeleins were a well-connected Nazi family living in the Munich area. They were also extremely close to their son. The CIC wanted Hirschfeld to win their confidence and uncover reliable leads as to what happened to their offspring—and to Hitler and Eva Braun.[4]

Hirschfeld suspected it would be very difficult to win the confidence of the general's parents, who had good reason to remain silent and keep their affairs private. Pondering how best to approach the couple, he decided to pose as a former SS officer who had played a major role in Operation Bernhard, the counterfeiting scheme run by the RSHA. Hirschfeld had become acquainted with the project during his work on the Josef Spacil case.

Hirschfeld arrived at the Fegelein residence on September 20 for the first of several visits. His knock brought forth Frau Fegelein, who admitted him, though with some reluctance, after discovering he was a former SS officer. Hans Fegelein was not nearly as receptive or accepting as his wife. Hirschfeld's initial concern was correct. "The work is very difficult," was how he began the day's report. "These people are well informed about the work we did at Fischhorn. They have good communications with Austria." Hans Fegelein was distinctly distant and circumspect. "The elder Fegelein is more than careful; his wife is somewhat less cautious," Hirschfeld observed. Fegelein continually pressed Hirschfeld "for substantiation." He asked him for his address and then wrote it down as if to later confirm it. (According to Hirschfeld, a man followed him when he left the house later that afternoon.)

"Why are you here," demanded a suspicious and obviously hostile Fegelein.

Hirschfeld took a deep breath and launched his tale. "I buried large quantities of gold, silver, and diamonds in Austria during the war's closing hours, and I am trying to establish communication with your son, General Fegelein."

The elder Fegelein barely blinked in response. Hirschfeld cleared his throat and continued. "He is one of the last high ranking representatives of National Socialism still at large, and I must turn over to him maps and sketches of where these valuables are hidden. We can use this money in the future." It was a convincing display of lying and acting, and Hirschfeld was an expert at both. The wary Fegelein listened closely but said little.

Quiet seconds ticked past. "I am in Munich to sell some rings I took from one of the hiding places."

"We have almost no money left," Fegelein broke in. "If Hermann were to return, he'd have nothing left." Was he asking for money? wondered Hirschfeld.

Have you heard anything from the general?" asked Hirschfeld. "How can I contact him?"

"I telephoned my son only two days before the capitulation," Fegelein replied, beginning to thaw a bit around the edges. "I heard from a reliable source that the English radio has broadcast that they captured him in good health. I don't believe it, though, that they have found him.

Besides, it was said to have been broadcast only once." Fegelein paused for a moment before resuming. "Even if the English do have him, that is better than having him fall into Russian hands. They have already sentenced him to death. Twice!" Apparently the elder Fegelein knew about his son's actions in the Soviet Union.

Hirschfeld sensed the general was alive and that his parents not only knew it, but knew where he was. They also seemed to know more than they let on about what had transpired at the SS-dominated Fischhorn castle during the war's final weeks. Each time Frau Fegelein tried to tell Hirschfeld about something that had happened there Hans would admonish her to silence. "Be still! That would not interest Herr Hirschfeld at all!" They were hiding something. But what?

It was slow and careful work, but as the hours slipped past Hirschfeld managed to gain a confidential toehold inside the Fegelein home. Gently but expertly he guided the conversation around to the topic of hidden assets and Franz Konrad. Did they know him?

"Konrad!" spat Fegelein. "No, I did not get any money from him. They should rather have given me the money. I would have distributed it honestly. That crook is certain to have kept it all for himself."

"Do you think he has much?" asked Hirschfeld.

Fegelein nodded knowingly. "I know that Konrad has a lot of money. He and [Captain Erwin] Haufler had a tin trunk or chest, you know, the kind the officers always have. There was gold and jewelry in it. They were going to give me some, but then decided to bury it." The old man paused. "Did you know that Haufler is in Dachau? I also heard Konrad has been arrested."

Hirschfeld feigned ignorance. As the conversation continued Hirschfeld thought it rather macabre that neither parent discussed the fate of their son who, more likely than not, was dead. "Not one word was spoken of the death of Hermann Fegelein, Eva Braun, or Hitler," he recorded in his first report. Instead, the Fegeleins spoke of the trio in the present tense as if they were alive and little had changed. Were they indeed still among the living? Hirschfeld was told that a large amount of Eva's baggage had been removed from Fischhorn castle and taken to a farm owned by Andreas Hofer. The Austrian native had been a high ranking member of the Nazi party and one of Hans Fegelein's closest confidants. Hofer's remote homestead now served as a safe house and message center for Nazi party members and former SS officers. Part of the jewelry was buried and the remainder stored with a "Doctor Winkler" in Zell am See. "The doctor has a large, fine house and surely no one will look for them there," added Frau Fegelein before her husband could shut her up. She was too talkative now to silence completely. Ursula Göhler, the wife of SS Sturmbannführer (Major) Johannes Göhler, she continued, "sent a Boeckling painting, a gift to her from her husband, to the Hofer farm." As Hirschfeld later discovered, Eva's sewing machine, toy wagon, and several trunks, contents unknown, were sent to Traunstein, where Eva's father worked at the hospital.[5]

The discussion inevitably turned toward Gretl Braun, Eva's sister and the Fegelein's daughter-in-law. "Gretl was here just last week," Frau Fegelein announced. "She bore a girl. She's now in Garmisch-Partenkirchen and is living with another woman. She is not in arrest."[6]

Before Hirschfeld could make further inquiries about Gretl, Frau Fegelein changed gears and began speaking about their difficult journey from Zell am See to Munich. The Fegeleins had hooked two horses to a large wagon with a tarp on it, packed it with food and a few paintings and luggage, and traveled home. "We did not bring much with us because we were afraid everything would be taken from us at the border," she said. "With the help of a few bottles of schnapps we were able to get everything through." We were followed by Eva Braun's dog, "which she loved so much. Suddenly it was missing at the Mangfall Bridge. And, can you imagine it? That dog went alone to Munich and hung around Eva's house there for three days. Later, it left and we don't know where it is."

By now it was late afternoon and Fegelein was obviously tiring. But the old man had taken a liking to Hirschfeld. "Will you have breakfast with me tomorrow? I have some good beer. Perhaps I can tell you more." That was exactly what Hirschfeld wanted to hear.[7]

The agent returned the next day, September 21. This time a warm and friendly atmosphere greeted the SS-officer-turned-thespian. He jump started the conversation by wondering aloud whether his dangerous work after the surrender was in vain. "No!" Fegelein said emphatically. "You need not worry that your work is in vain. You will receive proper thanks one day. The man will call for you himself and give you a commendation."

Did Fegelein believe or *know* whether Hitler was still alive? "Yes, the man is our Führer," Hirschfeld replied carefully. "But he is supposed to be dead."

"I think I can say with certainty that the Führer is alive," nodded the old man. "I have received word through a special messenger. That was not before the death of the Führer was announced, either. It was later after the capitulation, after his death had already been announced. My son hinted that he is with the Führer and that the Führer is still alive." Was Fegelein's son alive and in contact with his parents? "I hope they were able to get through. I am now awaiting word any day, myself. Gretl brought me news [the Americans] are looking for the possessions of Eva [Braun] in Austria."

Seeing an opening, Hirschfeld explained that he would have to go to Austria soon to see his associates there. "Naturally I would appreciate if you would stop to see my daughter-in-law in Garmisch," said Hans Fegelein. It was more an order than a suggestion. "I will give you a message to take along." Fegelein admonished Hirschfeld to be wary. "If you visit Gretl, be very cautious. I think things there are very different from here. I am not being watched," he said without knowing just how wrong he was, "but my daughter-in-law is certain to be watched. The Americans are very correct there," he cryptically added.

Of special interest to Hirschfeld that day was the traffic running through the Fegelein household. Several people arrived that morning to speak with the couple. One in particular stood out as important to the CIC's investigation—a well dressed and bejeweled Polish woman Hirschfeld understood was "the fiancée of an SS man." With her was the wife of General Fegelein's driver, Frau Klickow. Hans Fegelein rambled on while Hirschfeld listened with great interest to the conversation taking place in the next room between the mysterious women and Frau Fegelein. The pair were planning to make a trip to Bruck, Austria, to "bring back some things with them." A truck, they said, was going to be sent to Fischhorn in a few weeks to bring "everything" back.[8]

Hans, meanwhile, confided additional information of interest to Hirschfeld. When asked about the chest of gold he had mentioned earlier, Fegelein confirmed the story a second time. "Captain Haufler had a chest which was supposed to contain gold which had been sent by the Gruppenführer [General Fegelein]. I was supposed to pick it up," he whispered. "I buried a number of things about which even my wife doesn't know. In particular, I left a lot with acquaintances." Fegelein was telling him that the contents of the chest had actually reached him, and that he had deliberately not informed his chatty wife.

The conversation changed course again, quickly. "Believe me," Fegelein fantasized, "the Führer is sure to return."

This time Hirschfeld played it differently. "How can that be? That's impossible!"

Fegelein leaned closer and lowered his voice. "I know for certain that we will have a second war next spring, against the Russians. . . . I heard that from good sources. . . . They have released the SS [they captured] and have drafted them into their army. [Walther von] Seydlitz-Kurzbach and [Friedrich von] Paulus [two generals captured in the Stalingrad debacle in February 1943] are supposed to be busy reorganizing all of their old troops into an army. . . . Everything will be different. The Führer will then return and will call for you!"

The bizarre conversation persisted, the old man's fanatical SS beliefs rising to the fore. "The Americans are holding SS troops only because they know them to be elite troops! They are certainly retaining their services for the future war. That's why," he said, shaking his index finger at Hirschfeld, "they don't release the SS!"

Hirschfeld's second day with the Fegeleins wound down following lunch. He had to be careful not to overstay his welcome. "Well, Herr Fegelein," he said, rising from his chair, "I guess I must go now and see what my group is doing. I must see whether this woman has sold the rings."

"Please keep us in mind," he replied. "Perhaps you could bring us something tomorrow?"

"Would you like some cash? Do you need money?" asked Hirschfeld.

"Yes, cash is all right, though we"d rather have jewelry."

Hirschfeld reached into his coat and pulled out 15,000 Reichsmarks. He handed the money to Fegelein. The generous offer was made to win the old man's confidence. As far as Hirschfeld was concerned, the money could be "used as evidence against him upon arrest." The unsuspecting Fegelein thanked him profusely. "Naturally you must have breakfast and lunch with us tomorrow. It did not occur to me that you haven't any ration cards." Hirschfeld was heading for the door when Fegelein offered to provide him with a "letter" that would allow him to operate more freely and without suspicion.[9]

The third and shortest of Hirschfeld's meetings with the Fegeleins took place the next day on September 22. Like the others, it also went smoothly. The night before, during his debriefing, Hirschfeld had been instructed to try again and determine whether Fegelein had any concrete knowledge of Hitler's whereabouts or fate. The effort was largely fruitless.

The day began with fantastic tales of attempted murder, atomic weapons, and Hitler's state of mind. Fegelein wove a chimerical story about a plot hatched by Himmler and the Führer's doctor to kill Hitler during the war's final days. Himmler had the responsibility of getting the atomic bomb into action, explained Fegelein with a straight face, but Himmler sought peace instead and sabotaged the effort. "It would meant a change in the course of the war," he said with sadness.

"Yes. The Americans used it against Japan to end the war in the Pacific," observed Hirschfeld.

Fegelein scoffed at the statement. "As far as that atomic bomb is concerned, the Americans need not be so proud of that. I know for certain that this invention was turned over to the Russians. It is a German invention anyhow," he said. "The engineers who were in the Führer's headquarters at the last, and the Führer himself, were awaiting daily the use of the atomic bomb in combat. I would only like to know why it was not used against the Russians," he asked wistfully. "When the Russians entered Germany there was still time, and plenty of opportunities. The Führer realized fully that the atomic bomb could decide the outcome of the war, and for that reason he believed in a German victory up until the last minute."[10]

Mindful of his charge, Hirschfeld asked Fegelein directly about Hitler. "Do you really believe the Führer is still alive?"

"Yes, I am positive of it," he snapped back telling him again about the message he had received.

"When you got the message, were they [Hitler, Fegelein, and Eva Braun] still here in Germany?" inquired Hirschfeld.

"Yes. The courier told me that my son said, 'The Führer and I are safe and well. Don't worry about me; you will get further word from me, even if it is not for some time.' This man—an SS Sturmbannführer—also said that on the day when the Führer, Hermann, and Eva Braun left Berlin . . . there was a sharp counter-attack in Berlin in order to win a flying strip where they could take off." The elder Fegelein was confident in his facts.

Hirschfeld persisted. "Where did this Sturmbannführer come from?"

"He came from Berlin. He was on his way through."

"But that all sounds so unreal!" exclaimed the acting agent. "Many SS officers claim the Führer is dead and his body was burned!"

"Don't let yourself be taken in by propaganda," said Fegelein with deadly seriousness. "They are all trusted and true SS men who have been ordered to make these statements." He paused. "Keep your eye on South America."

At that moment another visitor was announced. Hirschfeld did not catch the name. Fegelein waved his wife off and told her to have him come back later. "You can't leave this man waiting," she admonished. Fegelein agreed and told Hirschfeld to wait outside in the garden. As he was leaving the man entered the room and shot a startled look in Hirschfeld's direction. The undercover agent immediately recognized him as one of Hitler's architects and someone he had dealt with briefly in the past. Hirschfeld excused himself and stepped outside.

After the brief conference Fegelein called him back inside. Something had changed. "Fegelein's attitude toward me was somewhat retrained and hesitant," noted Hirschfeld, and it took some time for the old man to warm up again. The conversation resumed without anything concrete being learned. "The Führer is in Argentina," and he got there "on a submarine." When Hirschfeld decided Fegelein had told him everything he knew or would reveal about Hitler, he turned to the subject of stolen loot. What of Haufler's chest of gold?

Fegelein surprised Hirschfeld with his forthcoming answer. "Haufler gave me the chest of gold. . . . Konrad wanted to have it, but I said I would take it with me. I gave the chest to Andreas Hofer, who was to bury it, and I think he buried it under some automobiles." Fegelein also had Hofer bury a few other items, including his son's riding trophies and various articles of jewelry, all of which were concealed inside a hay shed. "They are buried so deep that they are sure not to be found."[11]

And so Hirschfeld ended his third encounter with General Fegelein's parents. Overall the meetings had been very interesting and revealed much about the psyche of elder, well-placed Germans in postwar Germany. Other than fanning the rumor mill, they had produced few substantial leads. The best was a direct connection to, and credibility with, Gretl Braun Fegelein. The next night at 8:30 p.m. Hirschfeld called on her. Gretl answered the door. The strikingly pretty woman with brown hair and distinctive features lived with Herta Schneider in a small house in Garmisch-Partenkirchen. As an SS general's wife and the sister of the Führer's mistress she had learned to be naturally skeptical of everyone, and Hirschfeld was no exception. To his dismay and surprise, the letter of introduction penned by her father-in-law did not allay her suspicions. Neither woman, Gretl nor Herta, was talkative—especially Frau Schneider, who would not initially answer any of Hirschfeld's questions. "Instead," he reported, "they subjected me to a close cross-examination on the personalities of the RSHA, the Waffen-SS, and the General Staff of the Wehrmacht."[12]

Frau Fegelein was especially wary Hirschfeld might be an undercover agent working for the Americans. "I have visited Fischhorn personally with an American officer," she warned him, "and I have exact information about what is going on there." She paused. "I also know that Germans have a role in the work there."

Eventually, however, Hirschfeld "overcame the doubts displayed as to my identity." The undercover actor finally convinced the women that as an SS officer he had played a major role in a counterfeiting operation run by the RSHA. Their fitful conversation lasted until midnight. In accordance with Hans Fegelein's wishes, he offered Frau Fegelein 15,000 Reichsmarks. She declined claiming she did not need the money, but invited Hirschfeld to stay overnight in the apartment.

The next morning Gretl led him into a small bedroom. In a night stand was a small red leather chest. Inside was a complete set of turquoise and diamond jewels, necklaces, rings, brooches, ear rings, and pendants. One gold bracelet was studded with nine gigantic (8 to 14 karat) diamonds. "Eva sent me her jewelry at the end of the war with a will naming me as principal beneficiary," she said with both pride and sadness. "My mother had even more of Eva's jewelry. She is going to give it to my sister Miezi in accordance with Eva's will." The testamentary document had been smuggled out of Berlin by Julius Schaub, Hitler's personal staffer, and delivered to Gretl at the Berghof on

April 26, 1945. "It must be somewhere in Frau Fegelein's apartment," Hirschfeld noted in his report. Gretl told Hirschfeld that Eva had requested her to look after private letters, films, and other items of interest.[13]

Briefly the conversation turned to the fate of Gretl's husband, Hermann Fegelein. "Do you know where he might be?" asked Hirschfeld.

According to Gretl, Frau Schaub (Julius Schaub's wife) told her that her husband had been seen in Berchtesgaden after the fall of Berlin. "The Führer originally intended to go there," she explained. "Eva wrote to me in April that they were preparing to move out, but that the Führer changed his mind and decided to direct the defense of Berlin in person."

"But he never made it," said Hirschfeld.

"No. Herr Fegelein [Hans Fegelein] told me he had received a radio message one day before the fall of Berlin, in which the Gruppenführer [her husband] stated 'I am coming to Fischhorn tomorrow.' He did not arrive at Fischhorn," she said sadly. "I know nothing further about where he is."

"And what of Hitler's writings and the other items?" inquired Hirschfeld.

"Eva requested that I look after her letters from Hitler and the film," which showed the Führer and his inner circle of associates. "I gave these things to Captain Erwin Haufler, in person, at the Fischhorn, and requested him not to destroy these items, but rather to bury them." When asked why she did not destroy them she answered, "I wish to retain them as keepsakes and perhaps for eventual publication. I intend someday to write a book about all these events."

"And what about his diaries? Haufler told me he had seen them in the Berghof shelter." Hirschfeld held his breath and waited.

Silence hung for a few moments between the pair. Gretl shook her head. "Hitler did not keep any diaries," she answered. "The books standing in the air-raid shelter in the Berghof were not diaries, but minutes of the day's activities, which were kept by whoever was the Führer's adjutant at the time." Gretl had been there many times and was part of Hitler's inner circle. She would know. But was she telling the truth?

"And what of our Führer's personal belongings?" Hirschfeld inquired.

Gretl shrugged. "I am unable to concern myself with them. Julius Schaub arrived at Berchtesgaden drunk in the company of his mistress," she spat. "She was present and supposedly burned Hitler's personal effects." Schaub, however, refused to allow two of Hitler's secretaries there to get involved. "I know Schaub," Gretl declared. "He selected the most interesting items with the help of his mistress and hid them away."

At that point Hirschfeld began what he described as "playing off the statements of the father-in-law [Hans Fegelein] against Frau Fegelein." He tread gingerly so as not to arose suspicion. Small streams of information he had learned from the elder Fegelein were slowly dribbled into the conversation, including her husband's potential whereabouts, Hitler's ultimate fate, the fact that her father-in-law had hidden away gold and various items of value that belonged to her husband, and other similar matters. "[Gretl] did not find it strange that he told her nothing about any of these things," wrote Hirschfeld. "She pointed out she had only been married a short time, had had little contact with her husband's parents," and that the father "stood closer to his son than she did." Still, she asked Hirschfeld to visit Herr Fegelein again and "ask him where he had obtained all the information." The old man may not have told her, Hirschfeld shrewdly observed in his report, "because he did not fully trust her, since she had been seen often with American officers, and her father-in-law might have gained a false impression from that."[14]

"And what have you heard of the fate of the Führer?" asked Hirschfeld. "Do you think the story Herr Fegelein told me that he and Eva and the Gruppenführer escaped is true?"

"You are of course familiar with the rumors going around," she replied. "I would think the story . . . most likely is that the Führer attached himself to an SS patrol and was killed with them. That they all escaped is very dubious, but not impossible."

Unable to learn any additional information Hirschfeld prepared to leave. In an abrupt about face, Gretl blurted out that she had 18,000 Reichsmarks, but could use the additional money he has offered her the night before. In order to retain her confidence Hirschfeld pulled the currency from his coat pocket and pressed it into her hands.

"You will of course revisit whenever you have a chance," Gretl smiled at Hirschfeld. "We will exchange the latest news." Gretl may have had more on her mind than exchanging news. During the war years she acquired a reputation as a woman of loose morals; in Hirschfeld she would have met her match in that department.

"I gained and achieved this woman's confidence, and believe she will give me further information at a later date, and will also inform me if she should hear from her husband," reported the agent.[15]

* * *

Hirschfeld took the opportunity to carry out Gretl's wishes by visiting the Fegeleins one last time the next afternoon. This time the agent reversed the tables and used the daughter-in-law's statements as a means of extracting additional information from Hans. The effort gleaned little of value.

"I don't think Hitler is alive," Hirschfeld coldly provoked the old man. Fegelein, who was in bed that day with an injured leg, "raised himself up on his elbows . . . as the tears rose in his eyes."

"Herr Hirschfeld," he admonished, "You can believe me, I've told you no lies and no fancy stories. I know for certain that the Führer and my son Hermann are still living; otherwise, my life would be finished." His attempt to convince himself of the impossible was pathetic to watch.

"But your stories sound almost fanciful," responded Hirschfeld.

"I have no reason to mislead you, and have no intention of lying to you, one of the last true National Socialists." Hirschfeld must have enjoyed a quiet chuckle. "You must understand I have not told my daughter-in-law everything," the unsuspecting Fegelein continued. "As a woman, she must be satisfied when I tell her that her husband is living."

For the first time the old man acknowledged that a credible report was circulating that his son was no more. "Don't let yourself be taken in by rumors! They are saying that my son was shot on orders from Hitler because he was found running around in civilian clothing! That is nonsense!" he shouted. "I know positively that the Führer would never have done such a thing! Do not be taken in by those other rumors either, which state that the Führer and Eva Braun poisoned themselves and were burned in the courtyard of the Reich Chancellory." He looked directly into Hirschfeld's eyes, adding, "None of that is true."[16]

In fact, most of it was true. The father, mother, and wife all waited in vain. None of them ever heard from Hermann Fegelein again.

*   *   *

The final fate of Gruppenführer Fegelein is a lingering mystery. Hushed rumors of a summary execution sketched with elements of treason and desertion undergird the tale. It took decades before enough facts and clues became available to flesh out the plausible end of this loathsome individual. Although his destiny is not entirely germane to this study, he brushed against so many of the major and minor players in our story that his end is worth recounting.[17]

On April 23-24, 1945, a fateful meeting was held near the Danish border at Flensburg. The participants included Heinrich Himmler, Hermann Fegelein, the chief liaison officer between Himmler and Hitler's headquarters, General Walter Schellenberg, the chief of Bureau VI, Foreign Intelligence, and Count Folke Bernadotte, the vice president of the Swedish Red Cross and nephew of King Gustav of Sweden. During the war's final months Schellenberg sought to convince Himmler that Germany was losing the war because of Hitler's poor decision making, a direct result of his obviously deteriorating health. He urged Himmler to take whatever action necessary to gain the reins of power and make peace with the Allies. Himmler, slowly but surely, lifted one leg and straddled the fence Schellenberg had dared him to step over. Several diplomatic meetings between Himmler and Bernadotte followed. Each dealt with questions regarding the release of concentration camp prisoners and ending the war; tangible results proved elusive. After one meeting Schellenberg tried to arrange for Bernadotte to convince General Dwight D. Eisenhower to set up a conference with Himmler to discuss the surrender of the German Army. "The Reichsführer no longer understands the realities of his own situation," responded Bernadotte prophetically. The meeting of April 23-24 was but another effort by Himmler to craft a German surrender to the Western Allies rather than be crushed by the merciless Russians.[18]

Late on the evening of April 25 Fegelein flew into Berlin. Although he arrived in time for the regular midnight conference, he chose not to attend. That was not so unusual since he had been shuttling back and forth between the headquarters of Himmler and Hitler for some time now. Thursday, April 26 passed as well. No Fegelein. Hitler finally took note of his absence the next afternoon—the Gruppenführer had skipped six meetings in a row, a most unwise course of action. The Führer, his suspicions immediately aroused, ordered Gruppenführer (Major General) Johann Rattenhuber, his security chief, to locate the errant SS officer and bring him in. Rattenhuber placed a call to Fegelein's small flat on the Bleibtreustrass, just off the more upscale Kurfürstendamm. Foolishly, as it turned out, Fegelein picked up the receiver. He was drunk, but sober enough to convince Rattenhuber he would clean up and reach the bunker within a couple of hours. Fegelein, however, had no intention of ever visiting the bunker again. He was leaving to save himself. The intoxicated SS officer proceeded to make another serious mistake by phoning Eva Braun and telling her as much. He even advised her to do likewise. A hidden microphone in the switchboard channeled every call into Hitler's private study. In all likelihood, the Führer heard every word. Fegelein was a deserter and encouraging others to follow suit!

Rattenhuber immediately dispatched three soldiers under SS Captain Helmut Frick in a jeep to deliver Fegelein to the bunker. He was still drinking when they arrived; evidence of earlier consumption was visible in the empty bottles of cognac littering a nearby table. The Gruppenführer had not even taken the time to dress or shave. When Frick asked him to accompany him back to the bunker, Fegelein declined the invitation. Frick hesitated. Drunk or not, Fegelein was a prominent high ranking officer, and captains simply did not arrest generals—especially in the German army. The frustrated Frick left without him.

Hitler and Martin Bormann, the Führer's powerful private secretary, ordered out a full SS colonel and squad to bring in the deserter. The men returned a couple hours later, kicked in Fegelein's apartment door, and rushed inside. They found him standing at a table, freshly shaven and in a crisp uniform. A woman was with him, tall with shoulder-length blond hair. Both were busily packing her hand bag. The colonel reminded his superior of the outstanding order that he return to the bunker—immediately. Fegelein, still deeply intoxicated, agreed to accompany them. Meanwhile, the Gruppenführer's mistress excused herself and walked into the kitchen with a platter of empty glasses to fill with water for the cognac Fegelein had offered his SS arresters. Several minutes ticked by, but the faucet continued running. One of the SS men grew suspicious and pushed his way into the kitchen, only to find the window open and the mysterious woman gone. But her travel bag and lover remained behind. Both were seized and transported to the bunker.

The dangerous trip was a comic-tragedy of Shakespearean proportion. Like a prisoner of old, riding in a wheeled lorry to greet his executioners, Fegelein shouted and sang his way through the combat-ridden Berlin streets. The former unfortunates, however, knew death was waiting around the next corner; Fegelein was too inebriated to rationally analyze the seriousness of his predicament. Once in the bunker Hitler reduced Fegelein to the rank of private and ordered Gruppenführer (Major General) Wilhelm Mohnke to convene a drumhead court-martial. Contrary to popular belief, no trial ever took place. A stickler for military protocol, Mohnke knew the German Army manual inside and out. It clearly stated that no soldier could be tried unless he is of sound mind and body and in a condition to hear and respond to any evidence presented against him. Fegelein was "roaring drunk, with wild, rolling eyes," remembered the general after the war. "He acted up in such an outrageous manner that the trial could not even commence." Fegelein rejected a right to counsel and then "refused to defend himself." Simply put, the doomed Gruppenführer "was in wretched shape," Mohnke told investigative author James P. O'Donnell many years later. "Bawling, whining, vomiting, shaking like an Aspen leaf. He took out his penis and began urinating on the floor. He really was drunk; he was not acting." Mohnke steadfastly insisted it was Fegelein who "tore off his own shoulder [epaulets] and threw them to the floor," and not Hitler as some sources claim. "He called us all a collection of German assholes." The general could not try Fegelein in this condition and dismissed the court.[19]

While Mohnke pondered his dilemma Bormann rummaged through the mystery woman's valise Fegelein had with him when he was apprehended. Inside was a chamois pouch, out of which spilled diamonds, rubies, amethysts, opals, necklaces, diamond-studded gold watches (including one Eva Braun had given Fegelein to have repaired), and about $50,000 in various currencies. Of more importance to the Gruppenführer's fate was a pair of passports made out to the same woman, one British and the other probably Hungarian. (The names were different but the pictures identical.) Bormann already knew Fegelein was a deserter. Now, before his very eyes, was evidence of treason.

For months Hitler's headquarters had been the scene of an intelligence seepage, the source of which had been driving the Führer, quite literally, insane. Confidential conversations, promotion lists, and other information generated within Hitler's inner circle had been broadcast on British radio. Who was *das Leck* (the leak)? Now it was obvious. The woman who had been allowed to climb out of the apartment window was a spy! Fegelein—a notorious womanizer and drinker—had been sharing intimate intelligence with her in his bed chamber and she had been sending the information back to the Allies. Gestapo chief Heinrich Müller had been in the bunker for some time specifically to investigate *das Leck* when Fegelein and the story of the mystery woman tumbled into his lap. On Bormann's orders Müller's thugs dragged the disgraced, drunken officer to a secret Gestapo cellar dungeon in the nearby Dreifaltigkeit chapel. Throughout April 28 a now thoroughly sober Hermann Fegelein was beaten and tortured. Of primary concern to Müller was information concerning the identify and whereabouts of the female spy. Whether he ever revealed the information (or whether he even knew it) is not known.[20]

And then the dam broke: news of the Himmler–Bernadotte meeting at Flensburg reached the Führer's ears. The BBC broadcast the shocking news that peace negotiations had taken place between the SS Reichsführer and the Swedish Red Cross representative. "When the news was handed to Hitler the eruption was spectacular," wrote Himmler's most recent biographer. According to pilot Hanna Reitsch (who would soon leave the bunker) Hitler raged like a madman, thrusting the message into the direction of anyone he met inside the dank complex. How could his loyal Heinrich betray him as the Thousand-year Third Reich tottered on the brink of defeat? Himmler was beyond his immediate reach; his golden boy, the battered Hermann Fegelein, was not.

Hitler ordered his execution. Later rumors that the Gruppenführer was hauled out into the Chancellery garden and shot are unlikely. The most plausible account is that he was murdered in the basement of the chapel the same way others who had conspired against Hitler (i.e., traitors) were dispatched: hung with piano wire from a hook cemented into the wall and strangled to death. Just one hour later Hitler and Eva Braun married. The timing was impeccable. Fegelein, the traitor married to Gretl Braun, would never be Hitler's brother-in-law.[21]

Exactly how Hermann Fegelein came to breathe no more will probably never be solved to everyone's satisfaction. We do know that his corpse was never located. The final disposition of Eva Braun's fabulous jewelry collection is, likewise, an enduring mystery.

Chapter Notes

1. "Top Secret, Report by Walter Hirschfeld," September 19, 1945.

2. "Top Secret, Report by Walter Hirschfeld," September 19, 1945.

3. 307th Counter Intelligence Corp Detachment, CIC Team 970, "Recommendation of Walter Werner Hirschfeld," by Robert Gutierrez, November 15, 1945.

4. Padfield, *Himmler*, p. 294; CIC, "Report of Conversations of Mr. and Mrs. Hans Fegelein with Walter Hirschfeld, Acting as Undercover Agent," September 22, 1945.

5. "Report of Conversations of Mr. and Mrs. Hans Fegelein with Walter Hirschfeld, Acting as Undercover Agent," September 22, 1945. The statements are all contained in the detailed reports filed by Walter Hirschfeld. The conversations are reconstructed from these detailed reports. The CIC was well aware that General Fegelein's parents had spent a substantial amount of time living with Hofer near Fischhorn castle. American agents also knew that an SS sergeant named "Reinicke" had left Berlin with some of General Fegelein's personal possessions on one of the last flights out of the embattled city. The son's possessions were delivered to the Hofer place and eventually turned over to Hans Fegelein. The CIC had already searched the farm and recovered some of the general's valuables.

6. "Report of Conversations of Mr. and Mrs. Hans Fegelein with Walter Hirschfeld," September 22, 1945. Gretl Braun Fegelein gave birth to her daughter, whom she named after her sister Eva, on May 5, 1945. Despondent in the wake of a failed love affair, Eva Braun Fegelein committed suicide in 1975 at the age of thirty. O'Donnell, *The Bunker*, p. 186. It is said that after the war the name Fegelein was never again uttered in the Braun household.

7. "Report of Conversations of Mr. and Mrs. Hans Fegelein with Walter Hirschfeld," September 22, 1945.

8. The mystery woman was almost certainly Polish Countess Barbara Kalewska. Whether Hirschfeld had learned of her earlier visit to Rudolf Meier's home, and put two and two together, is unknown.

9. "Report of Conversations of Mr. and Mrs. Hans Fegelein with Walter Hirschfeld," September 22, 1945. The currency used by Hirschfeld was obtained from Captain Erwin Haufler's wife, and represented part of the money Haufler had received from Franz Konrad for safekeeping.

10. "Report of Conversations of Mr. and Mrs. Hans Fegelein with Walter Hirschfeld," September 22, 1945. Fegelein's observation about Russian knowledge of the nuclear program is very interesting. It was not publicly disclosed for many years that the American atomic program had been infiltrated by Russians spies. Was the German high command aware of this in 1945 as the old man's comments suggest? And if so, had the information, through General Fegelein, been passed on to his parents?

11. "Report of Conversations of Mr. and Mrs. Hans Fegelein with Walter Hirschfeld," September 22, 1945.

12. "Report of Conversation Among Gretl Fegelein, Frau Herta Schneider, and Walter Hirschfeld," on September 23, 1945. The report itself is undated.

13. "Report of Conversation Among Gretl Fegelein, Frau Herta Schneider, and Walter Hirschfeld," on September 23, 1945. The will was seized on November 6, 1945. It was dated April 23, 1945.

14. "Report of Conversation Among Gretl Fegelein, Frau Herta Schneider, and Walter Hirschfeld," on September 23, 1945.

15. "Report of Conversation Among Gretl Fegelein, Frau Herta Schneider, and Walter Hirschfeld," on September 23, 1945; O'Donnell, *The Bunker*, p. 186.

16. "Walter Hirschfeld, Report of Conversation with Hans Fegelein," September 22, 1945.

17. This brief reconstruction of General Fegelein's final few days is primarily (and shamelessly) lifted from O'Donnell's, *The Bunker*, pp. 177-215. Of all the accounts surrounding the Fegelein mystery, O'Donnell's remains the most compelling. The chapter devoted to this affair, "The Lady Vanished," is a model in historical detective work and the best effort in the book.

18. Folke Bernadotte, *The Curtain Falls: Last Days of the Third Reich* (New York, 1945), pp 105, 110, 144, 145; Padfield, *Himmler*, pp. 592-593.

19. O'Donnell, *The Bunker*, pp. 177-215. 180-183, 192-195.

20. O'Donnell, *The Bunker*, p. 197. O'Donnell presents substantially more detail corroborating the woman's ties with espionage and confirming her identity as *das Leck*.

21. Padfield, *Himmler*, p. 596; "Interrogation of Hanna Reitsch," October 8, 1945. The BBC learned of the Himmler-Bernadotte meeting after Winston Churchill's Foreign Secretary mentioned it to another British official, who in turn informed Reuters news service. Padfield, *Himmler*, p. 596; O'Donnell, *The Bunker*, pp. 214-215. Hanna Reich provided her interrogators with news of Fegelein's execution by firing squad, but admitted years later that all the details were hearsay. "Interrogation of Hanna Reitsch," October 8, 1945.

The Perpetrators

Reichsführer Heinrich Himmler (above left) and SA head Ernst Röhm (above center) are all smiles in 1934—even as Himmler was orchestrating Röhm's ouster from power and murder by firing squad. Himmler's *Reichssicherheitshauptamt* (Reich Security Main Office or RSHA) implemented the Holocaust and wholesale looting of Europe. *NA* (Below) A smiling Himmler looks on as his golden boy, Hermann Fegelein, meets with Adolf Hitler. Fegelein helped rape Warsaw's civilians of their property, and slaughtered thousands in the Pripet Marshes region in Russia. *NA*

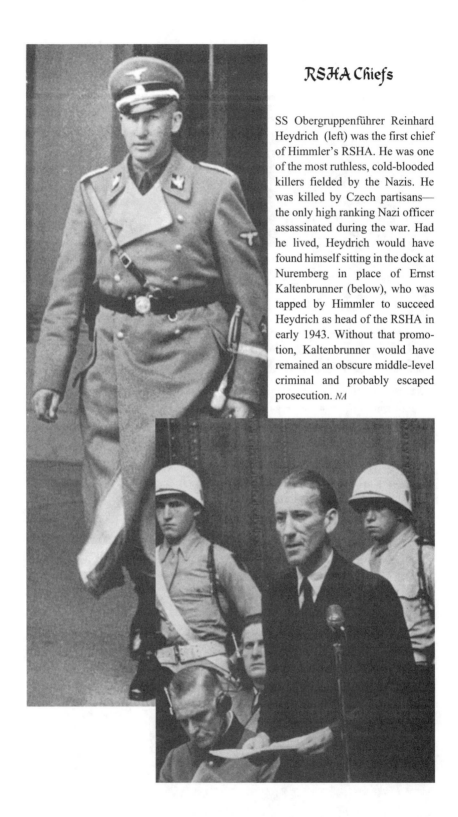

RSHA Chiefs

SS Obergruppenführer Reinhard Heydrich (left) was the first chief of Himmler's RSHA. He was one of the most ruthless, cold-blooded killers fielded by the Nazis. He was killed by Czech partisans— the only high ranking Nazi officer assassinated during the war. Had he lived, Heydrich would have found himself sitting in the dock at Nuremberg in place of Ernst Kaltenbrunner (below), who was tapped by Himmler to succeed Heydrich as head of the RSHA in early 1943. Without that promotion, Kaltenbrunner would have remained an obscure middle-level criminal and probably escaped prosecution. *NA*

Oberturmbannführer Kurt Becher as an SS officer during the war (top left) and as a rich businessman during the postwar years (above right). His bloodcurdling deal with Rezsö Kastner (above left) in Budapest, Hungary, came within a whisker of earning Becher a well deserved hangman's noose at Nuremberg. At the end of the war he was found with a fortune in stolen loot. How many of his millions were actually earned in the business world after the war, as opposed to money recovered from secret bank accounts or hidden caches, is open to debate. *NA*

SS Hauptsturmführer Franz Konrad poses here with his wife Agnes just before the outbreak of World War II. Konrad's heinous activities in Warsaw helped him acquire a king's ransom in gold, currency, jewels, and other valuables. Much of it was hidden in Austria at war's end. But alas, a return trip to Poland awaited the "Ghetto King." *CIC File*

The Ghetto King

CIC Entrapment

The only known image of SS Obersturmführer Walter Hirschfeld (top left). The SS officer-turned-spy helped American Intelligence capture Einsatzgruppen leader SS Brigadeführer Franz Six (top right). Hirschfeld's postwar activities as a CIC agent were shocking displays of excess. *NA.* The bloodstained clothes Adolf Hitler was wearing during the assassination attempt of July 20, 1944 (above), were hidden by SS officer Franz Konrad, and later recovered. Though ostensibly these items were burned in 1947, CIC agent Robert Gutierrez (above left, in later life) may have ended up with the uniform. *NA* and *New York Times*

The Moneymakers

This grainy image (right) depicts SS Oberführer Josef Spacil, the head of RSHA Bureau II. Spacil helped launder hundreds of millions in fake English pounds. During the war's final days, Ernst Kaltenbrunner ordered Spacil to shuttle truckloads of gold and currency out of Germany into Austria in an attempt to keep it in SS coffers and out of Allied hands. He may have largely succeeded. *NA*

This drawing (below) shows the plates used in the counterfeiting of English Pound notes in Sachsenhausen concentration camp. Declassified documents reveal for the first time that part of the operation was so secret even Berlin was not aware of it. *CIC File*

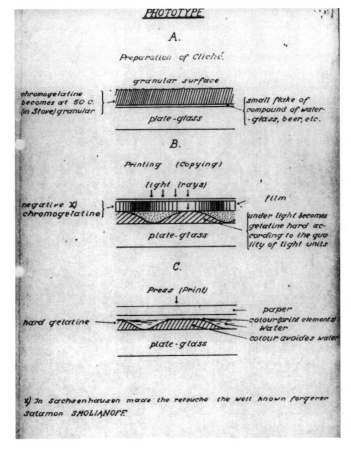

Gold in Blaa Alm

Lovely Blaa Alm (above) near Altaussee, Austria. Several SS groups hauled multiple millions in gold, jewels, and currency into this area in 1945; only some of it was recovered. Gold bars and coins are still occasionally found here by farmers and treasure seekers. Did RSHA chief Ernst Kaltenbrunner's lost truck of gold end up here? His adjutant, Arthur Scheidler, oversaw the transfer of at least six large sacks of gold coins from Berlin to Austria. A mistake resulted in a near miss: the truck made it into Upper Austria—where the gold vanished. Scheidler (below on a CIC file card), never told Kaltenbrunner about the mix-up. Evidence indicates the gold ended up in Altaussee. *NA*

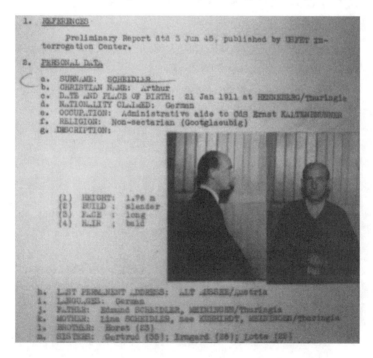

1. REFERENCES

    Preliminary Report dtd 3 Jun 45, published by USFET In-
terrogation Center.

2. PERSONAL DATA

    a. SURNAME: SCHEIDLER
    b. CHRISTIAN NAME: Arthur
    c. DATE AND PLACE OF BIRTH: 21 Jan 1911 at HENNEBERG/Thuringia
    d. NATIONALITY CLAIMED: German
    e. OCCUPATION: Administrative aide to CdS Ernst KALTENBRUNNER
    f. RELIGION: Non-sectarian (Gootglaeubig)
    g. DESCRIPTION:

        (1) HEIGHT: 1.76 m
        (2) BUILD : slender
        (3) FACE : long
        (4) HAIR : bald

    h. LAST PERMANENT ADDRESS: ALT AUSSEE/Austria
    i. LANGUAGES: German
    j. FATHER: Edmund SCHEIDLER, MEININGEN/Thuringia
    k. MOTHER: Lina SCHEIDLER, nee KUEHLMDT, MEININGEN/Thuringia
    l. BROTHER: Horst (23)
    m. SISTERS: Gertrud (35); Irmgard (26); Lotte (22)

United States Army officers inspect Nazi treasures. Tons of large solid gold bars (below left) were smelted from dental filings, rings, and even coins. Most of the Blaa Alm gold bars were thin pencil-size ingots—but from the same repulsive source. The cloth sacks shown in the remaining two photos (below right and bottom) were stuffed with currency, coins, and other valuables. Ernst Kaltenbrunner had a half-dozen similar sacks full of gold coins. All six disappeared in the Aussee region of Austria in May 1945. *NA*

Eichmann's Holocaust Gold

SS Obersturmbannführer Adolf Eichmann is the face of the Final Solution. At the end of the war "SS Group Eichmann" hauled millions in gold bars, coins, and currency to the Blaa Alm Inn. With the Americans and Russians closing in, and with the snow deep and heavy, Eichmann attempted to flee on foot. He was apprehended and later released by accident. Some of his gold bars and coins were later discovered; the bulk of his treasure was not. The Nazis smelted stolen gold from dental fillings and rings (like those shown below) into gold bars to erase the scent of death. *NA*

Eva's Letters and Jewels

Gretl Braun Fegelein (far left) and her sister, Eva Braun. Gretl married in 1943 SS Gruppenführer Hermann Fegelein, and bore his daughter days just before the war ended. It is doubtful whether she learned his true fate. Gretl ended up with much of Eva's jewelry, papers, and other valuables. The Polish 18th century silverware (below) was looted for Eva and stamped with her initials. Part of the collection was stolen at war's end by a CIC agent, the rest supposedly turned over to the U.S. Army. Where it ended up is anyone's guess. The silverware (and Eva's letters, diary fragments, jewelry, and other items) is largely unaccounted for. Odd pieces of "EB" silverware still surface at military shows. *NA*

The Bloody Red Cross?

SS officer Walter Schellenberg (left), the crafty counter-intelligence chief who ran Bureau VI of the RSHA, escaped a lengthy prison sentence (or worse) after the war by assisting Allied prosecutors during the Nuremberg trials and by providing intelligence on the Soviet Union he had gathered during World War II. Recently disclosed documents prove for the first time that he arranged for assets to be sent abroad during the war. CIC agents opened the investigation, dubbing it "Walter Schellenberg's External Assets." *NA*

One of Schellenberg's partners in his effort to secret wealth was none other than Count Folke Bernadotte, the Swedish Red Cross dignitary who thus far holds a respected place in the world's history books. He was dispatched by the U.N. in 1948 to Jerusalem to help broker a peace agreement during the First Arab-Israeli War. Israelis promptly denounced him as a Nazi collaborator, and gunmen executed him in a roadside ambush. Was the killing retribution for the Count's wartime collaboration with Schellenberg and perhaps others yet unknown? A new and important avenue of historical exploration beckons. *New York Times*

Chapter 11

"If, in any shape or form, Dr. Kempner should be mentioned as a protector of Becher's, the author and publisher [Sie und Er] will have to bear the consequences."

— Robert Kempner, American Prosecutorial Team, Nuremberg

Kurt Becher—The Only White Sheep in the Black SS?

ike so many of his comrades, SS Standartenführer (Colonel) Kurt Andreas Ernst Becher was feeling the heat in early May 1945. Spring had arrived weeks earlier, but the rising mercury was not what was bothering him. In fact, Austria was still in the grip of a cold snap and deep snow blanketed much of the country. The uncomfortable warmth Becher was experiencing came from within. Some who knew him would call it a guilty conscience. Was his inner voice tugging at him, reminding him of deeds wished undone? Perhaps. Others might hold his growing level of stress was the result of a clear conscience that only wished more could have been done to save the trapped souls under his charge.

The prospect of unconditional surrender was looming. Soon, very soon, he would have to answer to Allied and Jewish authorities for his wartime activities. The instinctive desire for self-preservation in every human being had been guiding Becher's every move for months.

Constructing an alibi-strewn dossier and an image of a savior of Jews became one of the immediate priorities of his life.

The only question now was whether he could pull it off.

* * *

The Allies were mopping up the last remaining pockets of organized German resistance when Kurt Becher drove up to the ominous gates of Mauthausen, a concentration camp in Austria. He had a specific purpose in mind for the visit; he only hoped he was not too late. Once inside he sought out Dr. Nicholaus Mosche Schweiger, an inmate who had lived within the barbed wire enclosure for a long while. Dr. Schweiger had been a member of the Relief and Rescue Committee, an organization founded by Dr. Israel Rezsö (Rudolph) Kastner ostensibly to help European Jews escape the clutches of the Nazis. Some had slipped away to freedom; many more had not. Becher knew both Schweiger and Kastner well. Both had negotiated with him for Jewish lives during Becher's tenure in Budapest.

Dressed in the distinctive black uniform of the SS, complete with tall black leather boots and a sidearm, Becher approached Schweiger. The sight of an SS officer was anything but uncommon in occupied countries; the only uncomfortable consideration was the purpose of the visit. Rarely did the SS make social calls. To Schweiger's surprise, this meeting proved the exception. The Mauthausen mission was to free Schweiger. Becher's benefaction was delivered with one eye on his ambiguous past, the other on an uncertain future. The doctor accompanied Becher to his car where, to his surprise, several boxes of gold and jewels were presented to him. Freedom, even in May 1945, came with a price: the safe transport of the fortune to Dr. Kastner in Switzerland. Becher also asked Schweiger to write out and sign a letter attesting to the fact that his wartime activities had permitted large numbers of Jews to escape from Hungary, and thus certain death. Before they parted Becher asked Schweiger for one last request: Would he send a card to his Budapest lover, Graefin Hermine, so she would know that he was still alive? "Since you have been in a concentration camp for such a long time, maybe you don't remember how to treat a lady," he added. "Don't forget to send flowers!" His Budapest whore would get good wishes and flowers; his wife and child received bombs and starvation rations in war-torn Berlin.[1]

When Schweiger agreed with his terms, Becher left Mauthausen and the pair drove back to his house in Weissenbach, a few miles north of Altaussee. He was there when the war officially ended. As an SS officer he knew he was subject to automatic arrest. He was not disappointed. On May 18, 1945, several CIC agents arrived in Weissenbach and apprehended Becher and a few of his comrades without incident. All were hauled away to Internment Camp No. 5. The agents fanned out and searched the premises. One entered a bedroom. When he knelt down and looked under a bed his jaw probably dropped open in disbelief. Like fiery dragons of myth and lore, Becher had been sleeping atop a king's ransom. The agent pulled out solid gold in the form of four plates and eight bars weighing more than twenty pounds. Platinum plates, platinum wrist watches, two hundred and six diamond rings, diamond earrings, and bracelets and much more. The whole cache required four pages just to inventory. Dr. Schweiger, who had remained behind when Becher was sent away, told the agents "he was liberated from a concentration camp by Becher." He, too, was in possession of a large amount of English pound notes. All of the seized valuables were turned over to Lieutenant Colonel Homer Keller, Property Control Officer of Salzburg. The loot was assigned the property number S3.3002 SA. In his report, which was filed in Bad Ischl, the arresting CIC agent noted that "Becher was in charge of transferring Jewish goods from Hungary . . . [he] is a very dangerous subject in this respect."[2]

On May 20, Becher was transferred to Ried, and three days later entered the prominent Natternberg Prisoner of War Camp in Bavaria, halfway between Passau and Regensburg. Weeks would pass before the obligatory interrogation all SS members endured. To his discomfort and dismay he was one of the higher ranking SS officers in custody there, a prominence he could have done without. Somehow he had to turn that to advantage, and he set about doing so right away. He made sure his military bearing was always perfect, his person always well groomed, and his manner always polite. Somehow he managed to keep his fitted uniforms, made in all probability by a Jewish tailor in Budapest. Throughout his stay in Natternberg, Becher steadfastly maintained to anyone who would listen that he had labored ceaselessly to save

Hungarian Jews. Even the morally self-assured American guards grew to admire him. On one occasion they even allowed him to jump into their jeep for the short ride to Deggendorf, where he dined with them in the Officer's Mess. Salutes were occasionally exchanged. Something was seriously wrong in Natternberg.[3]

One month after his capture CIC agents located another large cache linked to Becher in the nearby Austrian village of Bad Ischl. The Americans had arrived just in time to prevent the treasure from being appropriated by an unnamed French officer allegedly assigned to George Patton's Third Army. The fortune consisted of several hundred gold coins, including 132 Swiss 20-franc pieces. Other rumors about Becher also bubbled to the surface. According to Hungarian mechanic Joseph Lakatos, the bulk of the Manfred Weiss art treasures (probably looted by Becher) were stored in the underground tunnels at Redl Zipf, the same location the Nazi counterfeiters had used to hide some of their illegal product at war's end. Hungarian government officials in Budapest and the Hungarian Minister for Foreign Affairs made a request for competent American authorities to investigate the report.[4]

On July 5, 1945, investigators finally got around to interrogating Kurt Becher. He knew he could not lie about the basic and verifiable facts of his existence. So he did not. Yes, he admitted, he was born in Hamburg in 1909, and he was a member of the SS and of the Nazi party. Yes, he had served on the Russian Front and during the last year of the war had been stationed in Budapest, Hungary, where his duties including acting as a purchasing agent. And what about his actions there, asked the agents? His association with the SS or NSDAP seemed of little concern to them. Their focus instead was his behavior in Budapest and how he came into possession of so much wealth—at best, a poorly understood matter. The Americans, as Becher grasped it, were unclear about his war record. The proud SS man stood to his guns, stuck out his chin, and proudly recounted his wartime activities in Hungary. Or at least some of them.

His only noteworthy position in Budapest, he declared, was his position on the staff of SS Sturmscharführer (Major) Dieter Wisliceny, deputy to Adolf Eichmann, from March until December 1944. But their activities had nothing to do with mine, he adamantly insisted. Thousands of Jews were alive today because he had arranged for them to flee Hungary for Switzerland and Portugal. He had been in contact in St. Gall with Saly Mayer, the head of the Swiss Federation of Jewish Communities, and Roswell McClelland, an American diplomat representing the War Refugee Board and the personal representative of the now-deceased President Franklin Roosevelt. The entire purpose of these missions was humanitarian, explained Becher. The former SS officer showed his moxie by producing a copy of the letter from Dr. Schweiger documenting his testimony. And the wealth discovered in his home after the war? He had no explanation for how the gold and jewels ended up beneath a bed in the house he occupied. After all, many people came and went during the war's final days.[5]

Becher continued telling anyone who would listen—and even some who would not—how well he had treated Hungary's Jews. It was the same boastful story in Natternberg, and later in Budapest and eventually, Nuremberg. His jailers and some of the Germans in custody gave him the nickname "Juden-Becher." Some unnamed American went even further. Becher had stood up to the Nazi-sponsored Holocaust in the face of substantial personal danger. He was, claimed the soldier, "the only white sheep in the black SS." But Becher's SS colleagues knew better. SS Standartenführer (Colonel) Eugen Steimle, a former power figure in the Einsatzgruppen squad (and thus a prominent war criminal), laughed when he heard of Becher's new nickname. "When it became known in Nuremberg that the Americans called Becher the only white sheep in the black SS," he said, "a tremendous roar broke out in the cells of the Nuremberg prison, it seemed so grotesque!" Few German prisoners were about to inform the Americans about the man now in their custody. Ultimately they were all in the same boat, and who knew what information Heinrich Himmler's trusted former officer had up his sleeve about their own activities? Silence was the safer course of action.[6]

On October 3, 1945, Becher was transferred to the camp in Oberursel, near Frankfurt. A few weeks earlier American authorities had sent a notice to the Hungarians that Becher was in custody and that he may be of interest to them. To Becher's dismay they took the Americans up on the offer and he was shipped to Budapest on November 3, 1945. The Hungarians had a different take on the Hamburg native than his Allied jailers and they moved against him with breathtaking speed. Before the end of the year he was sitting in the dock for war crimes. Unfortunately little is known about this trial. The Communists purged their archives in 1948 and again in 1956. As a result, much of the internal documentation of Hungary's World War II history is simply no more. We do know that Becher continued denying having anything to do with the killing of Jews. In an effort to cleanse himself through association he sung the praises of his relationship with Dr. Wilhelm Billitz, the former Manfred Weiss manager who had died a mysterious death in 1945 while in Becher's company in Vienna. "I had a close men's friendship," he testified, "and therefore I was attacked by Hungarian as well as German persons of high standing. . . . In connection with this, I should mention that, because of this, personal and social connections with other Hungarians and Germans were ruined." The story was a bald-faced lie spun from whole cloth. Becher had no social relationship with Billitz and had never even seen the inside of his home. Mrs. Elisabeth Billitz testified she only saw Becher twice—once in her husband's office, and again when she passed him on the stairs leading up to the factory office. Her husband, she explained, never spoke of Becher in a way that led her to believe an enduring friendship existed. What Becher did not reveal was just as telling. Not a word was mentioned about how Billitz had tried to sabotage the dismantling of the Weiss factory or that he had been forced at the point of a gun to accompany Becher to Vienna. Without these key bits of testimony Billitz looked like a collaborator in the eyes of many Hungarians. Of course Becher had contact with a large number of Jews—that was unavoidable given his duties as Himmler's industrial thief. But the story dovetailed nicely with the public relations framework of lies Becher constructed around himself. Apparently the Hungarian judges decided they did not have enough evidence to convict Becher.[7]

Although it was not his intent (and he would not have cared anyway) Becher's claim of a close friendship with Billitz during his trial in Hungary hurt both the image of the dead man and the living widow. Elisabeth Billitz was the one who suffered as a result. Many now looked upon her as the wife of a traitor. Following the war the she took a job with the Hungarian Equestrian Organization. She lost her work and was questioned extensively by the police when her employer learned she had met Kurt Becher and the Eichmanns during the war. Later, when she tried to scrape out a living driving a taxi the communists took away her driver's license. Not until 1956 was she left alone to earn a meager existence as an insurance agent. She knew her husband had accumulated a substantial bank account in Switzerland before the war with money earned through a partnership he had set up with a pipe-making factory in South America. The information for the account was with her husband in his briefcase when he left with Becher for Vienna. She never gained access to the account. Perhaps the money still resides in a Swiss bank account; or, more likely, someone found the information inside Billitz's briefcase and took possession of it.[8]

*   *   *

Kurt Becher narrowly escaped the hangman's noose in Hungary, but his problems were only beginning. As he soon learned and probably long suspected, the Allies were now beginning to consider him a war criminal. The Americans had clamored for his return from Budapest to Oberursel so they could prepare a case against him for crimes committed at the Melk Concentration camp, a sub-camp at Mauthausen. Although Melk was not a death camp, it was a slave labor operation that resulted in the death of several thousand people. A large, new and advanced gas chamber and crematorium were built there in early 1945—stark evidence the Nazis intended to turn the camp into an extermination facility; only the end of the war prevented their use. Becher later claimed he did not visit Melk until the end of April 1945. He also insisted that the first concentration camp he witnessed on the inside was Bergen-Belsen on April 10, 1945. It looked like he would have an opportunity to present his case when the Americans got their hands on him again on January 8, 1946, when the Hungarians shipped Becher back to Oberursel.

There, he was grilled over a period of two weeks by Lieutenant Richard A. Gutman, an Allied interrogator who quickly grew to despise the former SS officer. "When Becher was brought to me the first time, I only knew that he was an imprisoned SS-Officer," explained Gutman. "Only as such did he interest me." On March 26, Gutman had Becher transported via jeep to the jail at Nuremberg. "During the trip, he suddenly sprang to attention, while seated, and addressed me by my military rank, and thanked me respectfully for [agreeing to] keep him in isolation," recalled Gutman, who had inserted Becher in isolation because he simply could no longer stand his constant bragging about how many Jews he had saved. According to Gutman, Becher told him that the "isolation" had given him the opportunity to think about all the horrible events that had taken place. Gutman remembered the moment clearly. It was "an illustration of the fact that people like Becher either attack you or squirm at your feet. It is the Master-Slave concept; when they know that they are no longer the master, they act like a slave—at least as long as it is to their advantage."[9]

The Becher case, in particular, bothered Gutman for the rest of his days. As he later put it,

> After several interrogations and in Becher's writings of his life's story, I learned about his background and close relationships with Himmler and Eichmann, and about his activities in Hungary. I remember the interrogations (which lasted 2 weeks) and many details very well, because they were among the most important of my charge. They never satisfied me, because I could not prove my inner conviction that this man was a war criminal. I have to underscore that the interrogations were only short interviews, to determine whether the prisoner was of interest for the International Military Court in Nuremberg. It was not my duty to investigate the war criminals, for which I didn't have the necessary staff, nor the time and equipment. But in all those years since 1946, I have questioned myself, if I didn't neglect bringing a notorious criminal to justice.[10]

Matters continued to look bleak for Becher when in late April 1946 the Americans prepared "List Number 8," an updated accounting of those men the United States considered to be war criminals. Kurt Becher's name was prominent on the register, a man noted as being "wanted by the United States for murder." The American Army did not place someone on a list of war criminals for murder without careful consideration and just cause. The prosecution of someone in a concentration camp court case was a very serious matter. Curiously, Becher was added to the list *after* he was interrogated repeatedly by Lieutenant Gutman, who specifically recollected that he was not sure whether Becher was a war criminal or not. If Gutman did not recommend Becher for indictment, who did? We don't know. We do know that a lack of personnel, the general chaotic situation in postwar Europe, and the ongoing Nuremberg trials of the major war criminals made it difficult to move against second or third tier men like Becher. And so he and hundreds more like him sat in custody awaiting their turn at the bar of justice.

Becher languished in jail for several months while the Americans determined whether to try him for war crimes. Luck, however, was about to waltz on his shoulders—this time in the form of Dr. Israel Rezsö (Rudolph) Kastner. Becher's erstwhile Hungarian acquaintance and partner in the selling of Jewish lives for gold and jewels appeared suddenly that July. He arrived from England, where he had been venerated by the English as a hero since September of 1945. Kastner had executed a sworn statement in England on September 13, 1945, in which he claimed that "SS Standartenführer Kurt Becher took me under his wing . . . He was anxious to demonstrate after the Fall of 1944 that he disapproved the deportation and extermination and endeavored consistently to furnish me with the evidence he tried to save the Jews." At Nuremberg Kastner portrayed himself to the Americans as an important Jewish voice speaking for the Jewish Agency and the Jewish World Congress. He had arrived, he boldly announced to the stunned Americans, to plead for the release of Kurt Becher. Robert Kempner, a representative of the primary American prosecutor in Nuremberg, introduced Kastner to several prominent judicial officials including Lieutenant Kurt Ponger and Captain Walter H Rapp, members of the American legal delegation who were also preparing cases against major Nazis like Hermann Göring and Ernst Kaltenbrunner.

To the best of Kempner's knowledge Kastner had traveled to Nuremberg voluntarily to testify on Becher's behalf. The fact that a prominent Jew would travel at his own expense across Europe to assist in the defense of a prominent former SS officer shocked many observers. Until the Hungarian arrived, Becher was just one of many under Kempner's jurisdiction awaiting formal indictment. The persistent Kastner visited with the judicial officials regularly. His repeated pleas on Becher's behalf slowly but inevitably tilted the balance in Becher's favor. From that day on the Americans extended to him many kindnesses and courtesies withheld from other inmates.[11]

The results of Kastner's efforts were soon noticeable to anyone paying attention. Several people on Captain Rapp's staff begin treating Kastner like royalty and went out of their way to help him. Rapp even noticed that court officials engaged in friendly conversations with Kurt

Becher, behavior the American captain considered both against the rules and shocking given his SS background. When he complained, Rapp's superiors told him that Becher was a special case and the behavior was justified. After all, how many times does a prominent member of the Jewish race voluntarily offer proof that a former high-standing SS officer personally intervened to save thousands of Jews? Therefore, went the mushy reasoning, Becher simply could not be a war criminal.[12]

Soon after his arrival Kastner submitted the sworn statement (Document 2605-PS) on Becher's behalf that he had executed in England: the SS officer had helped save tens of thousands of lives and had worked hard during the war's final year to slow down and even stop the mass execution of Hungary's Jews. Maybe the Americans were right after all—they had found the only white sheep in the black SS. A stalemate of sorts ensued as the fervor to investigate and prosecute Becher waned. Captain Rapp was smart enough to see the way the tide was running: SS Standartenführer Kurt Andreas Ernst Becher would never be prosecuted. Someone, somewhere, was protecting this man. Rapp and his staff had better things to do than waste their time on a dead end. According to Rapp, "all further investigations . . . were discontinued when Kastner informed them about Becher's self-sacrificing, if not heroic deeds." Richard Gutman, the man who had interrogated Becher, also confirmed that Dr. Kastner's intercession led to a halt of his investigation. An obvious war criminal with intimate ties to Heinrich Himmler and Adolf Eichmann was about to go free. Within a few weeks the SS's most opportunistic survivor was transferred from the jail at Nuremberg to the voluntary witness wing of the Nuremberg prison. He was one step away from becoming a free man.

*   *   *

From the witness wing, Becher followed with deep interest the ongoing trials of the major war criminals sitting in the court's dock. The large number of death sentences could not have come as a surprise to him. In early 1947 he felt compelled to pen a nineteen-page "explanation" of his alleged humanitarian activities in Hungary during 1944-1945. It was impossible to report everything in detail, he wrote, but he had worked "at great personal risk" to save lives. According to his calculations, between 120,000 and 150,000 Hungarian Jews were not deported from Budapest because of his efforts. The 80,000 Jews crammed into the Budapest ghetto were not evacuated to the death camps because of his objections and exertions on their behalf. He alone, he continued, had helped mold and influence Heinrich Himmler's orders seeking a halt to mass executions and deportations during the war's final months. Credit for gaining humane treatment of Jews in several concentration camps, and for the destruction of the gas chamber and incinerators in Auschwitz near war's end, he averred, should be deposited on his doorstep alone. The master of half-truths and outright lies was still busy weaving his safety net. In truth, he was not a savior of people, but rather a manager of lives. If he ever saved anyone it was only a means to an end, an avenue to increase the holdings and wealth of the SS at the expense of the innocent. He was a good SS officer, and in Hungary and elsewhere he had done his duty well.

At some point Becher was allowed to move into an apartment close to Nuremberg during the final months of his detention. How long this house arrest charade continued is not known. Nor do we know exactly when he was released from custody, but by Christmas 1947 or shortly after the turn of the year 1948, Kurt Becher was a free man.[13]

While Becher was busy writing his outrageous apologia, others were determining what would happen to the ill-gotten fruits of his Nazi past. Those treasures seized in Austria and deemed "of an unrestitutable character," concluded the Americans, would be turned over to the International Government Committee on Refugees and the Jewish Agency for Palestine. A large portion of this confiscated fortune included what was labeled "the Kurt Becher Deposit," a holding containing "gold coins, bullion, and assorted jewelry." The files inventorying this "looted property" were numbered S 3.3001 SA, and S 3.33002 SA. The fortune had been sitting for almost two years in the Austrian National Bank in Salzburg. On March 10, 1947, tens of millions of dollars worth of gold and jewels—including Becher's large cache—were loaded onto several trucks and driven to Buchs, Austria, on the Swiss border. At 5:00 p.m. the following day, Drs. Dagobert Arian and Meir Benzion Meiry, Palestine citizens and members of the Jewish Agency for Palestine, signed for the valuables, assumed full responsibility for the property, and vanished into Switzerland. Exactly what happened to this booty is unknown.[14]

*   *   *

Dr. Kastner's efforts on Becher's behalf would come back to haunt him. After his intervention in Nuremberg, Kastner and his family emigrated to Palestine. There, he joined Ben-Gurion's government and occupied several prominent positions, including spokesman of the Trade and Industry Ministry, Director of Broadcasting in Hungarian and Rumanian, chief editor of the Hungarian newspaper *Uj Kelet*, and Chairman of the Organization of Hungarian Jewry. His past, which had been running just a few steps behind him, finally caught up with him in 1953. A staunchly pro-Zionist journalist named Malchiel Greenwald published a pamphlet in Jerusalem accusing Kastner of collaborating with the Nazis—and worse. The doctor, he claimed, had knowingly assisted the Nazis in their extermination of 500,000 Hungarian Jews. Greenwald called for a public inquiry. Kastner was a conspicuous member of the ruling party. The Attorney General of the State of Israel stepped up on his behalf and prosecuted Greenwald for criminal libel. The case blossomed into one of the largest and most sensational litigations in the history of the young country.

The trial quickly careened out of control for Kastner and the government. No longer was the issue whether what had run out of Greenwald's pen was credible, but exactly what role Kastner had played during the war—and especially his controversial collaboration with Kurt Becher. News leaked out that Kastner had saved the SS officer from the gallows by intervening on his behalf at Nuremberg. Kastner's response can only be explained by a guilty conscience: he denied having ever assisted Becher. Documents and testimony were introduced that proved he was lying. Greenwald effectively left the litigation stage. Kastner, a mere witness in a criminal case brought by the state of Israel, had (at least metaphorically) changed places with the accused. The matter was a general embarrassment for the Israel government and dragged on for months on end. On June 21, 1955, Greenwald was acquitted on three of the four original counts brought against him. The court found that Greenwald had leveled "an unproven accusation" regarding the fourth charge (that Kastner had collected money from the Nazis for his help) and fined him a single Israeli pound. The judge also ordered that the government pay Greenwald two hundred Israeli pounds for court costs.[15]

Greenwald's general acquittal, coupled with the unusually harsh language of the court, was a symbolic conviction of Kastner. Judge Benjamin Halevi, one of the judges who would try Adolf Eichmann three years later, wrote:

> The support given by the extermination leaders to Kastner's Rescue Committee proves that indeed there was a place for Kastner and his friends in their Final Solution for the Jews of Hungary–their total annihilation. The Nazi's patronage of Kastner, and their agreement to let him save six hundred prominent Jews, were part of the plan to exterminate the Jews. Kastner was given a chance to add a few more to that number. The bait attracted him. The opportunity of rescuing prominent people appealed to him greatly. He considered the rescue of the most important Jews as a great personal success and a success for Zionism. It was a success that would also justify his conduct–his political negotiation with Nazis and the Nazi patronage of his committee. When Kastner received this present from the Nazis, Kastner sold his soul to the German Satan. . . . .
>
> All of Kastner's answers in his final testimony were a constant effort to evade this truth. Kastner has tried to escape through every crack he could find in the wall of evidence. When one crack was sealed in his face, he darted quickly to another.

Judge Halevi was not quite finished. Blunt words sealed Kastner's historical fate:

> Kastner perjured himself knowingly in his testimony before this court when he denied he had interceded in Becher's behalf. Moreover, he concealed the important fact that he interceded for Becher in the name of the Jewish Agency and the Jewish World Congress. . . . As to the contents of Kastner's affidavit, it was enough for the defense to prove Becher was a war criminal. It was up to the prosecution to remove Becher from this status, if they wished to negate the affidavit. The Attorney General admitted in his summation that Becher was a war criminal. The lies in the contents of Kastner's affidavit, the lies in his testimony concerning the document, and Kastner's knowing participation in the activities of Nazi war criminals, and his participation in the last minute fake rescue activities—all these combine to show one overwhelming truth—that this affidavit was not given in good faith. Kastner knew

well, as he himself testified, that Becher had never stood up against the stream of Jewish extermination, as Kastner has declared in the affidavit. The aims of Becher and his superior, Himmler, were not to save Jews but to serve the Nazi regime with full compliance.

Why had Kastner intervened on Becher's behalf knowing the SS officer was a mass murderer? The answer, concluded Judge Halevi, was clear: "Just as the Nazi war criminals knew they needed an alibi and hoped to achieve it by the rescue of a few Jews at the eleventh hour, so Kastner also needed an alibi for himself." By extension Kastner's fall from grace was an indirect conviction of Becher. Dr. Shmuel M. Tamir, Greenwald's defense attorney, was the first person who looked into Becher's soul and saw it for what it was: a black and cold morass. For the first time in a public forum Becher was portrayed for what he was: a ruthless war criminal who deserved a hemp dance. But he was a second or even third-tier malefactor, many years had passed, and few had any desire to reopen the case against him.

Two months later the verdict was appealed. The five judges sitting on the high court bench published their findings on January 17-19, 1958. Two upheld Judge Halevi's verdict; three found Greenwald guilty on three counts of libel. But all five agreed that in the face of overwhelming evidence and knowledge to the contrary, Kastner's efforts had saved Becher at Nuremberg from his well deserved punishment. Rampant rumors that Kastner himself was about to be brought up on charges of collaboration with the Nazis swept through Israel.

*   *   *

An interesting aspect of the Kurt Becher case lingers even today: almost all of the official documents collected by American investigators relating to his case have gone missing. Where are they? Who removed them from the files? Who ordered them removed? Were they removed for security reasons? More likely than not, these documents contained significant evidence that Becher had indeed committed serious war crimes. The publication of these interviews, interrogations, and other written memoranda would embarrass the American delegation and government that had ultimately freed him.

Benno Selcke, Jr., who had applied for Becher's transfer to the voluntary witness wing in the Nuremberg prison, came face-to-face with the former SS officer on a street in Frankfurt many years later. An embarrassing bit of small talk ensued. A short time later Selcke received a letter from Becher offering him "something" for the nice treatment he had given him in Nuremberg. Selcke cannot recall whether the offer was for money or employment. Selcke doubts Becher's freedom was won solely because of Kastner's intervention. Rather, members of the American team simply failed to vigorously prosecute him for his crimes. Why? The Americans, he explained, were just not that interested in Becher before Kastner appeared. It was almost as if they were looking for an excuse to free him. The Hungarian's efforts provided the whitewash needed to justify releasing Kurt Becher.[16]

Except for Selcke, most people who had anything to do with the Bremen-based millionaire treat the matter with some circumspection. Robert Kempner, one member of the prosecuting team at Nuremberg, sent a letter from his office in the United States in 1963 to the investigative magazine *Sie und Er*. "If, in any shape or form, Dr. Kempner should be mentioned as a protector of Becher's," the letter threatened, "the author and publisher [*Sie und Er*] will have to bear "the consequences."[17]

Chapter Notes

1. Headquarters, XV Corps, CIC Detachment 215, "Gold and Jewelry Found in Weissenbach," Major Theodore H. Possieck, May 30, 1945; Von Kurt Emmenegger, *Sie und Er* (April 1963), p. 29, Magyar Országos Levéltár, Hungarian National Archives, Budapest, Hungary.]

2. "Subject: Gold and Jewelry Found in Weissenbach," May 30, 1945. This document incorrectly lists May 12, 1945, as Becher's arrest date. The official arrest report lists the date as May 18, 1945. See "Kurt Becher Arrest Report," dated May 18, 1945.

3. Von Kurt Emmenegger," Das Einzige Weisse Schaf der Schwarzen SS?" (The Only White Sheep in the Black SS?), in *Sie und Er* (n.d., #14, 1963), p. 19, Magyar Országos Levéltár, Hungarian National Archives, Budapest, Hungary.

4. National Archives, Record Group 260, Austrian National Bank 1946-1950, Box 301; Verbal: American Legation, Budapest, April 12, 1947.

5. "Valuables Taken From SS Standartenführer Kurt Becher," February 1, 1946, by J. H. Hildring, Internal Affairs Division, Washington, D.C. See also, Tom Bower, *Nazi Gold: The Full Story of the Fifty-Year Swiss-Nazi Conspiracy to Steal Billions From Europe's Jews and Holocaust Survivors* (New York, 1997), p. 62. Becher's claim to have worked closely with Dieter Wisliceny was quite a gamble, especially since their wartime roles were so eerily similar. Wisliceny, Eichmann's deputy, was responsible for the mass deportation and murder of Jews in Slovakia, Greece, and Hungary. He was born on January 13, 1911, the son of a landowner. He failed as a theology student and worked briefly as a clerk in a construction firm before joining both the SS and SD in 1936. At that time Wisliceny was Eichmann's superior in the SS. As Eichmann rose through the ranks Wisliceny became one of his "Jewish experts" serving as an official in the Reich Central Office of Jewish Emigration. Like Becher, Wisliceny was more concerned with money than his career. He acquired a reputation in Slovakia and elsewhere for accepting bribes in exchange for lives. In 1942, he accepted $50,000 from the Jewish Relief Committee in Bratislava for delaying deportations from Slovakia. In Hungary, where he demanded the Jews address him as "Baron," Wisliceny was actively involved in the bargaining for Jewish lives. He readily took the money—and sent the people to Auschwitz anyway. Wisliceny and Becher were close acquaintances in Hungary, performed many similarly odious tasks there, and accepted gold in exchange for saving lives.

6. Von Kurt Emmenegger, "Das Einzige Weisse Schaf der Schwarzen SS?" (The Only White Sheep in the Black SS?), in *Sie und Er* (n.d., #14, 1963), p. 19, Magyar Országos Levéltár, Hungarian National Archives, Budapest, Hungary.

7. Von Kurt Emmenegger, "Mord of Dr. Billitz?" ("Murder of Dr. Billitz?"), in *Sie und Er* (n.d., #10, 1963), p. 19, Magyar Országos Levéltár, Hungarian National Archives, Budapest, Hungary; CIC Memorandum, "Investigation of War Crimes," September 26, 1945." It is interesting to note that the Communist Chinese have done the same thing with their archives. As far as their official records indicate, World War II was almost a non-event. Chinese history is largely blank from the early 1930s to 1948.

8. Von Kurt Emmenegger, "Mord of Dr. Billitz?" ("Murder of Dr. Billitz?"), in *Sie und Er* (n.d., #10, 1963), pp. 19-20, Magyar Országos Levéltár, Hungarian National Archives, Budapest, Hungary. Elisabeth Billitz survived the fall of Budapest, the withdrawal of the German occupying troops, and the ensuing Russian occupation. For several months she lived without knowing what had

happened to her husband. Finally, on May 4, 1945, Geza Varga, her husband's chauffeur, returned from Vienna where he had been detained by both Becher and the general course of the war. Billitz, he explains as gently as possible, was dead. All that was left was a small suitcase of his personal belongings. Varga told her that her husband had been feeling quite well during the trip to Vienna, and only fell ill with a high fever two days later. Ibid.

9. Von Kurt Emmenegger, "Das Einzige Weisse Schaf der Schwarzen SS?" ("The Only White Sheep in the Black SS?"), in *Sie und Er* (n.d., #14, 1963), p. 19, Magyar Országos Levéltár, Hungarian National Archives, Budapest, Hungary.

10. Von Kurt Emmenegger, "Das Einzige Weisse Schaf der Schwarzen SS?" ("The Only White Sheep in the Black SS?"), in *Sie und Er* (n.d., #14, 1963), p. 19, Magyar Országos Levéltár, Hungarian National Archives, Budapest, Hungary.

11. Von Kurt Emmenegger, "Das Einzige Weisse Schaf der Schwarzen SS?" ("The Only White Sheep in the Black SS?"), in *Sie und Er* (n.d., #14, 1963), p. 20, Magyar Országos Levéltár, Hungarian National Archives, Budapest, Hungary. Lieutenant Kurt Ponger, one of the interrogators from the American delegation, also has dirty linen to conceal: he was getting his instructions from Moscow, i.e., he was a spy. The last thing the Soviets wanted was a clear picture of what had exactly transpired in Hungary during World War II because they intended to pillage the country of its remaining wealth and blame it on the Germans. Thus Ponger had a strong incentive to see that Kastner's wish that Becher go free was acted upon. *History of the Counter Intelligence Corps*, "Occupation of Austria and Italy" (Vol. XXV, March 1959.)

12. Von Kurt Emmenegger, "Das Einzige Weisse Schaf der Schwarzen SS?" ("The Only White Sheep in the Black SS?"), in *Sie und Er* (n.d., #14, 1963), p. 20, Magyar Országos Levéltár, Hungarian National Archives, Budapest, Hungary.

13. Von Kurt Emmenegger, "Das Einzige Weisse Schaf der Schwarzen SS?" ("The Only White Sheep in the Black SS?"), in *Sie und Er* (n.d., #14, 1963), p. 90, Magyar Országos Levéltár, Hungarian National Archives, Budapest, Hungary. A March 1947 list of war criminals states that "Becher, Kurt, is wanted for torture at Budapest and Mauthausen." Yet, someone pulled enough strings to spring him from custody.

14. CIC "Informal Routing Slip," February 20, 1947; CIC Letter, Walter M. Treece, "Release of Looted Property to Jewish Agency for Palestine," March 3, 1947.

15. As it turns out, Kurt Becher was not the only SS officer who may have benefitted from Dr. Kastner's intervention. While at Nuremberg he had tried, unsuccessfully, to use his influence to assist the detestable Dieter Wisliceny. As noted earlier in this book, Wisliceny (Eichmann's subordinate) was wanted for his heinous behavior in Slovakia and Greece. Kastner also put in a good word for SS Haumptsturmführer (Captain) Hermann Krumey by way of affidavit. Research into recently released documents also uncovered evidence that Kastner helped SS Gruppenführer (Major General) Hans Juettner in 1948 by confirming the officer had not been responsible for a massive deportation of Jews on foot from Budapest from Vienna. Von Kurt Emmenegger,"Das Einzige Weisse Schaf der Schwarzen SS?" ("The Only White Sheep in the Black SS?"), in *Sie und Er* (n.d., #14, 1963), p. 94, Magyar Országos Levéltár, Hungarian National Archives, Budapest, Hungary.

16. Von Kurt Emmenegger, "Das Einzige Weisse Schaf der Schwarzen SS?" ("The Only White Sheep in the Black SS?"), in *Sie und Er* (n.d., #14, 1963), p. 94, Magyar Országos Levéltár, Hungarian National Archives, Budapest, Hungary.

17. Von Kurt Emmenegger, "Das Einzige Weisse Schaf der Schwarzen SS?" ("The Only White Sheep in the Black SS?"), in *Sie und Er* (n.d., #14, 1963), p. 94, Magyar Országos Levéltár, Hungarian National Archives, Budapest, Hungary.

Fall from Grace: Walter Hirschfeld and the Counter Intelligence Corps

On November 15, 1945, CIC Special Agent Robert A. Gutierrez sat down at his desk to prepare a lengthy report of the recent remarkable events he had overseen. A substantial portion of the memorandum concerned the stellar role former SS officer Walter Hirschfeld had played entrapping Josef Spacil, locating Franz Konrad, and interviewing Gretl Fegelein and her in-laws, Frau and Herr Fegelein. Gutierrez's report included a recommendation that Hirschfeld be officially "denazified."

Hirschfeld, wrote Gutierrez,

> has a natural talent for undercover work; he is very confident of his abilities, and knows the whole set up of the Nazi regime. In addition, he is German himself and knows the mentality of the German people. Hirschfeld knows the whole structure of the SS in detail, including personal acquaintances with several of Himmler's personnel. He also has his blood type tattooed under his left arm, and this mark gives him entree into SS circles in an undercover

capacity. All of these qualifications make him very valuable for work with U. S. Intelligence. . . . In addition, this agent feels safe in stating that Hirschfeld is definitely against the National Socialist Party and feels it is part of his duty to help break up the party completely and to establish a democratic form of government in Germany. . . . He can be relied upon to carry out intelligence assignments with good judgment and complete honesty.[1]

Gutierrez's intent was to do justice, but his glowing assessment of Hirschfeld was wide of the mark.

*   *   *

At the end of December 1945, a broad-shouldered man in a gray SS leather coat rang the doorbell at a home in Heidelberg. Owner Frau Martin opened the door. After the visitor introduced himself he requested to see Dr. Marianne Six, an attractive young pediatrician who rented a room in Martin's house. The pair conversed quietly for about twenty minutes before the stranger left. The visitor, Six excitedly told Frau Martin, is "an old SS comrade of my brother. He will help Franz, maybe he will be able [to] obtain papers for him too." She was referring to SS Brigadeführer (Brigadier General) Franz Six, a war criminal who had gone underground immediately after the war ended. Marianne had agreed to meet with the enigmatic visitor again the next day at the Odeonkellar, a local tavern. Her friends, who had seen him enter the home, warned her to beware of the stranger and stay away from him. He looked to them like "a habitual drinker" with a bulbous red nose complete with a blood wart. "No," she replied defensively, "he is a good man." She had questioned him closely and he knew the characteristics and number of the RSHA department for which her brother had worked. As scheduled, the pair met again the following day at the tavern. When Marianne returned home she told a close friend that she had found a decent man whom she would like to marry. His name was Walter Hirschfeld.

To the mortification of her friends Marianne left with the former SS asylum patient a few days later for Stuttgart. The purpose of the trip was ostensibly to "help" former members of the SS remove their blood-type tattoos by injecting bleach under the skin directly into the dye. The mark, which consisted of letters denoting the universal blood type codes (A, B,

AB or O), was about one-quarter of an inch long. It was needled into the underside of the upper left forearm about eight inches from the elbow and was required for everyone who served in the Waffen-SS (although not everyone received it). The tattoos were used after the war to identify whether a man had served in the organization. Removing the mark would help prevent arrest and shield the past from prying eyes. Marianne's efforts to remove the tattoos was only partially effective, but she returned "very low spirited" for a completely different reason. Someone had discovered what was taking place and all 180 of the SS men who had appeared for treatment were apprehended and imprisoned. What she did not know was that the entire affair had been a set up to lure SS men into a trap. Hirschfeld, Dr. Six's new friend and probable lover, was an undercover agent for the CIC.[2]

Once back in Heidelberg, Hirschfeld told Dr. Six—who was still completely unaware of his duplicity—that he could get her brother, Franz Six, a job at Leather Firm Christian in Schorndorf, a small company owned by his uncle Gerhardt Schlemmer. The shop was a front for CIC clandestine operations, and Schlemmer was Hirschfeld's former SS instructor. Like Hirschfeld, Schlemmer was also employed by American Intelligence. "All I need to know is how to contact your brother," explained Hirschfeld. Marianne hesitated revealing his whereabouts. Six had admonished her not to reveal his secret address in a small village south of Hannover because he was wanted as a war criminal. By the time Hirschfeld left, however, Dr. Six's brother's new alias and secret address were tucked away in his coat pocket.[3]

On January 17, 1946, Hirschfeld drove to Franz Six's hideout near Hannover in the company of another CIC agent. They found Six binding a broom in a shed. "A gentleman in a leather coat came in and asked me to come out," Six later remembered. "He said there was a friend from Heidelberg [waiting]." The "friend," remembered Six, was seated in the car and "looked at me very silly, and when I turned around . . . I found myself looking silly into the muzzle of a Colt." Hirschfeld handcuffed Six's hands behind his back, threw him into the backseat and drove into a nearby forest. Six was in serious trouble and he knew it.

"Which department are you from? American, British or Russian?" he asked in an effort to discover whether he was being officially arrested or about to be killed to satisfy an outstanding vendetta. Hirschfeld looked at him but did not answer.

"Maybe you are just going to complete it right here, in the forest?" asked an obviously distressed Six.

"We are not going to kill you," Hirschfeld told the pathetic bespectacled and deceivingly harmless looking man. "Taking you here is just a precaution."

In addition to the handcuffs the men shackled their captive with foot cuffs, stuffed him into a large sack "closed at the neck," and tied a heavy rope around his belly. Hirschfeld, however, was a better kidnapper than navigator: he got lost on the way back to Heidelberg and Six had to "show him the way." Six was turned over the American Intelligence agents as soon as they arrived.[4]

Marianne had no idea her brother had been secretly arrested. As far as she was concerned, Hirschfeld had taken him to work with Schlemmer at the leather firm. Proving again that love is indeed a blinding emotion, the young doctor continued aiding the undercover agent. At his request she provided additional names and addresses of SS fugitives. The dogged Hirschfeld hunted them down one by one. Sometimes he did the work alone, sometimes with the help of their friends and relatives. His modus operandi was always the same: he offered his services as friend, helper, negotiator, or representative. When they accepted his assistance he set a trap and arrested them. Hirschfeld loved his work. Although on occasion the former SS men were taken by American CIC agents, he often went into the field personally to apprehend his victims. But none of these arrests measured up to the capture of Franz Six, who was anything but a "harmless looking" SS officer.[5]

* * *

Alfred Franz Six was a native of Mannheim, Germany, born on August 12, 1909. After he graduated from the classical high school at Mannheim in 1930 he entered the University of Heidelberg. The study of sociology and political science fascinated the young man, who earned both high grades and a doctorate in the study of philosophy. For a time the paunchy scholar with a rapidly receding hairline and large, thick glasses taught college. Within four years he was a full professor at the University of Königsberg in 1938, and a year later was awarded the prestigious chair for Foreign Political Science at the University of Berlin. Later he served as that institution's first Dean of the faculty for Foreign Countries. He seemed destined for a stellar academic career.

But like so many who served the Third Reich in high places, Six had a dark side fighting to emerge. He had long been taken with the Nazi doctrine as espoused by Hitler and had joined the party in 1930. Voluntary membership in the SA followed two years later, and the SD three years after that. The onset of war only meant greater opportunity for advancement. When Germany invaded the Soviet Union during Operation Barbarossa, Six followed just behind the front lines as Chief of the Vorkommando Moscow. According to postwar court testimony, Six's bureau was organized well in advance of the campaign and his task was merely to collect important documents in and around Moscow after that city fell to the unstoppable German juggernaut. But this was a facade—a giant lie. In fact, Six and his underlings oversaw mobile killing squads. "Vorkommando Moscow" was a division of Einsatzgruppen B, which shepherded tens of thousands of men, women, and children to their brutal deaths. On November 9, 1941, Heinrich Himmler personally promoted Six for his "outstanding service in [the] Einsatz." After months of this odious work the Mannheim native accepted a prominent position in RSHA Bureau VII, the SS research wing that worked overtime furnishing a spurious scientific foundation for the Nazi doctrine of Germanic superiority. Marianne Six's beloved brother, the shy and studious scholar with an advanced degree from the University of Heidelberg, was a mass murderer.[6]

By the time 1945 rolled around Franz Six knew he was in serious trouble. He moved his beautiful blond wife and young baby out of Berlin to Mannheim to live with his parents. Just before the Russians arrived in April, he packed his personal belongings into his car and his chauffeur hauled them away. Six and two others donned civilian clothing and left. One witness described him as near "total nervous collapse" when they decided to go underground. The once-powerful and feared officer was on foot with a knapsack and empty briefcase looking for a place to hide when Germany surrendered. Dressed in a common laborer's clothes, Six hiked his way south toward the Austrian border and then headed northeast through American checkpoints passing himself off as "George

Becker." Americans were too busy to check for SS blood tattoos. He eventually reached Heidelberg, obtained papers there from his brother (who worked for the British Army), and then moved north and east about 80 miles to the small village of Kassel, where he performed menial labor until his path crossed with Walter Hirschfeld.

*   *   *

On February 13, 1946, almost four weeks after her brother had been arrested, Marianne and her father left Mannheim to return home to Heidelberg with a load of American cigarettes they had obtained on the black market. According to her father, Marianne was "happy and in good spirits." That evening her optimistic outlook began to crumble when the words shouted by her mother, "Marianne! There is a man who wants to arrest you!" greeted her return. "Come along," was all Walter Hirschfeld said to the confused woman, as he grabbed her by the arm and pushed her into his BMW.[7]

The next morning Marianne's other brother, Gustav Six, drove to his sister's rented flat to get the cigarettes she had obtained for him in Mannheim. Frau Martin answered his knock with bad news: Marianne had left the previous day with her father but never returned. Neither were yet aware that she had been snatched away by Hirschfeld in front of her parent's bombed-out home. Unsure of what to do, Martin and Gustav decided to walk downtown and ask around in an attempt to locate her. By sheer coincidence they spotted a nervous-looking Marianne walking quickly in and out of several stores.

"Where are you coming from, Marianne?" asked Gustav, who was troubled by her odd behavior. "We have been worried about you!"

Her baffling answer stunned both Martin and her brother. "I came from the American CIC [building.]. I was there last night and they gave me something to eat. I must return to the CIC."

"I will come with you," said Gustav. He could tell something was wrong, but did not know what it was.

"No! I have a feeling I am being observed. Go to my room and wait for me. I"ll come soon. Franz is arrested!" She hesitated a moment before adding, "Remember the name of Hirschfeld."

Gustav and Frau Martin watched as she walked away in the direction of the CIC building on Hauptstrasse. They, in turn, walked back to her rented room and waited for her there as she had asked them to do. She never returned.

Less than two hours later an elderly man noticed a young woman lying on the ground. She seemed intoxicated. Another woman approached and asked the man who she was. He shook his head and replied, "That is a GI sweetheart. She is stewed in typical American fashion." The half-conscious woman was alert enough to overhear his observation. She slurred in return, "I did not drink, the others drank." After uttering those few words she passed out.

The couple helped the woman up, leaned her against a nearby wall in the sunlight, and walked away. The owner of the wall watched from a window as the unconscious woman fell backward into her yard. The Red Cross and police were called to investigate. The authorities found the young woman senseless and seemingly paralyzed, her pulse barely discernable. Information obtained from her handbag revealed her identity: Dr. Marianne Six.

The police notified her parents, who contacted Frau Martin and a close family friend, Waldemar Hellweg. All of them hurried as fast as they could to the Ludolf Krehl Hospital. There, doctors told them Marianne was "in grave condition due to intoxication." The head of the clinic asked whether anyone knew what she had eaten or drunk in the last several hours. "It is a case of poisoning," he told them. "But I don't know what it is." The mystery deepened when Hellweg left the sick room and walked into the hall. There, he collided with a person he later described as "a tall, dark man." It was Walter Hirschfeld. According to a nurse, he had been inquiring about Marianne's condition. "Remember the name of Hirschfeld" Marianne had whispered to Martin and Gustav just a few hours earlier. The fives words rang in their ears when Hellweg explained that the mystery man was nosing around the hospital asking questions.

Marianne Six died three days later without regaining consciousness. The immediate cause of death was listed as "pneumonia." As far as the CIC was concerned she had taken her own life. Agent Rickmann of the Heidelberg CIC classified her death as a suicide. "We should also like to know what the matter was," he wrote. "Marianne had threatened to commit suicide when she learned of her brother's arrest. We did not believe her. It is my honest opinion that Marianne committed suicide." Everyone who knew Marianne strenuously objected to that conclusion. "It is out of the question that Marianne would have given up the idea of avenging the betrayal to which her brother had been subjected," retorted her surviving brother Gustav. "She had a lot of fight in her."

Herr Six was absolutely sure foul play was involved in his only daughter's death. Three days later he walked into the German police headquarters and asked authorities to file murder charges against Walter Hirschfeld. "Walter Hirschfeld murdered my daughter," he told them tearfully. They agreed to look into the case. Weeks passed without any further word from them. When the old man inquired as to the status of the investigation he was told "the case had been quashed under orders of the Americans." The Americans? Why in the world were they interested in his daughter's death? News that the autopsy had been botched and that the results were "inconclusive" only confirmed his suspicions that someone was hiding something. Dr. Messemer, the pathologist who had conducted the post mortem, explained that they had only examined the contents of her stomach, blood, and urine. Trace amounts of a chemical found in sleeping tablets was found. In all likelihood, however, Marianne's healthy body "had already excreted a considerable part of the toxin." In the case of suspected poisonings, Messemer told him, it was common practice to carefully examine the liver, gall bladder, and other parts of the body, including the roots of skin hair. These parts harbor poisons longer than other organs in the body. Unfortunately, Messemer explained, the procedure was not conducted "with the usual thoroughness," because investigators "did not care for such thoroughness." Messemer was never asked to provide a final opinion as to the cause of Marianne's death. The distraught family was outraged.[8]

CIC files contain an official record entitled "The Violent Death of Marianne Six"—an odd name for what the CIC officially proclaimed a suicide. No mention is made of the fact that Marianne's father accused Walter Hirschfeld of murdering his daughter. Nor is there any record or proof that Hirschfeld was ever interrogated by the police or CIC. When these facts are bound together with the botched autopsy, the utter absence of any record requesting the arrest or detainment of Marianne Six, or any record of any inquiry by the CIC into her affairs, one can not help but suspect that some powerful hand was stirring the pot to disguise what really happened to the young doctor. Was it murder or was she so distraught over playing a role in the discovery of her brother that she committed suicide? Since most or all of the participants in the affair are now deceased, it is unlikely a definitive answer will ever be reached.[9]

*   *   *

SS Standartenführer (Colonel) Emil Augsburg's war record was not one designed to make parents proud. The German native of Lodz, Poland, was born in 1904. Studious and dedicated, Augsburg earned a doctorate three decades later studying about the press in the Soviet Union. In 1934 he joined the SD; membership in the SS followed. In 1937, Augsburg became associated with the Wannsee Institute, the infamous SS institution that performed ideologically-based research on eastern Europeans. The Institute helped plan the logistics behind the "Final Solution." Augsburg was one of its departmental directors. In 1939-1940 and again in the summer and fall of 1941, he joined the Security Police to carry out what were called "special duties (*spezielle Aufgaben*), a euphemism for the executions of Jews and others the Nazis considered unworthy of life. Augsburg's superior officer was none other than SS Brigadeführer (Brigadier General) Franz Six. After Augsburg was wounded in an air attack in Smolensk in September 1941, he returned to Berlin to conduct research on Eastern European matters. The RSHA foreign intelligence branch formally absorbed the Wannsee Institute in 1943.

Augsburg realized long before Germany's final collapse that the writing on the wall was not a friendly message, and that surrender would expose him to charges of war crimes. He disappeared before the surrender. In order to escape capture, Augsburg slipped underground into the Benedictine cloister at Ettal, Germany, where he served as the private secretary to a Monsignor of Polish origin with connections to the Vatican and the SD or German Secret Police. Fearing the worst, the Monsignor and Augsburg fled to the Vatican in Rome during the final days of the war with important political documents. Empathetic to Augsburg's plight, the Monsignor obtained a commission for him (Augsburg spoke Polish and Russian fluently) in the Polish army of General Wladyslaw Anders, an organization popularly known as the 2nd Polish Corps. Anders's men were stationed nearby in northern Italy.[10]

Augsburg was still working (and hiding) inside the Vatican almost a year later in early 1946 when a surprise letter arrived for him. It was from his former commander Brigadeführer Franz Six. "I have important missions in South Germany. I need you very quickly. Come." A secret place of rendezvous was noted in the letter. Augsburg, still a proud and devoted Nazi, dutifully answered the call by doffing his Polish uniform and leaving Rome. He arrived at the appointed rendezvous in southern Germany right on time. Franz Six was nowhere to be found. Waiting for him instead was Walter Hirschfeld. The CIC agent identified himself as one of Six's deputies and produced orders signed by Six. They were going to work together to help former SS officers go underground or escape Europe. The papers satisfied the normally suspicious Augsburg. He worked hand-in-hand with Hirschfeld to gather together his former associates. Resistance movements were planned, secret committees were established, and "desperate deeds were performed" to help a number of former Nazis escape detection or relocate in other countries. All the while Augsburg and his friends believed they were helping their old chief Franz Six, who continued demanding, via written orders, absolute secrecy and silence. One directive followed another, all signed by Six. Each time Hirschfeld acted as Six's courier. Augsburg obeyed each order.[11]

The entire Six–Augsburg affair was a fraud organized by Hirschfeld on the orders of the CIC. The scam, officially known as "Operation Flower Box," was managed out of the CIC's Leather Firm Christian. Its purpose was to penetrate the shadowy Nazi European underground and arrest those who appeared on lists of war criminals. After many months had passed Augsburg began to suspect something was not right. "Why don't I ever hear directly from Franz?" he asked Hirschfeld. "Why am I not allowed to see or hear from him?" Hirschfeld advised him to be patient. But Augsburg was not a patient man. Smelling a rat he dispatched a trusted courier to Franz Six's wife's residence to bypass Hirschfeld and set up a personal meeting with his former friend. Franz's wife was astounded when she learned what had been going on over her husband's name. "My husband has been confined for over a year in Oberursel, Nuremberg, and Dachau!" she told the equally shocked courier, who returned and broke the bitter news to Augsburg.[12]

An angry (and probably embarrassed) Augsburg confronted Hirschfeld and demanded an explanation. To Augsburg's surprise

Hirschfeld did not deny the charges. Instead he "grinned" and admitted that every Franz Six signature and order had been forged. Without knowing it, Augsburg and his team had been carrying out orders for the CIC for more than one year. They were American agents and did not even know it. Several other notable Nazis, among them Klaus Barbie, had also been recruited into Operation Flower Box. Barbie, too, had joined the team believing he was working for Franz Six. Augsburg and his criminal pals were outraged by the deceit, but Hirschfeld had actually done all of them a lifesaving favor. Few of the former war criminals could have guessed that their illicit association was about to transmogrify into official employment with United States Intelligence. Fewer still could have known that their forthcoming relationship with the CIC and CIA would keep them out of prison and off the gallows, where so many of them belonged.[13]

*   *   *

Walter Hirschfeld's life was in an out-of-control spiral, and the CIC was growing increasingly embarrassed by his activities. He had been blackmailing former members of the SS and their relatives, running small-time money laundering operations, and had probably had a hand in murdering Dr. Marianne Six. More scandal bubbled into the public domain during Operation Flower Box when Hirschfeld began an affair with 27-year-old Frau Erna Hoffmann, the wife of Heinrich Hoffmann, Adolf Hitler's personal photographer. When he learned that Hoffmann was in Allied custody, Hirschfeld hatched a plan to steal his furniture and artwork and use it to decorate the leather shop and his own home. The piece-by-piece theft was underway when his romance with Erna hit the rocks. She reported Hirschfeld's larceny to local Schorndorf police and the items were restored to the Hoffmann home. Hirschfeld, thanks only to his connections with the CIC and local police, avoided a jail sentence.[14]

It was at this time that Hirschfeld also suffered a very public breakup of his friendship with Gerhardt Schlemmer. The pair had borrowed money from a local bank to spend on luxury items, alcohol, and women. When they were asked for collateral, the men offered up the inventory in the CIC-owned leather firm to secure the fraudulent loan. After Operation Flower Box ended and the leather shop closed, the bank demanded repayment. Neither man had any intention of paying back the funds. Schlemmer was the only one who signed the note, and he eventually ended up in jail. While he was interned his friend and comrade Hirschfeld had another affair—this time with Schlemmer's wife Barbara. Both were seen dancing and frolicking in a popular American bar in Stuttgart. The mortified Schlemmer made preparations to divorce his wife but eventually halted the proceedings. The longstanding friendship between Schlemmer and Hirschfeld, however, was kaput.

So was Hirschfeld's tenure with the CIC. Like every good bureaucracy the American Intelligence operation knew it had to have a record justifying his removal. Two men were employed to investigate and report on his outlandish behavior. Both were known mass murderers. One was Emil Augsburg, and the other was Klaus Barbie. These men were well suited for the task—the latter particularly so.[15]

*   *   *

Nickolaus "Klaus" Barbie was born in 1913 along the Rhine River in picturesque Bad Godesberg. Although most of his grades were mediocre at best, Barbie excelled in languages. He discovered Nazism while still in college and joined the party in 1933. Close association and comradeship with others experiencing similar feelings of angst over the deteriorating economic and social conditions appealed to Barbie. After several failed attempts to pass his final exams, he finally graduated in 1934. A voluntary six-month stint at a Nazi labor camp seared party propaganda deep within him. Service with the German resistance movement in the occupied Rhineland followed. Barbie claimed his father (whom he despised) had died in the 1930s from a festering French bullet wound inflicted during World War I. His death, he later explained, crippled the family financially and limited his own professional aspirations. Barbie turned this anger against the French. Years later, this personal wrath would inflict far more pain and suffering than a single French bullet fired over the berm of a muddy trench.[16]

The SS and Klaus Barbie were made for each other. He joined Himmler's organization in 1935 and the SD shortly thereafter. Instruction in Berlin on the finer techniques of interrogation (i.e., torture) and investigation followed. His stint in Amsterdam in 1940, where he oversaw the deportation of thousands of Jews, earned him an Iron Cross.

The award was bestowed after he publicly beat a man to death for a minor infraction. Now it was time for Lyon, France, to feel the sociopath's rage. In 1943 Barbie was assigned to "cleanse" the southern French city widely known as a hotbed of French resistance. As the head of the Gestapo there, Barbie freely murdered hundreds of people and deported thousands of Jews to the death camps. His personal sadistic actions are legion and well documented. His most notorious feat was the infiltration of the Resistance and the arrest of Jean Moulin, General Charles de Gaulle's chief representative in France and a hero of the Resistance movement. Moulin was beaten to death by Barbie himself. Another decoration from Hitler arrived. Barbie deserted Lyon and fled to Germany when the Allies approached. The French were anxious to get their hands on Barbie and searched ceaselessly but unsuccessfully for him. They tried the "Butcher of Lyon" in absentia and sentenced him to death. It was this man—a murderer and sadist of the worst order, but also an experienced interrogator with invaluable intelligence that would be useful in the budding Cold War with the Soviet Union—who was now investigating Walter Hirschfeld on the payroll of the United States Government.[17]

Both Barbie and Augsburg were more than pleased to assist the CIC with "Operation Happiness," the incongruous code name tagged to their assignment, if it meant avoiding jail or a trial for war crimes. Both relished the work. Detailed reports were compiled on the death of Marianne Six, Hirschfeld's affair with the wife of Heinrich Hoffmann, his failed business ventures, and his many attempts to blackmail relatives of former SS members. The report, which was turned over to U.S. Special Agent Camille S. Hajdu, successfully knocked out any support Hirschfeld had left within the American intelligence community. Who would stand up for this man in the face of this damning dossier? An unsigned CIC memorandum dated March 6, 1947, the probable result of the vindictive accomplishments of Augsburg and Barbie, recommended the following: "If any action is contemplated to remove Hirschfeld from his present precarious position . . . it [should] be done in such a manner as to preclude any further embarrassment to the CIC." Hirschfeld was dismissed from the CIC before year's end. Gone were his BMW, Mercedes, and luxury apartment. Gone, too, was his power and influence on the streets of postwar Germany. Augsburg and Barbie made sure Hirschfeld's name was publicized and blacklisted in the circles frequented by former SS members. "It must fill every German with shame, that a member of the so-called former 'leader society' denounces his former comrades for a vile Judas," wrote one underground German publication.[18]

Walter Hirschfeld's career was finished.

Chapter Notes

1. CIC, "Recommendation of Walter Hirschfeld for Further Work with U.S. Intelligence," by Robert A. Gutierrez, November 15, 1945.

2. 307th Counter Intelligence Corps, "Translation and Interpretation of *Der Speigel* (December 9, 1949), pp. 7-8.

3. "Translation and Interpretation of *Der Speigel* (December 9, 1949), pp. 7-8.

4. "Translation and Interpretation of *Der Speigel* (December 9, 1949), pp. 7-8.

5. "CIC Intelligence Report Number 98," N.A., September 17, 1951. Six later lamented having told his sister anything. "I did always have the funny feeling that one should not give addresses about illegality no matter whether she is the wife or the sister. . ." Ibid.]

6. Michael Musmanno, U.S.N.R, Military Tribunal II, Case 9: *Opinion and Judgment of the Tribunal.* Nuremberg: Palace of Justice. April 8, 1948, pp. 146-151. Ibid. If Operation Sealion (the invasion of England) had been a success, Franz Six would have been unleashed to murder innocent people one year earlier. In May of 1940, SS officer Walter Schellenberg put together the "Black Book," a list of 2,820 British subjects and exiles tagged for arrest—or worse. Franz Six was chosen to head the operation. Six was to have been based in London and provided with six Einsatzgruppen (killing squads) to murder his victims. Dear, *Oxford Companion to World War II*, p. 134.

7. 307th Counter Intelligence Corps, "Translation and Interpretation of 'Remember the Name Hirschfeld,'" (no date).

8. 307th Counter Intelligence Corps, "Translation and Interpretation of 'Remember the Name Hirschfeld,'" (no date).

9. 307th Counter Intelligence Corps, "Translation and Interpretation of 'Remember the Name Hirschfeld,'" (no date).

10. Folder of Emil Augsburg papers, in IRR Personnel File, Franz Six, Record Group 319, National Archives.

11. 307th Counter Intelligence Corps, "Translation and Interpretation of *Der Speigel* (December 9, 1949), pp. 7-8.

12. 307th Counter Intelligence Corps, "Translation and Interpretation of *Der Speigel* (December 9, 1949), pp. 7-8; 66th Counter Intelligence Detachment, "Subject: Walter Hirschfeld," by Eugene Whitaker, April 5, 1950. This document is stamped "Highly Secretive."

13. 307th Counter Intelligence Corps, "Translation and Interpretation of *Der Speigel* (December 9, 1949), pp. 7-8; 66th Counter Intelligence Detachment, "Subject: Walter Hirschfeld," by Eugene Whitaker, April 5, 1950. This document is stamped "Highly Secretive."

14. 66th Counter Intelligence Detachment, "Subject: Walter Hirschfeld," by Eugene Whitaker, April 5, 1950. This document is stamped "Highly Secretive."

15. 66th Counter Intelligence Detachment, "Subject: Walter Hirschfeld," by Eugene Whitaker, April 5, 1950. This document is stamped "Highly Secretive." The backgrounds and war careers of both men were fully available to the CIC. The Americans knew exactly who they were hiring.

16. For in-depth information on Barbie, see Brenda Murphy, *The Butcher of Lyon: The Story of Infamous Nazi Klaus Barbie* (New York, 1983), pp. 193-199.

17. Murphy, *The Butcher of Lyon*, pp. 193-199.

18. CIC, Agent Report: "Barbie Klaus," October 19, 1949; 66th Counter Intelligence Detachment, "Subject: Walter Hirschfeld," by Eugene Whitaker, April 5, 1950.

Chapter 13

"Knowing what a passionate rage Kaltenbrunner would fly into should
he learn that the gold had not arrived, I never informed
[him] of the mistake which had been made."

— SS Obersturmbannführer (Lieutenant Colonel) Arthur Scheidler

Ernst Kaltenbrunner's Missing Sacks of Gold

*T*he stranger came right to the point. "I am here to discuss buried treasures in the U.S. Zone of Austria." CIC special agent Robert Kauf leaned back and looked askance at the man who had settled into a chair on the opposite side of his desk. The alluring and intriguing subject came up for discussion on a beautiful sunny day in June of 1947, two full years after Germany's unconditional surrender. Any doubts Agent Kauf harbored at the outset of the meeting with the Chief of the Austrian Investigation Service of the Ministry of Property Control and Economic Planning were quickly put to rest. By the time Hofrat Reith left his office, Kauf was a believer. He and his agents were about to embark on a fascinating investigatory journey. The story they uncovered entailed war and corruption, pillage and mass murder, stolen and concealed fortunes, and black market trading in gold and currencies.

Reith had been investigating rumors that multiple millions in gold, jewels, and currency, had been buried or otherwise hidden by retreating SS officers during the war's final fleeting hours. "At first these rumors sounded too fantastic to be given credence," explained Kauf, "but interrogation of alleged eyewitnesses and cross-checking of their testimony have convinced Reith that treasures were actually buried at a number of different places between Salzkammergut and Zell am See." Even more amazing was that "the location of most of these spots is known to within a radius of two square miles, while in one or two cases even the exact location is believed to be known." Rumor also had it that large caches of arms and foreign currency—principally American dollars, Swiss francs, and English pounds—were waiting to be found.[1]

The Austrian appeared that day to request "full CIC cooperation" in recovering the treasures, something Reith deemed absolutely necessary. He counseled Kauf that his "experience has shown that his investigators were often viewed with suspicion by the local CIC," and that many American agents, "when they learned of the purpose of the inquiries, initiated investigations of their own, which jeopardized the success of the Austrian investigation." Full cooperation, he continued, would avoid "a duplication of efforts." Specifically, Reith asked Kauf for three areas of assistance: (1) The interrogation of specific witnesses being held in Camp Marcus Orr, Camp Dachau, and Camp Nuernberg–Langwasser; (2) Instruments, such as advanced metal detectors, to assist in the detection of buried treasures; and (3) Assistance in apprehending and interrogating "a number of persons who are said to have 'powerful American protectors,' and whom the Austrians, therefore, have not dared to approach."[2]

In his report to headquarters Kauf heartily endorsed Reith's requests. "Aside from the obvious result of recovering and returning the valuables to the rightful owners, a successful operation would also serve to eliminate a possible security threat by recovering hidden arms [and] depriving possible subversive elements of potential funds," he wrote. The Americans were not wholly unaware of the swirling rumors about hidden treasures and buried loot. In fact, the CIC had made several stunning discoveries of gold, jewels, currency, and other items of interest in the weeks and months following the close of the war. Kauf and his fellow agents had long suspected many high ranking ex-Nazi Party members, SS officers, and others living in the U.S. Zone of Austria "are only able to do so because they have access to some of the treasures." Reith's detailed information merely confirmed these suspicions.

After outlining Reith's solid investigatory credentials, Kauf concluded that it was in the best interests of the United States to offer the Austrians any help they required. I am under the impression, he concluded, "that Reith has accumulated a great deal of concrete evidence on the subject matter, so that a joint operation would . . . not . . . be a disadvantage to the CIC." Kauf's report and recommendations triggered the proposed operation. Kauf, however, did not know that a tentative investigation had been simmering on a back burner for several months. His conference with Reith merely cemented into place the pieces necessary to provoke full-blown CIC support.[3]

Reith's report focused on a half-dozen or so "credible" treasure stories. The first, he told Kauf, pushing the paperwork across the desktop, involved two men—Ernst Kaltenbrunner, the head of Himmler's notorious RSHA, and Arthur Scheidler, Kaltenbrunner's aide-de-camp—and a fortune in missing gold.

*   *   *

SS Obersturmbannführer (Lieutenant Colonel) Arthur Scheidler performed a myriad of tasks for the Third Reich, but as a bureaucrat within the RSHA he was, in essence, Ernst Kaltenbrunner's major-domo. Scheidler handled both official and personal matters for his powerful boss—everything from scheduling meetings to such tiresome tasks as paying rent, arranging for banquets, or sending funeral wreaths (a commonplace practice within RSHA). One of the perks Scheidler enjoyed because of his personal association with Kaltenbrunner was free travel and entertainment. Much of it was designed so that Scheidler could purchase presents and wine for Kaltenbrunner and his esteemed guests. A typical procurement trip would originate in Berlin with Austria or Hungary as the final destination. From the German capital Scheidler would drive Kaltenbrunner's armored car to Hindelang, south of Munich, where he would pick up Countess Gisele von Westarp, the chief's 24-year-old mistress. From there Scheidler and the countess would travel on to Salzburg, Austria, in order to pick up Scheidler's wife, Iris. Kaltenbrunner would fly in from wherever his duties had taken him and join the trio waiting for him in the beautiful medieval city. Days filled with luxurious shopping and dining sprees followed in Vienna or

Budapest, Hungary. Scheidler and his wife often purchased costly silk dresses, toiletry articles, and other commodities no longer available in war-torn Germany. He made sure to stock up on rare items his chief would want to offer his guests, including expensive clothing, fine cognac, American cigarettes, and Dubonnet wines. The two couples enjoyed a close friendship. They frequently traveled together to Altaussee in Austria in order to celebrate a birthday or holiday. The high life continued into 1945, even as their world crumbled into dust around them.[4]

The nightmare of the Second World War was unimaginable in tiny 1911 Henneberg, Germany. There, into a middle class family, Arthur Ernst August Scheidler was born, the second of five children. The early years for the quiet and aloof youngster were spent in Meiningen, where he attended primary and high school. An above average student with a keen eye for detail, Scheidler entered the business school in Meiningen in 1925 and graduated three years later. A thirst for ambition and success did not come naturally to the young man, so when an offer for a modest clerical position in town was made he promptly seized the opportunity—and remained there for the next six years. From within the confines of his small town the round-faced, short and balding bureaucrat-in-training quietly observed the rise of Adolf Hitler and the progressive acquisition of power by the Nazi party. Without fanfare he became a member of the SS in 1933, but remained in his position of employment. Aspirations for something beyond sitting at a desk in Meiningen were beginning to burn within. Before 1935 was over Scheidler had shed his civilian employment and enlisted with the infantry. The next eight months were expended undergoing rigorous training in an SS infantry school. That fall he joined the SD and was transferred to Berlin, where he served in a variety of administrative capacities for the next four years. Scheidler had finally found a comfortable home tucked away in the belly of the beast.[5]

While Poland was being cleaved in two by Hitler and Stalin, and raped by the likes of Franz Konrad, Kurt Becher, and Hermann Fegelein, Scheidler was promoted to serve as an administrative aide to SS General Reinhard Heydrich, chief of RSHA. He dutifully served Heydrich and was advanced to the rank of Sturmbannführer in 1941. When Heydrich was assassinated in Czechoslovakia in 1942, Scheidler was assigned to serve the new chief, a tall Austrian with a horse-shaped head accented with fencing scars and punctuated by cold, dead eyes—Ernst Kaltenbrunner. Exactly how much Scheidler knew about the murderous activities of the RSHA and Kaltenbrunner is subject to some debate. Certainly he was exceedingly familiar with the intricate internal politics infesting RSHA and the oddball personalities that slithered within its confines. He freely admitted after the war that he was "familiar" with his chief's personal life, but claimed that his duties were "purely administrative." His official work only provided him with "a sketchy knowledge of Kaltenbrunner's confidential affairs." Scheidler "never participated" in the important conferences held or attended by Kaltenbrunner, or at least he so testified, although he did admit learning "of confidential matters from dinner-table conversations and occasional remarks by Kaltenbrunner and his guests."

Scheidler's professional tasks, however, were inextricably inter-twined with Kaltenbrunner's "principal interests," which according to Scheidler were Bureaus I (personnel), III (security), and VI (military intelligence and counter-intelligence). The operations of Bureau III "were a closely guarded secret," explained Scheidler, "never discussed at the dinner table." There was good reason for the suppressed conversation: within the confines of Bureau III operated the Einsatzgruppen—the killing squads responsible for some 2,000,000 murders in Poland and Russia. According to Scheidler, of all the RSHA bureau heads, Otto Ohlendorf, chief of Bureau III, was the one "Kaltenbrunner had the greatest confidence [in] and whom he saw the most frequently." Scheidler may have attended few if any formal "conferences"; no evidence exists one way or the other on that issue. It is inconceivable, however, that someone holding his rank and tenured credentials inside the RSHA, and who enjoyed such intimate professional contacts with the likes of Heydrich and Kaltenbrunner, did not know that his paper shuffling represented hundreds of thousands of dead men, women, and children. It also represented a fortune in gold, currency, and jewels.[6]

By the beginning of 1945 the number of individual conferences Scheidler arranged for Kaltenbrunner with his bureau heads steadily diminished. Meetings once held daily were now weekly or bi-weekly affairs. Many officers never sat down at a table across from Kaltenbrunner again. The war was clearly lost, all of them knew it, and many of them were busy conducting parallel lives, going through the motions of their official duties while cobbling together plans for escape. The strategic situation was deteriorating so quickly, however, that military situation conferences were held twice daily at 4:00 p.m. and 11:00 p.m. With the English and Americans closing in from the south and west, and Stalin's dreaded Russian divisions rolling over the landscape from the east, it became obvious to Kaltenbrunner and his cronies that any climactic military defense (and, for that matter, means of escape) would be found in mountainous southern Germany and Austria.

As March fell away and the calendar turned to April, plans were crafted for a grand finale. It was decided that leading SS officers and soldiers, together with RSHA assets and staff, would be funneled into the Altaussee region of Austria where they would mount a spirited final defense. Scheidler's primary duty was to arrange the transfer of SS files, liquor, and the large foreign exchange fund kept in Kaltenbrunner's office for purchasing their luxurious gifts and personal items. Kaltenbrunner's slush account contained about "600,000 units" in stable foreign currencies, including $100,000 American dollars. It also consisted of a fortune in gold. The precious metal was in the form of thousands of gold coins stuffed into six large cloth sacks weighing 30kg. (or sixty-six pounds) each. The loot was stuffed into silver boxes 36" long, 18" inches wide, and 24" tall. Scheidler's task was to see that this treasure made it to Kaltenbrunner's office in Altaussee. The pace of Scheidler's war increased to a dizzying speed. Maps listing evacuation points, future supply depots, and other vital locations for carrying on the war were printed and distributed to select RSHA personnel. As officers and staff dispersed to carry out their orders, the various departments fragmented. Bureau VI dispersed in several directions. Some of its officers found themselves operating out of a Bavarian barracks in Franconia; others set up headquarters along the Munich-Salzburg Road or in a hotel on the way to Innsbruck.

While staffers (in typical German fashion) continued filling out requisitions in triplicate for supplies they would never need, a special train formerly belonging to Reinhard Heydrich (which he never used), and reserved solely for RSHA use, pulled into Fürsteneck, Germany. The rail cars arrived from Thuringia for use as a mobile evacuation headquarters for Kaltenbrunner and his key officers. Few RSHA officials intended to utilize the train for official duties. Instead, the precious space was jammed with expensive furniture, food, liquor, artwork, and other valuables, all of which—together with wives and mistresses—were shuttled south into Austria. Scheidler saw to it that Kaltenbrunner's gold and currency were safely stashed aboard.[7]

As the RSHA train smoked and wound its way south toward Austria on April 22, many of the bureau chiefs and related staffers made the same journey by plane. Scheidler, however, was already in Salzburg administering to a variety of pressing concerns for Kaltenbrunner, who was laboring in his office at Altaussee. The aide-de-camp's stress level rose considerably when a phone call was patched through to him. "The train has been almost completely destroyed by artillery fire," crackled the voice of an RSHA officer known only to Schiedler. The rail-based caravan derailed into a smoking mess after being repeatedly strafed by American fighter planes. While disheartening, the news could not have been a complete surprise. Scheidler was well aware the Americans controlled the skies over southern Germany. Arrangements, with Kaltenbrunner's approval, were made to transfer the boxes into a truck and haul them to their final destination. Scheidler's orders were very specific: the gold and currency were to be sent straight to Kaltenbrunner in Altaussee; the SS files, liquor, and other supplies were to be dispatched to Schloss Glanek near Salzburg. SS Sturmbannführers (Majors) Reinhard Eimers and Lothar Kuhne were ordered to accompany the treasure and oversee its safety. The cases were off-loaded from the broken boxcars "in late April," stuffed into a large truck, and transported to Gmunden, Austria, near Bad Ischl. There they were divided for their separate destinations. As one CIC report put it, "a mistake, either deliberate or unintentional, was made." The files and whiskey was sent to Kaltenbrunner and the gold to Schloss Glanek, "from which it was further transported in the direction of Imst."[8]

Exactly what happened next is, according to one American intelligence officer, "somewhat vague." As the distance between the gold and whiskey widened, Scheidler was putting distance between himself and Salzburg, which he was fleeing for Altaussee. Advancing Russian and American troops made the move unavoidable. As later witnesses testified, "a state of frenzied confusion existed." Scheidler learned of the botched transfer when he reached Altaussee. "Knowing what a passionate rage Kaltenbrunner would fly into should he learn that the gold had not arrived, I never informed [him] of the mistake which had been made," explained Scheidler. The end was drawing near and the adjutant knew it as well as anyone and better than most. Within a few hours or a few days the fate of the gold would be of little consequence to anyone—especially Kaltenbrunner. Events proved him right. Several days later American forces closed in on Altaussee and Kaltenbrunner fled for his life. Scheidler bolted with him. Neither man had a clue where the gold and currency ended up.[9]

* * *

Until May 11, 1945, the Allies did not have any idea as to the whereabouts of Ernst Kaltenbrunner and Arthur Scheidler. That morning a leading figure of the Free Austrian Movement named Johann Brandauer walked into the 80th CIC office in Vocklabruck. He brought with him "some startling information," one agent later remembered. A forester had informed Brandauer that Ernst Kaltenbrunner, his leading adjutant Arthur Scheidler, and two SS officers "had been seen in a cabin at a spot named Wildensee," in the Totes Gebirge range of the Austrian Alps. Rumors as to Kaltenbrunner's whereabouts were rampant even before the surrender took effect. Few Nazi's ranked as high on the list for capture as the ruthless head of the RSHA. The news, which Brandauer assured the Americans was trustworthy, was welcome indeed.[10]

Special Agent Robert E. Matteson, the man who had already apprehended Kaltenbrunner's wife, "hastily arranged with Brandauer for a group of reliable mountain climbers to accompany him up to the cabin retreat." Ten American soldiers and two officers joined the search team. Matteson was determined to catch Kaltenbrunner alive, but was also prepared to kill him rather than allow him to escape justice. His plan included donning the party in "native Austrian clothes" to facilitate an easier approach to the hiding place. His Austrian guides suggested the team depart at midnight and undertake the trek at night. The journey would consume an estimated five hours, which would position the party near the cabin before daybreak. The fugitives would probably be asleep at that time and vulnerable to a surprise visit.

The excursion began just a handful of minutes after midnight on May 12. Five men dressed in Austrian clothing formed the vanguard and another dozen American infantrymen brought up the rear. Seventeen pairs of boots crunched the thick crust of frozen snow as the team climbed Wildensee, traversed a valley and continued on through thick timber where the white powder was piled in places thirty feet deep. The Austrian guides had judged the situation well. By 5:00 a.m. the advance party could see the cabin. By 6:30 a.m. the entire team was positioned in a skirt of timber 250 yards south of the lodge, "concealed behind the last slope of intervening ground." The former RSHA chief was enjoying his last few minutes of sleep as a free man. Whether he was sleeping well is something that will never be known.[11]

Dressed like a forester, Agent Matteson tiptoed toward the cabin. He was completely unarmed so that if he was spotted his presence would not arose much suspicion. The infantrymen were ordered to remain stationary until he reached the porch and signaled for their advance. Matteson made his way to the west side of the cabin because that side of the building was without windows or doors. Once there, he worked his way around to the cabin's solitary door. A gloved hand tried the knob; it was locked. The few windows were also bolted tight and shuttered. He lifted his hand and knocked quietly on the door. Matteson heard only a few "indistinct groans" from within. The occupants were sound asleep. Repeated knocking, this time louder and more forceful, "aroused an SS man who, after calling out for identification, opened a shutter."

"Who is there?" His voice still sounded sleepy.

"My name is Matteson. I was sent here by Frau Kaltenbrunner and Frau Scheidler with four other mountain climbers to persuade their husbands to give themselves up to the Americans." A few seconds of silence followed.

"I don't know either man. You must be at the wrong cabin." The speaker was suddenly wide awake.

Matteson signaled his advance team forward. He had to buy a few more seconds of time. "Please open the door so that I may ask you a few more questions," he instructed, peeking through a corner of the shutter.

In the semi-darkness the agent watched as the SS officer scurried across the room, withdrew a pistol from a briefcase, and tucked it into his coat pocket. He was making his way back to the window as Matteson's four well-armed guides were making their final approach to the cabin. It was at this point, remembered Matteson, that the fugitive "sensed something was wrong and slammed the shutter closed." Matteson signaled again and the entire cabin was quickly surrounded. To everyone's surprise, a few minutes later the cabin door opened and the SS officer walked out onto the porch and looked around. Perhaps he thought the small group of mountaineers had left. "When he saw the troops ringed around the building, he reentered the cabin in a hurry and bolted the door," Matteson recorded in his report. The Americans were prepared for a shootout. Kaltenbrunner and company were not going anywhere.

"There is no need for bloodshed!" shouted Matteson. "Surrender now! Drop your weapons and come out with your hands in the air!"

Several seconds passed in silence. Only the wind blowing through the timber stirred the solitude of the early Alpine morning. Matteson ordered the infantry to kick in the door and storm the cabin. As they moved forward and "started to push against the door . . . [it] was opened from the inside and four men marched out, surrendering to the patrol."

A thorough search of the lodge produced important "papers of both Kaltenbrunner and Scheidler," as well as about fifty packages of "tax free American Chesterfield cigarettes, French chocolate bars, 1,500 Reichsmarks, two pistols, and a 'burp gun,' which had been hidden in the chimney." There was little doubt one of the four men was Kaltenbrunner, but which one? As odd as it seems today, neither Matteson nor any of his men knew what the RSHA chief looked like. Each man was interrogated in turn. One of them claimed he was a Wehrmacht doctor named "Unterwegen," and had papers supporting his assertion. "Another brought forth papers that also seemed authentic," remembered Matteson. All professed ignorance as to the whereabouts of Ernst Kaltenbrunner. Within an hour the patrol, augmented by four more men, began the journey down from the mountain now "uncertain if they had apprehended the persons whom they had sought." As they walked through the snow Matteson crafted a simple plan to determine whether the former head of RSHA was one of his captives.[12]

When Altaussee was reached at about 11:30 a.m., Matteson hustled his foot column to Scheidler's house. A brisk knock on the door brought forth Frau Scheidler, who "rushed out and planted a kiss on one of the men," reported Matteson with smug satisfaction. "This settled the identity of Scheidler." Now there was no doubt that one of the remaining three men was Ernst Kaltenbrunner. Matteson repeated the sly performance at Kaltenbrunner's mistress's house. The subterfuge "identified the phony 'Dr. Unterwegen' as the Intelligence Chief." Both the adjutant and his former boss, however, remained absolutely stoic. "Neither man was willing to admit his true identity until later in the day despite the conclusive evidence," recorded Matteson. A picture of a woman and two children was thrust in front of Kaltenbrunner, who was sitting at a desk in a CIC office. The smiling trio was his own family, lifted from his confiscated billfold.

"We know who you are! You are Ernst Kaltenbrunner. Admit it!" demanded Matteson. As the agent later remembered, the tall man with the long, drawn and scarred face "saw the futility of holding out further."

"Yes. I am Kaltenbrunner," he said quietly.

Soon after Kaltenbrunner's confession Arthur Scheidler came clean as well, and "the capture of two of the three worst war criminals at that time still at large in Europe was ended." His embellishment of Scheidler's significance in relation to the war crimes committed under the Nazi banner is easily forgiven. The faithful CIC agent had a right to be justifiably proud of his remarkable accomplishment.

The seizure of Ernst Kaltenbrunner was a law enforcement coup worth remembering for a lifetime. The lawyer-turned-murderer had been directly responsible for overseeing the apparatus that had implemented and made possible the Final Solution. As the head of the Gestapo and other equally heinous organizations he had administered crimes against humanity on a scale never before witnessed. The blood of millions was splashed across his grotesque features. On October 13, 1946, Countess Gisele von Westarp was allowed into the Nuremberg prison to bid farewell to her erstwhile lover. She later told CIC investigators that Kaltenbrunner had told her during the visit "of the existence of two chests of gold but not their location, since Kaltenbrunner himself did not know it."[13]

*   *   *

Of Kaltenbrunner's end there is no doubt. But what of the fortune in gold and currency that vanished after leaving Gmunden in the belly of a

Wehrmacht army truck? The CIC in Bad Ischl searched for the boxes filled with sacks of gold in vain. Countess von Westarp herself had pleaded that the Americans do so. Kaltenbrunner was not in possession of any of the gold when he was captured. He had with him nothing more than a healthy sum of marks, a valuable watch, and a few loose jewels. Perhaps one or both of the SS officers tasked with its protection concealed Kaltenbrunner's treasure. Conceivably they, or others, kept the secret and picked away at the contents after the war became a memory, living well in a changed world. Perhaps it was hidden away and is still waiting to be found.

The only thing we know for sure is that Kaltenbrunner's sacks of gold officially disappeared in the tumultuous final days of World War II.[14]

Chapter Notes

1. CIC Memorandum, "Buried Treasures in the U.S. Zone of Austria," June 5, 1947, prepared by Robert Kauf.]

2. "Buried Treasures in the U.S. Zone of Austria," June 5, 1947.

3. "Buried Treasures in the U.S. Zone of Austria," June 5, 1947.

4. CIC "Unsigned Statement of Mrs. Iris Scheidler," dated April 1947. In March of 1945, Countess von Westarp gave birth to twins fathered by Kaltenbrunner.

5. CIC, "Final Interrogation Report of Arthur Scheidler," July 11, 1945.

6. "Final Interrogation Report of Arthur Scheidler," July 11, 1945. According to Scheidler, "Its [Bureau III] personnel was of a higher caliber than that of the other bureaus, and many of its members had university degrees." Many of these well-schooled officers were also tried after the war as criminals and either executed or imprisoned.]

7. "Final Interrogation Report of Arthur Scheidler," July 11, 1945; "Assets of Gold and Foreign Currency of the RSHA Berlin/Dislocation in the Salzkammergut, Salzburg and the Tyrol," April 26, 1947; "Statement of Mrs. Iris Scheidler, Given to Hofrat Reith," April 4, 1947. The sources conflict as to whether each sack of Kaltenbrunner's gold weighed 30 kg., or whether the entire cache weighed 30 kgs. We believe the former is correct, for reasons that will become clear in the text.]

8. CIC Memorandum, "Concealed Gold, Jewelry, Foreign Exchange, and Weapons, Believed to be Located in the Salzkammergut, Zell am See, Salzburg, and in the Tyrol," July 3, 1947; Emanual E. Minskoff, "Preliminary Report on External Assets of Ernst Kaltenbrunner," 1945.]

9. "Concealed Gold, Jewelry, Foreign Exchange, and Weapons, Believed to be Located in the Salzkammergut, Zell am See, Salzburg, and in the Tyrol," July 3, 1947.

10. CIC Memorandum, "The Capture of Dr. Ernst Kaltenbrunner, Nazi Chief of Gestapo, Kripo and All German Intelligence—and his Adjutant Scheidler," May 13, 1945.

11. "The Capture of Dr. Ernst Kaltenbrunner," May 13, 1945.

12. "Concealed Gold, Jewelry, Foreign Exchange, and Weapons, Believed to be Located in the Salzkammergut, Zell am See, Salzburg, and in the Tyrol," July 3, 1947.

13. "Concealed Gold, Jewelry, Foreign Exchange, and Weapons, Believed to be Located in the Salzkammergut, Zell am See, Salzburg, and in the Tyrol," July 3, 1947.

14. "Assets of Gold and Foreign Currency of the RSHA Berlin/Dislocation in the Salzkammergut, Salzburg and the Tyrol," April 26, 1947. Even the small amount of cash and jewels taken from Kaltenbrunner when he was captured vanished. According to the foregoing CIC memorandum, "it is not known what has become of these."

Adolf Eichmann's Blaa Alm Gold

Less than two weeks after Austrian investigator Hofrat Reith walked into agent Robert Kauf's CIC office, a conference was held in Vienna to determine how best to proceed with the investigation. The June 17, 1947, meeting was overseen by Special Agent Frank P. Dierick and attended by Kauf, Reith, and Reith's section chief, Dr. Otto Gleich. The men drove to Altaussee the next day to meet with Inspector Auerboeck, whom Reith described in glowing terms as one of his best "confidential informers." Auerboeck, explained Reith, had been diligently working the case for almost one year. He would be able to help them hammer down the background of these stories, what valuables were buried where, and who was involved and still needed to be grilled for information.

The conference with Auerboeck at an office in Fischerndorf (Altaussee) was extremely productive. Hours were exhausted pouring through documents and interviews. The Americans listened carefully while Auerboeck and Reith brought them up to speed regarding some of the major personalities involved and the treasures they had allegedly hidden. The more information the agents read and heard, the more obvious it became that a sizeable chunk of European wealth had been funneled into Austria at war's end.

One of the stories related in detail by Reith concerned another man with deep Austrian roots who had once sported a pair of miniature lightning bolts on his stiff uniform collar. He, too, had tried to abscond with gold and currency, though on a scale dwarfing Ernst Kaltenbrunner's puny effort. The SS officer's previous position and power had given him ready access to much of the gold and treasure generated by the implementation of the Holocaust. Unlike so many, however, he was more interested in bureaucratic mass murder by Führerbefehl (order of the Führer) than in milking the system to line his own pockets; others—the likes of Kurt Becher, Franz Konrad, and Josef Spacil—indulged in such matters. Like so many other Third Reich criminals, when the end arrived he loaded up his caravan with stolen loot and made a run, literally, for the hills. The Obersturmbannführer made it, at least for a while. His treasure, however, did not.[1]

*   *   *

Adolf Eichmann knew what would happen to him if he was caught by the Allies. Somehow the executioner of the Final Solution would have to make good his escape. The final weeks of the war found him in Prague, Czechoslovakia. Remaining there or returning to Germany was tantamount to suicide; there was no hope in either place of holding out against the Russians or the Americans. What to do? Like a good upper level manager he decided to pose the question to his superior. It took several attempts before he was able to get his boss, Ernst Kaltenbrunner, on the phone. The testy head of the RSHA was mired in his own problems, but he took the time to advise Eichmann to head for Altaussee in the Austrian Alps. The eventual strategy decided upon, sketchy at best, was to retreat into the mountains with as many assets and men as possible and conduct there a last ditch stand in the hope of staving off capture—or worse. Gauleiter August Eigruber was helping prepare a command post there for the Führer, whom many expected would soon would arrive from Berlin to direct the effort. If Eichmann vacillated on the issue he did not do so for long. At worse the journey and effort would buy days or perhaps weeks of additional freedom. His wife and children lived in Altaussee, and his parents in nearby Linz, Hitler's adoptive birthplace. That seemed to settle it. Upper Austria is where he would go.[2]

As April 1945 wound down and the German Sixth Army was beginning to disband in the Aussee region, the tattered remnants of SS leadership gathered in scenic Austria for a session of collective hand wringing. Eichmann, operating now under the alias "Dr. Müller," was prominent among them. According to at least one report he was the reputed "leader" of the resistance movement. In reality, he was the leader of a group thrown together to save his own skin. Traveling with him from Prague into Austria were an indeterminate number of Waffen-SS men, 150 Hitler Youth, and artillery pieces and other equipment including crates of weapons and a truckload or two of cargo, vigilantly guarded. The destination of this motley assemblage was the Blaa Alm, southeast of Salzburg, a small remote pasture land plateau about two miles square. The convoy made a stop at Altaussee and set up shop in the Park Hotel, a large luxury ski resort. A radio transmitter-receiver unit was erected and scattered bits of news of the outside world were received. None of it was good.[3]

Altaussee was a lovely, small village surrounded by Austrian lakes at the foot of the Dead Mountains (Totes Gebirge). When he arrived at headquarters, Eichmann was met by Kaltenbrunner's chief aide, "an old and trusted friend of mine, Major [Arthur] Scheidler." His RSHA boss was seated at a table in the next room, remembered Eichmann, "clothed in the uniform blouse of an SS general and some wedge-shaped ski pants tucked into some wonderful ski boots. It was an odd costume for the 'Last Days of Pompeii' feeling that then oppressed us all." Lunch had just ended. Few official duties remained for the once all-powerful head of RSHA. The tall figure was hunched over a table playing solitaire; a glass of cognac sat a few inches from his hand. Kaltenbrunner ordered up a snifter for Eichmann, who remembered (or imagined) that it tasted "good despite my gloomy mood."

"What are you going to do now?" inquired Kaltenbrunner.

Duty, as Eichmann later realized, had become of secondary importance. It was hard to concentrate on what was happening, and he later admitted as much. Nervous shock, which "hit him like a hammer" a few days later, was beginning to set in. His beloved Third Reich, to which he had sold his soul in exchange for the power of life and death over others, had all but exited history's stage. "I am going into the mountains," he answered.

"That's good," Kaltenbrunner responded. "Good for Reichsführer Himmler, too. Now he can talk to Eisenhower differently in his negotiations, for he will know that if Eichmann is in the mountains he will never surrender, because he can't." Kaltenbrunner was referring to the recent public announcement that Heinrich Himmler had been trying to negotiate a surrender to General Dwight D. Eisenhower through the auspices of Sweden's Count Folke Bernadotte.

As Eichmann remembered it, the pair "concluded . . . official business and I went off to become a partisan chief in Austria. I took my leave formally without any personal overtones, as did Kaltenbrunner. He remained sitting at his solitaire, only his expression revealing a certain friendliness to me."

"It's all a lot of crap. The game is up," Kaltenbrunner suddenly blurted pathetically as Eichmann left the room. They were the last words Eichmann ever heard "from my good friend Kaltenbrunner." Tens of millions of civilians and soldiers had been killed, millions more wounded or dislocated, and a large swath of the civilized world lay in smoking ruins, and the best parting phrase the RSHA chief could come up with was an analogy to excrement. The final words he would speak the following autumn would be no more meaningful.

Eichmann left Altaussee, "collected all the heavy equipment we had there and set out to organize a resistance movement in the Totes Gebirge, above the town. The whole thing had now been dumped in my lap." It had indeed. According to Eichmann he had with him:

> the regularly assigned people in my department . . . some groups of Waffen SS soldiers, and a wild bunch from [Walter] Schellenberg's Intelligence Section of the SS. Schellenberg's crowd had been burned out of the [Austrian] Kremsmünster monastery. I think they set it on fire themselves, but they managed to get a few truckloads out with them. In the trucks were scattered piles of uniforms, all kinds of uniforms except winter equipment and ski gear. Instead they had down sleeping bags and emergency rations—chocolate, hard sausage, etc., of the sort we hadn't seen for a long time. They also brought a small chest full of dollars, pounds and gold coins.

One small chest of gold? Perhaps not.[4]

*   *   *

April had given way to May by the time part of Eichmann's entourage took up temporary quarters at the (as yet unburned) monastery in Kremsmünster. A series of encounters and experiences with Eichmann at the monastery, in Altaussee, and on the Blaa Alm, seared themselves into SS Oberscharführer (Technical Sergeant) Rudolph Doskoczil's memory forever. Doskoczil was a native of Vienna and had been a member of the SS since 1938. As far as he was concerned the organization provided food, shelter, and pay. It kept him off the streets. From the perspective of the 1930s he could not see what was lurking in the decade that would follow. By 1943 he had reached the rank of Obersturmführer (First Lieutenant). He was also demoralized by the war and the role played thus far by his SS. Doskoczil spoke out on the subject and was demoted to sergeant. As an administrative aide to Dr. Wilhelm Höttl, Doskoczil found himself quartered in Kremsmünster as the war wound its way to a fitful conclusion. Just when it looked as though the end would arrive without much fanfare, Adolf Eichmann's men came calling that final May of the war.[5]

Doskoczil was returning to his quarters in the Kremsmünster monastery on May 2 when he spotted several heavily armed SS men milling about. Discreet inquiries revealed they were part of "SS-Group Eichmann." Unsure exactly what that meant, Doskoczil entered the monastery and discovered, to his complete surprise, "great amounts of gold and foreign exchange . . . being packed into sheet-iron chests by the administrative officer of the group." The next day Doskoczil was ordered to take command of a truck supposedly filled with food, weapons, clothes, and other items, and see to it that it arrived safely in Altaussee. His carefully worded orders were to report to the police station in Altaussee and make a phone call to the Villa Kerry "for further instructions." In the company of a Ukrainian driver, Doskoczil did as he was told and arrived at the police station on the evening of May 3. "The phone call was answered by a woman's voice telling me to wait in front of the police station . . . until somebody came and gave me further instructions," he told his postwar Austrian investigator. A few minutes later a pair of civilians on a motorcycle arrived and instructed Doskoczil to drive the truck to the Park Hotel. Curious, but smart enough to keep his mouth shut and do as he was told, Doskoczil followed the men to the inn. He was ordered to leave the truck in their custody, which was fine with him. The exhausted solder took a room and fell promptly to sleep. To Doskoczil's dismay, he discovered the next morning that the truck was missing and he had forgotten to remove his personal trunks from the back of the vehicle. Everything he owned, which was not much, was stuffed into those missing trunks. He promptly reported the truck stolen to the local police, but all they would tell him was that he "would learn where the lorry was [later]."

More surprises were in store for Doskoczil that morning of May 4. Without advance warning an assembly of SS men was called in front of the Park Hotel. Doskoczil was still a member of the SS so he fell in with the rest of them. He was standing there waiting to see what the gathering was all about when a second heavily loaded truck arrived from Kremsmünster carrying food, ammunition, office equipment and, as he later discovered, more gold. His attention snapped back to an SS lieutenant colonel. A new "fighting-group" led by a "Dr. Müller" was being formed, he barked at them. While Doskoczil looked on as "the alleged 'Dr. Müller' was introduced as the new commander." Doskoczil's mouth fell open. "I at once recognized that man; he was SS Obersturmführer [Adolf] Eichmann, whom I myself had known for many years." At least part of the fog surrounding the puzzle was beginning to lift. Eichmann walked slowly in front of the men, his heavy leather boots crunching in the snow. With his hands on his hips, the SS officer called out, "Who knows how to ski?"

Doskoczil and many others unwittingly raised their hands.

"You will step forward and select ski equipment at the hotel," Eichmann snapped. "You will then prepare to head out to the Blaa Alm in order to defend the mountain post against the approaching U.S. Forces."

Doskoczil realized immediately his mistake, but did as he was told. In the milling confusion that followed, he quietly slipped out of the group and a few hours later headed to see Dr. Höttl, who was visiting his wife and family at their home in Altaussee. When Doskoczil told him about his new mission at Blaa Alm, Höttl cut him short. "You cannot be party to this undertaking," he advised his subordinate. "It is nothing but a suicide mission aimed at buying the high brass a few more days to make good their escape." Doskoczil agreed to take this good advice and remain in

Altaussee. After his afternoon visit with Höttl he learned that both trucks—the one he had driven to Altaussee and the one that had arrived during the SS assembly—had departed for Blaa Alm.[6]

There was still the matter of his missing personal belongings. While other SS men drank boisterously or prepared themselves for the ski mission, Doskoczil searched about for his trunks. He was under the impression they had been off loaded at the hotel. "I supposed that they were still at the Park Hotel as numerous boxes and trunks were lying around there," he later explained. The sergeant poked his head into each room occupied by the SS, inquiring about his belongings. No one had seen his things. One of his last stops was the office of the administrator of Eichmann's group. What he observed inside remained with him for the rest of his life. "I saw a table, 2 meters long, which was entirely covered with piled-up foreign exchange and gold coins, the heap having a height of nearly half a meter," he remembered. "On the floor there were also cases containing foreign exchange and gold coins." One of Eichmann's assistants, a man Doskoczil had never seen before, was casually counting and sorting the stolen loot as though he were sitting in a toy aisle of a store taking inventory. In his hand was a list on which he was scribbling numbers. The sandy-haired officer looked up at the stunned, and by now a bit embarrassed, Doskoczil. Inquiring about misplaced underwear and toiletry items seemed ridiculously out of place. Still, they were the only things he owned. The officer, whom history has not named, waved Doskoczil away with a gruff, negative reply.[7]

Unable to find his things in Altaussee, Doskoczil hitched a ride in a jeep with two SS officers heading for Blaa Alm. They were seeking Eichmann to obtain food rations; Doskoczil simply hoped to find his belongings inside one of the two trucks already at that place. The jeep bumped along the single-lane mountain dirt road, but the two miles were slow going. Mud, slush, deep tire ruts, and eventually blowing snow forced the men to pull the jeep over and walk the last several hundred yards to the Blaa Alm Inn. The trucks were parked about fifty meters from the building next to a radio car. As the three men approached, two SS guards armed with machine guns refused to allow them near the vehicles. Doskoczil and his comrades raised their hands to show they understood and then backed away, heading instead for the inn. Perhaps they would find Eichmann there. Music, laughter and song rose to greet them as they entered a taproom. Inside were a dozen fully armed SS men throwing down cognac as fast as it could be poured. All of them were "drunk and in a state of complete helplessness," remembered Doskoczil with some disdain. [A few years ago, author Kenneth Alford enjoyed a dark ale in the Blaa Alm Inn, which was rebuilt on the original foundation. It is still located at the end of the same, single dirt lane in a remote splash of Austrian pasture land.]

Eichmann and his adjutant were quickly located. One of Doskoczil's companions approached and requested "emergency rations by order of Obergruppenführer Kaltenbrunner." Eichmann immediately took a dislike to the unnamed solder, whom he later described as "a fresh, arrogant fellow." SS Hauptsturmführer (Captain) Anton Burger, one of Eichmann's top aides, asked for permission to shoot him, but Eichmann declined. "I told the man he could have half a case and no more. Otherwise, I'd have [him] done in." On their way back to their jeep the trio passed the watchful, wary (and obviously sober) machine gun-wielding guards standing next to the parked trucks. "It struck me" at that time that the [trucks were] so strongly guarded that the assets of gold and foreign exchange were stowed away in [them]," recalled Doskoczil. He walked with his companions to the abandoned jeep and motored back that night to the Park Hotel in Altaussee. He never saw his personal belongings again, but he did have some vivid memories that would last a lifetime.[8]

*   *   *

Adolf Eichmann had already discovered just how difficult it was to reach Blaa Alm. The SS leader described the remote place, "a stretch of mountain pasture land about an hour's march from Altaussee." Late April and early May are usually snowy months in this region, and the early spring of 1945 was no exception. "I had the Bürgermeister order out 150 of the Hitler Youth—they were all we had—to shovel the snow out of our path," he recalled in his postwar memoirs. "It was already one or two meters deep in spots. At least we could get through with the vehicles." (Eichmann's vehicles and marching soldiers left behind the deep truck ruts and churned mud that Doskoczil's jeep was ultimately unable to navigate.) There was only one place to stay on the Blaa Alm, and Eichmann headed directly for the small inn. He was requisitioning a room when "an old party man in the town warned me about the innkeeper. He said I would do well to have the traitorous anti-Nazi clerk done in, and I decided to do so." As Eichmann breezily noted, "it was the time when everybody was doing everybody else in." When the innkeeper was brought to him for execution, Eichmann decided to spare his life—not because it was the moral or just thing to do but because he was "a little sausage of a man," and not a threat to anyone. A number of SS men discovered a large barrel of wine in a nearby storehouse. "I set it upon the street so that all the soldiers coming up to the mountain could stop for a few glasses before going on," explained Eichmann. "I allowed each man only a five-minute stop. The barrel was soon empty."

At about this time, another SS man stopped by seeking gold. His orders bore Kaltenbrunner's signature. "I knew the writing and it seemed genuine to me," remembered Eichmann, "although I had no reason to test its authenticity. In any case gold or money meant nothing to us in the mountains, while bread and emergency rations were everything. Although I was harsh to this fellow at first, I finally had . . . our paymaster pay out the gold that he requested, thus translating Kaltenbrunner's wish into fact." Exactly how much gold he gave the officer, who the officer was, and whether the metal ever reached Kaltenbrunner, is unknown.[9]

Eichmann surveyed his ragtag command and estimated his chances of survival. What he saw did not please him. "What a bunch of good-for-nothings you have here, I said to myself. There were guys from the Waffen SS, who probably were just out of [the] hospital and at the disposal of almost any unit, rounded up and turned over to me by the Security Police; this absolutely insubordinate gang from the Intelligence Section, a few women, my own men. And add to this 150 Hitler Youth. Then there were some Romanians on my neck, too. With this I was supposed to fight a war." He was at least well armed. "I had plenty of the most modern weapons, however, I had never before seen assault rifles, and now I had piles of them. I had never seen as much ammunition as I had up here—bazookas lying in heaps."[10]

One may legitimately doubt whether Eichmann ever seriously considered conducting a last stand in the snowy mountains of Austria. He was a bureaucrat, not a front line soldier. His stomach was cast iron when it came to shipping unarmed people to their deaths; picking up a rifle and directing a military action was not in his psychological play book. Even the pretense of a redoubt-style defense was finally, irrevocably, abandoned when he ordered most of his weapons and ammunition dumped into a stream and "the majority of the men" released from duty. Discipline by this time was all but nonexistent. "I had 5,000 Reichsmarks paid out to each one against his signature," he later wrote. "I was hard and brusque with them. Each man, on hearing he was no longer needed, gladly took off down the mountain without further formalities. I was even hard on a little SS girl, an office worker, who had begged and implored me to take her along. Scorning all her feminine wiles, I said, 'Pay out 5,000 marks. Dismissed!'" The trip from Prague to Altaussee and beyond merely bought Eichmann a few additional days of semi-organized freedom, its end uncertain but its purpose clear. Orders were issued to the remaining small group of men "to evacuate the Blaa-Alm and go farther away to the Rettenbachalm, which lies even higher." Captain Burger, Eichmann's "best skier," was sent ahead to investigate the condition of the mountain roads and seek advance lodging. In all likelihood, the volunteer skiers gathered in front of the Park Hotel, accompanied him.[11]

Eichmann's smaller motorized party was moving, snail-like, higher into the mountains when, as he recalled it, "an orderly arrived from Kaltenbrunner with a directive from Reichsführer Himmler ordering us not to shoot at Americans or Englishmen. I countersigned it and the boy rushed off back to the valley." Eichmann passed the directive down to his men. "It looked like the end." Kaltenbrunner was resigned to defeat; his actions in Altaussee at the card table bespoke as much. Eichmann was simply angry. "The Americans were now sitting in Bad Ischl, not very far away, and we heard that our girls were already dancing with the Americans in the marketplace," he scribbled with undisguised contempt almost two decades later. "Even the huntsmen were hostile to us. Gangs of them—home guardists they called themselves—were crawling around us in the hills, all of them punks. They were probably people who had shouted themselves hoarse yelling 'Heil Hitler!' in 1938. Now they prowled about us, with weapons of course. Whether or not my men shot at them I did not know, nor do I know now if they ever did. There was shooting everywhere at that confused time."[12]

One would have had to have been blind and deaf to have not recognized for many weeks that "the end" was near. The Americans arrived faster than even the Germans anticipated, and by now Altaussee was firmly in their grip. The Russians had reached Liezen in the Enns Valley. Now even his faithful inner circle began to unravel. Eichmann's driver, "Polanski," sought him out and asked for a vehicle or two "so that he might go off and set up a peacetime trucking concern on his own." Eichmann saw no harm in the request. After all," he thought, he had served me loyally for many years. "Take a truck for yourself," he told him, "or whatever you need from the Blaa-Alm, and make off with my Fiat Topolino."

Captain Burger also sought out Eichmann for a private conversation. "Obersturmbannführer, you are being sought as a war criminal," he said candidly. "The rest of us are not. We have thoroughly discussed the matter. We feel that you would be doing your comrades a great service if you would leave us and appoint another commander." Eichmann professed neither surprise nor anger at the direct remark. He had already decided to break away from the crowd and seek an escape on his own. "I will leave you alone on the Rettenbachalm," he replied to his men. "The war is over. You are not allowed to shoot at the enemy any longer. So take care of yourselves." With those two dozen or so anticlimactic words, the terrible wartime reign of Adolf Eichmann, one of the most feared men in Europe, fizzled to its conclusion.[13]

Eichmann took leave from the official stage for what would be a lengthy turn on the lamb. As he slogged through the heavy snows he regretted not having "done more for my wife and children." While the war had been winding down he had been in such a "shock" he failed to make provision for them ahead of time. "I, too, could have had my family securely wrapped in a very comfortable cocoon of foreign exchange and gold," he lamented years later, implying that many other officers has done exactly that. "In fact, I could easily have sent them on to the farthest, the most neutral of foreign countries. Long before the end, any of the Jews I dealt with would have set up foreign exchange for me in any country I had named, if I had promised any special privileges for them." The manager of statistics had been too busy driving the Holocaust train to think ahead for a life after defeat, for when the twin iron rails would reach their inevitable end. Instead, all he was able to give his family was "a briefcase full of grapes and a sack of flour before going into the mountains from Altaussee." Gold and safety he failed to provide, but poison he had in abundance. "I [gave] them poison capsules, one for my wife and one for each child, to be swallowed if they fell into the hands of the Russians." Eichmann and Josef and Magda Goebbels', it seems, were cut from the same piece of cloth.[14]

*   *   *

Advance elements of the American Army captured Altaussee and the deserted mountain defense post at Blaa Alm on May 8, 1945. The pair of trucks and radio car Doskoczil had seen parked and guarded outside the inn were recovered. The trucks were empty, but intact. The radio car had been burned. Not a soul was to be found. Adolf Eichmann, the SS troops, the Hitler Youth—all were gone now, scattered to the blustery Austrian winds. So were the boxes holding Eichmann's millions in gold and currency.

The mystery of what happened to Eichmann's gold remains. Could it have been shipped elsewhere during the war's final hours? Rudolph Doskoczil argues passionately and persuasively against this scenario. The gold, he believes, "must have remained on the Blaa Alm." He went on to observe that the trucks did not get back to Altaussee before the Americans arrived there on May 8. "It is out of the question that further transportation was made to Bad Ischl because the Americans were at that time already at Bad Ischl." Moreover, he added, "the road leading to that place [Bad Ischl] was impassable [because it] was blocked by avalanches," not to mention deep mud and slush.

So the trucks never left Blaa Alm, a small plateau a mere two miles square. Could Eichmann and his men have carried away the valuables? "Impossible," concludes Doskoczil. "These things existed in such large quantities that they could not be transported by means of rucksacks" on foot up hillsides through deep snow. Besides, he added, "The other members of the 'SS-Group Eichmann' are partly in flight, the majority of them however, are in several American concentration camps in Bavaria and Glasenbach." Was some of the gold hauled out in the pockets or rucksacks of a few men? Almost certainly. Then what happened to the large bulk of the treasure? "Buried by Eichmann and his administrative officer," concludes Doskoczil, "because such actions were taken by various SS groups."[15] None of Eichmann's gold was ever officially recovered by U.S. Forces.

Evidence that it never left the area was not long in coming. After the war small amounts of gold were regularly found in the Blaa Alm–Altaussee region. According to a local official, several kilograms of gold coins were found in one of the many hay huts that dotted the Blaa Alm in 1982. (A kilogram weighs slightly more than 2.2 lbs.) As one might imagine, the sensational discovery triggered a widespread treasure hunt by the local populace. No additional gold, however, was recovered. Or perhaps it is more accurate to write that no one *reported* finding any additional gold. Revealing that information would expose the finder to taxes and a whole host of other problems.

In July 1987, author Kenneth Alford traveled to the Aussee region and met Frau Eggers at the Blaa Alm. The woman was wearing tall black rubber boots and a large cloth dress attending a handful of cows. "I was a young waitress at the Blaa Alm Inn during [Adolf] Eichmann's stay there," she told Ken after he struck up a conversation with the woman. The subject of Eichmann's lost gold quickly came up for discussion.

"It is too bad they never found it," Alford told her.

The elderly Austrian woman smiled knowingly, tapped her walking stick into the ground, and shook her head. "Small bars of gold are every year found concealed in hay sheds or buried."

"Really?" Alford replied. "I am conducting research on this subject. Can you put me in touch with anyone who has found some of this gold?"

At that Frau Eggers merely smiled, clucked her cows along, and walked away.[16]

Chapter Notes

1. "First Progress Report: Concealed Gold, Jewelry, Foreign Exchange, and Weapons, Believed to be Located in the Salzkammergut, Zell am See, Salzburg, and in the Tyrol," July 3, 1947.]

2. The entire idea of a last ditch "Alpine Redoubt" defense in Bavaria and northern Austria was absurd, but some truly believed in its viability. After it became obvious that the Allied drive across Europe and final German defeat was a *fait accompli*, officers and politicians in positions of authority, including German propaganda minister Josef Goebbels, began to seriously consider

reinforcing the southern mountainous area for a final defense. Bunkers, training facilities, and airstrips would be built there, supplies stored there, conventional armies would eventually retreat there, and the Führer would arrive and direct an impregnable defense. Most informed higher-ups knew that a prolonged defense with conventional forces was no longer possible. Thus the idea of a final Alpine defense strategy was proposed and propagated as a strategic ploy to convince the Allies it would be too bloody and costly to overrun the area. The only hope was for a negotiated peace. Intertwined within this fantasy was "Operation Werewolf [Wehrwolf]," whereby regular soldiers and militia would act as partisans before and after any surrender and cut roads, destroy rail lines, and poison wells behind the lines [i.e., in occupied Germany]. Partisan activities (whether part of "Operation Werewolf" or not remains unclear) were reported in southern Germany and Austria as late as 1947. For more information on this fascinating and overlooked aspect of the war, see Perry Biddiscombe, *Werewolf! The History of the National Socialist Guerrilla Movement, 1944-1946* (Toronto, 1998).

3. Eichmann, "Memoirs," Life Magazine, p. 155, 156. "Alm" means pasture or field.

4. Eichmann "Memoirs," *Life Magazine*, pp. 154-155. Eichmann's small mindedness is evident in a passage he penned about the Park Hotel's proprietor, who " years afterward kept railing against 'that dog Eichmann' who requisitioned his hotel and let his gang run it, inflicting all sorts of fancied damages. The complaint was merely something rooted in his wretched shopkeeper's mind. By no means did we wreck everything in his hotel. On the contrary, I finally yielded to the pressure of the doctor in charge of the neighboring field hospital, who had tearfully begged me to take my combat troops out of Altaussee so that he might declare it an open city. So we evacuated. Before my troops left, I personally saw the Red Cross nurses scrubbing and cleaning up, room by room, since the overcrowded hospital had to expand into this pig's hotel. It was set up as a hospital annex. The beneficiary of all this clean-up operation was thus enabled to feather his own nest." Ibid., p. 154.

5. CIC Memorandum, "Statement of Rudolph Doskoczil," interviewed by Inspector Auerboeck, April 24, 1947.

6. CIC Memorandum, "Statement of Rudolph Doskoczil," interviewed by Inspector Auerboeck, April 24, 1947.

7. "Statement of Rudolph Doskoczil," interviewed by Inspector Auerboeck, April 24, 1947.

8. "Statement of Rudolph Doskoczil," interviewed by Inspector Auerboeck, April 24, 1947; Eichmann, "Memoirs," *Life Magazine*, p. 156. SS Captain Anton Burger, an Austrian, was an aide to Eichmann and had been deputy commander of Theresienstadt concentration camp in Czechoslovakia. Burger helped deport 10,000 Greek Jews to concentration camps, where most of them perished. "Concealed Gold, Jewelry, Foreign Exchange, and Weapons, Believed to be Located in the Salzkammergut, Zell am See, Salzburg, and in the Tyrol," July 3, 1947.]

9. Eichmann, "Memoirs," *Life Magazine*, p. 156.

10. Eichmann, "Memoirs," *Life Magazine*, p. 156.

11. Eichmann, "Memoirs," *Life Magazine*, p. 156.

12. Eichmann, "Memoirs," *Life Magazine*, p. 156.

13. Eichmann, "Memoirs," *Life Magazine*, p. 156.

14. Eichmann, "Memoirs," Life Magazine, p. 155, 156. Josef and Magda Goebbels poisoned their six children in the Berlin bunker before they themselves were either killed or committed suicide.

15. "Statement of Rudolph Doskoczil," interviewed by Inspector Auerboeck, April 24, 1947.

16. Author Interview with Mrs. Eggers, Altaussee, 1987.

Chapter 15

"It became apparent during this period that further amounts of gold, foreign currency, and jewels confiscated by the Gestapo in Vienna [and elsewhere] were hidden in the area of Altaussee."

— Hofrat Reith, Chief of the Austrian Investigation Service of the Ministry of Property Control and Economic Planning

The Frau Connection: Iris Scheidler and Elfriede Höttl

*H*ofrat Reith smiled at his American counterparts and pulled out another pair of files. The conference in Inspector Anton Auerboech's office was going better than even he had hoped. The CIC agents were impressed with what he and Auerboech had thus far accomplished. Now it was time to explain how it was that the Austrians learned so many details about what had transpired at war's end in Upper Austria.

Rumors of gold and other treasures and priceless artifacts piled up as thick and fast as Alpine snow in the days leading up to the German capitulation. Shortly after the Americans occupied Altaussee, explained Reith, "seventy-five kilograms [165 lbs.] of buried gold were discovered by civilian members of the Austrian Resistance Movement." These men, he continued, were on "sentry duty" when the gold was discovered. The soldiers were both diligent and honest. The entire cache was delivered to Captain L.A. Degner, a member of the 319th Infantry Regiment. Almost simultaneously, four Wehrmacht Sixth Army cash boxes containing 4,700,000 marks and diverse kinds of foreign exchange were found a few miles to the east in a salt factory at Bad Aussee. This mammoth currency cache, which was about to be burned by "two German military officials," was also delivered into Degner's hands. "It became apparent during this period that further amounts of gold, foreign currency, and jewels confiscated by the Gestapo [and SS] in Vienna [and elsewhere] were hidden in the area of Altaussee," Reith told the American CIC agents.[1]

On May 17, 1945, Anton Auerboech, who had been a policeman before the war and an infantryman in the Wehrmacht after 1938, assumed police duties in Bad Aussee. The quaint market village, just three miles south of Altaussee, is nestled tightly in the Valley of Traun at the confluence of a pair of branch like fingers from a river bearing the same name. Surrounded by lakes, timber, and mountains, the salt- and mineral-spring spa is one of the most lovely spots in all of Austria. The new policeman's arrival was marked by an early growth of narcissus. Within two weeks the hillsides and pastures would be in full bloom, an ancient sign of renewal that winter was a memory and European spring had arrived. The flowers were lovely, but it was what might be hiding under their beauty that interested the inspector. "I began to hear numerous rumors about concealed gold," he told agents Kauf and Dierick, "but I had little time to investigate because of my many duties. But I kept them in mind and continued to be alert for more of them." His duties carried him back and forth between Bad Aussee and Altaussee, where three of the inhabitants of that small village of seventy-five families included the wives of SS men Adolph Eichmann, Wilhelm Höttl, and Arthur Scheidler. The Allies seeded the area with agents and Auerboech took it upon himself to pry into the lives and secrets of the latter two women.

The following year passed quickly. In September of 1946, Hofrat Reith and section chief Dr. Otto Gleich drove from Vienna to Salzburg to take custody of a fortune in priceless artwork that had been recovered there by the Americans. On the way the pair stopped in Bad Aussee, where they "became acquainted with Auerboech" for the first time. The new inspector "told them about the steady stream of rumors and the gold and currency that had been found immediately following the surrender." Reith, a survivor of Dachau and Buchenwald, was keenly interested in the story. "He told me to investigate further," explained Auerboech, "and that he would be in touch with me in the future for additional reports."[2]

Another five months slipped past. When Auerboech received word that he was about to be transferred to a new post, he drove to Vienna in February 1947 and informed Reith. A relocation, he complained, would completely disrupt his ongoing investigation. Reith had enough clout to pull strings halfway across the country and arrange for the inspector to remain in Bad Aussee. There, he informed him, you will "devote [your] time wholly to the subject matter." Reith also devoted significant energies helping Auerboech track down leads. They seemed to be as plentiful as narcissus in June. Credible clues led them from Salzburg to Zell am See, Innsbruck to Vienna, and Altaussee to points north in southern Germany and beyond. The pair visited "numerous sites in the region of Altaussee and accumulated considerable evidence to substantiate the validity of reports which had hitherto been regarded as somewhat fantastic." Reith reached the conclusion that "the exact location of sizeable amounts of gold could be determined."

In order to achieve this end, however, interrogations of key individuals were necessary. He and Auerboech cobbled together a list of thirty-six people, some still under U.S. arrest and some now free, for questioning. Satisfied he had done all he could with his means at hand, Reith prepared a preliminary report in April 1947 and submitted the memorandum up the chain of command to the Federal Minister of Property Control and Economic Planning. The report ended with a plea for American assistance in a joint operation, which Reith deemed "absolutely necessary" for success. His boss agreed. Evidence was gathered together and Reith, briefcase in hand, contacted Agent Robert Kauf. And that is how the group of men ended up sitting at Auerboech's desk in Bad Aussee on June 18, 1947.

If there was any one particular catalyst that propelled Reith to pen the report seeking American support, it was the success Auerboech enjoyed interviewing two women: Iris Scheidler and Elfriede Höttl. Both were married to men who had close ties to the upper echelon of Nazi power brokers. Both husbands were now marking time in Allied hands. Both women told incredible stories any professional would deem worthy of additional investigation.

*   *   *

Thousands of middle and high ranking German officers found themselves pacing in detention cells at war's end. Arthur Scheidler was one of them. Ernst Kaltenbrunner's former right-hand man was languishing in jail while his ex-chief sat in the dock at Nuremberg staring at evidence of his crimes under the harsh light of public scrutiny. Another detainee was Dr. Wilhelm Höttl who, in a delicious twist of irony, was interned at Dachau twelve miles north of Munich. The former concentration and death camp, where tens of thousands has been murdered or starved to death, had been converted into a large prison camp and trial court by the U.S. Army. Many of Höttl's former superiors has sent entire families to languish and die within its confines.

During Scheidler's internment, his wife Iris, a lithe and attractive 34-year-old native of Vienna, took up with a U.S. Army colonel stationed in Nuremberg. The pair were in love and wanted to marry. Unfortunately, the sticky situation of an existing marriage kept them from exchanging wedding vows. In an effort to alter the status quo, the colonel arranged for Iris to visit Scheidler and obtain his consent for a divorce. No one could have predicted the simple visit designed to end a marriage contract would trigger one of the largest treasure hunts in history.[3]

Exactly when Frau Scheidler first met with her jailed husband is uncertain. When they did meet, Scheidler took the opportunity to inform his unfaithful wife, sitting a handful of feet away across a table, that he and Kaltenbrunner had hauled a fortune in gold and currency from Berlin to Austria in April 1945. "The treasure was in the vicinity of Altaussee and is now missing," he told her. If Scheidler revealed this information to his wife in an effort to buy her loyalty and keep her from running off with the unnamed American colonel, it worked. Iris dropped plans to divorce her husband and marry the officer, and instead returned immediately to her Altaussee residence. She would find it impossible to keep the story secret.[4]

In early April 1947 (whether weeks or months had passed since Frau Scheidler's initial visit with her husband is unclear), another rumor of a golden cache hidden away in Upper Austria reached the keen ears of Inspector Auerboech. Unlike so many others, however, this one was tethered directly to a person living in Altaussee: Frau Iris Scheidler. The officer energetically followed through with a visit to her home, where "he eventually gained her confidence and was given the information contained in Exhibit V." This memorandum detailed her husband's responsibilities during the war and his working relationship with Ernst Kaltenbrunner. Some of it was very personal; the Allies, though, already had much of the same information. Of far more interest to Auerboech was the news concerning Kaltenbrunner's gold and how Iris came to possess the information (as just related, her husband had told her during her visit to the Nuremberg jail). She professed to know nothing more than that the fortune had existed in April-May 1945 and was now missing. She had been trying to discover what happened to it, she explained to Auerboech, but had not been successful. The fact that she had not been allowed to see her husband "since March 1947" only made finding the gold that much more difficult.

Auerboech's developing leads had also guided him to the front door of Frau Elfriede Höttl, the wife of SS officer Dr. Wilhelm Höttl. She, too, was tied into the network that had information about the mobile wealth that had deposited itself into Austria's scenic highlands. When Auerboech informed Reith of these important developments, the pair devised a plan of action. At Auerboech's insistence, both women agreed "to cooperate in finding out the hidden assets of gold and foreign exchange." In exchange, their husbands would be treated well and perhaps released from custody. A meeting was organized on or about April 12, 1947, between Frau Scheidler and her husband in Nuremberg. The only question now was whether Scheidler knew more than he had thus far disclosed, and whether he would talk fully about it. As it turned out, he knew a great deal. So did his wife, and much of it had yet to be revealed.[5]

Tired of jail and anxious to be free, Scheidler agreed to cooperate fully with the investigation. In return he was allowed "a leave for several days" with his wife. Out spilled a slew of information, including how the RSHA train was damaged by Allied fire, the mix up between boxes filled with personnel files and other boxes filled with gold and currency, and the final disappearance after the cases were put on a truck in Gmunden and driven in the direction of Imst under the control of a couple SS men. "These people are known to me," he told his wife, but he could not mine the proper parties for more information sitting behind barbed wire in the camp at Nuremberg. "I will be able to give more particulars concerning the precise location of the gold at our next meeting," he said, hoping that freedom would soon strike in his direction.[6]

When debriefed on the matter, Frau Scheidler volunteered additional facts of which neither Auerboech nor Reith was aware. In September 1946, she and her sister-in-law, Irmgard Gottschalk (Arthur Scheidler's sister), had met with Scheidler in Nuremberg. There, Gottschalk related a strange, though reasonably credible, story. "Just before the surrender, gold and silver coins as well as an amount of weapons were buried or rather sealed in the canal . . . before the gate or beneath the gate to the former concentration camp of Ebensee." The notorious death camp at Ebensee, Austria, was a sub-camp of the larger complex at Mauthausen located at the southern tip of Traun Lake about 50 miles southwest of Linz. It was liberated by the Americans on May 9, 1945. By the end of the war some 350 inmates were dying there each day, stacked up like cord wood in front of the buildings. Each concentration camp was a repository jammed with individual stories of mechanized death and hardship and suffering beyond imagination. Did Ebensee's library of secrets also include hidden gold? Frau Gottschalk did not witness these things. She had been told about the treasure trove "by a member of the aide-de-camp's office in Berlin, who was present when the burying or the sealing was performed." Arthur Scheidler confirmed the story and even produced a sketch of the location for his wife who, in turn, passed it along to Auerboech and Reith. "These assets would be immediately seizeable," she told them, "but whether that is advisable I must leave for the decision of the Austrian Government."[7]

Frau Scheidler was not yet finished. She had also learned from "the wife of a non-commissioned officer of the aide-de-camp's office who stayed for a short time in Bad Aussee that a considerable quantity of gold has been found in the cellar of a house at Altmünster, in which a certain Mrs. Koplin lived." When pressed for additional details Frau Scheidler declined, claiming, "Further particulars are not known to me." She admitted having so little verifiable information on this story that she could not say "whether this rumor is founded by truth." But, she stressed, "it would certainly be interesting to check the matter. It would also be possible to learn the address of Mrs. Koplin, who lives in Germany at present." Auerboech dutifully scribbled the information into his notebook for use at a later time, recording that "further examination and investigation will have to be carried through."[8]

As earlier indicated, Inspector Auerboech's investigation was running on parallel tracks. One of the rails comprised the Iris Scheidler saga; the other, the Elfriede Höttl story. Iris Scheidler's statements confirmed a few of the same things 35-year-old Elfriede had told Auerboech just two weeks earlier. Of particular interest to Auerboech was Elfriede's marriage to Dr. Wilhelm Höttl, the former SS officer and chief of the Sicherheitsdienst, or SD, for southeast Austria. Her husband had been an important and fairly powerful Nazi bureaucrat, and authorities had good reason to suspect he had intimate knowledge concerning several aspects of their investigation. Auerboech's interviews with Frau Höttl confirmed these suspicions.

*   *   *

Opportunistic. That single word sums up SS Obersturmbannführer (Lieutenant Colonel) Wilhelm Höttl's career. Indeed, by 1945 he had honed opportunism to a razor's edge. The future member of Himmler's notorious SS was born on March 19, 1915, in Vienna, Austria. His scholarly bent, which had been obvious from a young age, matured into something tangible when he graduated in 1938 from the prestigious University of Vienna with a doctorate in world history. A few months before graduation Höttl's application for service with the SD (Sicherheitsdienst, or Secret Service of the SS) was accepted. Five months later he had achieved the rank of Haupsturmführer (Captain), a full member of the organization in charge of handling "church affairs." Though Höttl's genesis with the SD was smooth, his tenure with the organization soon developed into a stormy love-hate relationship that almost cost him his life.

By summer of 1939 Höttl was being scrutinized by more fanatical elements within the SD. Whispers of "political unreliability" wafted through the halls of the intelligence service. A formal disciplinary investigation was launched. The exact findings are not known, but the Austrian was quietly transferred to a sub-department of the Foreign Intelligence bureau of the RSHA in Vienna. There, Höttl and his fellow SD members monitored goings-on in southeastern Europe and southern Russia. Two years passed in relative quiet while Höttl labored beneath the radar screen of the extremists who permeated his department. Although few others foresaw defeat early in the war, Höttl appreciated early and often that the spreading conflict could only bring death and destruction to Germany and his beloved Austria. As early as 1941 he may have been trying to establish a reliable contact within the Vatican in the hope of organizing a negotiated settlement of the war. Someone got wind of his efforts and word seeped up to RSHA chief Reinhard Heydrich. In October of that year another disciplinary investigation was initiated. This one had teeth. "I was called before the SS and Police Court for having religious ties and for lack of political and ideological reliability," he recalled in his testimony at the main Nuremberg trial. To put a finer point on it, Höttl was not a good and true believing Nazi. Like Admiral Wilhelm Canaris and many other generally honorable officers serving Hitler's Third Reich, Höttl had an intrinsic dislike for Nazism and what it stood for. He knew full well that evil paraded in parallel lock-step with Hitler's jack booted armies, and that an early peace was the only way to save Austria. His conscience tugged at his sleeve, but so did the burning desire of personal ambition and a call to duty—the twin glues that kept men like Höttl, Canaris, and Albert Speer in their positions of responsibility. The employment and labors of respected army generals, politicians, diplomats, and industrialists cloaked the German State's machinery of misery and death with a shroud of respectability. In Höttl's case inertia was trumps. He remained in place serving an ideology whose objectives were at odds with his own, even as he worked to undermine them.[9]

The charges brought against Höttl were serious. Somehow he managed to avoid a prison sentence (or worse), but punitive measures awaited. A demotion "to the ranks as an ordinary private" was followed by a transfer to the Russian front. Putting his brains to work, Höttl eluded service with a rifle by finagling instead a job as reporter and publisher of the SS Prinz Eugen Division newsletter. His pitiless boss, however, was not so fortunate. In June of 1942, Heydrich was assassinated by Czech partisans. Several months later Höttl was pardoned by Heydrich's successor, the equally merciless Ernst Kaltenbrunner, and recalled to duty in February 1943 as sub-department chief of Bureau VI for Southeastern Europe with headquarters in Berlin. His direct superior was the chief of Bureau VI, Walter Schellenberg. "I was in charge of matters relating to the Vatican, as well as of matters relating to some states in the Balkans. We had no executive authority," Höttl later explained to the Nuremberg judges while testifying on Kaltenbrunner's behalf. "The SD was purely an information service . . . Its task was to give to the highest German authorities and the individual Reich ministries information on all events at home and abroad."[10]

Dr. Höttl had no intention of remaining in Berlin. That December he arranged for a transfer with his staff to Vienna. Once again he delved head first into activities contrary to what was expected of a loyal SS officer. Murmurs that something was amiss circulated again around Höttl. The relocation, some whispered, was the result of contact he had established with the American embassy in Madrid, Spain. No charges were filed. Höttl opened communications with Austrians who held similar concerns that the entire ship upon which they were all passengers was heading for the shoals. Their united goal was to bring about the separation of Austria from Germany, keep the advancing Russians out of Austria, and avoid turning the country into a killing field. Securing for Austria and her citizens better treatment than the harsh retribution many expected would be meted out to Germany and her people was high among Höttl's many priorities. In late 1944, Höttl (by now a Obersturmbannführer, or Lieutenant Colonel) made an important breakthrough when he established contact with Allen Welsh Dulles, the head of the U.S. Office of Strategic Services in Europe with an office in Switzerland. With Dulles's assistance Höttl obtained a visa from the Swiss General Staff and traveled to that country several times. His hand was significantly strengthened when he latched onto a powerful issue to use as leverage to achieve his ends: the existence of a plan to wage a prolonged resistance from within a powerful German Alpine redoubt in Austria.[11]

"We used it [the existence of a redoubt defense] as a means to obtain better terms, if not for the whole of Germany then at least for that part of Austria which was affected," Höttl wrote after the war. Dulles was keenly interested (and worried about) the Alamo-like stand planned in Austria. "From the very first talks with Dulles it became clear that the Alpine redoubt was to be and would remain the main subject of discussion," remembered Höttl. He routinely furnished Dulles with specific data regarding the military strength of the German resistance movement slated for the mountainous region. The German army in Italy, he informed Dulles, was going to withdraw and hold a fortified line in the Bavarian Mountains. The plan sent shivers down the spines of Americans in high places, many of whom believed reducing the area might take years and cost tens of thousands of more lives. Ironically, the activities of Höttl and others acting in concert with him were sanctioned by Ernst Kaltenbrunner, himself an Austrian native who saw a noose or firing squad looming in his future. The chief of RSHA fervently hoped and arrogantly believed his actions would catapult him into a position of safety as a leading figure in the drive for a negotiated peace with the Western Allies, and thus earn him a place in the postwar political restructuring that would follow.

Höttl's effort bore mixed fruit. SS-Gruppenführer (Major General) Karl Wolff, who was sent with Heinrich Himmler's blessings to negotiate with Dulles, was hamstrung by his lack of diplomatic or official standing. Dulles was an experienced intelligence officer and was unwilling to plow any ground beyond terms for the surrender of the Southern German Army Group. Wolff was keenly aware that he was holding few cards he could play; the deck had already been dealt and all the cards were on the Allied side of the table. He offered to arrange the capitulation of all German and Italian troops in Italy. A complex and delicate series of negotiations— complicated by Russian involvement, President Franklin Roosevelt's untimely death, and Kaltenbrunner's bullying interference— eventually led to the execution of terms surrendering the Southern Army Group and Italian troops on April 29, 1945, to take effect on May 2, 1945. Thus did the war in Italy end about one week sooner than the rest of the fighting in Europe. "Without [this force]," explained Höttl, "the nucleus and the mass for manning the redoubt were both lacking. The Allies now had nothing more to worry about in the South, and in the meantime they had also come to know that their original misgivings had been exaggerated." Höttl, of course, had been pining for something much broader and lasting than Wolff's accomplishment. Still, with hindsight Höttl was generally pleased with the outcome. "Although we did not achieve the far-reaching results for which we had striven," he explained, "the contact of the German secret service with Dulles did at least ensure that the occupation of Austria and the reconstruction of government in that country were accomplished without vain bloodshed and senseless destruction." At the end of the war Dr. Wilhelm Höttl joined his wife in Altaussee, and surrendered there to American army solders on May 8, 1945.[12]

*   *   *

As he had with the Scheidlers, Inspector Anton Auerboech found Elfriede Höttl and her Dachau-fettered husband willing and ready to cooperate with his investigation. On April 4, 1947, Frau Höttl sat down with Austrian investigators in Vienna and executed a detailed statement on the subject of hidden treasures in Austria. She and her husband had always disliked the Nazis, she told the agents. "We always felt ourselves to be Austrians and have always behaved in an appropriate manner." The bromide was a standard refrain uttered amidst the smoking ruins of central Europe, but in the Höttls' case, it was largely true. When pressed about what she knew of hidden gold and other assets, the Austrian agents discovered that Elfriede Höttl, like Iris Scheidler, had quite a story to tell.

"As I believe it is already known to [you]," she began, "valuables of gold, foreign exchange, paper money, and so forth of [an incredible] amount have been especially brought to the area of Aussee and have been scattered afterwards." This news was common knowledge all over the region even before the surrender, she added. In addition to verifying the story of Adolf Eichmann's fortune in gold and Ernst Kaltenbrunner's missing truckload of bullion, Elfriede introduced other characters who had played a role in the drama still without end. During the final days of the war, one of her husband's fellow officers from Bureau VI-Vienna, SS Obersturmbannführer (Lieutenant Colonel) Wilhelm Wanek, had taken up temporary residence in the monastery at Kremsmünster before moving on to the Villa Kery and the Park Hotel. Wanek's group, she explained, was hauling with them a bundle in stolen loot. "The large amounts of gold and foreign exchange located there [Kremsmünster] were transferred to Altaussee." Frau Höttl adamantly claimed that "all Departments had to deliver [their] assets of gold and foreign exchange to Wanek's secretary," which was why he had so much of it with him when he moved into the Aussee region. "This gold certainly had a value of [many] millions." Frau Höttl referred several times to an unnamed "informant," known both to her and her husband, who could substantiate these claims. Although it was never explicitly stated, the clever woman was apparently using his identity as a means of springing her husband from custody. "All of these valuables were transported from Aussee to the Blaa Alm, and they were seen again by our informant [there.]" When pressed about their final disposition, Frau Höttl maintained that "it was impossible that they were further transported from the Blaa Alm because at that time the Americans were already at Ischl and because there prevailed such snow-conditions (90 cm.) on the Blaa Alm that they hardly could be moved on. Therefore, the searching should be confined [to that area]." She concluded by adding, "The gold which was found at the Villa Kery came certainly from the group Wanek."[13]

The Villa Kery gold to which Elfriede Höttl was referring was discovered shortly after the Americans walked into Altaussee. A salt miner and farmer named Johann Pucher stumbled across a pair of half-buried iron Wehrmacht cases. The chests were taken to the local police station and turned over to a commissioner in Bad Aussee. Pucher, who was later interviewed by Austrian agents, was present when the cases were inventoried. Inside were 10,176 gold coins, plus notes totaling 92,000 Swiss francs, $22,000 American dollars, and 25,000 Dutch gulden and Belgian francs. A gold cigarette case and gold bar were also found inside. A third case was discovered a few days later when Pucher made a thorough search of the Villa Kery and it grounds. The case was hauled to Bad Aussee one evening and placed inside the town hall safe. The next morning it was cut open with an acetylene torch. More gold coins were found inside. Pucher never saw the contents of the third chest, but "could hear them make a ringing noise when the chest was carried." The case, he remembered, "was extremely heavy."

The gold from these cases was inventoried properly and turned over to the correct authorities. However, a report drafted by investigator Hofrat Reith and shared with American agents concluded that "there exists no proof whatsoever at the Ministry of Property Control and Economic Planning that the large amount of paper currency was ever surrendered to the U.S. Military Government or to the Austrian Government." Reith went on to explain that receipts for a "considerable amount of gold" were filed away, but "no receipts for paper money" could be found. What happened to all that money? No one knows.[14]

*   *   *

Details on the Villa Kery gold were just the beginning of Elfriede Höttl's story. Two other SS officers, Obersturmbannführer (Lieutenant Colonel) Werner Götsch and Hauptsturmführer (Captain) Viktor Zeischka, both of whom she knew personally, had also been at the Villa Kery. The pair drove into Altaussee in a yellow-green Adler-Sturm automobile about 11:00 p.m. on May 8, 1945—the day of Germany's official capitulation. Just ahead of them was another car carrying three Obersturmbannführers. Americans were already in possession of the town, a fact of which the cars' occupants might not have been aware. The two automobiles approached a road check and were signaled to pull over. The vehicle with the three lieutenant colonels accelerated and sped out of town, bullets zipping around it. Götsch and Zeischka prudently decided to take their chances with the Americans and pulled over. Both were arrested and dispatched to the Altaussee jail. An informant came forward and told officials that Zeischka often "stowed in the luggage hold of the car 40 kilograms (88 lbs.) of gold bullion, which he was accustomed to take with him regularly for fear of losing it." Zeischka's gold was held inside a large rucksack. The news reached authorities too late to do them any good.

That same night, Maria Eibl, the owner of the Pension Eibl, in company with her lover Franz Fischer, pushed Zeischka's car "into the yard of the Pension Eibl." The servants of the place were "ordered to go to bed earlier than usual," and Frau Eibl was described as being "in a state of unusual excitement." The car disappeared. Authorities believe Fischer took the car to Vienna. After that night intelligence agents watched the pair closely. Before long they noted that both made "unusually large expenditures . . . The 40 kilograms of gold are thought now to be in the hands of the pair." According to a CIC report, "It is certain that the gold was not obtained by American authorities unless it is assumed that an American filched the gold for himself." Although the report recommended additional follow-up and even identified the names of servants to be questioned, the record is silent thereafter. Did the investigation go forward? If so, was anything of further use discovered? If not, why not? Unfortunately, CIC records do not hold the answers to any of these questions.[15]

Werner Götsch, Viktor Zeischka's traveling companion, may have had the last laugh in the matter. According to Frau Höttl, a high ranking

SD officer arrived at the Kremsmünster monastery from Romania in early May 1945. From there, "a transport, especially guarded and handled very cautiously, rolled to Schaz in the Tyrol. The Branch-Office was on the Vomperberg, a nearby mountain, "on top of which is a housing development formerly seized by a Nazi." One of its residents was a Frau Götsch—Werner Götsch's wife. "As it has become known to me," explained Höttl, "there are valuables actually lodged in this place, but it is at present impossible to approach . . . because the area is guarded by French guards." That part of Austria was in the French zone of control. She did not know "whether the watch is carried through for political or for financial reasons. It is certain, however, that the French did not find anything thus far." How was it that Frau Höttl knew that nothing had yet been discovered? No one seems to have asked the question. Did Zeischka's gold (or some other treasure) end up with Werner Götsch's wife?[16]

According to a CIC memorandum, Elfriede Höttl "is certain that the transport . . . carried gold and jewels," and that the fortune was buried in a well within the Vomperberg housing development. She offered even more specific evidence. "The wife of Franz Steindl lives on the Vomperberg and frequently makes trips to Salzburg in order to contact her husband, who is known by [Agent Hofrat] Reith actually to live in Salzburg and who is said to be an illicit dealer in gold and jewels." The CIC concluded that "Franz Steindl knows the location of the jewels and gold and avails himself of them from time to time." How Frau Höttl had discovered these specific details is not clear, but in all likelihood her husband had shared these details with her, feeding her with bits of information to tantalize Allied investigators in the hope of earning an early release. Was Frau Höttl telling the truth or spinning a yarn? The Austrian investigators interviewed her for hours and reached the conclusion her story had veracity.[17]

* * *

Stolen Russian church gold. That was the next story Frau Höttl shared with the Austrian investigators. Sketchy details on this particular conspicuous cache of loot were already in the hands of the investigators; Höttl's statements helped flesh out the story. Six Wehrmacht travel cases were delivered into Austria during the final days of the war. How they arrived there and who brought them is not known. As Höttl told it, between May 10 and May 15, 1945, "6 cases containing golden objects from [Russian] churches had been sent to Bad Aussee by officials of the police-station Altaussee, or by members of the [Austrian] Independence Movement." The shipment was in boxes or chests marked "typewriters" and had been specifically "demanded by the Minister of Finance for Ausseerland, by the name of Winkler, a merchant at Bad Aussee." The former chief of the Free Austrian Movement and Burgermeister of Bad Aussee, Albrecht Gaiswinkler, who had been planted in the Altaussee area as an informant, reported that the cases of priceless ecclesiastical treasures "were properly surrendered" to Austrian authorities. This statement was recorded on April 4, 1947. A later investigation seemed to contradict Gaiswinkler's declaration.

One of the six cases tracked to Bad Aussee was spotted there by an Austrian informer who told officials "he saw one of the chests in the Café Vesco at Bad Aussee, and upon opening it observed written on the inner side of the cover the word "Charkow" [a city in the Ukraine], beneath which were several Russian characters he could not read." The chest held a monstrance (a receptacle within which the host is held), an icon representing the Madonna with a golden veil, and a number of small gold statues of shepherds and saints. "The case is extremely heavy," he told them, "and the figures are as heavy as lead." This case was apparently "taken over" by a Croatian man and former SS soldier named "Schaghy." The mystery man was a cook in an American kitchen at Bad Aussee and "a typewriter mechanic by profession." Someone ordered Schaghy to deliver the treasures "to the local priest at Bad Aussee which, however, was never done." This case was supposedly transported to Grundlsee from Bad Aussee, and from that point by boat to Wienern. "From Wienern," concludes the report, "the trace was lost and may only be recovered by means of further investigations." Agents combed the area and discovered that several of the six cases had been left with Karl Rastl, a farmer in the village of Wienern. These cases, they concluded, "contain the so-called Russian church gold." The agent drafting the report wrote, "For reasons of restitution to the USSR, it would be of important significance for the Austrian State to recover this gold." A subsequent search of Rastl's property in July, however, turned up only "two

Wehrmacht chests . . . containing books, which belonged to a studious Wehrmacht soldier."[18]

Several Austrian citizens involved with this matter incriminated Albrecht Gaiswinkler and accused him of stealing the church gold. Further interrogations shed little additional light on the matter. Johann Pucher signed a CIC statement claiming Gaiswinkler was himself a crook responsible for stealing American, Dutch, and Swiss currency that had been turned over to American authorities. Pucher, it will be recalled, had discovered a fortune in gold after the war ended and had voluntarily turned it in to the proper authorities. On August 3, 1947, Special Agent Frank P. Dierick interviewed Gaiswinkler, who by this time was a member of the Austrian parliament. Gaiswinkler scoffed when confronted with the allegations uncovered by Austrian and American investigators. Reith, he spat contemptuously, was a "ridiculous man, lacking a knowledge of the most primitive investigation methods." As for the Russian church gold, "that was found in 1945." According to Gaiswinkler, an art expert named Wolfgang Gurlitt, a resident of Linz, was brought in to appraise the collection. "It was learned that the church figurines were made of tin, painted over with gold paint." These things "have little intrinsic value," he continued, "only an artistic value, and were surrendered to the Military Government in Bad Aussee."

Gaiswinkler's deposition conflicts with statements gathered from other witnesses, including the observation by one that "the figures are as heavy as lead." Tin is not a weighty metal. The communist-leaning politician refused to say anything more on the subject. No record that the Russian objects were turned in at Bad Aussee has been found. Was Gaiswinkler lying to block further investigation? Agent Dierick was unsure. My interviews with Gaiswinkler, he wrote, "elicited strong indications that [he] has kept for his personal use considerable quantities of gold and currency found in the Altaussee region." Dierick had been informed that "the Military Government has an extensive case against Gaiswinkler but that, because of the parliamentary immunity [he] presently enjoys, the case has been merely filed." Nothing ever became of the investigation into Gaiswinkler's suspected criminal activities.[19]

And there the trail ends. Whether the precious church treasures were ever located and returned is unknown, and no further records have been found on the subject.[20]

*   *   *

Was Heinrich Himmler's car at the bottom of an Alpine lake? According to Frau Höttl, that's exactly where it was. "About one year ago," she began, "I learned from a friend that shortly before the surrender a special car of Himmler's was brought to Zell am See and was dropped there into the lake. This special car contained large treasures of jewels, diamonds and gold." The location, she continued, "is watched even now by a man unknown to us," she said, referring to herself and her husband. She did not know who dumped the auto into the lake, or who ordered it done. "Incredible as this statement appeared in the beginning," wrote a CIC agent a few weeks later, "it was nevertheless confirmed by a report" filed in May of the previous year by Hofrat Reith. Additional investigation demonstrated "the possibility of the dropping of a special car does exist. . . . Two points are to be considered for the dropping." The first was "the southeast shore toward Fischhorn. This place can easily be reached . . . and is comparatively shallow. To all probability the car has been dropped there by the SS." However, there was one other spot along the north shore near the castle Prielsu, a former SS hangout during the war and the property of Josef Thorak, one of Hitler's favorite sculptors. "This part of the lake is shallow, overgrown with reeds and appears to be suitable for the dropping." These credible claims, concludes the report, "should be followed up with appropriate and extremely confidential investigations."[21]

The credibility of these early postwar reports was bolstered by later discoveries that confirmed the Nazis did indeed conceal valuables in Austria's remote mountain lakes. In 1963, the Austrian Interior Ministry sent divers into mile-long Lake Toplitz to determine whether the rumors of sunken treasure were true. Without much difficulty they retrieved several caskets of forged currency notes, the product of Operation Bernhard. A ban on further diving was implemented, ostensibly because divers attempting similar feats lost their lives. Until 2000, no modern equipment had ever been used to comb its 350-foot depth. Local authorities finally gave a company called Oceaneering Technologies a license to search to "once and for all clear up if there is anything down there and put the past behind us so we can get on with the future." Three weeks of painstaking searching located "a field of debris," including the remains of crates. Bundles of British counterfeit notes, most of them £10 denomination, were brought to the surface. In the fall of 2001, a Dutch sport diver discovered Ernst Kaltenbrunner's personal seal in the shallows of Altaussee Lake. While no gold or jewels have been discovered to date, the Nazis absolutely used Austrian lakes as a dumping ground for illicit items.[22]

Was Himmler's car pushed off into the resplendent lake spreading out below Fischhorn castle with the hope that its valuable contents could be retrieved at a later date? Like so many other golden threads this trail ends, abruptly. Not another whisper of Himmler's treasure car is found among the official records from this period. Perhaps Frau Höttl was right, and the sunken auto was being monitored by former members of the SS and its contents were secreted away without anyone being the wiser. Perhaps the car and its treasures remain buried deep in Austrian lake silt. Of course, Himmler's car might never have been pushed into the lake in the first place. Until definitive records of the recovered loot or a rusting wealth-laden auto breaks the surface of Zeller Lake, we will never know for sure.[23]

* * *

Fraus Iris Scheidler and Elfriede Höttl had eagerly cooperated and shared what appeared to be very valuable information with the Austrians and Americans. Enough strands of substantiation existed to corroborate the gist of their fantastic stories. Auerboech, Reith, Dierick, and others, however, did not fully trust them. The women, they concluded, "appear to have considerations for their personal advantage." What, if anything, were they hiding? What else did they know? The Americans, too, were becoming a bit suspicious. Their sights, however, were focused on Hofrat Reith and his investigatory methods.

One way to test the credibility of the women and Reith's investigation was to thoroughly search at least one of the sites. The assets hidden at the Ebensee concentration camp, Iris Scheidler had asserted, "would be immediately seizeable." Reith believed the information to be "ninety-five percent certain." Determined to find out for themselves, the agents traveled to the former concentration camp on July 21, 1947. A search of the area outside the gate for what might be a sealed manhole cover turned up a likely candidate in exactly the area described. With the assistance of Captain Nichols, the officer in charge of the U.S.F.A Ammunition Depot, Lambach, Upper Austria, the excited agents placed explosives around the manhole and detonated them. A cloud of smoke and flame rose into the air and a few seconds later chips of concrete rained down around them. The agents hurried over to the manhole and looked inside. Disappointment waited to greet them. "No valuables or weapons were found after the explosion. What had been believed by Reith to be a cement cover over a manhole was discovered to be merely the foundation of a former gatepost," wrote a disappointed Dierick. "Although [the camp is] the likely location of 'tooth gold' and jewels," he continued, "it may be necessary to search a broader area."[24]

The failure to quickly substantiate Scheidler's assertion that valuables had been hidden at Ebensee served to heighten a sneaking suspicion that she was playing games with them. Auerboech's invest-igation also pointed in that direction. He had been quietly gathering evidence that Kaltenbrunner's gold may not be missing after all. "In contrast to the statements made by [the] Scheidlers," explained Dierick in a detailed CIC report, "the opinion exists among former SD [and SS] personnel that the chests of gold and foreign exchange [destined] for Kaltenbrunner actually arrived at Altaussee [in May 1945]."

The level of the agents' suspicion rose when Iris Scheidler herself, perhaps without thinking about the consequences, breezily explained that Franz Steindl—"who is said to be an illicit dealer in gold and jewels"—had paid her a visit at Altaussee. The man whose wife lived on the Vomperberg had arrived without warning one day and demanded $20,000 "on the order of [SS Obersturmbannführer Wilhelm] Wanek's assistant, Kurt Auner," who had recently been released from Camp Marcus Orr. The agents knew Steindl dabbled in jewels and gold coins in the Salzburg area (his primary clients were American soldiers). Steindl's demand and Auner's order "seems not only to confirm the existence of the gold [in the first place]," explained Dierick, "but also to indicate that it is concealed." In other words, the gold supposedly hijacked by the SS men tasked to guard it had actually made it to Altaussee—and former SS and SD officers believed Frau Scheidler either had it in her possession, or had direct access to it.[25]

Proving it would be a whole different matter.

Chapter Notes

1. "First Progress Report: Concealed Gold, Jewelry, Foreign Exchange, and Weapons, Believed to be Located in the Salzkammergut, Zell am See, Salzburg, and in the Tyrol," July 3, 1947, p. 3.

2. "First Progress Report: Concealed Gold, Jewelry, Foreign Exchange, and Weapons, Believed to be Located in the Salzkammergut, Zell am See, Salzburg, and in the Tyrol," July 3, 1947, pp. 3-4. "A young attractive Jewish agent, against his will but under orders to do so, had become Eichmann's wife's lover in Altaussee after the war. He lived with her for about one year but was unable to obtain any useful information about either Eichmann's whereabouts or any valuables he may have hidden." Interview, Tuviah Friedman, Director of Documentation Center, Haifa, Israel, November 20, 1985.

3. "First Progress Report: Concealed Gold, Jewelry, Foreign Exchange, and Weapons, Believed to be Located in the Salzkammergut, Zell am See, Salzburg, and in the Tyrol," July 3, 1947, p. 7.

4. "Statement of Frau Iris Scheidler," undated (but probably April 16, 1947). The colonel, whose name was never revealed in CIC reports, apparently transferred back to the United States.

5. "Statement of Frau Iris Scheidler," undated (but probably April 16, 1947); "First Progress Report: Concealed Gold, Jewelry, Foreign Exchange, and Weapons, Believed to be Located in the Salzkammergut, Zell am See, Salzburg, and in the Tyrol," July 3, 1947, p. 7. During an interview in a CIC office Frau Scheidler discovered an American agent in possession of a silver case for a cologne bottle that belonged to her husband. The case, which had been confiscated at the time of his arrest, was returned to her at her request.

6. The story of this gold shipment is detailed in Chapter 13, "Ernst Kaltenbrunner's Missing Sacks of Gold."

7. "Statement of Frau Iris Scheidler," undated (but probably April 16, 1947).

8. "Statement of Frau Iris Scheidler," undated (but probably April 16, 1947).

9. *Trial of War Criminals before the International Military Tribunal*, November 14, 1945-October 1, 1946, 42 vols. (U.S. Printing Office, 1947-1949), vol. 21, p. 228 (commonly known as the "Blue Series").

10. CIC Memorandum, "Subject: Wilhelm Höttl," May 31, 1945; *Trial of War Criminals before the International Military Tribunal*, p. 228.

11. "Subject: Wilhelm Höttl," May 31, 1945. Frau Elfriede Höttl told investigators her husband was a Major, or Obersturmbannführer. CIC Memorandum, "Statement of Elfriede Höttl," April 4, 1947. Allen Welsh Dulles would become the future director of the Central Intelligence Agency from 1953-1961, an organization that grew out of the Office of Strategic Services, or OSS.

12. Wilhelm Höttl, *The Secret Front: The Story of Nazi Political Espionage* (New York, 1954), pp. 288-293; "Special Investigative Report on Höttl," June, 20, 1945; "Subject: Wilhelm Höttl," May 31, 1945. Höttl was so dedicated to the idea of undermining the German Redoubt effort that his activities during the last hours before the capitulation included the scrutinizing of Allied propaganda leaflets. He suggested the leaflets point out that only "war criminals" were continuing the fight to save their own skins. Ibid.

13. "Statement of Elfriede Höttl," April 4, 1947. Bad Aussee and Altaussee are 4.5 kilometers, or 2.8 miles, apart.

14. "First Progress Report: Concealed Gold, Jewelry, Foreign Exchange, and Weapons, Believed to be Located in the Salzkammergut, Zell am See, Salzburg, and in the Tyrol," July 3, 1947, p. 9-10. Hofrat Reith was wrong about the gold: it did not make it into the proper hands. After the Austrians issued the receipts for the precious metal, the gold disappeared. No one seems to have recognized this fact until the authors of this study determined that the gold discovered by salt miner Johann Pucher was never formally recorded as having been received at the Foreign Exchange Depository in Frankfurt, Germany. Somewhere between the time it was turned in and the time it was to have been turned over to the Americans, the gold vanished.

15. "First Progress Report: Concealed Gold, Jewelry, Foreign Exchange, and Weapons, Believed to be Located in the Salzkammergut, Zell am See, Salzburg, and in the Tyrol," July 3, 1947, p. 9.

16. "Statement of Elfriede Höttl," April 4, 1947.

17. "First Progress Report: Concealed Gold, Jewelry, Foreign Exchange, and Weapons, Believed to be Located in the Salzkammergut, Zell am See, Salzburg, and in the Tyrol," July 3, 1947, p. 3; "Statement of Elfriede Höttl," April 4, 1947.

18. "First Progress Report: Concealed Gold, Jewelry, Foreign Exchange, and Weapons, Believed to be Located in the Salzkammergut, Zell am See, Salzburg, and in the Tyrol," July 3, 1947, p. 3; "Statement of Elfriede Höttl," April 4, 1947; "Assets of Gold and Foreign Currency of the RSHA

Berlin/Dislocation in the Salzkammergut, Salzburg and the Tyrol," April 26, 1947, p. 5; CIC "Statement of Walter Grötzl," June 20, 1947.

19. "Concealed Gold, Jewelry, Foreign Exchange, and Weapons believed to be located in the Salzkammergut, in Zeller See, Land Salzburg, and in the Tyrol," p. 3, August 18, 1947. Albrecht Gaiswinkler seems an unlikely suspect. Recently declassified Austrian documents claim he rescued Leonardo da Vinci's *Mona Lisa* from the Nazis. Officials speaking on behalf of the Louvre in Paris (where the Mona Lisa was, and is today, exhibited) deny the report. They claim the painting never left France and that the occupying Nazis had absconded early in the war with a centuries-old copy of the priceless piece of art. Gaiswinkler, these same documents continue, deserted from the Wehrmacht and fled to France in June of 1944, where he hooked up with the French Resistance. Somehow the industrious Austrian managed to bring with him several truckloads of weapons and 500,000 francs. Gaiswinkler was later sent back into Austria, where he served with the Free Austrian Movement against the Germans. According to a newly published book by William Mackenzie, *The Secret History of SOE: Special Operations Executive 1940-1945* (St. Ermin's Press, 2001), which was written just after the war and until recently classified, Gaiswinkler turned over several mid-level Nazis to the Americans and "rescued a number of Nazi treasure hoards, including the Mona Lisa and the Austrian Imperial Crown Jewels."

20. "First Progress Report: Concealed Gold, Jewelry, Foreign Exchange, and Weapons, Believed to be Located in the Salzkammergut, Zell am See, Salzburg, and in the Tyrol," July 3, 1947, p. 3; "Assets of Gold and Foreign Currency of the RSHA Berlin/Dislocation in the Salzkammergut, Salzburg and the Tyrol," April 26, 1947, p. 5.

21. "Assets of Gold and Foreign Currency of the RSHA Berlin/Dislocation in the Salzkammergut, Salzburg and the Tyrol," April 26, 1947, p. 6. In August 1947, when the CIC began to doubt Hofrat Reith's "investigative work," an agent reported that "an investigation was conducted to determine whether it was possible to 'push' or 'drop' a car laden with gold and jewelry into the lake. An examination of the shore line of Zeller See convinced this source that such an act was impossible to execute." "Concealed Gold, Jewelry, Foreign Exchange, and Weapons believed to be located in the Salzkammergut, in Zeller See, Land Salzburg, and in the Tyrol," p. 3, August 18, 1947. This conclusion contradicts an earlier CIC statement that an investigation demonstrated a car could be pushed into the lake.

22. "Nazi Fake British Currency Found in Lake," *USA Today*, November 21, 2000; "Nazi Chief's Seal Found in Alpine Lake," by Michael Leidig, *London Telegraph*, November 16, 2001.

23. "Assets of Gold and Foreign Currency of the RSHA Berlin/Dislocation in the Salzkammergut, Salzburg and the Tyrol," April 26, 1947, p. 6.

24. "Concealed Gold, Jewelry, Foreign Exchange, and Weapons believed to be located in the Salzkammergut, in Zeller See, Land Salzburg, and in the Tyrol," p. 1, August 18, 1947.

25. "First Progress Report: Concealed Gold, Jewelry, Foreign Exchange, and Weapons, Believed to be Located in the Salzkammergut, Zell am See, Salzburg, and in the Tyrol," July 3, 1947, pp. 7-8.

Chapter 16

"Grötzl, this is a business in which I can earn something,
and I don't care about anything else!"

— Reinhard Haas to Walter Grötzl

The Gold Trade in Upper Austria

he fraus of Altaussee, Iris Scheidler and Elfriede Höttl, had seen an opportunity and worked overtime to deflect attention away from their own nests. Their detailed statements were varnished with veracity, but the depth of the finish was yet to be determined. Neither woman had come completely clean with the investigators, of that Hofrat Reith and the American agents were confident. Both women knew more than they were telling.

Evidence steadily amassed supporting the general thrust of their story. "By the evidence accumulated up to now," wrote a CIC agent two months after the initial round of interviews with the women, "it can clearly be seen that great amounts of gold and foreign exchange were a short time before the surrender hidden by the SS at several locations near Aussee and at other places." Moreover, he continued, "it is evident that already considerable amounts are in the hands of former Nazis and members of the SS, who use them for carrying on a thriving trade and for living an easy life unhampered by regular employment."

Allied intelligence officers had other concerns beyond their former enemy's living well off stolen loot. Many saw a dangerous storm cloud looming on the distant horizon. The report warned "that these people and the leaders of the SS will after their release have an opportunity to use these assets—they speak of X-millions and even of 10 billions—for establishing a new organization and thus precipitate not only Austria but the whole of Europe into another disaster." That fact alone, concluded the report's author, provides "the necessity for a thorough investigation of the whole case." The CIC's concern that the Nazis might rise again and seriously threaten Europe seems, from our perspective today, borderline delusional. The authors of this report, however, did not enjoy the historical benefits we have gleaned from a rearview mirror which looks back almost six decades into the past. In the immediate aftermath of the world's most destructive war, the threat of a resurgent Nazi movement was on everyone's mind. To those living in the second half of the 1940s the possibility seemed all too real.[1]

As it turned out, the Intelligence reports were misguided on one count but right on the money with the other. The last thing the vast majority of former SS officers (and even most diehard Nazis) who had survived the world conflagration desired was another deadly European war. One was enough for a lifetime. Many had already witnessed two. But dabbling in the lucrative postwar underground trade in gold and foreign exchange in Austria was another matter entirely.

*   *   *

"It was the summer of 1946, I believe, when the wife of Reinhard Haas showed me blank bills with official stamps of the police-station (Vienna)." So begins the extraordinary report of undercover Austrian informer Walter Grötzl, upon which much of this chapter is constructed. The informer-agent blended into war-torn Austrian society as an unemployed former soldier living hand-to-mouth. In this condition he took up an acquaintance with Reinhard Haas and his wife. Both lived comfortably without visible means of support. The blank bills facilitated that lifestyle. With the help of a typewriter, Haas used the official papers to forge, among other documents, travel and employment permits, which allowed him to slip in and out of the American occupation zone. Haas, as Grötzl soon learned, also trafficked in the thriving black market that had engulfed Europe. Small quantities of cigarettes, cocoa, bacon, diesel oil, and coffee were the common currencies of his trade. Austrian authorities had little interest in this facet of Haas's budding new career. It was his access to a continuous and reliable stream of gold that piqued their interest.[2]

As far as Grötzl could determine Reinhard Haas began dabbling in the black market gold trade in early 1947. By this time Grötzl had fully gained the Haas's confidence, and the subject of gold was a frequent topic between them. A few days into the 1947 New Year found Haas and Grötzl conversing in the former's modest flat at Puchen No. 81. Grötzl was a frequent visitor there. Conversation naturally tacked in the direction of the recent unpleasantness and its impact on their respective lives. Making a living in postwar Europe was difficult for almost everyone; most people found themselves mired in serious financial distress without much hope for the future. Haas and some of his associates, however, fell outside that wide circle.

Haas looked at his new friend intently and then spilled the beans. "At the surrender in 1945 a friend of mine named Hans took gold in small boxes, packed in cotton-wool, to a baker named Fritz Binder in Altaussee."

Grötzl's interest was suddenly aroused. "Gold? Where did he get it?"

"From the Park Hotel in Altaussee," Haas replied. "They were bars of gold. Hans had hidden them there." Grötzl, of course, knew of the rumors that the SS had trucked in gold and stored it, at least temporarily, at the hotel. The subject was a common one among the citizens of Upper Austria.

"Hans," as Haas explained to Grötzl, was Hans Herbert. He was German, but exactly where he was from is unknown. Herbert had spent the war marching in the ranks of the SS, and during the general retreat had ended up in the Aussee region. He was quartered at the Park Hotel in Altaussee when the capitulation was signed. Herbert may have been associated with SS-Group Eichmann, which arrived at the hotel with millions in gold and currency. Or, perhaps, he was with one of several other groups of SS that had streamed into the area that late April and early May two years past. What is firmly known is that somehow Herbert managed to get his hands on a sizeable amount of the precious metal while sojourning in Altaussee. The gold, or that portion not in the form of coins, was shaped in bars "half an inch square" and packed in boxes on a lorry of the SS-Group Eichmann.[3]

"On New Year's Eve I also took some gold away from the Park Hotel," continued Haas. "I opened the boxes and looked inside. They were full of gold." How much he took and where he transported it did not enter the conversation. But he did tell Grötzl that he had hauled away gold several times from the inn. Wasting time trading cigarettes or cocoa was a thing of the past. "From this time on," remembered Grötzl, "Haas carried on only trade in gold."[4]

A few days later, during another visit to the Haas flat, "a white-haired Russian woman" who was staying with a local doctor appeared and gave Haas several solid gold coins. Haas later told Grötzl he "sold these coins to a Jew at Goisern." It was apparently his first foray into actually selling gold. The intermediary who had introduced Haas to the Jewish buyer was none other than Hans Herbert, the same man who had stolen some of Eichmann's gold bars from the Park Hotel. "Grötzl, this is a business in which I can earn something, and I don't care about anything else!" exclaimed an excited Haas.

The same old Russian woman returned a week later with two gold rings and more good news for Haas: another Russian living in Bad Aussee "also has gold he wishes to sell." Any doubts Grötzl may have harbored of plentiful stocks of hidden gold in the Altaussee region of Austria vanished. Even poor displaced Russians had access to gold coins and rings. The metal brought in a comfortable living for Haas. For each gram of 14-carat gold Haas received thirty-five shillings, forty-five shillings for 18-carat gold, and sixty-five shillings for "mint gold," or 24-carat metal.[5]

Soon after Haas fired up his illegal livelihood, he struck up a friendship with Josef "Sepp" Kronberger, an unemployed former soldier living in a flat in Altaussee. The man appeared one day while Grötzl was visiting Haas. Kronberger eyed Grötzl with deep suspicion before turning his attention to Haas. The pair engaged in "low conversations" for a few minutes before Kronberger left the flat. Haas turned to Grötzl and smiled.

"These are good bargains," Haas said confidently as he reached into his pocket and withdrew several gold coins. "If Koller only knew! But he is much too silly to find out!" (Koller was a local policeman.)

From that day forward, Kronberger and Haas kept frequent company. In the aftermath of another visit, Haas fished out additional gold and fondled the yellow metal rounds in his hands as Grötzl looked on. "If Koller would see this," Haas giggled,"he would go mad!"

Puzzled, Grötzl asked, "Why?"

Haas laughed aloud. "Because he believed I lent him a hand in clearing up the gold-affair! He [can] go to hell!"[6]

As Haas's illicit activities increased, so did his need for transportation. In May of 1947 he began borrowing Grötzl's motorcycle for regular trips to Goisern. According to Grötzl, every time Haas "returned from such rides he brought with him considerable quantities of food, such as bacon, eggs, butter . . . and the Haas family had some feasts." Grötzl was often invited to partake in the delicacies. His host, however, shared few specifics with his dining partner when asked how he had obtained the food. "I have been with the Jews at Goisern selling gold," was all he would utter. A few weeks later Haas bought a green fiat complete with permits and disappeared for two weeks.

By now it was obvious that Haas and his friends were serious players in black market gold, and the price of the metal was beginning to escalate. The time had arrived to become pro-active. Grötzl was ordered by the Altaussee police, who were monitoring his efforts, to penetrate into the network. On May 31 he approached Kronberger who, like Haas, eventually grew to trust him completely. "I want to buy some gold," he explained. "I want to get a motor-car. How much do you charge for it?"

"The cost is 800 shillings per coin," replied Kronberger. "You should have told me a couple days ago. I had 2.2 kilograms [five and one-half pounds] but this is now in Graz. I will have more gold in two days. Find me then."

Two days later Grötzl sought out Kronberger. "I have it [the gold]," Kronberger told him. Come to my house at 7:00 p.m. tonight." The informant arrived on schedule but broke the news that he did not have enough money to buy all he needed. At this Kronberger grew visibly agitated. "I cannot lay up this much gold for so long! Tomorrow it goes to Linz." He drew out a small black leather purse, pushed a button and popped open the lid. Inside were two gold coins, or "samples," as Kronberger called them. One was French, the other Italian. "These are the kind you would have gotten," he explained, implying that there were several varieties floating around the local market. "And now the price has gone up to 1,000 shillings. The price of gold is climbing fast, and I can no longer afford to sell it for less."

"Where do you get this gold?" asked Grötzl.

Kronberger replied without hesitation. "From a Russian named Paul. He owns a considerable amount of it, but he is very cautious about selling it. I will get some for you when you have enough money."

Whether the pair ever did business is unclear because Kronberger is never mentioned again in the official records, either by Grötzl or any Intelligence agent. There is a possibility that Kronberger became suspicious of Grötzl and refused to do business with him.[7]

Just as Grötzl had become friends with Haas and Kronberger, so too did he curry favor with Hans Herbert, the man who had helped shepherd Haas into the gold trade. Based upon Haas's comments and personal observation, Grötzl was confident Herbert was sitting on the mother lode. They were sitting together at Herbert's house one day when Herbert nonchalantly told Grötzl that he bought the place from a Hungarian and paid cash for it. "Now," he said angrily, "I have to hire a lawyer because that rogue [Inspector Anton] Auerboech seized my [deed]!" Deed or not Herbert was still living in the house, and inside was a fortune in gold. The German pulled out a small box—"similar to a pencil case," remembered Grötzl—containing several thin bars of gold packed in cotton-wool. "These bars were about 20 cm. [8"] long and had a diameter of about 1 cm. [.25"]." Emboldened by his wealth Herbert did little to hide his affluence. In addition to buying his house outright, he frequented the Caffee Vesko, where he routinely bought drinks for everyone and "contributed 2,000 shillings to the band's kitty." Herbert, as far as the CIC was concerned, "disposed of rather large amounts of cash, which he certainly must have gotten by ill means . . . [He] is also not engaged in regular employment and is living in a grand style."[8]

Eventually Herbert disclosed to Grötzl what he had done with the boxes of gold he had snatched away from Eichmann's gang at the Park Hotel. "I hid it in the Pension Alpenland in Altaussee. I am going to get it soon. It is worth several [hundred] thousand shillings!" he exclaimed. "I never have to work again!" This conversation was prompted by the splintered friendship that had once existed between Hans Herbert and Reinhard Haas. The latter had tried to rob the former of his gold. Herbert had foolishly told Haas (just as he was about to unwisely tell Grötzl) that his fortune, or much of it, was hidden away in his former room at the Pension Alpenland. Exactly how Herbert discovered Haas's perfidy is not known, but he was furious when word reached him that his "friend" and accomplice in crime had tried to rip him off. "Haas," he hissed, visibly angry and shaking his head, "is a great scoundrel. But he will never find my gold!" Looking like the cat that ate the canary, Herbert explained that his treasure "was hidden too well to be found."[9]

Haas, meanwhile, confirmed the story when Grötzl called by his flat. After Herbert had told him of the gold's location, he had visited the small boarding house to search for the cache. The outwardly simple task, he told Grötzl, proved harder and more complicated than he thought it would be. Inside the boarding inn was a young "foreign major" living in Herbert's old room. "I asked him to help me search for the gold and that I would give him half of it," he explained to Grötzl, "but we could not find it!" Although he could not locate Herbert's primary cache, he did manage to acquire another, rather grand, source of gold. "Look at this!" he told his friend as he brought out a brown case and opened it. Inside was what Grötzl later described as "a square block of gold." As we know today, much of the SS gold molded into bars or "squares" had once filled the teeth of human beings. Haas beamed. "It belongs to me!" Whether he sold it or disposed of it in another manner is unknown. "I never asked him more about it because he never tells me the truth," Grötzl penned in his statement.[10]

*   *   *

Walter Grötzl's undercover effort was not quite worth its weight in gold, but it did substantially further the investigation. American and Austrian agents were now in possession of tangible names, dates, and addresses, and had an eyewitness informant who could account for much of the illegality. Two days after he filed his June 8, 1947, statement Grötzl was "questioned anew" by CIC agents. He had more to tell them, and this time a pair of names familiar to the CIC were the subject of conversation.

A few days ago, began Grötzl, an acquaintance named Stefan Kumeritsch told him that he "maintained good connections with Mrs. [Iris] Scheidler." The smooth-talking frau also apparently maintained "good connections"—if Kumeritsch's information was accurate.

Kumeritsch confided to one of Grötzl's contacts, "Mrs. Wallicek," that "he had seen gold at Mrs. Scheidler's." Ever since the wife of Arthur Scheidler had let slip that a former SS officer had come to her door in 1945 demanding money on behalf of another high-ranking SS officer, CIC agents had suspected she was housing stolen gold and currency, or knew where it was hidden. Certainly prominent ex-SS and SD officers believed that was the case. According to the same witness, Iris's friend Elfriede Höttl, "also possesses such gold." Given all that had transpired thus far, nothing surprised the investigators. Grötzl's own spying seemed to confirm that something was amiss at the Scheidler residence. The informant had been keeping a close eye on Frau Scheidler's flat. "Three local lads frequently came to Mrs. Scheidler's and are in constant contact with her," he reported. They were always the same three. "I don't know the nature of these connections," he admitted.[11]

Something surely was afoot. While her husband was languishing in the camp at Nuremberg, Iris Scheidler was kicking up her heels and living the good life. (This was the same woman who was ready to abscond with an American colonel soon after the end of the war.) According to one informant, she often danced and drank her way into the wee hours of night at the Kaffeehaus Fischer. She ordered and paid for expensive rounds of drinks—over and over—and yet had no visible means of support and her husband was in jail. At least two of the three "local lads," as Grötzl called them, comprised her customary retinue at the nightspot. On or about May 31, 1947, remembered one female informant, two of the lads dropped by her table for an anxious exchange of whispering. One of them angrily demanded the keys to her car, left in a huff, and returned an hour later. "I observed the whole matter very furtively," related the informant, "and gathered from the state of things that it must have been about something quite mysterious."[12]

*   *   *

It was indeed all rather "mysterious," and the mystery continues to this day. Few records have surfaced to indicate what further efforts were made to track down these leads. On July 24, 1947, Hans Herbert was arrested and subjected to an intense interrogation. He signed "a lengthy statement," and was released. The statement has not been located. If it was indeed lengthy it was also devoid of value. "The only information of any significance to be found in the statement is Herbert's avowal that in 1945 he overheard an SS sergeant, Walter Ries, of Kremamulenster, remark to a truck driver, 'Come quickly, we still have to take care of the gold,'" concluded a summary report.[13]

The inability of the Austrian and American investigators to turn up a substantial cache of hidden loot caused Agent Dierick and other CIC men to reach the conclusion (at least officially), that the fault rested in Hofrat Reith's weaknesses as an investigator. "It is believed that Reith is an experienced investigator, with years of police experience behind him," began Dierick's summary on this point. "However, Reith has had little experience in actual investigative work." The distinction between "experience and mere official tenure of office" was stressed. Dierick was not finished. "It has been proven several times that Reith's credulity is no way checked by the exercise of good judgment. Reith pants after the most fantastic rumors and gossip and accepts as truth all he hears about concealed valuables." My investigation, concluded Dierick, "has established the unreliability of Reith's informants . . .[and] also the unreliability of Reith himself." Dierick may have gotten it right. Reith may not have been the world's most experienced detective. And many of his leads may have been dead ends offered by unscrupulous people bent on tricking the authorities.[14]

But two indisputable facts loom large and tip the scale back into the balanced position. Dierick himself confirmed the first. "There is no doubt that large quantities of gold were transported to Altaussee by retreating SS forces shortly before the surrender of the German Army," he wrote in a summation intended to crucify the credibility of both Reith and his partner, Anton Auerboech. Dierick continues:

> Indeed, the subject of buried gold has been a favorite conversational topic at Altaussee for the past two years. But due to the time lapse since the gold was concealed, because of the multitude of rumors which have sprouted since the end of the war and have grown to fantastic proportions, and because of the exceedingly poor investigative methods of Reith, it is felt that the possibilities of discovering the hidden gold in cooperation with Reith and the Austrian police, are too slight to warrant the continuance of this case.

Dierick's statement is indeed interesting. The CIC agent seems to want it both ways. Were there really vast quantities of gold hidden in the region? Yes, he admits, in abundance, *but* the rumors are so plentiful that sorting through them all and determining which are credible is now impossible because two years have passed. Dierick is blaming Reith for not being able to do what Dierick now claims can't be done—even though he admits that stolen treasures were secreted in the region. The second important point is that much of the information collected by Reith (and the Americans) came from highly placed former SS officers and/or their wives. Each was in a position to know about the "large quantities of gold" that everyone admits were hauled into the Altaussee area by SS officers—but not hauled out again.[15]

It is reasonable to conclude that some of the leads generated by Reith and Auerboech were nothing but gross caricatures of the truth or outright lies. Still, caches of gold and currency continued to be found in this region of Austria over the next five decades. Therefore, it is equally plausible to assume (especially given the sources) that some of Reith's leads were indeed authentic. Dierick had to know this.

Unfortunately, the termination of "official" American involvement made it impossible to ever separate the lies from the truth. And, exactly *when* this involvement ended is unclear, since many of the documents relating to this period have vanished. Whether Dierick or other agents continued their investigation in a less official capacity is unknown.

Chapter Notes

1. CIC "Summary Report," unsigned, June 20, 1947.

2. CIC, "Statement of Walter Grötzl," June 8, 1947, p. 1.

3. CIC "Summary Report," unsigned, June 20, 1947, p. 1. It is worthwhile remembering the statement filed by former SS officer Rudolf Doskoczil concerning Eichmann's gold. Doskoczil, it will be recalled, was looking for his personal belongings when he walked into a room in the hotel and spotted a table piled high with gold coins and foreign currency. See "Statement of Rudolf Doskoczil," April 24, 1947, p. 2. Assuming Doskoczil's statement is accurate (and circumstantial evidence on many fronts corroborates it), the room and table

held potentially millions in stolen loot. Yet, these thousands of gold coins represented just the tip of the bullion iceberg, for now we know that untold boxes holding bars of solid gold were also at the hotel at the same time, all under Eichmann's control.

4. "Statement of Walter Grötzl," June 8, 1947, p. 5.

5. "Statement of Walter Grötzl," June 8, 1947, p. 2. Troy weight is a system of units of weight in which the grain is the same as in the Avoirdupois system, but the pound consists of twelve ounces, or 5,760 grains. Most of the gold coins confiscated in postwar Austria were small, about the size of a dime, or 1/12 of a troy ounce. In 1947 a troy ounce was worth about $35 American dollars, so a small gold coin had a value between $3.00 and $4.00.

6. "Statement of Walter Grötzl," June 8, 1947, p. 2. Haas may have been involved in either discovering or recovering a treasure cache that was only partially turned over to the proper authorities.

7. "Statement of Walter Grötzl," June 8, 1947, pp. 3-4.

8. CIC "Summary Report," unsigned, June 20, 1947; "Statement of Walter Grötzl," June 8, 1947, p. 1. Anton Auerboech had become suspicious of Kronberger's activities and apparently pulled the deed so that he could not sell the property until his investigation was complete. It is not known what became of his investigation.

9. CIC "Summary Report," unsigned, June 20, 1947; "Statement of Walter Grötzl," June 8, 1947, p. 1. A "pension" is a boarding house or hotel in Europe, never very elegant and usually quite small.

10. CIC "Summary Report," unsigned, June 20, 1947; "Statement of Walter Grötzl," June 8, 1947, p. 6; CIC "Summary Report," unsigned, June 20, 1947, pp. 1-2.

11. "Statement of Walter Grötzl," June 8, 1947, p. 7. Exactly who Stefan Kumeritsch was and what he did for a living is unknown. The only place his name appears in the records is during the Walter Grötzl questioning session of June 10, 1947.

12. "Statement of Walter Grötzl," June 8, 1947, p. 7; CIC, "Statement of "Mrs. Sevecek," June 11, 1947, contained on page 7 of the Walter Grötzl statement. We have been unable to determine any additional information on "Mrs. Sevecek." The only place her name appears in the records is the statement appended to the Walter Grötzl questioning session of June 10, 1947.

13. "Concealed Gold, Jewelry, Foreign Exchange, and Weapons believed to be located in the Salzkammergut, in Zeller See, Land Salzburg, and in the Tyrol," p. 1, August 18, 1947.

14. "Concealed Gold, Jewelry, Foreign Exchange, and Weapons believed to be located in the Salzkammergut, in Zeller See, Land Salzburg, and in the Tyrol," p. 2, August 18, 1947.

15. "Concealed Gold, Jewelry, Foreign Exchange, and Weapons believed to be located in the Salzkammergut, in Zeller See, Land Salzburg, and in the Tyrol," p. 3, August 18, 1947.

Chapter 17

"There is no doubt [Schellenberg] has at least
skirted the truth on many matters involving his own skin."

—Agent Emanual E. Minskoff

The Bloody Red Cross?
Walter Schellenberg's "External Assets"

D id intelligence officer Walter Schellenberg conceal a fortune in gold, jewels, and currency outside Germany during the war? Recent declassified documents strongly suggest he did indeed do so. Unfortunately, the asset trail developed by American investigators leads directly to the doorstep of one of Sweden's prominent and beloved historical personalities.

* * *

We know Walter Schellenberg as the head of RSHA Bureau VI, the SS counter-intelligence operation. Except for a biographical sketch in an earlier chapter, the young Gruppenführer's connections to this study have been infrequent and cloaked in shadow. He was not a major war criminal on par with Heinrich Himmler or Ernst Kaltenbrunner, but his crimes hover just one rung lower on the same ladder upon which these nefarious individuals stood. Schellenberg never pulled a trigger or ordered executions (that we know of), but it follows that anyone who worked closely with Reinhard Heydrich during his murderous reign in Czechoslovakia and hoped to succeed him as the head of RSHA was complicit in, and knowledgeable about, the Final Solution. His captors certainly believed as much. Following one of the 200 interrogations he endured an American agent wrote, "There is no doubt [Schellenberg] has at least skirted the truth on many matters involving his own skin." One "matter" deeply interested his jailers: the amount of wealth he had managed to conceal before Germany's collapse.[1]

Schellenberg was extradited from Sweden into Allied custody in June 1945. For much of the next two years the British and Americans questioned him closely and opened a special investigation into whether he had transferred assets out of Germany. Investigators quickly reached the conclusion that he had done so; the only question was how much he had squirreled away, and where it was hidden. Otto Ohlendorf, the former Einsatzgruppen leader and head of RSHA Bureau III, told Allied agents that "sufficient funds were put at Schellenberg's disposal so that he could live in appropriate style." More than that he would not reveal. As a counter-intelligence chief, Schellenberg possessed a Swiss passport and traveled to that neutral country many times during the war. Repeated interrogations focusing on these excursions proved largely fruitless in terms of information gleaned. "He had excellent contacts for hiding assets abroad if he chose to do so," concluded Agent Emanual E. Minskoff. Schellenberg adamantly denied he had taken anything to Switzerland. The trips, he explained, were "purely political."[2]

The real information bombshell, delivered "reluctantly," came about when Schellenberg admitted "my friend, Count [Folke] Bernadotte is keeping 3 or 4 thousand Swedish kronen of my personal money for me, which I did not wish to take into captivity." The news shocked the Americans. The internationally respected head of the Swedish Red Cross was holding illegal loot for an SS war criminal complicit in the liquidation of Jews? Was such a thing possible?

Following the shocking disclosure, wrote one agent,

> Schellenberg . . . deftly combined fact and fiction in describing the source of these funds, the manner in which possession was acquired by Count Bernadotte and the circumstances under which he was holding the Swedish crowns. He intentionally left vague the subject of whether 'my friend' Count Bernadotte was holding the Swedish

crowns as a personal favor to Schellenberg or officially on behalf of the Red Cross.

As far as Agent Minskoff was convinced, it was the former and not the latter.[3]

The SS officer was interrogated a second time on the Bernadotte revelation. "Schellenberg, still clinging to his attempt to make it appear that Count Bernadotte was acting in some official capacity in holding the funds for [him], nonetheless was compelled to admit that to the extent that such funds have not been dispersed by Count Bernadotte, he is holding the money for Schellenberg." It was a damning disclosure.

"This was purely a friendly arrangement?" asked one agent.

"Yes," admitted an exhausted Schellenberg.

After additional questioning, Schellenberg claimed he no longer recalled how much money Bernadotte was holding. Speculation put the sum at 10,000 Swedish kronen. When his interrogators asked him to prepare a sworn statement to that effect, Schellenberg experienced an epiphany: the funds were not Swedish kronen at all, but had been converted into Swiss francs by Swedish authorities. American invest-igators eventually extracted and pieced together this fascinating end-of-war saga.

Count Bernadotte and the 35-year-old Schellenberg had become good friends during their several wartime meetings. On May 4, 1945, Schellenberg left Germany for Sweden. His secretary, "Miss Schinke," followed him there the next day. In her possession, wrote the agents, was "Schellenberg's cash box which contained his private papers and also 'a small money reserve' which Schellenberg had always taken into the air raid shelter." According to Schellenberg, "Miss Schinke did not have specific instructions to bring the box to Sweden," but that she had permanent standing orders from him to bring the box any place he went. Inside the small chest was almost 30,000 Swiss francs and $28,000 in U.S. dollars. The francs, explained Schellenberg, "were my personal funds which were at my disposal as Chief of the Bureau VI, and I did not have to account for it in detail." When asked about the American money, Schellenberg offered the "somewhat cryptic remark" that the dollars "would be in excess of the moneys I was entitled to dispose of personally." Beyond that he would not elaborate. He had earlier told investigators that the "U.S. dollars were Amt. [Bureau] VI funds," and that Kaltenbrunner had "ousted" him from his high bureau perch several weeks before the end of the war. In that case, he would have no right of office to claim the money. When confronted with these seemingly incongruent details, Schellenberg launched into a contorted explanation of how he had obtained the currency. "[He] claimed that he was entitled to draw one year's salary in advance," apparently for his new function in the Foreign Office, reported Agent Minskoff. Further explanation included that his intent was to pay his secretaries and small staff out of that sum; whatever remained he described as his "personal property." Minskoff was an experienced intelligence officer and he did not buy any of Schellenberg's prevarications.[4]

Upon further questioning, Schellenberg told investigators that on the day Germany surrendered, May 8, 1945, he turned over the money in the box (28,000 Swiss francs and $28,000 American dollars) to the Swedish government—through Count Folke Bernadotte. The money, claimed Schellenberg, was intended to pay for the costs of internment in Sweden for his staff of seven, including Schellenberg and his secretaries, for a period of three months. The Swedish government, he continued, authorized the Count to "release" back to Schellenberg some 19,000 Swedish kronen, which he in turn distributed to his staff members. The balance remained with Bernadotte. "Schellenberg," explained Minskoff, "tried to elude the fact that this balance was being held for him personally" by lying about how the balance would be spent. "Pressed further, he admitted that Count Bernadotte was holding the money for him." In his final statement, Schellenberg concluded that his friend Bernadotte was holding "the approximate sum of 10,000 crowns [kronen]."[5]

Minskoff's gut told him that Schellenberg was lying, or at least was not fully forthcoming, about his activities. Ernst Kaltenbrunner's justification for canning Schellenberg seems to confirm Minskoff's suspicion. The former head of RSHA "had accused Schellenberg of establishing a fund abroad to use for private income after defeat." Minskoff sought out others who knew Schellenberg. Former SS agent Dr. Theodor Paeffgen, who knew the counter-intelligence chief well, "did not believe [Kaltenbrunner's] accusation." However, Paeffgen clarified, "if Schellenberg had made such a transfer, it would probably have been to Switzerland since Schellenberg was supposed to have a Swiss passport and the necessary papers to get across the Swiss border as a Swiss citizen." Schellenberg scoffed when confronted with these statements. "They were only used as an excuse for removal [by Kaltenbrunner]," he explained.[6]

More damning evidence, however, was soon uncovered. On September 11, 1945, the American Legation in Bern, Switzerland, sent an air gram to CIC agents investigating Schellenberg. A former "anti-Nazi German national" testified that Schellenberg, Kaltenbrunner, and Martin Bormann, Hitler's private secretary and power broker, "without the knowledge" of other authorities, "arranged to procure and place free currency in secret deposits in Switzerland, Turkey, Spain, and Sweden in order to carry on special Nazi political tasks." Schellenberg, claimed the informant, "directed the operations from within France." The informant included names, dates, locations, and specific details about numerous transactions. Intense questioning of Schellenberg on this issue only served to further frustrate the agents. Yes, he admitted, he did know many of those allegedly involved in this scheme. But, he explained, "this seems to be a chapter with which I never had any connection."[7]

Like Josef Spacil and Franz Konrad, Walter Schellenberg was a magnificent liar and smooth operator. The master of facts used his quick mind to confuse and shade the truth. He knew enough not to deny the undeniable, and yet obfuscate any role he might have played in the event in question. Did he transfer wealth generated as a result of illegal activities abroad for his own benefit? The money carried by Count Folke Bernadotte proves he did so at least to the extent of 10,000 Swedish kronen and $28,000 in U.S. Dollars.[8] Was this Swedish link but one of his threads of gold? How much more did he hide away?

Unless or until other documents surface, it is doubtful we will ever know.

Chapter Notes

1. CIC, "Preliminary Report on External Assets of Walter Schellenberg," pp. 2-3, prepared by E.E. Minskoff, undated (probably early 1946).

2. CIC, "Preliminary Report on External Assets of Walter Schellenberg," p. 3, prepared by E.E. Minskoff, undated (probably early 1946).

3. CIC, "Preliminary Report on External Assets of Walter Schellenberg," p. 7, prepared by E. E. Minskoff, undated (probably early 1946).

4. "Preliminary Report on External Assets of Walter Schellenberg," pp. 7a and 7b.

5. "Preliminary Report on External Assets of Walter Schellenberg," pp. 7c and 8.

6. "Preliminary Report on External Assets of Walter Schellenberg," pp. 7c and 8.

7. "Preliminary Report on External Assets of Walter Schellenberg," pp. 8-13, Appendix A, and Air gram letter from Bern, September 11, 1945.

8. For more information on Count Folke Bernadotte, see his entry in the Postscript, pp. 292-293.

Postscript

"I have not, contrary to some sensational reports in the German weekly press, managed to discover and squander the buried treasure that they [Nazis] are said to have left here in Aussee. . . . All I have found here has been solitude and peace."

—Wilhelm Höttl, *The Secret Front: The Story of Nazi Political Espionage*

Loose Ends

SS Colonel Emil Augsburg's life after World War II was much better than he deserved. After the former Einsatzgruppen leader-turned-informer filed his reports on Walter Hirschfeld, Augsburg joined German Federal Intelligence. This outfit is better known as the Gehlen Organization, and a brief history of this infamous association is now in order.

Brigadeführer Reinhard Gehlen was the chief of Adolf Hitler's Soviet intelligence unit. He had organized and maintained a vast network of undercover agents, and by war's end was in possession of a mountain of information about Soviet personalities, organizations, military secrets, and the like. He hid his files and offered them to his captors. With the Cold War heating up, American Intelligence officers fully realized his value and the CIA hired him. In one fell swoop the entire Gehlen network (about 350 agents) fell into the anti-Soviet camp. On his orders hundreds of German army and diehard pro-Nazi SS officers were released from internment camps to serve under him—employed with American tax dollars. Gehlen's unit operated out of a headquarters near Munich under the name South German Industrial Development Organization. It eventually numbered more than 4,000 agents, most of whom worked behind the Iron Curtain. Gehlen was instated as the new head of West German intelligence in 1955, and maintained this powerful post until 1968. He died in 1979.

Gehlen's expertise proved invaluable during the early postwar years, but as one writer put it, "the vilest of the vile" worked within his ranks. Dozens were wanted war criminals, including Klaus Barbie, Alois Brunner, Adolf Eichmann's chief deputy—and Emil Augsburg.

By the late 1950s, it was known that Soviet agents were trying to contact Augsburg. In the early 1960s, many people operating in intelligence circles believed Augsburg was working as a double agent. Perhaps he was blackmailed by his murderous past, a tactic routinely employed by the Russians to turn foreign agents. Ironically, Augsburg suffered the same fate he had helped mete out to Walter Hirschfeld. He was increasingly viewed as a liability and a record of his nefarious wartime activities was compiled to force his quiet resignation. In 1966, Augsburg was dismissed for "unauthorized intelligence activities."[1]

* * *

"The Butcher of Lyons," Klaus Barbie, was also a survivor. Like so many jackbooted thugs, his journey through the rest of his life was smoother and easier than his deeds warranted. His employment with the CIC, CIA, and Gehlen Organization protected him for many years. How ironic that a man sentenced to death in absentia by the French worked for the Americans during the postwar years just a few hundred miles away from French soil. Soon after the war, Father Krunoslav Draganovic, a Croatian Roman Catholic priest, moved to Rome and labored there as a secretary at a training seminary for new priests. When not training priests Draganovic operated what is now known as the "ratline," a clandestine escape route into South America for Nazi war criminals seeking freedom from their would-be hangmen or jailers. There is some evidence that the ratline was supported by the Catholic Church and endorsed by Allied intelligence. Eventually, Barbie's presence in Europe became problematical. With the help of Draganovic's ratline, Barbie and his entire family emigrated to South America in the early 1950s.[2]

He eventually settled in Bolivia and obtained citizenship there in 1957. Under the alias Klaus Altmann, he worked in his element as an interrogator (and worse) for several far-right governments. His cover was blown in 1971 when he was discovered and identified in Bolivia. Thirteen years passed before he was finally extradited to France to stand trial for his crimes. By that time the French had become too politically correct to implement the sentence Barbie so justly deserved (and had been given almost four decades earlier). Instead of death he was sentenced to life in prison in 1987. He died of cancer four years later.

*   *   *

Kurt Becher's black star followed him to his grave. Rezsö Kastner's testimony at Nuremberg may have brushed away the Sword of Damocles that had been hanging over Becher's head, but the stench of his activities lingers to this day. When he was finally released from Allied custody at the end of 1947 or early in 1948, Becher returned to his native Hamburg. Within a few months, Bremen beckoned. Becher moved to the historic seafaring city and set himself up as an exporter of wheat in the autumn of 1948. Still, the threat of prosecution lingered in the shadows. As the years passed, the chance he would ever be indicted receded. Becher went on to become the president of several corporations and headed up the sale of grain to, of all places, Israel. His corporation, the Cologne-Handel Gesselschaft, ended up doing extensive business with the Israeli government. By the late 1950s, he was considered by many to be one of the richest men in West Germany.

As those in attendance at the Bremen Seafaring Association discovered, Becher's failure to appear at the annual meeting was somehow related to Adolf Eichmann's recent arrest in South America and trial in Israel. There is sketchy evidence to support the charge that Becher was about to be indicted, and that someone moved to quash the attempt. Eventually he provided written testimony in Bremen on May 23, 1961, which was submitted for use in the Eichmann trial. Perhaps that was his ace in the hole. He was never sent to Israel to testify in person.[3]

Becher died a rich old man in August 1995. It is left to the reader to determine whether all of his wealth was the result of outstanding business acumen.

* * *

Count Folke Bernadotte survived World War II only to perish as a martyr in western Jerusalem three years later. Or so popular history has written.

On September 17, 1948, Bernadotte found himself in the center vehicle of a three-car convoy stopped at a roadblock in the Katamon suburb of Jerusalem. He was in the Middle East at the request of the United Nations in an attempt to broker a peace in the four month old Arab-Israeli war. This first of many conflicts was triggered when the United Nations partitioned a geographic area referred to as Palestine into Arab and Jewish states. Five Arab armies opened aggression the day after Israel declared itself a nation. While two gunmen shot out the tires of the convoy's vehicles a third man trotted along the sides of the cars peering inside to examine the occupants. When he spotted Bernadotte, he stuck an automatic pistol through the open rear window and sprayed the interior with bullets. Six of them dug deeply into the 54-year-old diplomat. Bernadotte and French United Nations observer Andre Seraut, seated beside him, were killed outright.

The killers belonged to an organization called Lehi (Lohamei Herut Israel, or Fighters for the Freedom of Israel). History knows the group as the Stern Gang. According to the world press at the time and historians thereafter, the Swedish diplomat was executed by "Jewish zealots" because (generally speaking) he favored and was pushing a partition of Jerusalem under Jordanian rule that favored the Arabs. However, *before* the assassination Lehi had called Count Bernadotte a British agent and accused him of collaborating with the Nazis. Hyperbole? Rhetoric? Contemporary news agencies, and historians thereafter, casually brushed aside the seemingly ridiculous accusation leveled by what they viewed as nothing but a bunch of murderous thugs.

The assassination was strongly condemned by the Israeli government and arrests were made. The indictment and trial, however, does not appear to have been vigorously pursued. When international outrage died down rather quickly and the United States failed to act in any meaningful way, the members of the Lehi organization were quietly released. It is widely claimed that future Israeli prime minster Yitzhak Shamir had a hand in the assassination. Sweden launched an official inquiry and in

1950 accused the Israelis of "gross negligence" and failing to "bring the inquiry to a positive result." Tempers flared on both sides. What is generally not known is that Israel formed a committee to study the charges, and a report of the matter was made available to a few ranking Swedish officials. Israel apologized for the death, conceded some of the Swedish accusations, and paid the United Nations $54,628—ostensibly for its negligence in handling of the matter. Thereafter the Swedes dropped the matter. The full content of the Israeli report to Sweden has never been made public and is today unavailable.

Recently declassified documents (see Chapter 17, "The Bloody Red Cross: Walter Schellenberg's External Assets,") prove that Bernadotte did indeed collaborate with the Nazis—just as the "Jewish zealots" alleged a short time before his murder. The *New York Times* eulogized Bernadotte as a "man of integrity." It now seems as though the former Swedish Red Cross diplomat had a price. Was there a connection between his actions with Walter Schellenberg and Company during World War II and his assassination in Israel? How extensive were Bernadotte's ties with the Nazis? The manner of the diplomat's death fits the *modus operandi* traditionally employed by the Israelis as retribution for past wrongs.

It is time historians dig deeper into Count Folke Bernadotte's World War II activities to determine the breadth and depth of his collaboration with the Nazis, and whether a connection exists between his actions and sudden demise in a Jerusalem suburb.[4]

*   *   *

After the war, Adolf Eichmann aide and champion skier Anton Burger was arrested and interned at Camp Marcus Orr. He escaped in the spring of 1947, went underground, and was never rearrested. As the years passed, interest in him waned. Burger deposited large sums of money in Swiss bank accounts following the war and continued to live in Germany under the assumed name of "Willi Bauer." He died at the age of 79 in 1992 in Germany.

*   *   *

Adolf Eichmann's race into the snowy hills of Austria was unsuccessful. He was arrested shortly thereafter and placed into an American internment camp—but only because of his membership in the SS, not because anyone recognized who he really was. As amazing as it seems today, his name was not yet widely known through Allied circles. The next year he was mistakenly released. He eventually fled to South America and ended up in Argentina. He lived there in a suburb of Buenos Aires under an assumed name until Israeli agents found him in May 1960. He was kidnapped and sent to Israel, where he was the subject of one of the most sensational trials of the century. On December 2, 1961, Eichmann was sentenced to death for his heinous crimes against the Jews and against humanity. He was hanged on the last day of May 1962. The preface of this book details his final minutes.

*   *   *

August Eigruber, the vicious SS Governor of the Upper Danube in Austria, worked tirelessly during the war's final months to prepare the Alpine Redoubt for Hitler's expected arrival and the final, cataclysmic, campaign of the war. He was tried after the war for war crimes and sentenced to death. On May 28, 1947, the Americans stretched his neck at Landsberg Prison just a few yards from where his beloved Führer had penned *Mein Kampf* two decades earlier.

*   *   *

Little is known of Gretl Braun Fegelein's life after the war. Eva had nicknamed her "Mogerl" because she sulked so much. It is likely her remaining years were unhappy ones. According to popular rumor, the name Fegelein was never mentioned again in the Braun household. The daughter Gretl gave birth to on May 5, 1945, was named Eva after her dead aunt. Tragedy (and one might posit, mental instability) seems to have coursed through the Braun genes. When a love affair ended in failure in 1975, the despondent younger Eva committed suicide. She was just thirty—three years younger than her aunt when she, apparently, killed herself in the Berlin bunker. In March 1965, Gretl was living in Munich under the name Gretl Berlinghoff. She is probably deceased, but when and how she met her end is not known.[5]

*   *   *

CIC agent Robert Gutierrez conducted and oversaw some of the most productive investigations during the early postwar period. He also managed to profit from his experiences in Austria. At the close of the war, former SS members, regardless of rank, were incarcerated. In an effort to forge a better existence, many wives of these imprisoned men took American soldiers as lovers. When SS Sturmbannführer (Major) Johannes Göhler was interned in a POW camp in Germany, rumor has it that his eye-catching young wife Ursula serviced agent Gutierrez as his mistress. Twenty-five years later, Frau Göhler told British historian David Irving that she had personally packed Adolf Hitler's and Eva Braun's diaries into Gutierrez's suitcase just before his departure to New Mexico. It will be recalled that CIC agents searched high and low for these journals and questioned Franz Konrad, Josef Spacil, and many others repeatedly without success. This subject ignited the historical community in the 1980s when the German magazine *Der Stern* foisted the fake Hitler diaries onto the world's stage. To this day, historians still debate whether Hitler even kept diaries.

There is no doubt, however, that a considerable body of his personal papers survived him. In a phone call just ten years ago, Gutierrez confirmed to author Kenneth Alford that he had indeed acquired "a large quantity of valuable documents," but that years ago his sister-in-law had "burned them." Willi Korte, a representative of the German Government, traveled to Gutierrez's home and, through sympathetic persuasion, obtained from him a handmade silk dress that had once belonged to Eva Braun, together with some of her silverware. On March 13, 1993, the *New York Times* published a report that Michael Walsh, a writer for *Time* and *Life* magazines based in Munich, Norman Scott of Global Explorations, and Marian Earnest, a London specialist in the authentication of documents, flew to Gutierrez's home to copy Hitler and Braun correspondence that was reported to be in his possession. Scott told the former CIC agent that they would pay him "a substantial sum in the neighborhood of two or three million dollars" if the letters could be authenticated. (Author Kenneth Alford had furnished Scott with 642 pages of documentation regarding Gutierrez's activities during the closing days of World War II and the postwar months that followed.) Gutierrez may have obtained these precious historical documents during the early postwar period while acting for the CIC. He declined Scott's offer.

In the middle of the 1990s, Gutierrez offered to sell the coat that Hitler was wearing during the July 20, 1944, assassination attempt. This was the same coat that had so excited Josef Spacil and Franz Konrad. Gutierrez's asking price was $25,000. A prominent Texas collector and real estate dealer, Mike Bauman, immediately flew to Albuquerque with cash in hand, but Gutierrez turned down the offer.

Gutierrez's son, retired astronaut Sidney Gutierrez, reportedly told several people, including Mike Bauman, that he will talk freely with them after his father's death. At last report the elderly and ailing Gutierrez was in a nursing home, where he has been for several years.

*   *   *

SS Captain Erwin Haufler's postwar life is a blank slate. The privacy laws in Germany are extremely strict, and tracing former SS officers who don't wish to be found is almost impossible.

*   *   *

Heinrich Himmler, whose power grew as Germany's military circumstances waned, was captured by the British and eventually admitted his identity. Not man enough to stand trial for his horrendous crimes, the former chicken farmer instead snapped an ampule of cyanide between his teeth.

*   *   *

Like Himmler, Adolf Hitler was also too cowardly to face the world after his grand plans fell away to ashes. He died in his dank Berlin bunker, probably by his own hand, on April 30, 1945.

*   *   *

When we last left this disreputable character, Walter Hirschfeld had been blackmailed and booted out of the CIC. Unemployed and now trusted by no one (courtesy of Emil Augsburg and Klaus Barbie),

Hirschfeld married an English woman named Josephine Gratius in 1948. For a time he managed a small studio owned by his peroxide-blond wife, who worked as a sales lady in the American House in Heidelberg. Hirschfeld was under constant CIC surveillance. British intelligence agents were also keeping an eye on him. Unbeknownst to the Americans, Hirschfeld's activities had been much wider and deeper than previously believed. MI5, the British security intelligence agency, revealed a very embarrassing fact about their former employee: Walter Hirschfeld was a double agent. He had been working for the CIC and the Soviets at the same time. His aliases, none of which were previously known to the CIC, included "Alois Hirschfeld," "von Bredus," "Eberling," "Wittgenstein," and "Herr Blaw." Official documents dealing with Hirschfeld's actions have been redacted or withheld from the authors by the U.S. Central Intelligence Agency. Government bureaucrats have invoked the Executive Order for National Security for documents withheld in their entirety.[6]

Hirschfeld's later years are like a chalk board wiped clean. He disappears from the record in the 1950s and nothing more of his whereabouts or activities have been located. In 1990, author Ken Alford was told by a German friend that Hirschfeld had died in Innsbruck, Austria in the late 1980s.

*   *   *

Wilhelm Höttl is one of the war's mystery men. He is difficult to evaluate because we know he played so many different roles both before and after the war. Immediately after hostilities ended, Höttl was interrogated closely about his experience in Germany's intelligence service. He apparently cooperated fully with CIC agents, who realized his expertise would be of great assistance in setting up a network of former German agents to use against the Soviets in postwar Europe. He was directed to contact his former agents in Budapest by wireless transmission, a technology with which the CIC was absolutely fascinated, and one often used by Höttl's agents. With Höttl's assistance, and under the supervision of American soldiers, the CIC established a working network in Soviet-occupied Eastern Europe.

His cooperation, however, did not prevent his arrest and imprisonment in Dachau because of his prior service with the SS. The figure of 6,000,000 Jewish dead, so often repeated in literature published on the subject, originated with Wilhelm Höttl. How he obtained the information is an interesting story. His path crossed Adolf Eichmann's in Budapest in August 1944 when Eichmann dropped by Höttl's residence seeking information about the deteriorating situation on the Eastern Front. Höttl was in communication with front line agents because of his position with SS Intelligence. He told Eichmann frankly that there was nothing the Germans could do to stop the Russian advance. "Then we shall probably never see each other again," was Eichmann's reply.

Eichmann was convinced that if Germany lost the war he stood no chance of survival because the Allies would consider him to be a major war criminal. Höttl took the opportunity to ask him for reliable information about the extermination program—and particularly about the number of Jews that had been killed. To his surprise, Eichmann answered his inquiry. The number of murdered Jews, he explained, was a top Reich secret, but given the situation he was facing he could tell Höttl something about it—particularly since Höttl was a historian. According to sworn testimony, Höttl later submitted testimony at Eichmann's trial in Israel in 1961, that the SS officer told him that "approximately 4,000,000 Jews had been killed in the various concentration camps, while an additional 2,000,000 met death in other ways, the major part of whom were shot by operational squads of the Security Police during the campaign against Russia." When Höttl displayed shock at the number, Eichmann responded that Heinrich Himmler thought the figure of 6,000,000 was "not correct," and that the figure had to be *higher*. Eichmann displayed neither emotion nor excuse; he simply answered Höttl's question and left it at that.

What to do with this important former SS intelligence officer? A memo written by an American agent on February 19, 1947, and sent to Third U.S. Army recommended that "Höttl be denied any facilities to resume outside contacts with Allied Intelligence Agencies. He is a dangerous man; thoroughly unprincipled and likely to cause a lot of damage if left to his own devices." The author of this memo had no idea just how prescient his observation would turn out to be. Höttl was released later that year and took a job with the CIC monitoring Soviet activities in Eastern Europe and keeping American agents fully briefed so they could prevent the Communists from sabotaging U.S.-backed interests in that region. Höttl organized a team of former members of the SD, Waffen-SS, and refugees from Eastern Europe. His network turned Salzburg into the central intelligence hub of Western Europe. Höttl and his CIC-financed agents burned through American money like there was no tomorrow. The CIC directed Höttl to cut back on spending and fully account for his organizational expenses. To the astonishment of the CIC, Höttl instead resigned and his network of experienced agents disappeared with him. Salzburg CIC agents swore they would one day have their revenge.

In one connection or another Höttl was, or had been, in contact with virtually every intelligence organization operating in Europe. After he dropped out of CIC ranks, he began working with the West German agency headed by super spy and former SS General Reinhard Gehlen (see Emil Augsburg entry). His contact was through his friend Baron Harry Mast, whose wife Edith Berndt was involved with the Czech intelligence service. Information gleaned by Höttl or his agents was sent back and forth between Salzburg and Munich twice a month. Baron Mast supervised Höttl's network while posing as an employee in Höttl's Nibelungen publishing house. Höttl once told an intelligence officer in Munich that he considered himself to be "the administrator of the [Walter] Schellenberg legacy."[7]

About the same time Höttl also began spying for the French. His contact was French Captain Maurice Blondell, who was stationed in the French Occupation Zone. The captain provided Höttl with fake identification papers so that he could travel without hindrance in Switzerland and Italy. He was also provided with a French army truck so that he could ship illegal cigarettes, coffee, and other items across the German-Austrian border without fear of inspection. Two of the recipients of this illicit largesse were Höttl's friends Kurt Ponger and Otto Verber, both of whom he had met while interned in Nuremberg.

Was Höttl also a Soviet spy? The U.S. Army thought so. In March 1953 he was arrested for his involvement with two former OSS officers who also happened to be Communists and Russian agents: Lieutenant Kurt Ponger and Lieutenant Otto Verber. Both Austrians had fled to America in 1938 to escape Nazi oppression. The brothers-in-law became citizens and served in U.S. Army Intelligence units during the war. Both also served as interrogation officers for the International Military Tribunal at Nuremberg (and had helped Kurt Becher by sabotaging his pending indictment). After they played their parts exposing Nazi atrocities to the world, Ponger, Verber, and their wives settled down in a luxurious apartment in their old home town of Vienna. All of them were up to their necks in felonious activities. Their extravagant lifestyle was made possible by a scholarship from the U.S. Army for studies at the University of Vienna, jobs as analysts for Eastern affairs with the CIA, the sale of CIA information to Soviet agents—and an extensive black market operation courtesy of Wilhelm Höttl. When they were arrested and confronted with their guilt, both men waived trial and entered guilty pleas. Ponger was sentenced to a prison term of five to fifteen years; Verber received three to ten years. Höttl was the key to their arrest.[8]

Höttl, too, was apprehended. Members of the U.S. Army searched his home in Altaussee. Inside they found four blank Austrian identity cards, 1,265 British pound notes (curiously, these notes were issued between 1935 through 1937), 20,000 pages of written material (some of it classified), and more than 100 letters written between Ponger, Verber, and Höttl. Höttl was placed in solitary confinement. Grueling interrogations and at least one polygraph test followed. The CIC was unable to determine to its satisfaction whether the master spy was in fact a Soviet agent. They concluded he was not "physiologically testable by polygraph." The CIC extracted some measure of revenge by releasing a press report "to insure that Höttl is discredited once and for all with German Intelligence Services, and thereby to prevent his continued harassment of the United States by processing through various channels fabricated intelligence."[9]

Höttl hailed from a very modest background (his university education was paid for by the Nazi party), yet he maintained a lavish postwar lifestyle. In their ongoing quest for Nazi loot CIC agents monitored Höttl's movements closely in the late 1940s and early 1950s. They estimated his monthly expenses topped $1,000—an extravagant sum for that period. He purchased a home for his mother, supported her and his wife's parents, and had a housemaid, nursemaid, and private secretary. From humble SS origins Höttl was now a sleek figure in canary yellow leather coats and hand-painted neckties. How, exactly, did he support himself?

In the early 1950s Höttl established (or purchased) the Nibelungen Publishing House. The business was registered in his wife Elfriede's maiden name. Writing under the pseudonym of Walter Hagen, he published his first book entitled *The Secret Front: The Story of Nazi Political Espionage* (London, 1953). Höttl eventually admitted he was the author of this remarkable book. Knowing of the suspicions that surrounded his postwar life, he ended the book thusly:

> I have not, contrary to some sensational reports in the German weekly press, managed to discover and squander the buried treasure that they [Nazis] are said to have left here in Aussee. I have taken to publishing and printing. All I have found here has been solitude and peace. . .

Wilhelm Höttl lived comfortably in Altaussee until his death in 1997. His wife predeceased him by many years.

*   *   *

Polish Countess Barbara Kalewska vanishes from the world's stage after leaving Kitzbühl for Vienna—allegedly with a fortune in gold removed from the burned ruins of her small house.

*   *   *

Rezsö (Rudolf) Kastner did not live long enough to extract whatever small satisfaction there was to be gleaned from the paper-thin legal victory awarded by the Israeli appellate court—or to face charges for his wartime decisions and subsequent perjury. In early March 1947 he was shot and killed outside his flat in Tel Aviv. The shooter, Israeli Ze'Ev Ekstein, was driven away by Dan Shemer in a stolen jeep. The police arrested them in their homes that same night. Confessions quickly followed. A third man, Joseph Menkes, was arrested a short time later. Shemer and Ekstein were former employees of the Israeli Secret Service. On the day of the assassination an agent of the Secret Service warned his superiors that Kastner would be killed that night. No precautions were taken.[10]

Ben Hecht, a prominent son of Russian Jewish immigrants and a native of New York, is the author of a remarkable book called *Perfidy* (New York, 1961). *Perfidy* chronicles the Greenwald-Kastner trial and its far-reaching implications. The book outlines in great detail the 1953 court case and indicts not only Kastner but many wartime leaders of the Jewish Agency for their actions in Hungary during World War II. Hecht's study was banned in Israel for almost three decades. The public exhibition involving Greenwald and Kastner, coupled with the appearance of Hecht's book a few years later, wove a trail of collaboration deep into Israel's ruling Labour Party. Another, more thorough hearing would have been disastrous for many prominent politicians. According to one source, one of Israel's leading political journalists investigating the Kastner case, Dr. Moshe Keren, was murdered because of what he might discover; Kastner was shot dead before he could stand trial for collaboration; and Hecht may have been the last victim. He died in 1964 in what has been described as a "suspicious death" by some. Whether one believes in conspiracy theories or not, the implications of the Kastner case are substantial.[11]

*   *   *

Captain Franz Konrad's ticket to Poland was stamped "one-way." This time there was no escape, no loose floorboards, no midnight runs through open countryside. Unfortunately, at this point in his story the stage curtain descends almost completely to the floor. Little is known of Konrad's journey through the Polish justice system. We do know he stood trial for war crimes, but the full transcript and record of the proceeding have never been released. On a date uncertain, "Ghetto Konrad" was convicted and sentenced to death. The deed was carried out, probably by firing squad, in 1951. The only surprise is that it took the Poles that long to dispatch him. His widow Agnes had assumed he was already dead and had applied for a death certificate two years earlier. It is doubtful whether Polish officials even bothered to respond to her request.

*   *   *

Friedrich Walther Bernhard Krüger, the SS officer who had overseen the Sachsenhausen counterfeiting operation, was the subject of a global search that lasted for a decade. He and his mistress had reportedly absconded with a fortune at wars's end. Ten years later he was discovered working as a clerk in a small store near Hannover, broke and without his girlfriend. He was released after questioning. No charges were ever brought against him. Although invited to do so by many journalists and historians, he steadfastly refused to discuss Operation Bernhard. We have been unable to determine whether he is still living.

* * *

One of the most cold blooded SS killers, Otto Ohlendorf turned himself in to the British in the third week of May 1945. He was interrogated extensively and provided chilling details about the Einsatzgruppen and RSHA operations. He testified at length at Nuremberg. Thereafter the table was turned and Ohlendorf found himself sitting in the dock as the leading defendant in one of the dozen later Nuremberg trials sponsored by the United States Army (Case No. 9, The Einsatzgruppen Case). He was sentenced to death and after four years was hanged for his crimes.

* * *

Unfortunately nothing has been discovered as to the postwar lives of Arthur and Iris Scheidler.

* * *

Walter Schellenberg escaped both a death penalty and a lengthy prison sentence by assisting the Allied prosecutors during the Nuremberg trials and by providing intelligence on the Soviet Union gathered during World War II. An extraordinarily light sentence of six years in prison was meted out in April 1949. While in jail Schellenberg penned his memoirs, *The Labyrinth: The Memoirs of Hitler's Secret Service Chief* (New York, 1956), an interesting but wholly sanitized account of his wartime activities. While in prison Schellenberg developed a serious liver disease and was released after having served just two years. He died on March 31, 1952, in Turin, Italy.[12]

*   *   *

After working undercover with the CIC in the early postwar world, Gerhardt Schlemmer ran into trouble with Walter Hirschfeld, spent some time in jail for his fraudulent loan scheme—and vanished.

*   *   *

Former SS General Friedrich Schwend, the master organizer of a large network for the distribution of forged bank notes, was arrested shortly after the war in the company of fellow con man George Spitz. He was released in September 1945 and returned to Italy, where Spitz convinced him that as a high-ranking SS officer he could not safely remain in Europe. Spitz provided Schwend with falsified Jewish papers and a new alias as Vencel Turi. Another set of fake Red Cross papers listed him as a Croatian exile named Wenceslas Turi. With the help of the notorious "ratline," Schwend and his wife escaped through Milan to South America. He lived comfortably in Lima, Peru, where he worked as a senior engineer for Volkswagen. Schwend traveled extensively, and American Intelligence believed he was the leader of a pro-Nazi group and that he helped shield Josef Mengele from arrest.

Schwend's luck ran out when he was hauled before a Peruvian court for his involvement in a murder and other crimes. During the long trial that followed, the prosecution's lead witness died under mysterious circumstances. A conviction on a minor charge followed and Schwend was expelled from Peru. German authorities then took him into custody for his role in a World War II-era murder in Italy (perhaps the time he had spent in a Rome jail during the war years was related to this matter), but the case had gone cold and Schwend was released after about one year. Peru lifted the expulsion order during his sojourn in a German jail, and Schwend returned to Lima. He lived, some say lavishly, until his death in 1980.[13]

*   *   *

Brigadier General Franz Six, cleverly arrested by Walter Hirschfeld with the unwitting help of Six's sister Marianne, was tried in Nuremberg in 1947-1948. The mass murderer promoted by Himmler for his methodical work with Einsatzgruppen B was more than worthy of a seven-foot drop through a swinging door. Somehow he managed to escape the death penalty and was sentenced to a mere twenty years in prison. That paltry sentence was subsequently commuted to ten years, and he was released after serving just four. Forty-eight months for tens of thousands of lives. Six probably joined the Gehlen Organization (see Emil Augsburg entry) and was later an advertising consultant in the German town of Kressbronn. The date of his death is not known.

*   *   *

SS Lieutenant Colonel Otto Skorzeny, Adolf Hitler's daring commando and ritual sword fighting duelist (one scar on the left side of his face resembles a perpetual grimace), was arrested by the Americans one week after his meeting with Josef Spacil on May 15, 1945. He was tried for war crimes in 1947, but prosecutors were unable to secure a conviction. Skorzeny was turned over to the German authorities, who probably did not have the stomach to put the former (and still popular) war hero on trial. He escaped custody the following summer and fled to Spain, where Fascist General Francisco Franco shielded him from extradition. Skorzeny had an endless supply of money. He created and organized ODESSA, a clandestine organization that helped SS criminals escape Europe. The former commando lived affluently in Spain until his death in Madrid in 1975. His memoirs are available in English as *My Commando Operations: The Memoirs of Hitler's Most Daring Commando* (Schiffer, 1995).

*   *   *

Counterfeiter Salomon Smolianoff was arrested in 1947 by the U.S. Army for selling a $500.00 bill on the black market. He spent but a short time in custody. He married later that same year and emigrated first to Uruguay and then to Brazil. In 1955 he was painting and working on (apparently legitimate) commercial art projects. His fate is not known.

*   *   *

Colonel Josef Spacil was never charged with war crimes for his plundering activities or criminal SS past. After CIC agents finished with him and his mandatory imprisonment for serving in the SS ended, the nervous wreck of a man was released in the summer of 1948. He returned to Munich. There, he gathered himself together and established a chain of supermarkets. He lived untroubled for the rest of his days. Whether he gained access to the stolen loot he had buried in Austria has not been determined. We know nothing of Spacil's final years.

*   *   *

Star swindler George Spitz was arrested shortly after the war. Speaking with a New York City accent, the smooth one volunteered to help the Americans recover some of Herman Göring's stolen loot. Despite widespread knowledge of his multi-country pilfering, he was never charged with a crime. One CIC official called him a "snake, very difficult to catch." It was therefore better to squeeze him for "as much information as possible." Spitz tried to distance himself from his Nazi past by marrying his mistress in a Munich synagogue. He later told U.S. officials that he married her because she knew too much about his activities and was afraid of what she could be forced to reveal if they were not husband and wife. His efforts to convince the CIC that he was indeed a Jew and coerced into working for the Nazis were eventually successful.

*   *   *

SS Major Dieter Wisliceny, Adolf Eichmann's deputy and the man on whose staff Kurt Becher admitted having served in Hungary, was the originator of the "Jewish Star" badge. His actions rounding up and deporting Jews from Slovakia, Greece, and Hungary earned him a trip to Czechoslovakia. Unlike the French, the Czechs knew a capital case when they saw one. Wisliceny breathed his last on a gallows in February 1948, just a few miles from the scene of some of his crimes.

Postscript Notes

1. Richard Breitman, "Historical Analysis of Twenty Names from CIA Records," National Archives and Records Administration (NARA). This fascinating and detailed document can be found online at the NARA site at: http://www.nara.gov/iwg/declass/rg263.html#augsburg.

2. For a recent and interesting article on the "ratline," Father Krunoslav Draganovic's role, and Allied intelligence operations, see Tom Rhodes, "Nazi Loot Used in Cold War Fight," *Ottawa Citizen*, September 10, 2000.

3. Hecht, *Perfidy*, pp. 58-60.

4. Donald, Neff, "Jewish Terrorists Assassinate U.N. Peacekeeper Count Folke Bernadotte." *Washington Report on Middle East Affairs* (September 1985), pp. 83-84; *New York Times*, September 18, 19, and 20, 1948.

5. O'Donnell, *The Bunker*, p. 186.

6. 303rd Counter Intelligence Corps, "Examination of Political Background, Character and Ability," June 17, 1946; 970th CIC report, "Subject: Hirschfeld, Walter," July 7, 1947; "Biographical Report by Walter Hirschfeld," June 22, 1946; British Counter Intelligence Corps Group, "Subject: Hirschfeld, Walter," June 1949; CIC, Agent Report: "Barbie Klaus," October 19, 1949.

7. "Interrogation of Wilhelm Höttl, Preliminary Report," April 1, 1953; National Archives, RG 319, IRR Case Files, Personal, Box 617. Walter Schellenberg ran the German Foreign Intelligence Service, Bureau VI, RSHA.

8. *History of Counter Intelligence*, "Occupation of Austria and Italy," (U.S. Army, March 1958), Vol. XXV, p. 48.

9. CIC, "Interrogation of Dr, Höttl, Preliminary Report," April 1, 1953.

10. Von Kurt Emmenegger, *Sie und Er* (n.m., 1963), "Das Einzige Weisse Schaf der Schwarzen SS?" p. 92, Magyar Országos Levéltár, Hungarian National Archives, Budapest, Hungary.

11. For more detailed information on this topic, please see http://www.ahavat-israel.com/ahavat/protest/shoa.asp.

12. See also the entry on Count Folke Bernadotte, above.

13. For more information on Schwend and related matters, see generally, Linklater, Hilton, and Ascherson, *The Nazi Legacy: Klaus Barbie and the International Fascist Connection*.

Bibliography

A bibliography of sources used in the preparation of this book appears below. Secondary sources were utilized for general biographical and background information, such as the rise of Adolf Hitler and Nazism, the formation of the SS and SA, the progression of Allied arms, and so forth. However, the vast bulk of this study is based upon tens of hundreds of pages of manuscript sources, including interviews, interrogations, summation reports, accountings, inventories, telegrams, letters, and related memoranda. Most of this material has been recently declassified.

MANUSCRIPT SOURCES

Fort Meade, Maryland
    U.S. Army Intelligence and Security Command

Each specific document extracted from these institutions are listed in the end notes.

National Archives

Record Group 38—Records of the Chief of Naval Operations
Record Group 56—E.E. Minskoff, Reports on the Assets of the RSHA
Record Group 238—War Crimes Records
Record Group 260—U.S. Forces Austria, and Finance Division
Record Group 319— G-2, folder Hitler File, Volume I and II
Record Group 319—IRR Case Files

Each specific document extracted from these institutions are listed in the end notes.

NEWSPAPERS AND PERIODICALS

Der Spiegel
Life Magazine
London Telegraph
New York Times
Ottawa Citizen
Sie und Er
Stars and Stripes
USA Today
Washington Report on Middle East Affairs

BOOKS

Alford, Kenneth D. *The Spoils of World War II.* New York: Birch Lane Press, 1994

———. *Great Treasure Stories of World War II.* Mason City, Iowa: Savas Publishing Company, 2000.

Arendt, Hannah. *Eichmann in Jerusalem: A Report in the Banality of Evil.* New York: Viking, 1964.

Axelrod, Alan, and Phillips, Charles. *The Macmillan Dictionary of Military Biography.* New York: MacMillan, 1998.

Bernadotte, Folke. *The Curtain Falls: Last Days of the Third Reich.* London: Cassell Publishers, 1945.

Black, Peter R. *Ernst Kaltenbrunner: Ideological Soldier of the Third Reich.* New York, 1959.

Bloom, Murray T. *Money of Their Own: The Great Counterfeiters.* New York: Scribner's, 1957.

Bower, Tom. *Nazi Gold: The Full Story of the Fifty-Year Swiss-Nazi Conspiracy to Steal Billions From Europe's Jews and Holocaust Survivors.* New York: Harper Collins, 1997.

Dear, I. C. ed.. *The Oxford Companion to World War II.* Oxford, 1995.

Eisenhower, Dwight D. *Crusade in Europe.* New York: Doubleday & Co., 1948.

Fest, Joachim C. *The Face of the Third Reich: Portraits of Nazi Leadership.* New York: Pantheon, 1970.

Gutman, Israel. *Resistance: The Warsaw Ghetto Uprising.* New York: Houghton Mifflin, 1994.

Hecht, Ben. *Perfidy.* New York: Julian Messner, 1961.

Hoehne, Heinz. *The Order of the Death's Head.* New York: Ballantine Books, 1969.

Höttl, Wilhelm. *The Secret Front: The Story of Nazi Political Espionage.* New York: Praeger, 1954.

Lebor, Adam. *Hitler's Secret Bankers: The Myth of Swiss Neutrality During the Holocaust.* New York: Birch Lane Press, 1997.

Linklater, Magnus; Hilton, Isabel; and Ascherson, Neal. *The Nazi Legacy: Klaus Barbie and the International Fascist Connection.* New York: Holt Reinhart and Winston, 1984.

Machtan, Lothar. *The Hidden Hitler.* New York, 2001.

Mitcham, Samuel W. Jr. *Hitler's Field Marshals and Their Battles.* London: Leo Cooper, 1988.

Murphy, Brenda. *The Butcher of Lyon: The Story of Infamous Nazi Klaus Barbie.* New York: Empire, 1983.

Nickolas, Lynn, H. *The Rape of Europa.* New York: Alfred A. Knopf, 1994.

O'Donnell, James P. *The Bunker.* Boston: Houghton Mifflin Company, 1978.

Padfield, Peter. *Himmler: Reichsführer SS*. London: Cassell Publishers, 2001.

Schellenberg, Walter. *The Labyrinth: The Memoirs of Hitler's Secret Service Chief*. New York: Harper and Brothers, 1956.

Skorzeny, Otto. *My Commando Operations: The Memoirs of Hitler's Most Daring Commando*. Schiffer, 1995.

Shirer, William L. *The Rise and Fall of the Third Reich*. New York: Simon and Schuster, 1960.

Toland, John. *Adolf Hitler*. New York: Doubleday, 1976.

Trevor-Roper, Hugh R. *The Last Days of Hitler*. London: The Macmillan Company, 1947.

Weissberg, Alex. *Desperate Mission: Joel Brand's Story*. New York: Criterion, 1958.

INDEX